T0394325

Pilgrimage and Economy in the Ancient Mediterranean

Religions in the Graeco-Roman World

Series Editors

David Frankfurter (*Boston University*)
Johannes Hahn (*Universität Münster*)
Frits G. Naerebout (*University of Leiden*)
Miguel John Versluys (*University of Leiden*)

VOLUME 192

The titles published in this series are listed at *brill.com/rgrw*

Pilgrimage and Economy in the Ancient Mediterranean

Edited by

Anna Collar
Troels Myrup Kristensen

BRILL

LEIDEN | BOSTON

Cover illustration: The Athenian Treasury at Delphi (photo: Troels Myrup Kristensen).

The Library of Congress Cataloging-in-Publication Data is available online at http://catalog.loc.gov

Typeface for the Latin, Greek, and Cyrillic scripts: "Brill". See and download: brill.com/brill-typeface.

ISSN 0927-7633
ISBN 978-90-04-42868-3 (hardback)
ISBN 978-90-04-42869-0 (e-book)

Contents

Preface

The majority of the chapters in this volume are based on presentations at the symposium "Economies of Sacred Travel", organised by the editors, in the Department of History and Classical Studies, Aarhus University, 17–18 September 2015. This symposium was the second in a series of three organised as part of the collaborative research project "The Emergence of Sacred Travel: Experience, Economy, and Connectivity in Ancient Mediterranean Pilgrimage" (www.sacredtravel.dk), directed by Troels Myrup Kristensen and generously funded through the Danish Council for Independent Research's *Sapere Aude* excellence programme. The first symposium was published as T.M. Kristensen and W. Friese, eds. *Excavating Pilgrimage. Archaeological Approaches to Sacred Travel and Movement in the Ancient World* (Routledge 2017). We wish to thank the council for their generous support of our project. We are equally grateful to Jakob Engberg, Neville Morley, Brent Nongbri, Tessa Schild, the RGRW editorial board and an anonymous reader for helpful advice and suggestions for improving the manuscript. Finally, we thank Niels Bargfeldt for editorial assistance.

AC/TMK
Aarhus and Southampton, November 2019

Author Biographies

Hélène Aurigny
is Associate Professor of Greek History at the Centre Camille Jullian, Aix-Marseille University, France. She has been a member of the French School at Athens and studies the sanctuary of Delphi and its evolution through votive material, including bronzes and marble statuary. Her work in Argos, where she studies terracotta votives offered to Aphrodite in her sanctuary near the agora, constitutes a parallel study of ancient crafts and cults in Greece.

Louise Blanke
is Lecturer in Late Antique Archaeology, University of Edinburgh, UK. She specialises in the archaeology of the Eastern Mediterranean in the late antique and early Islamic periods and is the author of *An Archaeology of Egyptian Monasticism: Settlement, Economy and Daily Life at the White Monastery Federation* (2019). She has participated in the survey and excavation of several monastic sites in Egypt and has years of archaeological experience from Jordan, Qatar and Denmark. She currently directs the Late Antique Jerash Project in Jordan.

Anna Collar
is Lecturer in Roman Archaeology at the University of Southampton, UK. Her research focuses on the material culture of religion, social networks, and landscape, migration, emotion and memory. She is the author of *Religious Networks in the Roman Empire: The Spread of New Ideas* (2013), and co-editor of *The Connected Past: Challenges to Network Studies in Archaeology and History* (2016). She has excavated in Crete, Turkey and the UK, and is co-director of the Taseli-Karaman Archaeological Project in Cilicia, Turkey.

Esther Eidinow
is Professor of Ancient History at the University of Bristol, UK. Her area of expertise is ancient Greek culture, with specific focus on religion and magic. Her latest monograph is *Envy, Poison, and Death. Women on Trial in Classical Athens* (2016).

Marietta Horster
is Professor of Ancient History at Johannes Gutenberg University Mainz, Germany. Recent publications have focused on the self-shaping of Roman intellectuals, the Roman economy and the management of Greek sanctuaries.

Robin M. Jensen

is the Patrick O'Brien Professor of Theology at University of Notre Dame, USA, where she also is concurrent faculty in Art History and Classics and a Fellow of the Medieval Institute. Her research and publications explore the intersection of Christian iconography, architecture, and material culture generally with early Christian liturgy, lived practices, and theological discourse. Her most recent books include *The Cross: History, Art, and Controversy* (2018); *Christianity in Roman Africa: The Development of Its Practices and Beliefs* (2014); and *The Routledge Handbook to Early Christianity*, edited with Mark Ellison (2018).

Barbara Kowalzig

is Associate Professor of Classics and History at New York University, USA. Her field is the religion and anthropology of ancient Greece and the Mediterranean. She has published widely on song-culture, drama, and the social contexts of music and performance, on pilgrimage, and at the intersection of religion and economic history, notably in *Singing for the Gods: Performances of Myth and Ritual in Archaic and Classical Greece* (2007). Her current book project is entitled *Gods around the Pond: Religion, Society and the Sea in the Early Mediterranean Economy*.

Troels Myrup Kristensen

is Associate Professor of Classical Archaeology at Aarhus University, Denmark. He directed the collaborative research project from which this volume arises: "The Emergence of Sacred Travel: Experience, Economy and Connectivity in Ancient Mediterranean Pilgrimage" (2013–2017). His research focuses on the archaeology of pilgrimage, ancient visual culture, and the uses of classical heritage in the contemporary world. He is currently writing a book on the archaeology of ancient Mediterranean pilgrimage.

F. S. Naiden

is Professor of Ancient History at the University of North Carolina, Chapel Hill, USA. Naiden specialises in Greek law, religion, and warfare, with attention to comparanda among the Western Semites. He has previously written about pilgrimage in connection with the topic of his first book, *Ancient Supplication*. His contribution to this volume developed from his work on sacrifice in *Smoke Signals for the Gods* (2012). His most recent book is *Soldier, Priest, and God: A Life of Alexander the Great* (2018).

Dan-el Padilla Peralta

is Associate Professor of Classics at Princeton University, USA, and holds affiliations with the university's Program in Latino Studies, Program in Latin American Studies, and Center for Human Values. He has co-edited a volume on appropriation in Roman culture, *Rome, Empire of Plunder: The Dynamics of Cultural Appropriation* (2017) and is the author of a monograph on religion and state formation in fourth- and third- century BCE Rome, *Divine Institutions: Religions and Community in the Middle Republic* (2020). He has also authored *Undocumented: A Dominican Boy's Odyssey from a Homeless Shelter to the Ivy League* (2015). His work in progress includes a manifesto for "Racing the Classics"; a book-length study on the semiotics of mid-republican Rome; a co-edited volume on the long fourth century BCE; and a co-authored book on 338 BCE.

Max Ritter

is a Postdoctoral Fellow at the Johannes Gutenberg University Mainz, Germany. He read Byzantine Studies, Classical Archaeology, and Political Science at the Freie Universität Berlin and the National and Kapodistrian University in Athens. His 2017 PhD is in press under the title *Glaube und Geld: Zur Ökonomie des byzantinischen Pilgerwesens (4.-12. Jh.)*. Intermediately, he worked for a DFG project on the administration of Byzantine ports under the supervision of Prof. J. Pahlitzsch. Furthermore, he is part of a long-term excavation project in Pompeiopolis (Paphlagonia, Turkey), where his field of study is the late antique and Dark Age developments of the city and its wider region. Since 2018, he is working in a new collaborative DFG project supervised by Prof. M. Horster (JGU Mainz) and Prof. G. Brands (MLU Halle) which aims at a comprehensive digital commentary, a new English translation and accompanying studies of Procopius' *Buildings*.

Marlena Whiting

is a Postdoctoral Fellow at Johannes Gutenberg University Mainz and Martin Luther University Wittenberg-Halle, Germany. Whiting has a doctorate in late antique archaeology from the University of Oxford, specialising in pilgrimage and travel infrastructure of the late antique Near East. She currently works on the DFG-funded project "Procopius and the Language of Buildings". From 2015 to 2019 she held a Veni grant from the Netherlands Organisation for Scientific Research (NWO) investigating gender, pilgrimage, and lived religion in the late antique Near East. She has held visiting fellowships in Jordan and Turkey, and worked on several archaeological excavations in the Middle East and Europe.

Illustrations

Abbreviations

AASS	Acta Sanctorum quotquot toto orbe coluntur
AASS Nov. prop.	H. Delehaye, ed. 1902. Synaxarium ecclesiae Constantinopolitanae e codice Sirmondiano nunc Berolinensi adiectis synaxariis selectis opera et studio (Propylaeum ad Acta Sanctorum Novembris), Brussels.
AnBoll	Analecta Bollandiana
AR	Archaeological Reports
BHG	F. Halkin, 1957. Bibliotheca Hagiographica Graeca, third edition, 3 vols., Brussels.
CIG	A. Böckh, 1828–1877. Corpus Inscriptionum Graecarum, 4 vols. Berlin.
CCCM	Corpus Christianorum, Continuatio Medievalis
CCSG	Corpus Christianorum, Series Graeca
CCSL	Corpus Christianorum, Series Latina
CFHB	Corpus Fontium Historiae Byzantinae
CSCO	Corpus Scriptorum Christianorum Orientalium
CID	Corpus Inscriptionum Delphicarum
FD	Fouilles de Delphes
FGRH	Die Fragmente der griechischen Historiker, ed. F. Jacoby, Berlin 1923–1929.
GGR	M. Nilsson, 1967. Geschichte der Griechischen Religion, third edition, Munich.
IE	Eleusis. The Inscriptions on Stone = K. Clinton, 2005–2008. Eleusis. The Inscriptions on Stone: Documents of the Sanctuary of the Two Goddesses and Public Documents of the Deme, 2 vols., Athens.
IG	Inscriptiones Graecae
IGLS	Inscriptions grecques et latines de la Syrie
I.Ilion	Die Inschriften von Ilion, ed. P. Frisch, Bonn 1975.
IMT	M. Barth – J. Stauber, eds. 1993. Inschriften Mysia & Troas, München.
IvP	Die Inschriften des Asklepieions, ed. C. Habicht, 1969. Altertümer von Pergamon, Band VIII, Teil 3, Berlin.
LSAM	F. Sokolowski, 1955. Lois sacrées de l'Asie Mineure, Paris.
LSCG	F. Sokolowski, 1969. Lois sacrées des cités grecques, Paris.
LSCG Supp.	F. Sokolowski, 1962. Lois sacrées des cités grecques, supplement, Paris.

LSJ	H.G. Liddell – R. Scott – H.S. Jones, 1996. *A Greek-English Lexicon*, ninth edition, Oxford.
MGH SS	*Monumenta Germaniae Historica Scriptores*
ODB	A.P. Kazhdan *et al.*, eds. 1991. *The Oxford Dictionary of Byzantium*, 3 vols., New York.
OGIS	W. Dittenberger, 1903–5. *Orientis Graeci inscriptiones selectae*, 2 vols., Leipzig.
PG	*Patrologia cursus completus, series graeca*, ed. J.P. Migne.
PL	*Patrologia cursus completus, series latina*, ed. J.P. Migne.
SC	*Sources Chrétiennes*, eds. H. de Lubac – J. Daniélou.
RE	*Paulys Realencyclopädie der classischen Altertumswissenschaft*, Stuttgart – Munich.
RO	P. Rhodes – R. Osborne, eds., 2003. *Greek Historical Inscriptions 404–423 B.C.*, Oxford.
SEG	*Supplementum Epigraphicum Graecum*
SGDI	F. Bechtel *et al.* 1884–1915. *Sammlung der griechischen Dialekt-Inschriften*, 4 vols., Göttingen.
Syll.[3]	W. Dittenberger, ed. 1917 *Sylloge inscriptionum Graecarum*, third edition, Lepizig.
SubsHag	*Subsidia Hagiographica*
TAM	*Tituli Asiae Minoris*
ThesCRA	*Thesaurus Cultus et Rituum Antiquorum*

CHAPTER 1

Embedded Economies of Ancient Mediterranean Pilgrimage

Anna Collar and Troels Myrup Kristensen

1   Introduction

In our world today, global pilgrimages number around 100 million a year, with enormous economic impact at all stages of the process in the regions involved: from the point of departure at the pilgrim's home, to the destination at a holy place, and finally the return journey.[1] The annual income generated by Islamic pilgrimage to Mecca (*hajj*) alone was estimated in 2011 to be some $10 billion,[2] a figure projected to increase in the coming years as Saudi Arabia continues to invest heavily in the infrastructure to house and sustain pilgrims while undertaking *hajj*.[3] Scholarship on contemporary pilgrimage has emphasised some of these economic dimensions of the practice, for example, in *Pilgrimage in the Marketplace*, Ian Reader articulates the close links that exist between commercial interests and the creation of pilgrimage sites in many different countries.[4] Reader shows how pilgrimage operates as an interweaving of the 'market' and the 'sacred' to such a degree that it is impossible to pull the threads apart. Instead of being vilified as kitsch or dismissed as detracting or separate from the sacred purpose of pilgrimage, religious consumerism and the acquisition of material goods and souvenirs are crucial to the success of modern pilgrimage.[5] The same can be said of medieval Christian pilgrimage practice where the concepts of sin, debt, and redemption through pilgrimage operated together to form a 'market model'. Recent work has emphasised three major economic elements of medieval pilgrimage: the journey and end donation at a shrine, the 'franchised' business of shrines themselves, key to which were saintly relics and the marketing and distribution of miracles and indulgences,

---

1 Ellyatt 2012.
2 Maher 2012. In 2017, 2.4 million pilgrims undertook *hajj* – Cochrane 2018; with pilgrimage close second to oil as Saudi Arabia's main income stream.
3 The Abraj Kudai hotel in Mecca is set to become the world's largest, offering 10,000 rooms as well as 70 restaurants, a shopping mall, prayer halls and multiple helipads – Aswad 2017.
4 Reader 2014.
5 Reader 2014, 15.

and ancillary pilgrimage services which operated between the private sector and church authorities.[6]

Such observations of the contemporary and medieval economic significance of pilgrimage also have a bearing on the study of the ancient world. In antiquity, pilgrims made significant investments in terms of time, money, goods and even risking personal safety through the visitation of sanctuaries, becoming part of a crowd during festivals and sacrifices, and giving individual or communal gifts to the divine, and these investments gave back to the people involved by adding both symbolic and material value to communities and individuals. Although some scholars have argued that the term 'pilgrimage' is dangerously anachronistic when applied to ancient Graeco-Roman beliefs and practices, its introduction to the study of the classical Mediterranean over the course of the last thirty years has inspired a wave of scholarship that uses it to present the ancient evidence in a new theoretical and methodological light.[7] One of the advantages of using 'pilgrimage' to think with is indeed that it facilitates comparative and diachronic research that juxtaposes different periods, regions, cultures, beliefs, and practices, thus offering a useful interpretive framework for studying both commonalities and differences across many different contexts. While there are significant differences between the types of Greek, Roman and late antique Christian pilgrimage that are discussed by the contributors to this volume, there are also striking similarities, for example, in the ways that social, 'religious' and not least economic practices intertwined. A shared element that runs through all of the different traditions under scrutiny is thus the extent to which pilgrimage is embedded within other significant aspects of the ancient Mediterranean economy, be it emerging urbanism, production, exchange, or votive behaviour.

The express aim of this volume is to explore the socioeconomic dynamics of ancient Mediterranean pilgrimage across a broad historical canvas. The papers gathered here investigate 'sacred' aspects of economic practice and economic aspects of the 'sacred', through a series of chronologically and geographically wide-ranging case studies, from archaic Greece through to Late Antiquity, and from the Greek mainland to Egypt and the Near East. These case studies allow us to get a better picture of how our modern concepts of religion and economy intertwined in the ancient world, and by taking material culture as a

---

6 Bell – Dale 2011, 602.

7 Elsner 1992; Dillon 1997; Coleman – Elsner 1995; Frankfurter 1998; Elsner – Rutherford 2005; Petsalis-Diomidis 2010; Harland 2011; Kristensen 2012a; 2012b; Rutherford 2013; Kristensen – Friese 2017; Drbal 2018; Kristensen 2018; 2019; Friese – Handberg – Kristensen 2019. On the historiography of ancient Mediterranean pilgrimage, see further Bremmer 2017; Elsner 2017; Friese – Kristensen 2017.

starting point, to focus in on the ways that landscapes, architecture, and things shaped the pilgrim's experiences. The volume combines the comparative perspective on pilgrimage with an investigation of the economic infrastructures of ancient Mediterranean sanctuaries, an area where the plentiful archaeological evidence may contribute in a confident and systematic fashion.[8] Inspired by the notion of the 'embedded economy' that originates from the work of the economic historian Karl Polanyi, the volume furthermore goes beyond the understanding of economy as related to quantification, buying and selling, redistribution of resources, and supply and demand, and instead looks towards the broad, complex and manifold ways in which economy, belief and ritual behaviour intertwined, specifically through the processes and practices that were part of ancient Mediterranean pilgrimage over the course of more than 1,500 years.

This introductory chapter first discusses a number of controversial terms and topics that inform this study: the concept of pilgrimage itself and the ways that archaeology can access some of the practical, experienced aspects of pilgrimage; the separation and entanglement of the categories of 'religion' and economy, from Weber onwards; the notion of 'embedded' economy as a productive method to bring these categories together, and the problems inherent in these new methods of viewing 'religion' as an identifiable, separate category in the ancient world. Our own view is that pilgrimage constitutes a counterbalance to recent approaches to both 'religion' and economy in the ancient world, where these aspects of life are seen as segmented and separate from each other, as well as to those 'primitivist' approaches which would see the ancient world as insular, local, and fragmented. The work of Peregrine Horden and Nicholas Purcell has been instrumental in demonstrating the importance of connectivity and mobility to the functioning of the cultures of the ancient Mediterranean, and pilgrimage, in all its forms, offers a key lens on this re-imagined ancient world: a world of movement, exchange, networks, and connections, in which the economic and the 'sacred' are two sides of the same coin.[9]

The second part of the chapter discusses the individual contributions to the volume within the wider context of the 'embedded economy' of ancient Mediterranean pilgrimage. The contributions are organised into four sections. The first three focus on broadly conceived facets of pilgrimage practice: 'Movements', 'Communities', and 'Transactions', chosen because they clearly showcase the intertwining of 'religion' and 'economy' in practical, material

---

8   See also Kristensen – Friese 2017 for an earlier attempt to do this.
9   Horden – Purcell 2000.

ways. By looking closely at the material evidence for economic aspects embedded in pilgrimage practice, we bring the provision of ancillary services and the role of physical infrastructure and scaffolding for pilgrimage into the foreground and demonstrate the diversity of material that an archaeological approach can bring to the discussion. The final section of the volume, 'Sociological and Comparative Perspectives', outlines two different approaches to the future directions that can and should be taken in the study of ancient pilgrimage and the relationships between 'sacred' and 'economic' behaviour across the *longue durée*.

2   Pilgrimage: 'Sacred' and Economy Entwined

Pilgrimage offers perhaps the most readily apparent example of the intertwined nature of the 'religious' and the economic in antiquity. These terms, however, require a little more unpacking, so to begin this exploration of the entanglement and interdependence between 'religion' and economy in antiquity, we start by briefly situating the issues investigated in this volume within the longer-term scholarly discourse on the broad categories of 'religion' and 'economy'. This discussion begins with Max Weber, but has been given renewed exposure in more recent studies that have proposed the notion of 'embeddedness', and which have problematised the concept of ancient 'religion' itself. We then focus in on the study of ancient pilgrimage itself and the issues that have been taken with the use of this term, the ways in which this phenomenon has been defined and understood, and the basis for our claim that it offers a unique perspective on some of the transactional aspects of cultic life in antiquity.

The fundamental relationship that exists between religion and economy was articulated clearly by Weber at the very start of *The Sociology of Religion* (first published in 1920), when he observes that 'religious or magical behaviour or thinking must not be set apart from the range of everyday purposive conduct, particularly since even the ends of the religious and magical actions are predominantly economic'.[10] His account of the inseparability of Protestantism and the rise of capitalism in Northern Europe underscores this point.[11] Weber's analysis of religion was as a communal, social phenomenon that revolved around social action and social meaning — *contra* contemporary discussions which placed religion in the sphere of the irrational — and which saw participants as gaining meaning through belonging to religious communities in

---

10   Weber 1968, 1.

11   Weber 2011.

particular,[12] communities that were understood as causally interrelated to the economy. Weber argued that institutional religion required a basis in economic power,[13] a need which could be at odds with core doctrinal elements (for example, Christian ethical teaching relating to poverty), and it is the ethical dimension of some religions that he sees as bringing them into conflict with the political sphere.[14] This conflict between religious ethics and political and economic power is not so clear when thinking of pre-Christian beliefs and practices however, perhaps because the diverse ways of engaging with the supernatural that are witnessed across the Mediterranean world prior to the rise of Christianity did not have such a clear ethical dimension. Certainly some of these diverse cults could begin to be seen as institutionalised, and the economic bases that they developed is something that we will see emerging in some of the studies collected in this volume, specifically through the development of sanctuaries that attracted large numbers of participants.

One of the more problematic elements of Weber's discussion of 'religion' when thinking about pre-Christian beliefs and practices, is precisely the term 'religion' itself. In the past forty years or so, the use of the term 'religion' has been questioned and challenged, largely because of its Christian implications: 'religion', as the term is generally used, refers to 'the belief in and worship of a superhuman controlling power, especially a personal God or gods,' and 'a religion' generally means something like 'a particular system of faith and worship.'[15] In an attempt to counter this issue when thinking about the ancient world, thirty years ago the ancient historian Robert Parker proposed the term 'embedded' to describe ancient Greek religion. This was borrowed from the work of economic historian Karl Polanyi, who argued that competitive market-based economic activity was fundamentally connected to the nation state and to industrialisation. Prior to this, he suggests, economic activity was 'embedded' in social structures and family households, describing the inseparability of economics from reciprocity and redistribution via the social relationships, cultural values, and political and religious institutions that together comprise society itself.[16]

Parker's use of 'embedded' enabled him to argue that, in a similar way to economic activity, 'religion' was a fundamental part of all aspects of Greek

---

12 Kippenberg 2005, 173.

13 Weber 1968, 219. On this paradox in late antique Christianity, see Brown 2012.

14 Weber 1968, 224.

15 Nongbri 2008, 444.

16 Polanyi 1957 [1944], 57, 61, 272. For a recent review of his concept of embeddedness and its use in subsequent scholarship, see Gemici 2008.

society,[17] rather than something that was perceived as a separate category as it has become in the post-Enlightenment period in the west. This has been a fruitful idea, with Mary Beard, John North and Simon Price similarly noting that there were no special institutions or activities for the Romans that were separated out from daily life, but instead observed a situation where 'religion' and ritual were part of all institutions and activities.[18] This perception of 'embedded religion' has become ubiquitous in scholarship looking at ancient beliefs and practices, in part because it attempts to act as a counterpoint to an overly Christianised idea of religion itself.[19]

However, attractive though this notion is in differentiating between a modern religious conception and that of the ancient world, Brent Nongbri has questioned the use of the term 'religion' itself to describe the collections of beliefs and practices in which ancient people were engaged. Nongbri has argued that these definitions of religion are more than simply 'Christianising', they demonstrate that 'religion' itself is an actively Christian phenomenon, and one that was created relatively recently as a descriptive category. Using the modern, western, Christian (and specifically Protestant) term 'religion' to gather together and describe the situations in antiquity is inappropriate, he argues, as the beliefs and practices of ancient peoples were not conceptualised as part of a unified system in this way. Exploring this tangle of terminology, he argues that the use of 'embedded' regarding 'religion' in antiquity in fact confuses the situation still further: it both acknowledges that the evidence is difficult to slot into a traditional category of 'religion', while simultaneously underpinning the idea that 'religion' was an intrinsic part of that culture and a native term of definition.[20] This potentially hinders effective discussion of the differences between ancient ways of conceptualising the relationships between humans and the supernatural and those of more recent times. Although Nongbri refrains from eliminating use of 'religion' regarding the ancient world, he emphasises that scholars must be clear that they are using it to describe a categorisation that is their own, and not one that is inherent in the material.[21] While these are

---

17   Parker 1986; reprinted as Parker 1988. For further discussion and development of this term
      in relation to Greek religion, see Bremmer 1999, 2–4; Kindt 2013, 16–9; and Eidinow 2015.
      The concept is central in many other disciplines, including economic anthropology, see
      Plattner 1989, 3–4.
18   Beard – North – Price 1998, 43.
19   See also Price 1999; and discussion in Nongbri 2008; 2015.
20   Nongbri 2008, 452.
21   In this volume, when the term 'religious' or 'religion' is used, we are using it as a short-
      hand, second-order analytic umbrella term to cover ritual practices and beliefs. Barton –
      Boyarin 2016 argues for the elimination of its use altogether.

in many ways important criticisms, the same could be said of any second-order description of any phenomenon in the past (including pilgrimage) and does not as such detract from its usefulness as a heuristic, interpretive tool.[22]

Pilgrimage too is a slippery term. The modern study of pilgrimage took a leap forward in the late 1970s with the publication of Victor and Edith Turner's study of its iterations in Christian culture,[23] in which they explored pilgrimage anthropologically as a rite of passage. The Turners argued that pilgrims actively and voluntarily underwent a change in identity through the process of pilgrimage, where their everyday lives were temporarily laid aside and replaced by a new social and spiritual world created through interactions with other pilgrims. They described this new social cohesion as *communitas*, a term that was taken up in much subsequent scholarship.[24] However, not all pilgrimages are accompanied by social cohesion. Subsequent studies of pilgrims and pilgrimage practices have thus emphasised the conflicts that also occur in such new social spaces. Contestation between religious authorities and pilgrims, and amongst different groups of pilgrims themselves, was the subject of a later volume edited by John Eade and Michael Sallnow, whose case studies focused on a range of global Catholic contexts, including Lourdes, Jerusalem, Sri Lanka and the Andes.[25] Rather than approaching pilgrimage as a closely structured universal phenomenon, Eade and Sallnow stressed the need to study its variations and contestations as a 'realm of competing discourses'.[26] However, there are also significant overlaps between these two 'schools' of pilgrimage studies, as Eade himself pointed out in the introduction to the volume's second edition, and as further discussed in a later paper by Simon Coleman.[27] Coleman furthermore points out that the concept of pilgrimage is only useful it we allow for a certain amount of slipperiness in its application to specific contexts.[28] Indeed, as we noted in the beginning of this chapter, pilgrimage intersects with many other arenas of social, religious and economic life, and we actively limit our understanding of the phenomenon if it is too narrowly defined.

Explicit discussion of the concept of pilgrimage in the study of the ancient world is relatively recent but has received considerable traction over the course of the last thirty years. In fact, it has generated considerable debate with regard

---

22   As also noted by Nongbri himself (2015, 156–9), see also remarks in Frankfurter 2015.
23   Turner – Turner 1978.
24   On the continuing influence of the Turners' model, see Kowalzig 2005 and Bailey 2013.
25   Eade – Sallnow 1991a.
26   Eade – Sallnow 1991b, 5.
27   Coleman 2002.
28   Coleman 2002, 363.

to its use in relation to pre-Christian contexts.[29] Jas Elsner and Ian Rutherford capture the difficulty inherent in this discussion succinctly when they say in their introduction to the influential *Pilgrimage in Graeco-Roman and Early Christian Antiquity. Seeing the Gods:* 'in the move from numerous polytheisms to Christianity [...] the denial of the term pilgrimage (over-) emphasizes difference (and hence change), while its employment (over-) emphasizes similarity and hence continuity'.[30] Their anthology has played a substantial role in kick-starting a new wave of interest in ancient pilgrimage, including the project from which the present volume arises (see Preface). The editors' introduction not only tackled head-on the problems of applying the concept of pilgrimage to pre-Christian cultic practices, it also proposed a typology to capture some of its manifold manifestations in different cultural and religious contexts. The first type on their list relates to ancient Greek *theoria* — sometimes translated as 'state pilgrimage' — that involved representatives from individual cities travelling to sanctuaries to oversee religious spectacles at such well-known destinations as Delphi, Nemea and Epidauros.[31] While *theoria* is primarily documented through epigraphy and literary sources, many other forms of pilgrimage may be glimpsed through material evidence,[32] including for example, consultations of oracles, travel to offer a dedication (to fulfil a vow, for example), to ask for healing, or to be initiated into a cult community.

Pilgrimage has also been applied as a productive category of analysis in work that does not exclusively look at this phenomenon, much of which has increased our awareness of the integrated role of cult and temples in ancient economies. Horden and Purcell in *The Corrupting Sea* reconsidered the relationship between subsistence, landscape, economy and the sacred in the ancient world, and developed the notion of the sacralised economy that amongst other things includes festivals, fairs and the embeddedness of sacred elements in the landscape, including land ownership, civic duties and production.[33] The 'embedded' economy of Greek sanctuaries was further explored by Beate Dignas in *Economy of the Sacred in Hellenistic and Roman Asia Minor*, focusing on a region where there is a particularly rich record of inscriptions that testify to the economic and political entanglements of individual sanctuaries.[34] She also discusses cases in the Near East, such as Baitokaike and its extraordinary

---

29   Chélini – Branthomme 1987 and Coleman – Elsner 1995 were two pioneering studies.

30   Elsner – Rutherford 2005, 3.

31   Elsner – Rutherford 2005, 12–3, see also Rutherford 2013.

32   Kristensen 2012b; 2018; Kristensen – Friese 2017.

33   Horden and Purcell 2000; for recent discussion of its place in historiography, refer to Concannon – Mazurek 2016, 7–9.

34   Dignas 2002.

dossier that offers insight into the economic life of a sanctuary in both the Hellenistic and Roman periods (further explored by Kristensen, this volume).

While these works have shed useful light on the embedded economies of ancient Mediterranean sanctuaries, there are still many underexplored aspects of how these connect to the broader social landscape through pilgrimage practices. For example, in his discussion of markets and fairs in Hellenistic Greece and Roman Italy, Jean Andreau highlights how 'commercial aspects of fairs have been studied in isolation from their cultural and religious aspects' and further observes that 'Panhellenic sanctuaries have never really brought centrally into the picture the commercial activities that went on in them'.[35] His point is that during pilgrimages, festivals and fairs, sanctuaries effectively functioned as economic as well as religious and cultural hubs, and it is unproductive to try to split these aspects apart. More generally, 'religion' (*pace* Nongbri) rarely forms part of (ancient) economic history in its most traditional forms.[36] The entanglements of economy and cult practices have generally remained underexplored in studies of the ancient Mediterranean, reflecting a long tradition across many different disciplines to treat 'religion' as set apart from all other aspects of society,[37] with a few notable exceptions.[38] Specifically, in relation to the study of the ancient economy, John Davies has argued that

---

35   Andreau 2002, 122.

36   A key work here is Moses Finley's *The Ancient Economy* (1973) that has an index without reference to religion, ritual, or sacred. Finley attended Polanyi's seminars at Columbia University and was instrumental in introducing the concept of 'embeddedness' to the field of ancient history, see Bang 2008, 23–4. In his archaeological approach to the Roman economy, Greene 1986 also does not mention religion; and see also Austin – Vidal-Naquet 1977, in which the term 'religion' or 'sacred' appear a total of nine times. More recently see Bresson 2016. For a similar critique of the study of medieval pilgrimage (but where the focus has been on cultural aspects, rather than economic), see Bell – Dale 2011. In terms of thinking about the integration of religion and economics from a modern perspective, in the collection of papers that make up the 2011 volume, *The Oxford Handbook of the Economics of Religion*, the ancient world is completely absent.

37   See also Reader 2014, 13; and Orsi 1997.

38   *Economics of Cult in the Ancient Greek World*, a symposium held in Uppsala in 1990, discussed a wide range of different sources, both epigraphic and archaeological, see Linders – Alroch 1992. Continuing this tradition of Swedish research, Gunnel Ekroth and Judy Barringer organised the conference "Logistics in Greek Sanctuaries: Exploring the Human Experience of Visiting the Gods" in Athens 13–16 September 2018. Recently, a comparable conference on the economics of Roman religion was held in Oxford and publication of the proceedings is eagerly awaited: http://oxrep.classics.ox.ac.uk/conferences/the_economics_of_roman_religion/ (accessed 10 October 2019). The main topic for the 19th International Congress of Classical Archaeology in 2018 was "Archaeology and Economy in the Ancient World" and included sessions on the archaeology of cult in the ancient world (http://www.aiac2018.de) (accessed 10 October 2019).

the continued separation of economics and religion is in part a legacy of the ideological frameworks that structure the field of economics itself. Both capitalism and Marxism actively diminish the role of the sacred in human life and focus instead on production and consumption as the overriding aspects of importance. Davies, by contrast, emphasises the importance of understanding the embeddedness of economic behaviour within broader social actions – in particular, the role of temples and cults as economic actors.[39]

Similarly, this modernising separation of religion and economy is also witnessed in the long-term habits of Classical archaeology. Excavations of sanctuaries and sacred places have been the focus of systematic attention for archaeologists since the late nineteenth century, and have produced rich data with huge potential for addressing economic questions.[40] In addition to their roles as local, regional or international social hubs or places for political negotiations, as arenas for physical competition among individuals as well as competitive display between cities, as special places where the supernatural could be accessed and petitioned, ancient sanctuaries were also sites of production and consumption. Olympia, for instance, has plentiful evidence of *in situ* bronze casting, such as miscasts and moulds, evidence that is interpreted as a signal of the growing international importance of the sanctuary from the seventh century BCE onwards (Fig. 1.1).[41] However, the work that has been done on this aspect of Olympia is in many ways an exception, and the sacred economies of many other sanctuaries across the ancient Mediterranean remain underexplored. Pertinent cases for further exploration include both monumental construction, such as the treasuries (*thesauroi*) that were present in Greek sanctuaries, and the full range of smaller votive dedications.[42] Both categories demonstrate some of the complex ways through which monetary and sacred value was enmeshed, as well as how the sanctuaries' economic networks operated at many different levels.

Of course, the bond between the 'religious' and the economic has a much deeper time depth than that under discussion here. Indeed, in order to stimulate further questions about the complex relationship between the economic foundations of ancient Mediterranean sanctuaries, it may be fruitful to consider work on prehistoric settings across the wider area. Recently, Ian Hodder has used the term 'religion at work' to explore the role of what he terms 'vital

---

39   Davies 2005, 131–2.
40   It should be noted that especially pottery specialists working on both urban and rural sites more generally have adopted a range of economic models in their work, see *e.g.* Brughmans – Poblome 2016.
41   Morgan 1990, 35–9.
42   See Arafat 2009 on treasuries and Pausanias' conception of value.

FIGURE 1.1   Miniature tripods from Olympia, Olympia Archaeological Museum
PHOTO: TROELS MYRUP KRISTENSEN, BY PERMISSION OF THE HELLENIC
MINISTRY OF CULTURE AND SPORTS, EPHORATE OF ANTIQUITIES OF
ELIA, ARCHAEOLOGICAL RECEIPTS FUND)

matter' at the Neolithic site of Çatalhöyük in central Anatolia: that is, how 'materials and substances … played active roles in forming and transforming societies … constituting the religious by drawing numinous forces into the interstices of daily life'.[43] The term 'vital matter' not only foregrounds the material evidence, it also provides an important theoretical framework for the interpretation of all material culture using a 'religious', 'spiritual', 'numinous', or 'sacred' vocabulary; perhaps such an approach might see all of daily life as 'embedded' in the 'religious', rather than the other way round. The approaches and methodologies proposed by Hodder and his colleagues may stimulate further research on the way in which 'religion', economy and culture interact in significant ways that can be studied through material culture.[44]

---

43   Hodder 2014, 1.
44   Such holistic approaches are yet to make an impact on general study: recent handbooks on ancient religion, for example, do not focus on the inter-relationship between religion and economy: Insoll 2011; Rüpke 2011; Eidinow – Kindt 2015; Raja – Rüpke 2015.

And it is on the material evidence for pilgrimage that this volume is focused, because it offers an ideal window onto the ways in which the 'religious' and the economic elide. As Horden and Purcell observe,

> pilgrimage [...] need not always be a journey undertaken exclusively or even principally for religious reasons. '*Hem ziyaret hem tifaret*', as the Arabic phrase had it, 'partly pilgrimage, partly trade.' The travellers who invoked divine protection for their essentially non-religious journey shade into the pilgrims whose religious voyage could embrace many material opportunities.[45]

Previous work on ancient Mediterranean pilgrimage has been concerned with the essential job of finding and detailing pilgrimage practices.[46] The central argument of the present volume is that economic activity has fundamentally always been embedded into pilgrimage, and to some degree, 'sacred' and pilgrimage activities also form part of economic life. This includes economic activity at and relating to sanctuaries, but also the extension of the bond between pilgrimage and economy across the broader productive and commercial landscape of the ancient Mediterranean.[47]

3   The Embedded Economies of Pilgrimage from Archaic Greece to Late Antiquity

The contributions to this volume focus on three key parts of the 'embedded economies' of ancient Mediterranean pilgrimage where 'religious' and economic practices are most closely or visibly connected. These three elements, movements, communities, and transactions, do merge into one another and overlap in important ways, for example, in the building of community while engaging in a pilgrimage journey; however, attending to the elements individually allows us to highlight specific features one by one. Taken together, the three groupings are broad enough to constitute a fruitful structural framework through which to study the embedded economies of ancient Mediterranean pilgrimage, and the ways in which these remained the same or changed through time. Subdividing these categories further to engage with specific moments in

---

45   Horden – Purcell 2000, 445.
46   Kowalzig 2007 is exceptional in considering choral *theoria* as part of economic networks.
47   For long-term perspectives on pilgrimage, see Coleman – Elsner 1995; McCorriston 2011; 2017.

pilgrimage practice, for example, feasting or communal meals, or 'seeing the god' itself, we felt would detract from the volume's broader aim of interrogating the embedded economies of ancient Mediterranean pilgrimage practices.

The pair of papers that make up the first part of the volume – 'Movements' – examine the economic elements and implications of how people in antiquity prepared for and undertook pilgrimage journeys, investigating means of transport and infrastructure, and the experience of travel itself. Study of contemporary pilgrimage practices often places a strong focus on the journey as an important spiritual and emotional preparation for the pilgrim: that is, by undergoing physical hardship on the way to the shrine, the pilgrim is more in tune with their spiritual needs, their emotional state of being, their hopes and fears, and their own selves.[48] In contemporary terms, the journey is a vital aspect of the framing that pilgrims often seek in their lives more broadly; and it is often the journey that is undertaken by non-religious individuals who are seeking a new perspective in their lives. However, it is unclear whether such inner focus or sense of personal spiritual journey formed any part in the practice of ancient pilgrimage; and some scholars have made the argument that focusing on the experience of the journey in antiquity detracts from the key element for ancient people, reaching the sacred place itself.[49] However, people did engage in journeys, both short and long, in order to reach a sacred centre, and even if they were not the main element, those journeys nevertheless merit at least some of our attention — not least because travel in antiquity was arduous, dangerous and costly, both economically and in time. The two papers chosen for this section both look explicitly at the journey to the sanctuary and the theoretical and practical aspects involved, from slightly different angles. Anna Collar grounds the discussion of pilgrimage through her investigation of the physical act of walking and the reconstruction of a particular walked journey, whereas Marlena Whiting broadens out the discussion to show the physically intertwined relationship between pilgrimage and secular infrastructure. Both papers demonstrate that attention to the journey as part of the pilgrimage is an important element to consider for antiquity.

Collar's argument rests on the proposition that we can look at the act of walking to a sanctuary or shrine as an element in the act of devotion, familiar from Christian and Buddhist contexts, but not considered as part of

---

48   See, for example, the work of Egan 2007 and Chemin 2015 which explore the companionship and phenomenology of contemporary pilgrimage, or observations of increased Papal indulgences given for longer distances travelled in the high medieval period, Bell – Dale 2011.

49   Frankfurter forthcoming.

pilgrimage further back in antiquity. The many mountaintop sanctuaries in the Mediterranean invite us to think differently about the arduousness of the journey in antiquity: not only are these locations highly sacred, but they are also 'difficult' to get to. Because the journey up to a mountain sanctuary required a 'hard walk' from participants, the act of taking time away from normal work and the expenditure of physical energy in journeying to such a place can be interpreted abstractly as an economic contribution. The second half of Collar's paper uses satellite imagery and GIS techniques to reconstruct routes up the holy mountain Kasios (Jebel Aqraa, on the border between Turkey and Syria). In so doing, she considers both the labour involved in such an ascent, arguing that we can reconceptualise the journey as part of a pilgrim's devotion to the deity, and the ancillary physical requirements of a pilgrim for shelter and refreshment on the steep climb up to the mountain sanctuary.

The practical needs of pilgrims on pilgrimage are explored in more depth by Marlena Whiting in the second paper of the pair, which demonstrates the intertwining of the 'religious' and the 'secular' precisely in the routes pilgrims took on their journeys to sanctuaries in late antique Sinai. Any traveller, she argues, no matter how 'sacred' their motivations or destination, used 'secular' infrastructure, and this created what she describes as a 'braided network' of road systems, lodgings and markets. The term captures the plurality of people moving for (ostensibly) different reasons who occupied the same physical environment, but which differentiates between the separate motivations and destinations of each group of travellers. The development of the pilgrimage network in this case influenced the state network of routes, so demonstrating their mutual dependency. However, were motivations for travel that clearly differentiated, prior to the adoption of Christianity? Horden and Purcell's 'part pilgrimage, part trade' observation is important to remember in relation to this question. Whiting's observation of apparently different motivations for travel and the dependency of the pilgrim and secular routes in Christian Sinai may in fact demonstrate this sliding scale between reasons for travel: perhaps to some degree, all traders were also pilgrims. Whiting highlights the social side of the journey to a sanctuary, showing the ways that formal or informal groups met and travelled together, perhaps for reasons of spiritual community, or for more practical reasons of safety in numbers. A sense of community and the sharing of a similar frame of mind with fellow pilgrims has become a commonly recorded phenomenon in observations of modern pilgrimage practice (viz. the Turners' sense of *communitas*), but it is perhaps less clear in antiquity and in the material evidence.

The social, community elements of pilgrimage and their economic implications are more conspicuous once the sacred destination was reached, and this moves us into the second group of papers in this volume, 'Communities'. Participation in communal processions was involved in visitation of many shrines, for example, the processions along the sacred way between Athens and Eleusis. Various sources document the performances along the way — dances, libations, singing of hymns, and ritual washing in particular places — that each had economic implications at different levels, from the individual to the *polis*.[50] New clothes, musicians, and sustenance along the way were all prerequisites. At the Eleusinion near the Athenian agora, the numerous excavated dedications demonstrate the level of economic investment of the participants in the cult in the starting point of the procession,[51] and the economics of ritual participation can be glimpsed in Aristophanes' *Peace*, which informs us of provision of piglets for sacrificial rites on the second day of the Eleusinian Mysteries, each costing a mere three *drachmae*.[52]

Sustenance for pilgrims is an essential economic element of pilgrimage. In such ritualised contexts, food consumption is often couched as feasting and is has major social, economic, legal, judicial, moral and religious functions, which Michael Dietler argues contribute to public demonstrations of social control.[53] Materially, the remains of ritual feasting events have been identified in a number of contexts from the Bronze Age onwards.[54] A Linear B tablet from Pylos seems to indicate that initiation of the king into mysteries (*mu-jo-me-no*) at a particular sanctuary was an occasion for large-scale feasting, with a list of the quantities of foodstuffs required to make up the banquet.[55] In the development of early Greek sanctuaries, where temples had yet to reach the level of monumentality that they did from the Archaic period onwards, feasting and drinking are the most archaeologically visible activities, as evident from the material record of ceramic cups and animal bones from sites such as that which later became the Panhellenic sanctuary of Poseidon at Isthmia.[56] At Eleusis, gathering together (*agyrmos*) is named in the initiation process, and in the days that followed, associated communal drinking of a specific ritual drink (*kikeona*) to break a communal fast played a central role in the rituals of the mysteries.[57] The experience of gathering as a community was mediated and

---

50   Bremmer 2014, 6.

51   Miles 1998.

52   Ar., *Peace*, 374; Dillon 1997, 63.

53   Dietler 2011, 182,

54   *Hesperia* 73 (2004) was entirely devoted to feasting in various contexts across the Bronze Age Aegean.

55   PY Un 2, see Palaima 2004.

56   Morgan 1994, 113.

57   Bremmer 2014.

staged through acts of consumption, such as sacrifice, feasting and dedication. These acts are also fundamentally economic, and can be interpreted as investments in dominant (or competing) power bases, as acts of redistribution of resources, as acts of social control, participation, or exclusion, and so on.

The experience of community was also mediated through performances in particular spaces. In terms of built architecture, theatres or buildings such as the *telesterion* at Eleusis offer examples of spaces with the capacity to seat many participants at the same time — the *telesterion* could seat 3000 people, even if, as Plutarch records, there was 'shouting and uncomfortable jostling' involved.[58] Equally, open spaces free of architectural structures were places for people to come together as a community, both for ritual purposes and as temporary homes to merchants and traders selling goods — both the stuff of ritual and religious souvenirs, as well as daily essentials. The religious and the economic were, at the fairs associated with festivals, perhaps at their most cheek-by-jowl, even co-dependent.

The three papers that make up the discussion of communities here examine the economic impacts of festivals and the ancillary services required by pilgrims across a diverse range of places and across a broad sweep of time. These range from the earliest evidence for non-local, temporary community at archaic Delphi, through the highly organised and regulated festivals of the Hellenistic period, when the commercial opportunities for civic publicity and self-aggrandisement expanded greatly, into the early Christian period, and specifically into how communities were catered for physically at pilgrimage shrines. Juxtaposing the evidence for these festival events from across a thousand-year period allows us to see how there are similarities between them, as well as bringing the development of the economic elements into sharp relief. At Delphi, Hélène Aurigny highlights the commercial side of the festival fair and the impact that large groups of pilgrims had on the physical layout and architecture of the sanctuary itself. Finding little evidence to suggest that at the earliest periods, provision was made for pilgrims' accommodation, she suggests that most people would have found lodging within the city of Delphi or camped on the plain of Itea below, underlining the economic relationship between private citizens in the city and the authorities in the sanctuary. In more concrete terms, Aurigny observes how the gifting of votive bronzes and treasury buildings can be viewed as the materialisation of pilgrimage to Delphi, and the political and social competition between individuals and civic communities that their dedication, display or construction entailed. This element of conflict or competition has been highlighted by Eade and Sallnow:

---

58   Bremmer 2014, 9; Plut. *De Prof. virt.* 10, 81de.

pilgrimage was not only a place for the building of *communitas*, as the Turners argued. The rivalry between cities and elites is most transparently visible in the treasuries that line the processional way to Delphi, and where the 'religious' and the economic melded into one.

Competition and rivalry certainly became a major element of hosting festivals in the subsequent world of the Hellenistic kingdoms, because a well-organised *panegyris* (festival fair) would add much to a city's status as an attractive and prestigious sacred destination. This was a period of huge increase in the numbers of civic festivals, in part because of the political possibilities for diplomacy, reciprocal invitations and inter-city support that they offered, but also representing a clear investment in the economy of building inter-regional communities around shrines and sanctuaries as an important part of the broader economic palette of the *polis*. Marietta Horster's focus is on the financial and infrastructural impact that festivals had on cities and sanctuaries. At the inception of many of these newly-founded Hellenistic festivals, cities had to build a new community, a process that required their festivals to be recognised across a broader region. This was achieved by means of official sacred ambassadors, *theoroi*; and receipt of such invitations was generally honoured by the sending of a sacred embassy, or *theoria*, to the festival in question in return. Reciprocity was a key part of this process of building inter-regional festival communities, and cities went to great lengths to make their festival appealing to outsiders: offering associated draws such as sporting competitions, dance or theatrical performances, feasts, markets and so on. This technique of 'added extras' is well-known in the medieval period,[59] for example, and it is useful to see this outlined for earlier periods too.

With the growth of the international Christian community and the engulfing of the ancient 'pagan' sanctuaries and festivals of the Mediterranean under a new message of belief and salvation, we see also a subtle change in the messages about community as witnessed in the archaeological record. Pilgrims and festival attendees in earlier times were generally housed in local elite houses or left to fend for themselves under canvas, but as yet, no accommodation that relates to the sanctuary in an official capacity has been categorically identified archaeologically. However, in Late Antiquity, pilgrims were catered for by accommodation provided at sanctuaries, in part relating to the capacity of these sanctuaries to offer healing for sick individuals. At the pilgrimage site of St. Crispina's martyrdom at Theveate in North Africa, for example, there is evidence for dormitories, stables, and locking-door cells. In this third paper looking at pilgrimage and community, Robin Jensen explores the key issue of

---

59   Bell – Dale 2011.

the overnight accommodation of pilgrims, looking at the different terms in the literary sources, how pilgrim accommodations were funded, and the subtle change that was enacted between hostel and hospital as healing became part of the Church's key role as caregiver. Although the provision of hostels and built structures certainly marks a shift in the economic investment by shrines in their community of visitors, Jensen notes that these buildings would have housed a fraction of the estimated pilgrims to Crispina's shrine, for example, and many pilgrims would have had to find alternative places to stay.

The next group of papers are perhaps the most explicitly 'economic' in the traditional sense, as they revolve around the notion of 'transactions'. We have chosen this term to deliberately set wide the angle through which we can examine different aspects of transaction as a pilgrim or at a sanctuary. This is intended to cover the buying and selling of daily goods as well as souvenirs or items of spiritual meaning which would have taken place at most festival fairs of the ancient world, but to extend beyond the market element of exchange to include also the process of exchange between pilgrim and deity at a more conceptual level. This includes sacrifice and nuances the discussion of the 'gift' in this context of the relationship between human and deity.

The gift as a central aspect of pre-modern economies has been part of sociological and anthropological scholarly discourse since Marcel Mauss' exposition of the subject in 1925,[60] which outlined the reciprocity inherent in giving, the social obligations that result from giving, and the power of objects in bringing about social exchanges because of the continuing association between the giver and the gift itself. The gift blurs the lines between modern categorisations of economy and the rest of human social life, not least as an aspect of pilgrimage, of which it was a key part.[61] In pilgrimage, the gift can be many things. Perhaps the most durable archaeologically are high-value metal votives, such as those discussed by Aurigny at Delphi, and the deposition of votive offerings in sanctuary settings has a long history of study within classical scholarship. The subject continues to receive fresh exploration and interpretation, with anatomical *ex votos* – the dedicated representations of body parts often discovered in ancient Greek sanctuaries – recently being discussed as metaphorical conceptions of the fragmentation felt by the sick human body.[62] In the context of late antique Christianity, recent work has also proposed increasingly

---

60   Mauss 2016.
61   See also Carlà – Gori 2014.
62   See, for example, Rouse 1902; Weinryb 2015; 2018; Hughes 2017.

sophisticated interpretations of the changing social, religious and economic dynamics of gifts and blessings.[63]

A gift in pilgrimage can be a sacrifice of something: animals and comestibles, the hard-won fruits of agricultural labour, were a standard sacrificial offering to the divine in the ancient world. In this section of the book, Fred Naiden explores the relationship between these physical offerings of blood, sweat and tears and their gradual replacement with offerings of commodities, bought for the express purpose of offering to the deity, and finally, the elision of the bought offering into the simple gift of money itself. By teasing apart the different possibilities for sacrificial offerings — first fruits, the purchase of commodities, and the giving of money — Naiden presents a serious challenge to views about the meaning of sacrifice offered in earlier scholarship.[64] In donating money, participants were involved not in the smoke and flames of an altar of death, but in the chink of coins in the collection box. The collection box is highlighted as a silent innovation, one that engendered subtle changes in the economy of Greek religious practice — and one which is now the most obvious form of sacrifice for the contemporary Sunday churchgoer.

People too were gifts, dedicated to deities:[65] the manumission of slaves was often achieved within a sacred setting, at least in the Hellenistic period.[66] Sacred manumission implies that freed people, given to, 'sold' to, or protected by the gods, were *gifts*: the sociologist Orlando Patterson observed that 'the whole complex of ideas and interactions involved in the release from slavery amounts to a classic instance of the anthropology of gift exchange.'[67] Collar has suggested in this volume that the time and labour involved in going to a sanctuary could be seen abstractly as comprising a gift, part of which can be expressed as performativity — the *act* of gift-giving perhaps also in some way comprises the gift itself. If euergetic contributions such as the funding of

---

63   Caner 2006.

64   For example, the view of William Robertson Smith, that sacrifice produced kin groups through sharing a communal meal, Smith 1889: Walter Burkert, that sacrifice was used to expiate the guilt of killing, Burkert 1972: or Detienne and Vernant (1979/1989), who argued that sacrifice was about the consumption and distribution of the meat as a political act. See Knust – Varhelyi, 2011.

65   In addition to the dedication of prisoners of war or slaves to temples, a common practice in Assyria, for example, free people could be dedicated to the temple. Children, especially of indebted families or during times of shortage, were sometimes 'given' to a sanctuary as a temple slave, for example, the two young sons of a widow who were given to the temple during a period of famine (Dougherty 1920, 154). The sale of children and siblings into slavery was not uncommon in the ancient Near East, see Mendelsohn 1949 for examples.

66   Kamen 2014, 284.

67   Patterson 1985, 211.

choral performances, or the provision of musicians can be understood as acts of giving to the deities, can the speech act or even the act of repeating a prayer also be seen as 'gifts'?

Essential to the act of giving is the implication of *receiving*, the contract between human and divine (or human and sanctuary, perhaps). It is trust that forms the critical emotional quality of reciprocity in gift-giving: the trust that the gift given will be received appropriately and that as gift-giver, you will be rewarded: that the gift will in fact turn out to be a transaction. Where supernatural exchange partners are involved, however, givers may experience a delay in the receipt of their reward — yet this does not hinder the giving of gifts to gods. Why? This is where trust elides into belief: the knowledge that in making the gift to the deity, *at some point* the transaction will be completed, in ways as yet unknown. Esther Eidinow turns this discussion on its head, and shows that it is the commitment by worshippers in this transaction that breathes life into the gods themselves. She explores the implied reciprocal relationship at the core of the human-divine interaction in ancient Greece: the *do ut des* transaction between people and gods, and the notion of expected divine beneficence that worshippers felt was due in return for their own material gift. Eidinow digs deeper into the concept of the transaction of gift-giving and the associated narratives about the identities of giver and receiver that the gift implies. She argues that this transaction is described and created through narratives, and that these narratives then construct the identities and roles of the individuals involved. This observation that the narrative of gift-giving and divine reciprocity constructs identities on both sides of the equation enables her to show how narrative is critical to the creation of the divine itself. Gods are given the gift of existence by their worshippers.

From the conceptual transactions that co-create people and their divinities, the papers in the second half of the 'Transactions' section move to the signature of more worldly transactions at and beyond sanctuaries in terms of the material record. Fairs and markets have been mentioned briefly by Horster as part of the discussion of the economic impact of large gatherings of people on the physical infrastructure of cities and sanctuaries, but here, Troels Myrup Kristensen focuses on the material evidence for fairs, markets and spaces of economic exchange in the context of Greek sanctuaries. Although such fairs are well-known from literary and epigraphical evidence, their archaeological 'footprint' is often difficult to locate. But it is important that we try to do so, because the open spaces in the ruins of Mediterranean sanctuaries should be re-imagined as full to bursting with stalls, traders, trinkets and the bustle of the marketplace, at least some of the time.

Much of the discussion to this point has been on communities and transactions in sanctuaries without consideration of broader context. Louise Blanke, however, looks at the impact of a changing socio-political milieu on minority Christian monastic communities of Egypt. The rise of Islam effected pronounced physical changes in the structure of these communities. Using hagiographical literature and the archaeological record in tandem, Blanke argues for an increase in regular pilgrimage to the monasteries, and the associated economic requirement made of pilgrims to provide a donation.[68] She highlights a community of spiritual users in the monastery's hinterland, consuming regularly-accessed spiritual services, including celebration of feast days, exorcisms, baptisms, funerals and so on. This repeated, lower-level, localised engagement with the monastic complexes provided the core of the reinvigorated spiritual economy in the sixth century, however, the external forces of decreasing patronage and increasing taxation that forced the re-engagement of the monastic communities with the wider world — and the wider world's money — were products of the socio-religious change from Christianity to Islam.

In a similar way, the production of sacred items and souvenirs was a key part of the economic activity of sanctuaries. Concluding the section on transactions, Max Ritter discusses the specific example of *eulogia*: semi-perishable oils, waxes or dusts that were rendered holy through their contact with saintly Christian bodies or places, and which come to prominence in the record for pilgrimage in Late Antiquity. *Eulogiai* were given to pilgrims as a blessing to carry home, to heal the pilgrim or her relatives, act as an apotropaic device, or to testify to a pilgrimage undertaken. *Eulogia* containers — often misunderstood as the *eulogia* themselves — represent an important archaeological indicator of this act of creation, distribution and use of sacred artefacts. Ritter argues that the *eulogiai* themselves (but *not* the containers) were given as a free, non-returnable gift to all pilgrims visiting any pilgrimage site, in return for which the pilgrimage centre expected an immediate reciprocal gift — a gift that contributed greatly to wages of the clerics that ran the centre and similar to that expected by the monastic communities of Egypt examined by Blanke. By contrast, specific 'branded' containers produced by certain pilgrimage sites (Jerusalem, Abu Mena, Qal'at Sem'an) formalised the implied reciprocity of the giving of *eulogiai* by offering the containers themselves for sale.

---

68   Blanke eschews the term pilgrimage here, preferring 'visitation' because of the implication of repetition that this term allows. Note Frankfurter's similar objection to the term pilgrimage for the same reasons, he too prefers the term 'shrine visit' (forthcoming).

The volume concludes with two papers which outline the bigger picture of ancient pilgrimage economies and present some future directions in which the study of ancient Mediterranean pilgrimage can be taken in order to understand the fundamental relationship between ancient sanctuaries and the economy more broadly. The first encourages us to look again at the gatherings of people that took place as part of pilgrimage, emphasising the inseparability of 'sacred' and economic through the festival fair — encompassing movements, community and transactions; and the second exhorts us to experiment with modelling and the application of modern economic theories in our attempts to understand social behaviour at ancient sanctuaries. Barbara Kowalzig's wide ranging overview of festivals and fairs as associated and intertwined events draws out a transnational and multi-period picture of the particular ways the religious and the commercial were connected: through movement, community and transaction. Emphasising the consistent use through time of specific language to describe these festival fairs — especially the 'multitudes of people' and the overwhelming shine, gleam and glitter of the events — she demonstrates the generation of a 'community of giving and receiving' in emotional as well as economic terms. It is through this temporarily-gathered community that Kowalzig articulates the twin religious and economic core of the festival fair: simultaneously those of giving and receiving, and of buying and selling. Her ideas about the creation of temporary community in geographically and temporally 'liminal zones' resonate with Victor and Edith Turner's ideas about pilgrimage offering participants a sense of *communitas*: a new social space which enables the pilgrim to step beyond their ordinary existence and become part of a group in which identities are temporarily blended and merged.[69]

The volume concludes with Dan-el Padilla Peralta's suggestion that we can employ modern economic theory to look at and model the ancient world. His subject is trust, the key contractual binding force between people; and his case study is the island of Delos, famous both for Apollo's sanctuary and renowned as an economic hub of international standing in the Classical and Hellenistic periods. He argues that Apollo's statue was an enticement to traders, in part because economic transactions were sanctified and sworn upon statues and altars, but Padilla Peralta goes further in advancing the theory that economic behaviour itself was regulated and influenced by the presence of the divine. He argues that the statues of the gods on the island acted as ecological signals to visitors, generating positive social capital, which in turn encouraged cooperative behaviour among the groups of traders. The investment by private religious associations in monuments and buildings for communities built up a

69   Turner – Turner 1978.

landscape of trust among diverse economic actors on the island. He argues that it is the religious aspect of these associations which is critical to understanding their function: in creating what Vincent Gabrielsen terms 'brotherhoods of faith' among those who participate in cult together, these associations worked to build up trust in other people: an imperative for the success of long-distance trade operations. Finally, it is the power of this place as both cultic and trading centre, he argues, that enabled the centuries-long slave trade to flourish here. He reminds us that future directions in the study of Delos in particular but ancient Mediterranean trade/pilgrimage more broadly too, must also account for the unwilling participation of people moved for somebody else's profit, and not for their own.

4   Conclusion and Future Perspectives

Together the chapters in this volume demonstrate the potential of approaching the economies of ancient Mediterranean sanctuaries as 'embedded' within a larger 'pilgrimage economy' that incorporates a very wide range of elements other than those that simply involve market exchange. They draw out some of the elements of pilgrimage practices in the ancient Mediterranean which can be usefully compared over time (for example, the physical infrastructure required to shelter pilgrims is explored in both Archaic Delphi and in the shrines of saints in Christian North Africa). They also highlight some of the impact of changing religious practices, institutions and beliefs on the material that we see on the ground, such as the gradual process of monetisation seen in ancient Greek sacrificial practice, the sale of *eulogia* containers as part of a new Christian pilgrimage economy, and the impact that Islam had on the economics of monastic communities.

By bringing together studies of specific elements of pilgrimage practice from a range of geographical locations and across a broad swathe of time, we hope to demonstrate the comparative power of using the term 'pilgrimage' to examine material and sanctuaries in the ancient Mediterranean, and to show that the lens of pilgrimage offers an exciting way to examine the on-the-ground entanglements of 'religion' and 'economy' in the ancient world. There are many others aspects of the embedded pilgrimage economy that some readers may miss — for example, none of our authors discuss feasting, divination or *darshan* (interactions of people with (images of) the deity) in depth — but we argue that the three facets we have identified here (movements, communities and transactions) have the capacity to include these more specific experiences of pilgrimage. Future studies may add these or other dimensions to the discussion and may also integrate the material evidence even more systematically into the historical narrative than that which is attempted here.

Many questions remain, such as whether pilgrimage generated economic activity beyond the demand for ancillary services or pilgrim souvenirs, for example, by lowering transaction costs between fellow devotees or initiates, or by altering the availability of information. Recent work by Sandra Blakely on the cult of the Great Gods of Samothrace implies that alongside the initiate's guarantee of safety at sea, the sanctuary functioned also as a place of legal contracts between cities to refrain from piracy, and as a place to give and receive information about sailing routes, for example.[70] Connected to this, we might also ask how far pilgrimage followed routes that were already in existence, or if sanctuaries saw opportunities for developing markets and economic activity, and so created festivals for the purpose of income generation. Certainly this could be said to have happened during the boom in festival foundations of the Hellenistic period, for example. And how far do different kinds of ancient pilgrimage start to create an intensely networked world through which other kinds of information could travel?[71] Scholars of the ancient world are only beginning to understand how pilgrimage may be used to reveal the richness and complexity of cult behaviours and motivations, and it is our hope that the field will continue to grow in diversity and approaches.[72]

Bibliography

Andreau, J. 2002. "Markets, Fairs and Monetary Loans: Cultural History and Economic History in Roman Italy and Hellenistic Greece", in *Money, Labour and Land. Approaches to the Economies of Ancient Greece*, eds. P. Cartledge, E.E. Cohen, and L. Foxhall, London, 113–29.

Arafat, K.W. 2009. "Treasure, Treasuries and Value in Pausanias", *The Classical Quarterly* 59.2, 578–92.

---

70   Blakely 2018.
71   A new research project, *Connecting the Greeks: multi-scalar festival networks in the Hellenistic world*, led by Onno van Nijf and Christina Williamson and funded by the Dutch Research Council (NWO) 2019–2023, suggests that network methods are a useful tool to model the interactions of sanctuaries, an approach that may also be fruitful for thinking about other forms of pilgrimage.
72   Future publications on ancient Mediterranean pilgrimage from the "Emergence of Sacred Travel" project include Collar – Kristensen forthcoming; Kristensen forthcoming.

Aswad, C. 2017. "Exclusive: Saudi Arabia to resume building mammoth Mecca hotel – sources". *Reuters*: https://www.reuters.com/article/us-saudi-hotel/exclusive-saudi-arabia-to-resume-building-mammoth-mecca-hotel-sources-idUSKCN1AU1LX (last accessed 21 June 2019).

Austin, M.M. and Vidal-Naquet, P. 1980. *Economic and Social History of Ancient Greece*, Berkeley, CA.

Bailey, A.E. 2013. "Modern and Medieval approaches to Pilgrimage, Gender and Sacred Space", *History and Anthropology* 24.4, 493–512.

Bang, P.F. 2008. *The Roman Bazaar. A Comparative Study of Trade and Markets in a Tributary Empire*, Cambridge.

Barrett, C.E. 2016. "Archaeology of Ancient Religions", *Oxford Research Encyclopedia. Religion*, DOI: http://dx.doi.org/10.1093/acrefore/9780199340378.013.48.

Barton, C.A. and Boyarin, D. 2016. *Imagine No Religion. How Modern Abstractions Hide Ancient Realities*, New York, NY.

Beard, M., North, J., and Price, S. 1998. *Religions of Rome. Volume 1. A History*, Cambridge.

Bell, A.R. and Dale, R.S. 2011. "The Medieval Pilgrimage Business", *Enterprise & Society* 12.3, 601–27.

Blakely, S. 2018. "Sailing with the Gods: Serious Games in an Ancient Sea", *Thersites* 7, 107–53.

Bremmer, J. 1999. *Greek Religion*, second edition, Oxford.

Bremmer, J. 2014. *Initiation into the Mysteries of the Ancient World*, Berlin.

Bremmer, J. 2017. "Pilgrimage Progress?", in *Excavating Pilgrimage. Archaeological Approaches to Sacred Travel and Movement in the Ancient World*, eds. T.M. Kristensen and W. Friese, London, 275–84.

Bresson, A. 2016. *The Making of the Ancient Greek Economy. Institutions, Markets and Growth in the City-States*, Princeton, NJ.

Brown, P. 2012. *Through the Eye of a Needle. Wealth, the Fall of Rome, and the Making of Christianity in the West, 350–550 AD*, Princeton.

Brughmans, T. and Poblome, J. 2016. "Roman Bazaar or Market Economy? Explaining Tableware Distributions through Computational Modelling", *Antiquity* 90 (350), 393–408.

Burkert, W. 1983. *Homo Necans: The Anthropology of Ancient Greek Sacrificial Ritual and Myth*, trans. P. Bing, Berkeley, CA.

Caner, D. 2006. "Towards a Miraculous Economy: Christian Gifts and Material 'Blessing' in Late Antiquity", *Journal of Early Christian Studies* 14.3, 329–77.

Carlá, F. and Gori, M. eds. 2014. *Gift Giving and the 'Embedded' Economy in the Ancient World*, Heidelberg.

Chélini, J. and Branthomme, H. 1987. *Histoire des pèlerinages non chrétiens. Entre magique et sacré: le chemin des dieux*, Paris.

Chemin, E. 2015. "The Seductions of the Way: The Return of the Pilgrim and the Road to Compostela as a Liminal Space", in *The Seductions of Pilgrimage. Sacred Journeys Afar and Astray in the Western Religious Tradition*, eds. M.A. Di Giovane and D. Picard, Abingdon, 211–32.

Cochrane, P. 2018. "The Economics of Hajj". *ACCA Global*: https://www.accaglobal .com/an/en/member/member/accounting-business/2018/07/insights/economics -hajj.html (last accessed June 21, 2019).

Coleman, S. 2002. "Do You Believe in Pilgrimage? *Communitas*, Contestation and Beyond", *Anthropological Theory* 2.3, 355–68.

Coleman, S. and Elsner, J. 1995. *Pilgrimage Past and Present. Sacred Travel and Sacred Space in the World Religions*, London.

Collar, A. and Kristensen, T.M. Forthcoming. *Pilgrims in Place, Pilgrims in Motion*, Aarhus.

Concannon, C.W. and Mazurek, L.A. 2016. "Introduction: A New Connectivity for the Twenty-First Century", in *Across the Corrupting Sea: Post-Braudelian Approaches to the Ancient Eastern Mediterranean*, eds. C.W. Concannon and L.A. Mazurek, London, 1–16.

Davies, J.K. 2005. "Linear and Nonlinear Flow Models for Ancient Economies", in *The Ancient Economy. Evidence and Models*, eds. J.G. Manning and I. Morris, Stanford, CA, 127–56.

Detienne, M. and Vernant, J.-P. 1989. *The Cuisine of Sacrifice among the Greeks*, trans. P. Wissing, Chicago – London.

Dietler, M. 2011. "Feasting and Fasting", in *Oxford Handbook of the Archaeology of Ritual and Religion*, ed. T. Insoll, Oxford, 179–94.

Dignas, B. 2002. *Economy of the Sacred in Hellenistic and Roman Asia Minor*, Oxford.

Dillon, M. 1997. *Pilgrims and Pilgrimage in Ancient Greece*, London.

Dougherty, R.P. 1920. *Records from Erech, Time of Nabonidus (555–538 B.C.)*. Yale Oriental Series, Babylonian Texts, Vol. VI, New Haven.

Drbal, V. 2018. *Pilgerfahrt im spätantiken Nahen Osten (3./4.-8. Jahrhundert). Paganes, christliches, jüdisches und islamisches Pilgerwesen. Fragen der Kontinuitäten*, Mainz.

Eade, J. and Sallnow, M.J. eds. 1991a. *Contesting the Sacred. The Anthropology of Christian Pilgrimage*, second edition, Eugene, OR.

Eade, J. and Sallnow, M.J. 1991b. "Introduction", in Eade – Sallnow 1991a, 1–29.

Egan, K. 2007. *In Defence of the Realm: Mobility, Modernity and Community on the Camino de Santiago*, unpublished PhD thesis, National University of Ireland Maynooth: http://eprints.maynoothuniversity.ie/5210/1/Keith_Egan_20140712073656.pdf.

Eidinow, E. 2015. "Ancient Greek Religion: 'Embedded'... and Embodied", in *Communities and Networks in the Ancient Greek World*, eds. K. Vlassopoulos and C. Taylor, Oxford, 54–79.

Eidinow, E. and Kindt, J. eds. 2015. *The Oxford Handbook of Ancient Greek Religion*. Oxford.

Ellyatt, H. 2012. "How Religious Pilgrimages Support a Multi-Billion Dollar Industry", *CNBC*: https://wwrn.org/articles/38133/ (last accessed 4 December 2019).

Elsner, J. 1992. "Pausanias: A Greek Pilgrim in the Roman World", *Past and Present* 135, 3–29.

Elsner, J. 2012. "Material Culture and Ritual: State of the Question", in *Architecture of the Sacred. Space, Ritual, and Experience from Classical Greece to Byzantium*, eds. B.D. Wescoat and R.G. Ousterhout, Cambridge, 1–26.

Elsner, J. 2017. "Excavating Pilgrimage", in *Excavating Pilgrimage. Archaeological Approaches to Sacred Travel and Movement in the Ancient World*, eds. T.M. Kristensen and W. Friese, Abingdon, 265–74.

Elsner, J. and Rutherford, I. eds. 2005. *Pilgrimage in Graeco-Roman and Early Christian Antiquity. Seeing the Gods*, Oxford.

Finley, M. 1973. *The Ancient Economy*, Berkeley, CA.

Frankfurter, D. ed. 1998. *Pilgrimage and Holy Space in Late Antique Egypt*, Leiden.

Frankfurter, D. 2015. Review of Nongbri 2015, *Journal of Early Christian Studies* 23.4, 632–4.

Frankfurter, D. Forthcoming. "Getting There: Reframing Pilgrimage from Process to Site", in *Pilgrimage in Place, Pilgrimage in Motion*, eds. A.C.F. Collar and T.M. Kristensen, Aarhus.

Friese, W. and Kristensen, T.M. 2017. "Introduction: Archaeologies of Pilgrimage", in *Excavating Pilgrimage. Archaeological Approaches to Sacred Travel and Movement in the Ancient World*, eds. T.M. Kristensen and W. Friese, Abingdon, 1–10.

Friese, W., Handberg, S., and Kristensen, T.M., eds. 2019. *Ascending and Descending the Acropolis. Movement in Athenian Religion*, Aarhus.

Gemici, K. 2008. "Karl Polanyi and the Antinomies of Embeddedness", *Socio-Economic Review* 6.1, 5–33.

Goldman, H. 2005. "*Economy and Society* and the Revision of Weber's Ethics", in *Max Weber's Economy and Society: A Critical Companion*, eds. C. Camic, P.S. Gorski, and D.M. Trubek, Stanford, CA, 47–69.

Greene, K. 1986. *The Archaeology of the Roman Economy*, Berkeley, CA.

Harland, P.A. ed. 2011. *Travel and Religion in Antiquity*, Waterloo, ON.

Hodder, I. ed. 2014. *Religion at Work in a Neolithic Society. Vital Matters*, Cambridge.

Horden, P. and Purcell, N. 2000. *The Corrupting Sea. A Study of Mediterranean History*, Malden, MA.

Horster, M. 2004. *Landbesitz griechischer Heiligtümer in archaischer und klassischer Zeit*, Berlin.

Hughes, J. 2017. *Votive Body Parts in Greek and Roman Religion*, Cambridge.

Insoll, T., ed. 2011. *Oxford Handbook of the Archaeology of Ritual and Religion*, Oxford.

Kamen, D. 2014. "Sale for the Purpose of Freedom: Slave-prostitutes and Manumission in Ancient Greece", *The Classical Journal* 109.3, 281–307.

Kindt, J. 2013. *Rethinking Greek Religion*, Cambridge.

Kippenberg, H.S. 2005. "Religious Communities and the Path to Disenchantment. The Origins. Sources, and Theoretical Core of the Religion Section", in *Max Weber's Economy and Society. A Critical Companion*, eds. C. Camic, P.S. Gorski, and D.M. Trubek, Stanford, CA, 164–82.

Knust J.W. and Varhelyi, Z. 2011. *Ancient Mediterranean Sacrifice*, Oxford.

Kowalzig, B. 2005. "Mapping Out *Communitas*: Performances of Theoria in their Sacred and Political Context", in Elsner – Rutherford 2005, 41–72.

Kowalzig, B. 2007. *Singing for the Gods. Performances of Myth and Ritual in Archaic and Classical Greece*, Oxford.

Kristensen, T.M. 2012a. "The Material Culture of Roman and Early Christian Pilgrimage: An Introduction", *HEROM* 1, 67–78.

Kristensen, T.M. 2012b. "Textiles, Tattoos and the Representation of Pilgrimage in the Roman and Early Christian Periods", *HEROM* 1, 107–34.

Kristensen, T.M. 2018. "Mobile Situations: *Exedrae* as Stages of Gathering in Greek Sanctuaries", *World Archaeology* 50.1, 86–99.

Kristensen, T.M. 2019. "New Approaches to Movement in Athenian Religion", in *Ascending and Descending the Acropolis. Movement in Athenian Religion*, eds. W. Friese, S. Handberg, and T.M. Kristensen, Aarhus, 11–9.

Kristensen, T.M. Forthcoming. *The Matter of Pilgrimage. Landscapes, Gatherings and Presence in Ancient Mediterranean Sanctuaries*, London.

Kristensen, T.M. and Friese, W. 2017. eds. *Excavating Pilgrimage. Archaeological Approaches to Sacred Travel and Movement in the Ancient World*, Abingdon.

Kyriakidis, E. 2007. *The Archaeology of Ritual*, Los Angeles.

Linders, T. and Alroth, B., eds. 1992. *Economics of Cult in the Ancient Greek. Proceedings of the Uppsala Symposium 1990*, Uppsala.

Maher, A. 2012. "The Economics of Hajj: Money and Pilgrimage," *BBC News*: http://www.bbc.co.uk/news/world-middle-east-20067809 (last accessed 4 December 2019).

Mauss, M. 2016. *The Gift*, trans. J.I. Guyer, Chicago.

McCorriston, J. 2011. *Pilgrimage and Household in the Ancient Near East*, Cambridge.

McCorriston, J. 2017. "Inter-cultural Pilgrimage, Identity, and the Axial Age in the Ancient Near East", in *Excavating Pilgrimage. Archaeological Approaches to Sacred Travel and Movement in the Ancient World*, eds. T.M. Kristensen and W. Friese, Abingdon, 11–27.

Mendelsohn, I. 1949. *Slavery in the Ancient Near East. A Comparative Study of Slavery in Babylonia, Assyria, Syria and Palestine from the middle of the Third Millennium to the end of the First Millennium*, New York.

Miles, M. 1998. *The Athenian Agora XXXI. The City Eleusinion*, Princeton, NJ.

Morgan, C. 1990. *Athletes and Oracles. The Transmission of Olympia and Delphi in the Eighth Century BC*, Cambridge.

Morgan, C. 1994. "The Evolution of a Sacral 'Landscape': Isthmia, Perachora, and the Early Corinthian State", in *Placing the Gods. Sanctuaries and Sacred Space in Ancient Greece*, eds. S.E. Alcock and R.G. Osborne, Oxford, 105–42.

Nongbri, B. 2008. "Dislodging 'Embedded' Religion: A Brief Note on a Scholarly Trope", *Numen* 55, 440–60.

Nongbri, B. 2015. *Before Religion. A History of a Modern Concept*, New Haven.

Orsi, R. 1997. "Everyday Miracles: The Study of Lived Religion", in *Lived Religion in America. Toward a History of Practice*, ed. D.D. Hall, Princeton, NJ, 3–21.

Palaima, T. 2004. "Sacrificial Feasting in the Linear B Documents", *Hesperia* 73.2, 217–46.

Parker, R. 1986. "Greek Religion", in *The Oxford History of Greece and the Hellenistic World*, eds. J. Boardman, J. Griffin, and O. Murray, Oxford, 306–29.

Parker, R. 1988. "Greek Religion", in *The Oxford Illustrated History of Greece and the Hellenistic World*, eds. J. Boardman, J. Griffin, and O. Murray, Oxford, 248–68.

Patterson, O. 1985. *Slavery and Social Death*, Cambridge, MA.

Petsalis-Diomidis, A. 2010. *'Truly Beyond Wonders.' Aelius Aristides and the Cult of Asklepios*, Oxford.

Plattner, S. 1989. "Introduction", in *Economic Anthropology*, ed. S. Plattner, Stanford, CA, 1–20.

Polanyi, K. 1957 [1944]. *The Great Transformation. The Political and Economic Origins of Our Time*, Boston.

Polanyi, K. 1977. *The Livelihood of Man,* ed. H.W. Pearson, New York.

Price, S. 1999. *Religions of the Ancient Greeks*, Cambridge.

Raja, R. and Rüpke, J. eds. 2015. *A Companion to the Archaeology of Religion in the Ancient World*, Malden, MA.

Reader, I. 2014. *Pilgrimage in the Marketplace*, Abingdon.

Rouse, W.H.D. 1902. *Greek Votive Offerings. An Essay in the History of Greek Religion*, Cambridge.

Rüpke, J., ed. 2011. *A Companion to Roman Religion*, Malden, MA.

Rutherford, I. 2013. *State Pilgrims and Sacred Observers in Ancient Greece. A Study of Theoria and Theoroi*, Cambridge.

Sheller, M. and Urry, J. 2006. "The New Mobilities Paradigm", *Environment and Planning A* 38, 207–26.

Smith, W.R. 1889. *Lectures on the Religion of the Semites. Fundamental Institutions, First Series*, London.

Turner, V. and Turner, E.L.B. 1978. *Image and Pilgrimage in Christian Culture*, New York.

Weber, M. 1968. *Economy and Society*, 3 vols., Berkeley, CA.

Weber, M. 2011. *The Protestant Ethic and the Spirit of Capitalism. The Revised 1920 Edition*, trans. S. Kalberg, Oxford.

Weinryb, I. ed. 2015. *Ex Voto: Votive Giving Across Cultures*, New York.

Weinryb, I. ed. 2018. *Agents of Faith: Votive Objects in Time and Place*, New Haven.

Wjuniski, B.S. and Fernández, R.G. 2009. "The Athenian Economy in Light of the Welfare State: Karl Polanyi's Work in Perspective", *Journal of Economic Issues* 43.3, 587–606.

PART 1

Movements

∵

CHAPTER 2

Movement, Labour and Devotion: a Virtual Walk to the Sanctuary at Mount Kasios

Anna Collar

> Wanderer, your footsteps are the road, and nothing else; wanderer, there is no road, the road is made by walking. Walking makes the road, and on glancing behind one sees the path that he will never tread again. Wanderer, there is no road – Just foam in the sea.
>
> ANTONIO MACHADO, *Proverbios y cantares XXIX*[1]

∵

1 Introduction

Walking makes the road. The act of moving through the world creates the path, both literally and metaphorically: the journey is both means and end. The pilgrim's footsteps and the road she creates are the starting point for this chapter, which focuses on the physical act of going to a sacred place as a key part of both the experience of pilgrimage and as one which has economic implications.

Although overarching themes of liminality, *communitas*, contestation[2] and rites of passage[3] continue to dominate discourse in pilgrimage studies, developments in geography as part of the New Mobilities Paradigm are turning attention to the meanings of movement itself, which offer a new perspective on the process of pilgrims getting to their sacred destination. There are many practical economic aspects to consider in thinking specifically about the journey: how far is the destination, local, regional, or international?[4] Who works

---

1 Machado 1912.
2 Eade – Sallnow 1991.
3 Turner – Turner 1978.
4 See Frankfurter forthcoming for a discussion of how scholarship has defined pilgrimage through the transformative aspects of a long journey, which he argues to be a modern, romantic notion and at odds with the real point, that is, getting to the holy site itself. He suggests instead that focus should be on the practice and materiality of the local or regional

while the pilgrim is away, or are festivals always timed to avoid periods of most seasonally-based agricultural labour? What about physical requirements that need to be met along the way: shelter, food, water, warmth, and the maintenance of the path? Who, human or supernatural, guarantees safety *en route* if the distances being travelled are unfamiliar or dangerous? These questions raise other issues, such as whether these things were necessary; whether they formed part of the ritual involved in the journey, for example, the abstinence from food through fasting, exposure to danger as part of the process,[5] or the need to 'sing for your supper' along the way; or whether they formed part of the requirements of a position, as in the *hieromnamones* of Delphi whose oath entailed the maintenance of the bridges providing access to the city and sanctuary.[6]

However, this chapter offers a more abstract suggestion concerning the practice of walking to a sanctuary as part of the economy of pilgrimage. The movement of pilgrims to the sanctuary was an important part of people's sacred experience,[7] requiring a commitment of both time and effort. Time and human effort are not free, even if they are freely given: the act of going to the sanctuary has physical effects with economic implications, of work not done, of bodies exhausted. Viewed from this angle, the time and effort involved in the act of walking to a pilgrimage destination can be argued to be part of a worshipper's embodied dedication to the deity, through having got themselves to the sanctuary, the pilgrim had already made an economic sacrifice.

In antiquity, walking was the only way most people moved through space. Perhaps conceptualising walking to a sanctuary as the embodiment of a 'gift' of human labour is easier if getting to the sanctuary is clearly difficult: whereby a hard journey is written into the experience by the sanctuary's physical location, as with many remote modern pilgrimage sites.[8] Urban sanctuaries still involve journeys that have been described as pilgrimage,[9] but a difficult journey entails time and/or effort, a journey that is either physically long, or physically

---

shrine-visit, regarding long-distance pilgrimage as anomalous. However, the collective emotional aspect of moving towards a sanctuary – the act of procession, whether formal or informal – must have been of importance in antiquity too: there are plenty of examples of sacred ways that reveal something of the role of processions in past ritual practice. Perhaps, as ever, the point of contention is over the use of the term 'pilgrimage' in this context?

5   See Whiting, this volume, which explores some of these issues.

6   See Rutherford 2013, 183.

7   Even if, as Frankfurter forthcoming argues, this aspect has been overemphasised in recent years.

8   Scriven 2014, 256.

9   See for example, Wigley 2016 discussing the journey to church as 'micro-pilgrimage'.

tough.[10] By focusing on the physical performance of the journey to a difficult to reach extra-urban sanctuary, it is possible to illuminate the requirement these sanctuaries place on pilgrims to express their devotion to the deity through bodily effort. Equally, it shows how the sacredness of the place is maintained through the repetition of these movements. Sanctuaries on mountaintops offer a prime example of a difficult extra-urban pilgrimage destination.

The discussion will first examine walking and the performance of pilgrimage, moving on to consider mountain sanctuaries in general before using satellite imagery to virtually reconstruct the archaeological evidence for the journey to the sacred summit of Mount Kasios, in Turkey. The focus on the physical, embodied aspects of the walked journey up the mountain helps to reconceptualise notions of cult participation, and to highlight the role that the practice of walking had in pilgrimage to ancient sanctuaries.

2   Sanctifying Movement: Feet and Earth

Core to pilgrimage is the movement of the body involved, the act of getting to the sanctuary or shrine. Recent studies of contemporary pilgrimage practice have focused on the experiences of pilgrims on the journey itself and discuss it as a process that brings together people, places, performance, emotions, and beliefs.[11] These new approaches emphasise the intertwining of the corporeal and the spiritual, and the individual and the communal in performance and action through landscape. Examining pilgrimage as a spatially specific intertwining of bodily and spiritual performance is informed by scholarship in the New Mobilities Paradigm, which seeks to understand 'how movements, flows, and activity shape places and how places in turn shape mobilities'.[12] This approach extends the spatial turn in the humanities that was largely driven by the theory of Henri Lefebvre, and through which space has been re-interpreted as inseparable from the social actions that happen through them. Pilgrimage is thus seen as mutually constructive: the act of going creates not only the pilgrim, but also the pilgrimage, and the sanctity of the spaces involved. This mobilities perspective means that 'places are formed, maintained and transformed by flows and embodied movements', and enables the movement element of

---

10   Remaining aware that different people will define physically demanding in different ways — children, pregnant women and the elderly are generally able to walk considerably less distance than non-gravid women and adult men.

11   Scriven 2014; Slavin 2003; Maddrell 2013.

12   Scriven 2014, 255.

FIGURE 2.1   Pilgrims ascending Croagh Patrick, Ireland
                  PHOTO: RICHARD SCRIVEN

pilgrimage to thus be seen as a key practice in 'sanctifying or marking out an area as special'.[13] Richard Scriven includes a photograph (Fig. 2.1) of modern Irish pilgrims climbing the rocky mountainside of Croagh Patrick on the annual pilgrimage day. He describes the difficult ascent as part of the penitential exercise, arguing that 'the exertions and belief of the Christian pilgrims continually sanctify both the place and the people'.[14] Embodied ritual action such as this has internally affective consequences, on the emotions and psychological states of the pilgrims, as well as externally visible effects such as blisters or exhaustion. Scriven does not explore physical exertion as embodied religious commitment further, however, this aspect and the ephemeral act of walking to a sanctuary that produce it merits further investigation.

Lack of attention given to feet and the act of walking is historical. The anthropologist Tim Ingold has argued that the feet, and the experience of life through walking, have been separated out from conceptualisations of the mind and the hands as the 'natural' locations of intelligence and rationality:[15] emphasised by the wrapping of feet in boots, the construction of paved surfaces and the

13   Scriven 2014, 257–8.
14   Scriven 2014, 251.
15   Ingold 2004, 321.

proliferation of the chair. He highlights the connection between foot-based travel and labour through the etymology of the word itself, from the French *travail* — painful and laborious effort — and the continued derogatory use of the word *pedestrian* in English. Ingold demonstrates the 18th century distinction between travel and walking: travel was for the wealthy, ideally by means other than their own feet, done in order to reach a destination and the knowledge it held,[16] meaning that by the period of the Enlightenment in Europe, walking was negatively conceptualised as lowly and quotidian. This changed during the 19th century, when walking became a leisure activity for the well-off, partly due to the increased availability of affordable public transport and the inverse decrease in the stigma of poverty attached to walking.[17]

In antiquity, walking was how most people moved through space, most of the time. Other methods of movement were available — mule, horse, cart, litter, boat — but for most people, there was no option other than their own feet: walking and going amount to the same thing.[18] There is little literary evidence about walking, beyond claims that it was healthy,[19] that a straight walk is better than a winding walk;[20] that it can be exhilarating;[21] and that it requires attention to the experience.[22] Walking practices were culturally different across the ancient Mediterranean, for example, Roman officers walked for pleasure, an alien concept to the Iberian Vetones.[23] Beyond Jan Bremmer's use of literary sources to explore the 'correct' ways to walk in Classical antiquity, according to social status and bodily performances of gender stereotypes, gestural indications of superiority and manliness or subservience and femininity,[24] the act of walking in antiquity has received little scholarly attention.

3   Beyond Everyday Labour: Wandering, Suffering and Pilgrimage

However, modern accounts of pilgrimage[25] pivot on the notion of the length of the journey, the extraordinary destination, the authenticity of the pilgrim,

16   This tallies closely with Frankfurter's opinion of pilgrimage (forthcoming).
17   Urry 2000, 51.
18   Arist. *Rh.* 3.2.7.
19   Arist. *Metaph.* 5.103a; *Eth. Eud.* 2.1227b.
20   Celsus *Med.* 1.2.
21   De *curatione diuturnorum morborum* 1.3.
22   Arr. *Epict. Diss.* 3.10.
23   Strabo 3.4.16.
24   Bremmer 1991.
25   Discussion of how to define a journey as a pilgrimage continue. One recent argument views the plurality of practices and meanings that comprise 'pilgrimage' as a 'fiction

and on a difficult journey,[26] 'a metaphor for the difficulty of reaching the desired goal, be it enlightenment, virtue, or strength'.[27] The early Christian church fathers' legacy of asceticism made explicit that acts of physical endurance and suffering were an appropriate way to demonstrate piety and commitment to the Christian faith. Examples can be found in pilgrims to Canterbury who proceed on their knees, or the spiritual value attached to pain at Lourdes, where pilgrims' suffering is likened to the sacrifice and Passion of Christ.[28] Extreme arduousness of movement is also an act of piety in Buddhism; pilgrims at Mount Kailash make body-length prostrations over the fifty-one kilometres of rocky path around the base of the mountain.

David Frankfurter argues that ancient Mediterranean pilgrimage was rather different from these Christian, Buddhist, or modern notions, being most often at a local or regional scale, with longer distances being travelled rarely.[29] However, people did still undertake longer-distance pilgrimages, as well as difficult ones. Philip Harland has explored the pursuit of divine wisdom through travel, and the example provided by a little-known author of a letter introducing a book of herbal medicines, Thessalos. In it, the pursuit of divine wisdom culminates through contact with holy persons, high priests, and through conversation with Asklepios after a period of rootless wandering. Harland shows how such journeys in search of divine wisdom were commonplace enough to be used as a satirical trope by Lucian[30] — the implication being that travel was seen as a way to access esoteric, spiritual knowledge or undergo spiritual transformation. Although it was probably the contact with holy persons that enabled access to spiritual knowledge, the preceding travel seems nevertheless to be an important part of the preparatory process.

Such travel or wandering in antiquity was dangerous and difficult, as Harland notes. Important in an ancient Greek context was the protection afforded pilgrims by the concept of *asylia* — the inviolability of the sacred place and of the pilgrims or *theoroi* on their journey to and from the sanctuary.[31] *Asylia* was generally observed, and there are only a few examples of physical violence

---

that makes sense of the past', a way of describing past practices for modern scholarship which may have little to do with the contemporary conception of the people involved. See Elsner 2017.

26   Arellano 2007; Scriven 2014.
27   Whiston Spirn 1998, 58.
28   Dahlberg 2000.
29   Frankfurter forthcoming.
30   Harland 2011, 127.
31   Rutherford 2013 suggests that one of the reasons many new festivals were set up during the Hellenistic period — see Horster, this volume — was "part of a strategy to have their city or sanctuary or both recognised as 'inviolable'" (p. 46).

against or death of pilgrims in antiquity.[32] Travel by sea was an important or even essential element for many Greek and non-Greek participants in the major festivals or initiation cults, for example Delos, sometimes in designated vessels (*theoris*).[33] Sea travel, even in the summer months when many of the Panhellenic Greek festivals occurred, could still be dangerous, with real possibilities of storms, wrecking or being attacked by pirates.[34] Matthew Dillon details some of the rituals preceding sea journeys;[35] however, there is no indication that the danger or suffering in travel was fundamental to the validity of the sacred journey as in Christian or Buddhist pilgrimage practice.

Ian Rutherford suggests that 'visiting sanctuaries and pilgrimage was probably one of the most common motivations for land travel, perhaps even for building roads',[36] and although wealthier pilgrims or state pilgrims on *theoria* may have travelled using carts, litters, or on horse or mule, most people visiting sanctuaries would have done so on foot. This may have been dangerous, even with the *asylia* granted pilgrims, and references to the 'civilising' effect of road-building and clearing the area of robbers suggest that the dangers associated with pilgrimage were substantial.[37] In many cases, sacred roads were built and maintained by the city/ies responsible for a festival, for example, the way from Athens to Eleusis, or the route from Miletos to Didyma.[38] These are relatively short land trips, less than a day's journey and not necessarily physically demanding, but even short trips break with daily routines and existence, and so mark out that time as special and memorable; the performance of something different. It is also the case that for many the pilgrimage did not begin in the city or area closest to the sanctuary being visited: although these were less regular occurrences, certain festivals entailed longer journeys. In such cases, the journey could be broken into sections: Socrates, in the words of Xenophon, explains how, if correctly planned, the journey from Athens to Olympia was a five- or six-day walk: a distance not to be feared (contra the feelings of an unnamed discussant), if the journey is broken down into a series of short walks, akin to those done much of the time at home, with regular rest and if one started a day early.[39]

---

32   Dillon 1997a, 27–9.
33   Rutherford 2013, 178–82.
34   The shipwreck of *theoroi* off Tenos around 200 BCE is recorded in SEG 40.690A7, see Rutherford 2013, 186.
35   Dillon 1997a, 29–34.
36   Rutherford 2013, 182.
37   See discussion in Rutherford 2013, 185–7.
38   Dillon 1997a, 34–6.
39   Xen. *Mem.* 3.13.5.

4   Labouring Up: Why Mountain Sanctuaries?

The journey from Athens to Olympia was clearly rather daunting because of its length, but there are other ancient sanctuaries that require a physically demanding journey, in particular, those on mountaintops. The many instances of archaeological remains of sanctuaries in inaccessible mountain places across Greece and the Near East, often located on or near the summits, demonstrate that these were special 'thin places',[40] physical zones where the raw supernatural could be encountered. In Greece, mountain landscapes were the natural habitat of non-*polis* deities of wildness and wild nature, Dionysos, Artemis, the nymphs,[41] and Pan — who has 'every snowy crest and the mountain peaks for his domain';[42] and Apollo also held 'all peaks and towering bluffs' dear.[43] However, across Greece and the Near East it is Zeus, or local manifestations of the sky-storm god, who is the archetypal mountain deity. Mountains are places where it is possible to touch the sky.

Mountains were also dangerous: 'inaccessible',[44] 'shadowy',[45] wilderness places.[46] They were places of mad bacchants,[47] for refuge in times of war,[48] or metaphors, for the enormity of woe or misfortune,[49] or the greatness of Yahweh in the Old Testament, who can melt mountains under his foot.[50] For Christian authors, mountains were wild and spiritually dangerous — Mark records the man with the unclean spirit who has his dwellings in the tombs and in the mountains.[51] Given the latent dangers, then, why are there so many mountain sanctuaries from antiquity? Going up a mountain stands in opposition to the

---

40   The term 'thin places' was coined in the 1930s, either by the Scottish writer George MacDonald, or the Reverend George MacLeod, founder of the Christian 'Iona Community', to describe the special quality of certain places which seem to bring together the spiritual and the material — enabling people to access the supernatural and the dead. See Power 2006.

41   Ar. *Thesm.* 990.

42   *Hom. Hymn Pan* 19, 6–7.

43   *Hom. Hymn Apollo* 3, 144–5.

44   Diod. Sic. 14.20.

45   Hom. *Il.* 1.130.

46   This modern preconception of attitudes to mountains in antiquity has recently been questioned by König, 2016.

47   Eur. *Bacch.* 33–4.

48   Paus. 7.9, Liv. *Ab urbe condita* 26.11.

49   Cf. Plaut. *Epid.* 1.1; *Merc.* 3.4.

50   *Micah* 3, Ps. 97.

51   Mk 5.

'logic' that people act to minimise effort and maximise efficiency.[52] Going up mountains is in some ways tantamount to madness: ancient authors explicitly make the connection between mountains and insanity; modern mountaineering is heavily tinged with the madness of the adrenaline junkie, the thrill-seeker poised between heaven and earth, between omniscience and annihilation.[53]

The wildness and extremity of mountain-top sanctuaries must mean the land-sky-weather-scape is fundamentally part of the understanding of the divinity worshipped there, and that being there, high above the rest of the earth, in the wind and the weather, must have contributed to the physical and cognitive experience. The act of ascent to a mountain sanctuary in antiquity must have been motivated by a (social or individual) desire to participate in experiencing the supernatural or the thinness of the place. Himalayan Buddhism suggests a way of looking at these places: 'The power of such mountains is so great [that] people are drawn to them from near and far, as if by the force of some invisible magnet; and they will undergo untold hardships and privations in their inexplicable urge to approach ... the centre of this sacred power.'[54]

Certainly some of the many mountains where cult was enacted in antiquity would not be considered 'dangerous' or even particularly high (for example, Kynthos on Delos, or Dülük Baba Tepesi, home of Jupiter Dolichenus, near Gaziantep in Turkey). However, plenty were: Mount Ida on Crete, Mount Lykaion in the Peloponnese, Mount Olympus on the Greek mainland, and Mount Kasios on the coast of the Levant, all sacred to versions of Zeus. Getting up them was physically hard, and this physical and cognitive expenditure would have impacted on the experience of attending ritual at the sanctuary.

5   Throne of Zeus: a Brief History of Mount Kasios

Here, I will focus on only one mountain — Kasios (Jebel Aqraa, 'bald mountain', Fig. 2.2), as a stage to explore the physical and cognitive implications of a walked journey to a sanctuary. The mountain forms the current Turkish-Syrian border at the mouth of the Orontes river where it meets the Mediterranean, and is at present inaccessible to visitors, in general because of the military zone it occupies and now because of heavy military activity in the region, which has

---

52   George Zipf formulated the 'principle of least effort in the 1940s that is the general tendency for things to occur in the easiest way possible. Variations on the principle have been used to approach many subjects, including moving through landscape in archaeology. See also n. 94.

53   Macfarlane 2003.

54   Govinda 2006, 271.

FIGURE 2.2   Mount Kasios (Jebel Aqraa), from Seleucia Pieria
                PHOTO: ANNA COLLAR

seen the unfortunate cutting of a major new road up the mountain and the construction of a military base on its summit (Fig. 2.3).

The mountain is around 1800m high, drops straight into the Mediterranean and is visible from Cyprus.[55] It was sacred from at least the Bronze Age, that is, the physical body of the mountain was an object of cult, as a manifestation of the deity's throne (and although it is not known whether or how the cult

---

55   See Lane Fox 2009; Collar 2017.

FIGURE 2.3   Screenshot of the summit of Mount Kasios on Google Earth in April 2014
PHOTO: MAXAR TECHNOLOGIES 2019/ANNA COLLAR

was continuous, or how it changed through time, the mountain was still referred to as 'the Throne' by late antique sailors and locals.[56]) The people of the
Late Bronze Age city of Ugarit to the south knew it as Sapanu, home of their
storm god Baʻal and site of his silver and lapis lazuli palace;[57] to the Hurrians
of the north, it was Mount Hazzi, a mountain-god in its own right, side-kick as
well as seat of their own storm deity, Teššub.[58] The Hittites continued Hurrian
cult practice with their political ascendance, with mythological song cycles
(*Song of the Sea, Kingship in Heaven*) being sung about it and upon it. In
the *Song of Ullikummi,* two brothers ascend Hazzi in order to witness the birth
of the rock monster Ullikummi from the mountain.[59] Hazzi was the landscape
of the action.[60]

Early Archaic Greeks settling and trading at Al Mina at the mouth of the
Orontes, below the mountain, adopted the Hurrian-Hittite name of the mountain, Hazzi, and called the mountain *Kasios.* Robin Lane Fox argues persuasively

56   *Stadiasmus Maris Magni* 143.
57   KTU 1.101, obv., see translation in de Moor 1987.
58   Schwemer 2008.
59   CTH 345.2A = KUB 33.113 i 10.
60   Popko 1994, 156–7; Popko 1999; Rutherford 2001; Haas 2006, 131.

that it was here that the Hurrian-Hittite myths of the battles between Kumarbi and Teššub, or Kronos and Zeus, entered the Greek mythological canon, and were transferred back to Greece via Euboea.[61] Hellenistic kings and Romans too understood the real and symbolic power of the mountain, and according to John Malalas[62] Seleucus I Nikator sacrificed in April in order to discover where he should build his new city. An eagle carried off some sacrificial meat and dropped it across the Samandağ plain, where Seleucus then founded Seleucia Pieria.[63] The city was named for the area of Greece where Mount Olympus was located, and Lane Fox argues that this connection implies that Kasios was perceived as being so sacred that it was understood as the Olympus of the East.[64] Some time later, Trajan and Hadrian ascended the mountain together to offer sacrifice to Zeus Kasios around 113–5 CE;[65] Hadrian composed an epigram in Greek to mark both the occasion and Trajan's dedications to the deity, of gilded auroch horn and two cups, spoils from his Dacian campaigns.[66] Hadrian returned around 129 CE, and climbed the mountain at night in order to witness the (fairly improbable) meteorological phenomenon described by Pliny,[67] whereby around 3am it is apparently possible to see the sun rising while the earth below remained in complete darkness, allowing the viewer to see both day and night at the same time. According to the story, Hadrian's experience was marred by a thunderstorm during which a lightning bolt struck his priest and his sacrificial animal, burning both up completely.[68] Julian visited the mountain too, around 363 CE, participating in a festival,[69] and according to Libanius, beheld the god at high noon.[70] With high profile pagans like Julian still visiting the mountain, the Christian authorities could no longer ignore its power, and St. Barlaam apparently settled there in order to dispel the demon of the mountain in the fourth century.[71]

What is clear is that the mountain has an extremely long (c. 3000 years) sacred history – with historians providing much of the information. There is meagre numismatic, epigraphic, and archaeological evidence to supplement these

---

61 Lane Fox 2009.
62 Not necessarily a 'trustworthy' source for these earlier periods, but certainly aware of the rhetorical power that the mountain was able to exert. Treadgold, 2007.
63 Ioh. Mal. *Chronographia* 8.12.
64 Lane Fox, 2009, 259.
65 Birley 1997, 68.
66 *Anth. Pal.* 6. 332; Arr. *Parth.* fr. 36.
67 Plin. *HN* 5.18.
68 Spartianus, *Vita Hadriani* 14.3.
69 Amm. Marc. 22.14.4.
70 Lib. *Or.* 18.172.
71 Lane Fox 2009, 263.

accounts, but what exists offers tantalising insights into the nature of worship and experience on the mountain. T.A. Sinclair reports a huge 'Hittite tumulus'[72] on the often snow- and cloud-shrouded summit; this mound of ash and debris from sacrifice was recorded as being 180 feet wide and 26 feet deep. Only the first six feet have been excavated, reaching Hellenistic-period levels;[73] it is safe to assume that the deeper levels of this open-air ash altar would have contained a wealth of information about earlier practices, cultural affiliations, and caesurae or continuities in practice.[74] However, the altar appears to have suffered irreparable damage through the construction of the military base at some point in 2012, with this information irretrievably lost (Fig. 2.3). A few hundred metres below the ash altar on the summit, a temple to Olympian Zeus was built, and a few inscriptions to Dios Kasios from the mountain perhaps marked out the boundaries of a sacred precinct.[75] Coins of Antioch minted by Trajan and Antoninus Pius feature a pyramid-roofed shrine of Zeus Kasios, which may be an impression of this temple, with four columns enclosing a holy stone or *baetyl*, or perhaps a representation of the mountain itself.[76] The temple is assumed to be located underneath the Georgian monastery of St. Barlaam, which dates from the 6th and 10th centuries, and which was abandoned in 1268 when it was sacked by the Mamluks.[77] The monastery was investigated in the 1980s, when Djobadze *et al.* discovered details of its water supply, some funerary tombs and chapels, and monastic dependencies.[78] Djobadze's team also noted that the limestone quarry for the monastery was located on the summit of the mountain with two columns still *in situ*.[79] Perhaps cutting out the rock here was a way to Christianise and tame the ancient, pagan power of the peak, still tangible in the huge ash-mound from times of bloodier sacrifice?

Further survey and excavation might reveal the extent of the breaks and continuities of sacrifice and worship on the summit and at the temple, but the smatterings of material that are known indicate that throughout the ages, people were making the journey up the mountain to the temple and the summit, accompanied by animals and perhaps other items, in order to offer

---

72   Sinclair 1990.

73   Lane Fox 2009, 257–9. The partial excavation of the mound took place in the 1930s but
      was curtailed by the appalling weather conditions on the summit.

74   As, for example, the excavations at Mount Lykaion in the Peloponnese or Dülük Baba
      Tepesi near Gaziantep have revealed. See Romano   Voyatzis 2014, Winter 2017.

75   Djobadze *et al.* 1986.

76   Cohen 2006, 134.

77   Sinclair 1990.

78   Djobadze *et al.* 1986.

79   Djobadze *et al.* 1986.

sacrifice and/or dedications to the deity in his presence, to participate in collective feasting or festival or celebration of some sort. The walked journey up the mountain to participate is an important part of this experience, and the provision for the journey an important part of the economy of the sanctuary.

6 Virtual Phenomenology: Reconstructing a Vanished Road Up Mount Kasios

The sanctity of the summit and the road(s) up Kasios were co-created by the repeated practices of pilgrims attending festivals and walking the paths. Just as the pilgrims have long gone, so have the paths vanished. There is very little evidence for this ephemeral process of walking up Mount Kasios. Pliny[80] describes the way to the summit as nineteen miles long and 'winding', although he does not specify from which town or direction this road went. Seleuceia is roughly 26km from the summit, making it a good candidate. In addition to Seleuceia Pieria, Antioch and Laodicea must also have been well connected with the site in the Graeco-Roman period: an Imperial period inscription discovered in the ruins of the monastery was given by a man from Laodicea, a two-day journey away.[81] Given the long history of worship on the mountain and the communal, festival aspect of this worship — for example, the singing of Hittite songs requiring many participants and which were sung on the mountain itself[82] — there must have been perhaps a number of well-worn paths to the temple and summit. There may have been shrines that were necessary to visit along the way, for example, Strabo reveals that there was a festival of the agricultural hero Triptolemos celebrated by the people of Antioch on the mountain, near Seleuceia.[83]

In addition to sacred or spiritually meaningful points along the journey, there may have been practical necessities — food and water — and their provision through wells, springs and water tanks along the way.[84] It may also be that the journey was conducted over a period of days (some Hittite festivals were conducted over many days[85]), meaning that there may have been animal

---

80   Plin. *HN* 5.18.
81   Aliquot 2015.
82   Rutherford 2001, 605.
83   Str. 16.2.5.
84   There is the possibility that there was a requirement for purity, perhaps through fasting or abstinence, but it is reasonable to assume that access to water must surely have been important, especially if the festival was held during the late spring–summer.
85   Gurney 1977, 31.

pens or enclosures, or places for participants to stop, rest and eat — perhaps something like inns, roadside places to rest, or permitted camp-sites.[86]

Walking through the landscape, attending to the phenomenological aspects of the journey as well as investigating the traces of some of the physical infrastructures would offer a way to begin to piece together the residues of these ephemeral paths and processes. However, the summit and much of the surrounding area is off-limits to tourists and scholars, and instead, this phenomenological approach has to be achieved remotely. Remote sensing — the identification of archaeological remains using photographic or digital observations made from the air — has been a part of archaeological survey practice since people invented aeroplanes.[87] Conducting live aerial survey over the military zone of Mount Kasios is not possible, and this prohibition extends across much of Greece, Turkey and the Middle East,[88] meaning satellite imagery is the only option in surveying the East Mediterranean from the air. Although satellite imagery can now be accessed at a high enough resolution to also be used in archaeological prospection, there remain issues with the method, in particular in the case of the Mediterranean: landscape and vegetation patterns can make it difficult to differentiate between natural and man-made features,[89] and ambiguities in identification of ground features can arise when using only one kind of imaging system.[90] Nevertheless, there is much to be gained by taking such an approach. Google Earth is invaluable here, delivering satellite imagery, a 3D landscape DEM (Digital Elevation Model) and a GIS in one.[91] In what follows, I have compared images taken at different times of year between 2010–2016 available on Google Earth,[92] to suggest possible features in the landscape that might help to virtually reconstruct something of the last stages of the journey to the summit of Mount Kasios and so shed light on the experiences and economic implications of walking to the mountain sanctuary.

---

86   It was forbidden to camp in some areas around Greek sanctuaries, with strict regulations as to where tents were allowed and what size tents were permitted, suggesting that there was a special area set aside for camping. See Dillon 1997b, 123.

87   See Conolly – Lake 2006, 64–77 for a detailed outline of the techniques and applications for remote sensing in archaeological work.

88   Madry 2006, 303.

89   Slattery et al. 2008.

90   Altaweel 2005.

91   Google Earth was described by the CTO of the Google Earth team as 'the GIS for the 5.999999 billion people of the world's 6 billion population who don't know or care what GIS is,' Madry 2006, 304.

92   Higher resolution satellite imagery is available commercially (for example, Quickbird), but financial constraints have precluded their use here.

Sinclair, who visited the mountain in person, reports that the lower slopes are relatively level, so the earlier stages of the journey were certainly easier, walking through a sometimes shaded and more even, hilly landscape. The lower hills are well used, with terracing and, despite winter snows, small, permanent villages in sheltered high valleys. One of these, Yeditepe/Bezge, has been identified as the Roman Bexa, where there are reported finds of mosaics, marble fragments and column capitals,[93] which suggests year-round occupation during the Roman period too. Reconstructing the routes to an upper-mountain entry point such as Bexa is almost impossible: the path used might depend on from which city you were travelling; in which historical context the ascent was made; or the purpose of the journey — there may, for example, have been a formal processional route. Were the same paths taken by different users of the mountain at different times — was the Hittite route still visible and used in the Archaic or Hellenistic periods, for example? It seems reasonable to assume that if a path were visible and known, it would have been used, even if the connection with previous cult activity was no longer perceived. The role of intergenerational communal folk memory of participation in festival or myth-topography may have played an important role in the continuities of practices or in the maintenance or disuse of Bronze Age roads in later periods. Unfortunately, there is too much modern activity in the lower reaches to ascertain anything about routes up the mountain to Bexa from satellite imagery, although survey in person might still yield useful results.

From Bexa, however, the true ascent begins (Fig. 2.4). The upper reaches of the mountain are steeper, starker, and offer little in the way of trees or protection from the wind, sun, rain or snow. Travellers and the excavators in the 1930s commented on the adverse weather conditions of these upper parts: cold wind according to Sinclair; Hadrian's violent thunderstorm; and the snow-covered mountainhead is often hidden under an April shroud. There is less modern agriculture here, as well as less vegetation to obscure the view from the air. Although there is still human activity, this is limited to herding, fruit trees and dirt tracks, and the military. It is notoriously difficult to try to ascertain past human use of landscape remotely without the opportunity to ground truth claims by an actual visit to a place. Nevertheless, places are formed, maintained and transformed by flows and embodied movements — and there are some pathways up to the temple/summit that may have been in use in antiquity that are still possible to trace, like foam in the sea.

I have examined Google Earth's satellite imagery from different seasons and different years for signs of built structures, paths, disused terracing and other

---

93   Djobadze *et al.* 1986, 55.

FIGURE 2.4   Screenshot of the landscape of Mount Kasios on Google Earth, from the
               north east
               PHOTO: 2017 MAXAR TECHNOLOGIES/CNES/AIRBUS/ANNA COLLAR

anomalies which may indicate past human uses of and movements through
the landscape. I have studied these alongside relief models from Google Earth
to visualise routes up the mountain; and I have checked these against GIS
least-cost path analysis,[94] which show the two 'most efficient' routes up the
mountain from Bexa: one showing the least-cost path without any additional
requirements, and the other calculated to take in a visit to the monastery of
Barlaam/temple of Zeus along the way, assuming that pilgrims would have attended other ritual activities at the temple on their way up or down.

From Bexa, the distance to the summit is c. 6 km. Although this is not a
huge distance, the elevation profile of the walk is steep, especially the final
kilometres. Pilgrims may have stayed overnight in Bexa before making the final
journey to the summit. The first part of a modern road might have taken pilgrims from Bexa up to the next valley, now in agricultural use. There are three
road options here (Fig. 2.5), all of which appear to be well worn dirt tracks;
I do not claim that these are ancient. The left-hand road (Route 1) is clearly
the main one in use today, threading along the valley floor, planted with fields

94   'Least-cost path' analysis in GIS is 'a route that minimises the total cost of moving be-
      tween two locations on an *accumulated cost-surface*'. Such analysis presents the most 'effi-
      cient' — framed in terms of cost-benefit — way to move through a landscape, and is often
      used without accounting for other factors that determine human behaviour (memory
      and spirituality suffer most). See Conolly – Lake 2006, 294; also the chapter by Whiting,
      this volume.

FIGURE 2.5   Screenshot of the three potential routes from Bexa to the next valley up the
                  mountain in Google Earth
                  PHOTO: 2017 MAXAR TECHNOLOGIES/CNES/AIRBUS/ANNA COLLAR

of trees around 2010, and which joins up with the newly bulldozed 2012 road
to the summit. Although requiring less effort, as the ascent is largely around
the middle of the slopes of the mountain, it does not take into account a visit
to the temple. Because of the modern road, it will probably be impossible to
reach any conclusion about previous usage of this route. The right-hand path
(Route 3) leads up the northern flank of the mountain, to further terracing,
and although the route is longer, this path leads to the temple area. The middle
path (Route 2) leads up the spine of the hill through the middle of a relatively
flat area, unused for modern agriculture, which has a number of circular and
other anomalies in, potentially representing rock-cut water tanks or remains of
enclosures or buildings. This area might have been suitable for camping, with
space for grazing and watering sacred animals.[95] Route 2 is the one followed

---

95   Possibilities for zooarchaeological analysis of faunal remains from the sacrifice have most
      likely been lost. I make this point because although sheep and goats are expert climbers
      and able to find grazing grounds almost anywhere, cattle are not so nimble and would
      have needed more even ground upon which to graze. Moreover, it is important to consid-
      er restrictions on grazing ground within sacred areas: farmers were often prohibited from
      grazing within the sanctuary, as at sanctuaries at Argos, Ialysos, Euboia or Koropos in the
      Classical period, and provisions were made specifically for grazing sacrificial animals, as
      at Delphi, Ios or Tegea. See Dillon 1997b, 120–2.

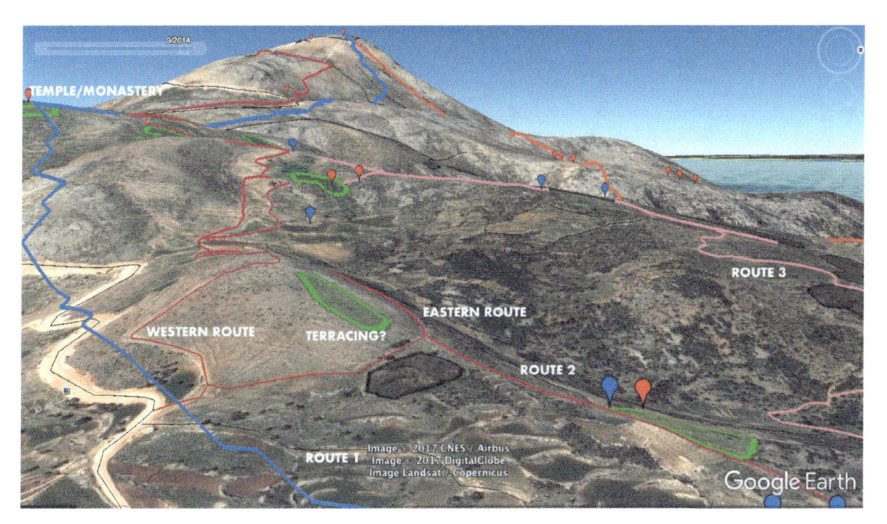

FIGURE 2.6 Screenshot of the path taken by Route 2 up the valley in Google Earth
PHOTO: 2017 CNES/AIRBUS/DIGITALGLOBE/ANNA COLLAR

here, chosen on the reasoning that a) it offers a relatively direct path to the temple, and b) it passes through this unused space that appears to contain potentially non-modern human activity.

Route 2 then makes a relatively steep ascent up the next part of the hill (Fig. 2.6). The path goes through a landscape with more circular structures, possibly water tanks, and some ancient terracing on the top of the slope. Two tracks lead over or around this hill, the eastern edge presenting a more gradual incline. From this point, the pilgrim must now climb 200m in altitude to reach the temple of Zeus (Fig. 2.7): possible routes here pass through remains of terracing as well as other structures and enclosures — located on the north-facing slopes, presumably cooler or more sheltered from prevailing winds — until it reaches a small circular structure and some other anomalies on the crest of this hill spine. It is easy to imagine that, after this arduous climb, pilgrims would need to refresh themselves and rest, and that this possible water tank would be very welcome. From this point, 1180m above sea level, the pilgrims still had another 100m in altitude to climb to reach the temple. The path turns to the south here, passing through the traces of more ancient terracing perhaps connected with later monastic land use, for another half kilometre, before pilgrims would have reached the base of the slope where the Hellenistic-Roman temple to Zeus stood (Fig. 2.8). Hellenistic-Roman period pilgrims would perhaps have stopped again here, to rest, receive instruction, participate in festival activities and so on. There are many structures visible on the satellite images

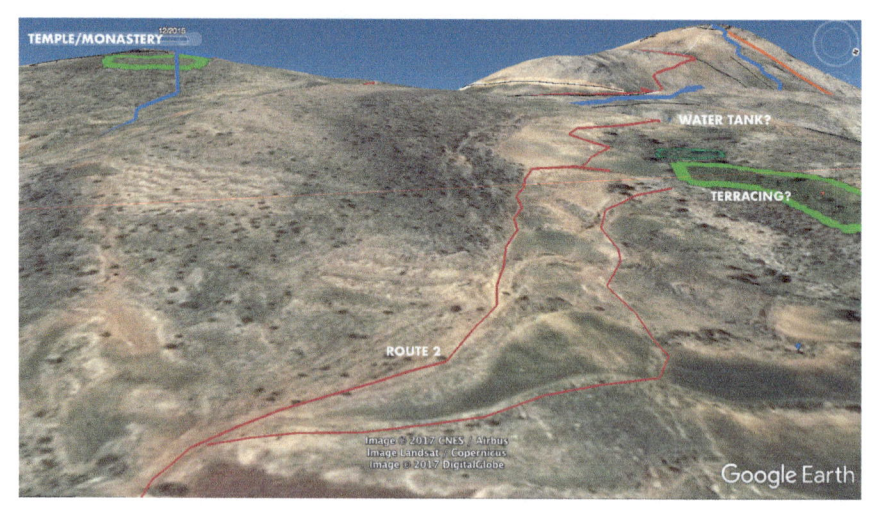

FIGURE 2.7   Screenshot of Route 2, looking up to the Temple of Zeus in Google Earth
PHOTO: 2017 CNES/AIRBUS/DIGITALGLOBE/ANNA COLLAR

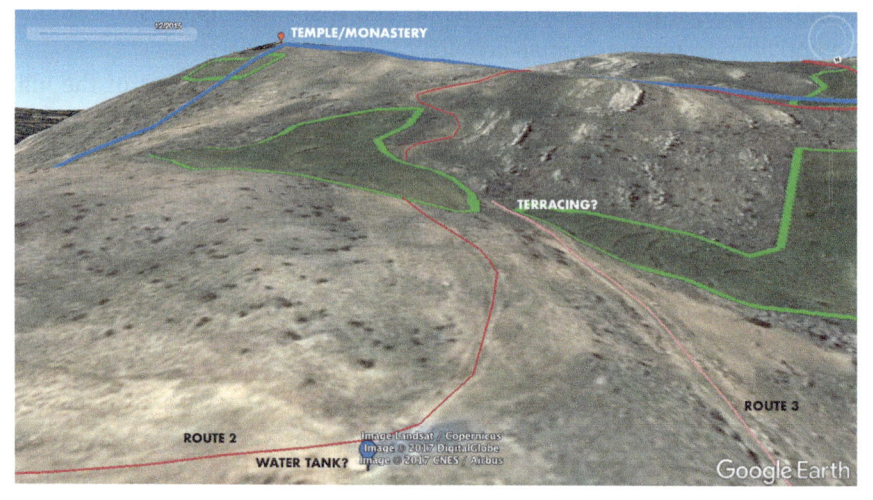

FIGURE 2.8   Screenshot of Route 2 from possible water tank to the Temple of Zeus in
Google Earth
PHOTO: 2017 DIGITALGLOBE/CNES/AIRBUS/ANNA COLLAR

FIGURE 2.9   Aerial view of the remains of the Monastery of St. Barlaam/location of the
Temple of Zeus in Google Earth
PHOTO: 2019 MAXAR TECHNOLOGIES

(Fig. 2.9), chiefly those related to the monastic complex of the first millennium CE, but perhaps there was also areas where pilgrims were permitted to camp or stay overnight.

It is a further 3km to the summit — but this 3km also climbs 500m in terms of elevation: it is an extremely steep walk. This part of the mountain is often covered with snow in winter, and there are no trees. Whether this was also the case in antiquity is unclear as the mountain is apparently below the tree line,[96] but ancient terracing here suggests that even if there were trees, they did not cover the entirety of this part of the mountain. Participants and their animals would have returned down the valley below the temple and headed north along it (Fig. 2.10), before turning to the south, along what is still in use as a drove road or dirt track, past further terracing (Fig. 2.11), then turning north to reach the base of the conical, rocky summit.

From this point, roughly 1350m above sea level, it is a very steep climb up the northern flank of the mountain — sometimes at a gradient of 47% (Fig. 2.12;

96   Vogiatzakis 2012.

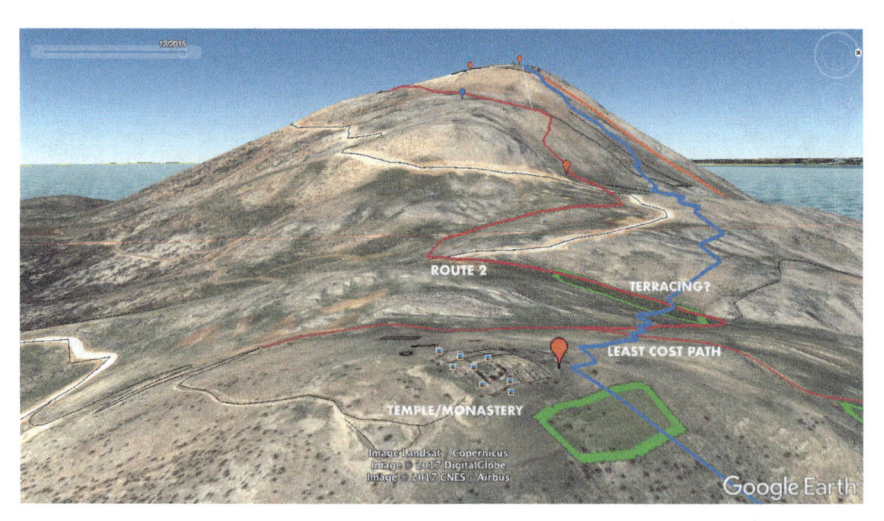

FIGURE 2.10   Screenshot of the path taken by Route 2 from the Temple of Zeus to the
                summit of Kasios in Google Earth
                PHOTO: 2017 DIGITALGLOBE/CNES/AIRBUS/ANNA COLLAR

FIGURE 2.11   Aerial view of terracing (possibly relating to monastic agriculture) in the
                valley between the Monastery of St. Barlaam and the summit of Kasios in
                Google Earth
                PHOTO: 2017 CNES/AIRBUS

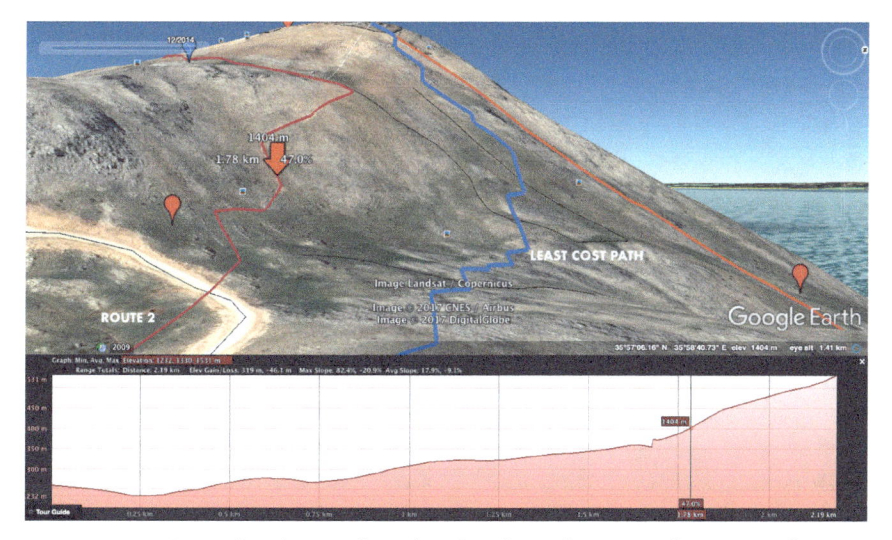

FIGURE 2.12   Screenshot showing the path and gradient of Route 2 to the summit of Kasios
in Google Earth
PHOTO: 2017 CNES/AIRBUS/DIGITALGLOBE/ANNA COLLAR

FIGURE 2.13   The path to the summit of Kasios in 2011
PHOTO: AHMET DERTSIZ

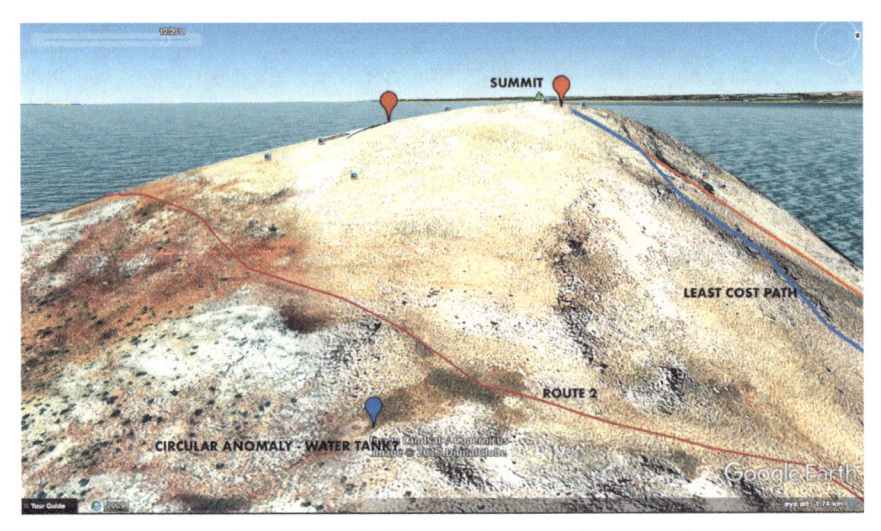

FIGURE 2.14   Screenshot of the path of Route 2 past a possible water tank in Google Earth
PHOTO: 2017 DIGITALGLOBE/ANNA COLLAR

Fig. 2.13 is a photograph taken from roughly the point of the red marker in
Fig. 2.12). Unless pilgrims preferred a further half kilometre at a similar incline,
the possible path then swings south along a flatter area around the base of the
final summit, past a circular depression (perhaps a rock-cut pool for gathering and storing rainwater? – Fig. 2.14), and then to two rhomboid enclosures
with regular internal walls on the southern flank of the summit (Fig. 2.15 –
raking light highlights the enclosures). Unfortunately, these have both been
half-destroyed by the construction of the 2012 road, but they may have served
as storage areas for festivals at certain times. They bear a resemblance to the
excavated storage magazines surrounding the great temples at the Hittite capital at Hattuša, offering the tantalising possibility that, perhaps in the Hittite
period at least, festivals on Hazzi were large enough to require permanent storage facilities. From here it is about a 400m climb to the summit, with the gradient ranging between 48% and 18%. By comparing images from 2011 and 2012
it is possible to see the new military base and the annihilation of the ancient
sacrificial altar at the mountaintop (Fig. 2.3; Fig. 2.16).

But once upon a time, here cult participants would have witnessed a huge
sacrificial fire. Cold wind and searing flames will have mixed with songs,
prayers, noise, blood, and sweat. Sky and earth met here and joined through
the pillar of smoke, as pilgrims may have engaged in or witnessed the enact-
ment or re-enactment of myths, stories, songs and rituals. Here was the zenith

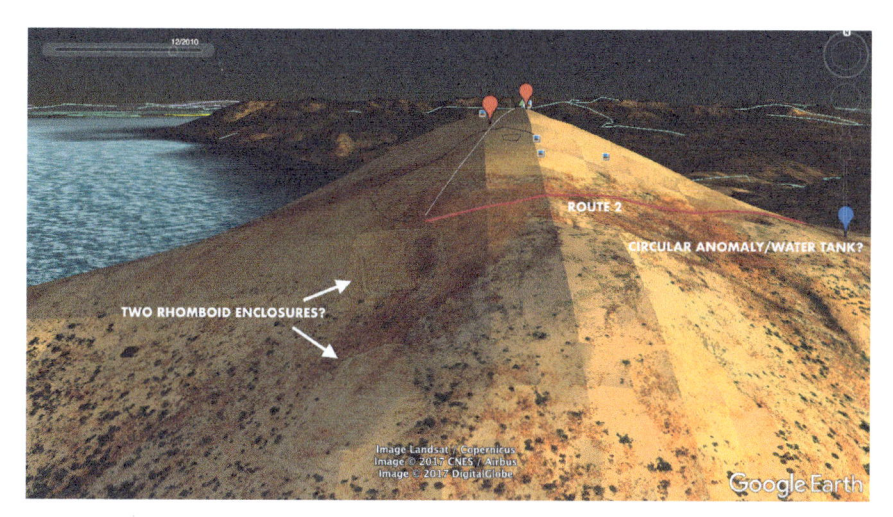

FIGURE 2.15   Screenshot of the path of Route 2 to the southern flank of the mountain and
the two possible enclosures in Google Earth
PHOTO: 2017 CNES/AIRBUS/DIGITALGLOBE/ANNA COLLAR

FIGURE 2.16   Screenshot of the summit of Mount Kasios on Google Earth in August 2011
PHOTO: MAXAR TECHNOLOGIES

of the physical journey, and, one could assume, also of the spiritual experience. At the summit of Kasios, human and divine were as close as they could be, and the pilgrims' bodies would have been tingling, sweating, exhausted and exhilarated from the climb, the view, the wild exposure, as well as the festival and the rituals themselves.

7   Movement, Labour and Devotion at Mountain Sanctuaries

Walking through the landscape, most of us do not attend to the traces of the
past; and maps, plans, or architect's drawings are flat, rootless, not-alive, they
do not account for the past as present.[97] Movement in the modern world is too
fast to understand the meanings and languages of landscapes, or the physical
labour required in movement. My exploration of the act of walking as part
of the devotional process pertaining to the experience and economy of sanctuaries has set out to reconnect with the traces of the past in the landscape
of Mount Kasios, to take account of what going to a mountaintop sanctuary
involved physically, but most of all, to set the metronome to *andante*. Tracing
the walked journey up Mount Kasios has highlighted a number of points.
Physically, the importance of the weather and time of year in the ways the
experience of the walk would be affected: some of the Google images show
the mountainhead under snow, and weather is critical to perception of landscape.[98] Certainly, if the mountain were climbed in August, participants might
be sunburnt or heat fatigued, yet the wind is still cold. The sharp gradients
mean that regardless of general states of fitness, pilgrims would have felt some
physical effects, and their bodily feelings would reflect the religious action they
had undertaken.[99] Even virtually walking the path to a significant mountaintop sanctuary has highlighted physical necessities required to get to a mountaintop sanctuary, such as water and shelter, as well as more abstract ideas of
spiritual transcendence or exhilaration that come with ascent.

Missing are the sensory and emotional aspects of the experience, both
natural and cultural: the smells and sounds — mountain herbs, birdsong, the
bleating of sheep and goats, the wind; the processional element of a festival,
including special clothes, scents, music or storytelling; the associated communal emotional affect of making the ascent together; and the marking out
of sacred areas or boundaries, and the potential for inclusion or exclusion
from these.[100]

---

97   Whiston Spirn 1998, 11.

98   Ingold 2010.

99   Experiences are different depending on whether the journey was a regular or one-off
       event. Ann Whiston Spirn explores both angles: 'in an unfamiliar place, senses sharpen …
       in familiar territory, senses dull, and it takes an effort to refresh them … reading landscape
       deeply requires local knowledge. On foreign ground, one needs an interpreter.' Whiston
       Spirn 1998, 4. Both of these elements may have been relevant in the ascent of Kasios for
       different people.

100   Some of these absences are addressed through reconstruction using multi-sensory Virtual
       Reality, see Collar – Eve in preparation.

The journey undertaken to the sanctuary must be considered as a fundamental part of the communal religious process of the experience of pilgrimage and as part of the economy of a sanctuary. Pilgrimage cannot be solely about the shrine being visited: by requiring pilgrims to move in order to reach them, the economy of any sanctuary extends out through the landscape. This is particularly physically demanding in the case of mountain sanctuaries: by requiring pilgrims to climb up to them, mountain sanctuaries can be seen to exert something akin to a sacred gravitational 'pull' upon pilgrims. When done communally, this act of movement also comprises an act of community creation, and by highlighting the physical labour and time involved in walking to a sanctuary on a mountaintop, it is possible to make the case that the movement to a sanctuary also in part constituted a pilgrim's dedication to the deity. Pilgrimage itself is a gift to god.

Bibliography

Aliquot, J. 2015. "A Laodicean on Mount Casius", in *Religious Identities in the Levant from Alexander to Muhammed. Continuity and Change*, eds. M. Blömer, A. Lichtenberger, and R. Raja, Turnhout, 157–68.

Altaweel, M. 2005. "The Use of ASTER Satellite Imagery in Archaeological Contexts", Archaeological Prospection 12, 151–66.

Arellano, A. 2007. "Religion, Pilgrimage, Mobility and Immobility", in *Religious Tourism and Pilgrimage Festivals Management: An International Perspective*, eds. R. Razaq and N.D. Morpeth, Oxfordshire, 89–97.

Birley, A., 1997. *Hadrian, the Restless Emperor*, London.

Bremmer, J., 1991. "Walking, Standing and Sitting in Ancient Greek culture", in *A Cultural History of Gesture from Antiquity to the Present Day*, eds. J. Bremmer and H. Roodenburg, Cambridge, 15–35.

Bremmer, J., 2017. "Pilgrimage Progress?", in *Excavating Pilgrimage: Archaeological Approaches to Sacred Travel and Movement in the Ancient World*, eds. T.M. Kristensen and W. Friese, Abingdon, 275–84.

Cohen, G.M. 2006. *The Hellenistic Settlements in Syria, the Red Sea Basin, and North Africa*, Berkeley – Los Angeles.

Collar, A.C.F. 2017. "Sinews of Belief, Anchors of Devotion: The Cult of Zeus Kasios in the Mediterranean", in *Sinews of Empire. Networks in the Roman Near East and Beyond*, eds. H. Teigen and E. Seland, Oxford, 23–36.

Collar, A.C.F. and Eve, S.J. In preparation. "Fire for Zeus. Using Virtual Reality to Experience Mount Kasios".

Conolly, J. and Lake, M. 2006. *Geographical Information Systems in Archaeology*, Cambridge.

Dahlberg, A. 1991. "The Body as a Principle of Holism. Three Pilgrimages to Lourdes", in *Contesting the Sacred. The Anthropology of Pilgrimage*, eds. J. Eade and M. Sallnow, Urbana, IL, 30–45.

De Polignac, F. 1995. *Cults, Territory, and the Origins of the Greek City-State*, Chicago.

De Moor, J.C. 1987. *An Anthology of Religious Texts from Ugarit*, Leiden.

Dillon, M. 1997a. *Pilgrims and Pilgrimage in Ancient Greece*, London – New York.

Dillon, M. 1997b. "The Ecology of the Greek Sanctuary", *Zeitschrift für Papyrologie und Epigraphik* 118, 113–27.

Djobadze, W. *et al.* 1986. *Archaeological Investigations in the Region West of Antioch-on-the-Orontes*, Stuttgart.

Eade, J. and Sallnow, M. eds. 2013. *Contesting the Sacred. The Anthropology of Pilgrimage*, Urbana, IL.

Elsner, J. 2017. "Excavating Pilgrimage", in *Excavating Pilgrimage. Archaeological Approaches to Sacred Travel and Movement in the Ancient World*, eds. T.M. Kristensen and W. Friese, Abingdon, 265–74.

Frankfurter, D. Forthcoming. "Getting There: Reframing Pilgrimage from Process to Site", in *Pilgrims in Place, Pilgrims in Motion. Archaeologies of Sacred Travel*, eds. A.C.F. Collar and T.M. Kristensen, Aarhus.

Govinda, L. 2006. *The Way of the White Clouds*, New York.

Gurney, O.R. 1977. *Some Aspects of Hittite Religion*, Oxford.

Harland, P. 2011. "Journeys in Pursuit of Divine Wisdom: Thessalos and Other Seekers", in *Travel and Religion in Antiquity*, ed. P. Harland, Waterloo, ON, 123–40.

Haas, V. 2006. *Die hethitische Literatur: Texte, Stilistik, Motive*, Berlin.

Ingold, T. 2004. "Culture on the Ground: the World Perceived Through the Feet", *Journal of Material Culture* 9.3, 315–40.

Ingold, T. 2010. "Footprints through the Weather-World: Walking, Breathing, Knowing", *Journal of the Royal Anthropological Institute* 16.1, 121–39.

König, J. 2016. "Strabo's Mountains", in *Valuing Landscape in Classical Antiquity. Natural Environment and Cultural Imagination*, eds. J. McInerney and I. Sluiter, Leiden, 46–69.

Lane Fox, R. 2009. *Travelling Heroes: Greeks and their Myths in the Epic Age of Homer*, London.

Machado, A. 1979. "Proverbios y cantares XXIX [Proverbs and Songs 29]", *Campos de Castilla (1912), in Selected Poems of Antonio Machado*, trans. B.J. Craige, Baton Rouge.

Macfarlane, R. 2003. *Mountains of the Mind*, London.

Macfarlane, R. 2012. *The Old Ways: A Journey on Foot.* London.

Maddrell, A. 2013. "Moving and Being Moved: More-than-Walking and Talking on Pilgrimage Walks in the Manx Landscape", *Culture and Religion: An Interdisciplinary Journal* 14.1, 63–77.

Madry, S. 2007. "An Evaluation of Google Earth for Archaeological Exploration and Survey", in *Digital Discovery: Exploring New Frontiers in Human Heritage. CAA 2006. Computer Applications and Quantitative Methods in Archaeology. Proceedings of the 34th Conference, Fargo, United States, April 2006*, eds. J.T. Clark and E.M. Hagemeister, Budapest.

Muir, S. 2011. "Religion on the Road in Ancient Greece and Rome", in *Travel and Religion in Antiquity*, ed. P. Harland, Waterloo, ON, 29–47.

Popko, M. 1994. *Zippalanda: ein Kultzentrum im hethitischen Kleinasien*, Heidelberg.

Popko, M. 1999. "Berg als Ritualschauplatz. Ein Beitrag zur Kenntnis der hethitischen Religion", *Hethitica* 14, 97–108.

Power, R. 2006. "A Place of Community: 'Celtic' Iona and Institutional Religion", *Folklore* 117.1, 33–53.

Romano, D.G. and Voyatzis, M.E. 2014. "Mt. Lykaion Excavation and Survey Project, Part 1", *Hesperia* 83, 569–652.

Rutherford, I.C. 2001. "The Song of the Sea (SA A.AB.BA SÌR): Thoughts on KUB 45.63", in *Akten des IV. Internationalen Kongresses fur Hethitologie, 4.-8. October 1999*, ed. G. Wilhelm, Wiesbaden, 598–609.

Rutherford, I.C. 2013. *State Pilgrims and Sacred Observers in Ancient Greece. A Study of Theoria and Theoroi*, Cambridge.

Schwemer, D. 2008. "The Storm Gods of the Ancient Near East: Summary, Synthesis, Recent Studies: Part II", *Journal of Ancient Near Eastern Religions* 8.1, 1–44.

Scriven, R. 2014. "Geographies of Pilgrimage: Meaningful Movements and Embodied Mobilities", *Geography Compass* 8.4, 249–61.

Siart, C., Eitel, B., and Panagiotopoulos, D. 2008. "Investigation of Past Archaeological Landscapes using Remote Sensing and GIS: A Multi-method Case Study from Mount Ida, Crete", *Journal of Archaeological Science* 35, 2918–26.

Sinclair, T.A. 1990. *Eastern Turkey: An Architectural and Archaeological Survey, Vol. IV*, London.

Slavin, S. 2003. "Walking as Spiritual Practice: the Pilgrimage to Santiago de Compostela", *Body and Society* 9.3, 1–18.

Stark, R. and Bainbridge, W. 1987. *A Theory of Religion*, New York.

Treadgold, W. 2007. "The Byzantine World Histories of John Malalas and Eustathius of Epiphania", *The International History Review* 29, 709–45.

Turner, V. and Turner, E. 1978. *Image and Pilgrimage in Christian Culture*, Columbia.

Urry, J. 2000. *Sociology beyond Societies: Mobilities for the Twenty-First Century*, London.

Vogiatzakis, I.N. ed. 2012. *Mediterranean Mountain Environments*, Chichester.

Whiston Spirn, A. 1998. *The Language of Landscape*, New Haven – London.

Wigley, E. 2016. "The Sunday Morning Journey to Church considered as a Form of 'micro-pilgrimage'", *Social and Cultural Geography* 17.5, 694–713.

Winter, E. ed. 2017. *Vom eisenzeitlichen Heiligtum zum christlichen Kloster. Neue Forschungen auf dem Dülük Baba Tepesi*, Bonn.

CHAPTER 3

Braided Networks: Pilgrimage and the Economics of Travel Infrastructure in the Late Antique Holy Land

Marlena Whiting

This volume is a testament to the momentum of current trends in the study of the materiality and phenomenology of ancient pilgrimage, within which the Christian pilgrimage of Late Antiquity is seen as a continuation of an ongoing tradition, rather than an innovation. Emerging from this trend have been studies on the pilgrim's experience of built space, and new studies on the *realia* of pilgrimage, such as pilgrim accommodation.[1] Despite greater awareness of the more mundane aspects of late antique pilgrimage (like economic aspects, often glossed over by pilgrims themselves in their accounts), so far little attention has been paid to the manner in which routes that originated for political reasons came to be used for economic or religious travel. The relationship of traders and pilgrims to the Roman imperial road system is seen as opportunistic or even parasitical without necessarily appreciating the potential that economic and religious concerns had to impact state decisions in the form of infrastructure investment.

This chapter examines this phenomenon as it occurred in the late antique Near East, encompassing 'the Holy Land', Greater Syria, and the Levant, but also Anatolia and the Sinai Peninsula (to which I will return in greater detail). To do this I will employ the heuristic aid of the 'braided network', offered as an alternative to the concept of 'embeddedness' as a way of describing the interactions between politically, economically, and religiously motivated travel.[2] Examining the evidence through this lens helps clarify some of the patterns apparent in the historical sources, while at the same time acknowledging the complexity and fluidity of the process. In this chapter, I will consider various travel networks in Late Antiquity, focusing in turn on the networks for military/administrative traffic, trade, and Christian pilgrimage. More significantly, I will show the influence that each network was able to exert on

---

1 See individual contributions in Kristensen – Friese 2017; for studies on pilgrim accommodation see Voltaggio 2011, Whiting 2016, and Jensen, this volume.
2 See Collar – Kristensen, this volume.

the others, as demonstrated through a combination of textual sources (pilgrim accounts, saints' lives, itineraries, legal codes) and archaeological evidence. This evidence shows that the different priorities and motivations of different kinds of travellers had an impact on the shape of networks and ultimately on routes and infrastructure. Considering this mutual impact of different networks on the road system of Late Antiquity through the lens of the 'braided network' provides us with a new way of conceptualising the interdependency of different travel networks in the ancient world, not just restricted to Late Antiquity. Pilgrimage cannot be studied in isolation from trade, for example, but neither can their differences be elided.

When we think of a road network, we often think of physical roadways, making their way through the landscape, following and yielding to its constraints, like mountain ranges and rivers. The idea of networks, however, can also be used to describe behaviours by human actors and their motivations.[3] Network theory is derived from a branch of mathematics that analyses objects ('nodes') and their connections ('edges'). When speaking of physical road networks, localities are the nodes and the roads are the edges. In social network theory, the connections between actor-nodes are socially determined (*e.g.*, friendship or kinship ties). In this article, when using the word 'network' I am referring to the socially-determined connections between nodes: a 'pilgrim network' is different from a "imperial communications network" for socially constructed reasons, even if they pass through the same physical nodes (*i.e.*, cities). To indicate the physical road network I use the term 'routes'.

By gathering papers together under the heading of 'sacred travel' it is automatically agreed that such a category can be differentiated from other categories of travel. However, what makes the travel sacred is the motivation of the traveller, combined with the destination and perhaps the ritual behaviours observed *en route*. However, even sacred travellers must move through a secular world to attain their destination, often relying on secular infrastructure, laid out for travellers with different motivations and behaviours. Soldiers, officials, merchants, and pilgrims all shared the same roads. This is fairly obvious, but for understanding the development of routes and sites in relation to the priorities of different networks it is helpful to have a clear sense of the way different networks shared physical space and infrastructure, how they combine, diverge, and exert influence on each other. In conceptualising this relationship it is helpful is to think of travel networks as 'braided', with various networks

---

3 For examples of using of social network theory to understand the social implications of travel and mobility in the Roman world, see *e.g.*, Collar 2013; Graham 2006.

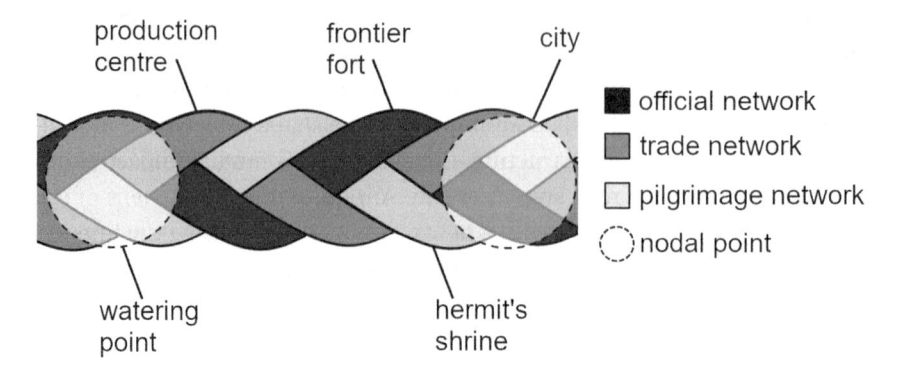

FIGURE 3.1   Schematic illustration of a braided network
(M. Whiting)

making up the 'strands' (Fig. 3.1). Each of these 'strands' is governed by its own priorities and motivations, which lead to 'points of divergence', but other factors, particularly relating to infrastructure, lead the strands to intersect at key nodes.

Although 'braided networks' can be conveniently if simplistically conceptualised as intertwined strands as in Fig. 3.1, a more apt analogy that better conveys change over time is with braided river systems. Unlike a braid of hair or fibre, a braided river is much more dynamic, with the various strands, or channels, exerting force over the others. Whereas strands of a braid remain distinct, in a braided river it is the force of water through the channels that determines the shape of the system. Channels can merge together, their barriers eroded. New ones can form. This is a more accurate description of the 'use-wear' that generates and changes travel networks over time, as we can perceive them in the historical and archaeological record.

'Points of divergence' are points along a route that only have interest for one of the network strands and limited or no interest to the others. They are often characterised by geographic remoteness, causing a deviation from the 'least-cost pathway' in pursuit of a particular goal.[4] For the military or state this could be a frontier outpost; for trade networks this might be a production centre or raw material source for trade goods; pilgrims could be drawn to a remote point where there is a sacred mountain or cave, or a shrine dedicated to a hermit or recluse. The nodal points that in turn draw the strands together

---

4   'Least-cost pathway' is a term derived from computer-based modelling where the computer determines the 'cheapest' route between two points based on factors ('friction surfaces') that influence the time, distance, and ultimately, resource use and financial cost of traversing a particular route. Douglas 1994.

can be the result of natural factors: water sources, river crossings, or mountain passes are 'pinch points' on routes and all networks must make use of them. Points where natural access routes converge become crossroads. These natural nodes or pinch points can be developed through human activity as settlements and the built environment expanded to accommodate and attract different road users.

Each braided network comprises two or more 'strands': networks which in and of themselves are potentially complex, but are differentiated primarily by the motivations of their users, the ends to which they use the road infrastructure. This is clearly exemplified, as shall be shown below, by travel in the Later Roman Empire, where clear strands making up the braided network include the military and imperial administration (who created and maintained the infrastructure system), merchants and traders (with their own, profit-making agenda, but also with mutual influence on the previous strand), and a clearly identifiable third strand of sacred travellers, pilgrims, with their own set of motivations and concerns.

The focus of this chapter is on the circumstances of the late antique Near East (third-seventh centuries CE). The emergence of Christian Holy Land pilgrimage as a popular phenomenon in this period, in concatenation with changes to imperial administration and a general period of economic prosperity in the region, make it an attractive case study to examine through the lens of 'braided networks'. I will proceed to consider generally the various strands (military/administrative, economic, and religious) and how they interacted. I will then present a focused case study of the development of the Sinai Peninsula as a pilgrim destination after the fourth century, which will show that contrary to the assumption that trade and religious travel follow in the wake of state mandates, sacred travel has the potential to influence economics and infrastructure.

In his *Holy Land Pilgrimage in the Later Roman Empire*, E.D. Hunt observed that concerns over the conflict between the more worldly aspects of secular travel and the spiritual aims of the pilgrim led to the creation of an 'alternative, and explicitly Christian framework' of hospitality.[5] Certainly monasteries and Christian hostels (*xenodochia*) were able to provide alternative accommodation to the inns and taverns that were mostly known for gambling, prostitution, and crime.[6] But it was not wholly possible to disentangle the strands,

---

5 Hunt 1982, 65.

6 On the variety of ancient inns, Constable 2003, Casson 1994, 87–8, 320; Christian objections, Hunt 1982, 70. On the reputations of commercial inns in the Roman West, see Le Guennec 2018, and in Rabbinic literature, Grossmark 2006.

especially in urban environments. Pilgrims were also at threat from violence on the road, not necessarily protected by their status as religious travellers.

The main theoretical underpinning of the braided network is that the basic constraints on non-motorised travel are the same for all. While there are variables, these are dictated by mode of transport (mounted on an animal or walking), and by terrain, and are easily quantifiable. However, the fundamental rates do not change: a 21st-century donkey does not move any faster than a fourth-century one. This is illustrated by the fact that the Baedeker guide of 1876 gives similar travel times to various locations in the Holy Land as do the early itineraries.[7]

A donkey – a typical animal of choice for a pilgrim in the late antique Near East[8]– walks at a rate of 6–8km/h. However, the majority of pilgrims were on foot. The average walking speed of a fit adult on level terrain is *c.* 5km per hour (5.07 for men, 5.29 for women).[9] This speed is reduced in inverse proportion to the gradient of the path, as quantified by Tobler's Hiking Function, developed by the geographer Waldo Tobler. Walking on unpaved paths slows the rate by 3/5, whereas riding on horseback increases it by 5/4.[10] The typical daily distance for a person on foot is usually estimated at 37km (7.4 h at 5km/h). This equates to 25 Roman miles, which is more or less the distance between *mansiones* on the *cursus publicus*, or the distance between military forts (allowing for variance due to terrain). This means that on average at 37km increments we should expect to find overnight accommodation – for all kinds of traveller on foot.

The basic needs of travellers can be divided into three categories: food, water, shelter. It is essential that these be available at regular intervals for travellers to survive.[11] For Christian pilgrims it is necessary to add a fourth category: ritual, since it is ritual or spiritual activity and motivation that differentiates a pilgrim journey, not just the sanctity of the destination. This distinction is far from definitive. Late Antiquity was a period imbued with piety – not just Christian piety – and ritual observances would be an important part of ensuring safety on any journey. I would, however, argue that Christian pilgrims appear to regard the journey itself as providing opportunities for performing piety. Egeria

---

7   Wilkinson 2002, 33; Baedeker 1876.
8   Egeria mentions riding on donkeys: *It. Eg.* 11.3, 6.1.
9   See Browning *et al.* 2006, 390–8.
10   Tobler 1993, 2, Fig. 2.
11   The Piacenza Pilgrim mentions water rationing in the desert of Sinai, where opportunities to replenish water supplies were scarce. *It. Ant. Plac.* 36.

prays and reads from the Bible at every holy site she visits.[12] Melania the Elder
and Melania the Younger both seem to use the hardships of travel as a way
of displaying their asceticism, by eschewing comfort or praying despite harsh
conditions.[13] The proliferation of holy sites and churches throughout the
fourth, fifth, and sixth centuries encouraged this mentality of travel by providing frequent opportunities for prayer. In some cases the distances between
these minor shrines is 5–10km, reflecting the universal hourly walking rate
mentioned above, meaning that shrines (and the opportunities for rest and
refreshment they provided) were available every few hours.

The Roman road system of the Near East is primarily a product of the
first and second centuries CE, as Rome extended and consolidated its power
throughout Syria, Palestine, and Arabia. The milestones that stand as testimony to this process record the role played by the military in the construction of
the roads, as well as the role of the imperial officials. There are of course overlaps and divergences in the competencies of the administrative and military
networks, but it is not necessary to go into them here. It was to meet their joint
needs for rapid communications, troop movement, and supply that the road
infrastructure was built up, and maintained.

From the late third century onward, however, the disposition of the legions
in the Near East underwent considerable change. There were also reductions
in number of garrisoned troops, culminating in the sixth century with the em-
ploying of *foederati*, local nomadic tribes under the leadership of the Ghassanid
dynasty, to patrol the frontier regions. The diminution of the workforce that
could be potentially used for large infrastructure projects like roads and bridges
is evident in the fragmentation of the formerly important major military high-
ways such as the *Via Nova Traiana*, which from the second century CE had

---

12   *It. Eg.* 10.7: 'And it was always our practice, when we managed to reach one of the places
      we were able to see, to have first a prayer, then a reading from the book, then to say an
      appropriate psalm and another prayer. By God's grace we always followed this practice
      whenever we were able to reach a place we wanted to see' (trans. Wilkinson).

13   Palladius, *Historia Lausiaca* 55: 'How dare you at your age ... thus coddle your flesh ... I am
      in the sixtieth year of my life and except for the tips of my fingers neither my feet nor my
      face nor any one of my limbs have touched water ... never in my travels have I rested on
      a bed or used a litter' (trans. Lowther Clarke). Although the chapter is titled 'Silvania' it is
      likely that it is Melania the Elder who is speaking. Gerontius, *Vit. Mel. Jun.* 56: 'At that time
      the winter was so fierce that the Galatian and Cappadocian bishops asserted that they
      had never seen such a winter ... Melania, who was like adamant, did not let up on her
      fasting at all' (trans. Clark).

connected Bosra in Syria with Aila on the Red Sea.[14] Infrastructure projects which had previously been the responsibility of military or civic officials, came under the auspices of the very highest imperial offices (*comes Orientis*, the praetorian prefect, and the *comes sacrarum largitionum*, the imperial officers in charge of collection and disbursal of public funds). As former civic wealth came to be concentrated in the hands of the church, bishops, as public officials, oversaw infrastructure improvements, such as improvement of roads or building of bridges.[15]

One salient aspect of the imperial administrative network was the system for rapid communications, the *cursus publicus*.[16] The *cursus publicus* should be thought of as a set of amenities (*e.g.*, relays of horses, fodder, food and lodging for travellers) made available at state expense (via taxation on local provincials). The system comprised horse-changing stations (*mutationes*) and rest-stops (*mansiones*) at regular intervals,[17] that enabled riders on horseback to carry messages long distances very swiftly. From the fourth century this aspect of the *cursus publicus* came to be called the *cursus velox*.[18] There was also a slower option, the *cursus clavularis* or *vehicularis*, used for freight, usually the transport of taxes (levied in coin or in kind). Individuals might also be granted permission to avail themselves of the government horses, if they were travelling on imperial business. The stations were maintained at the cost of the state and local authorities; it was a very expensive operation. The horses of the *cursus publicus* were worked so hard they only had a working life of four years.[19] It was also a system open to abuse: of the vast legislation from the fourth and fifth centuries dedicated to the *cursus publicus* in the *Codex Theodosianus*, the majority is aimed at curtailing the issuing of unnecessary permits, and against people requisitioning more animals than they were entitled to.

---

14   On the fragmentation of the *Via Nova Traiana*, see Fiema 1993, 549–50; MacDonald *et al.* 1982, 117–31; Bauzou 1998, 105–255.

15   Theodoret, bishop of Cyrrhus in northwest Syria, in a letter dated *c.* 449, mentions paying for two bridges out of the revenues of his see. *Ep.* 81.

16   This particular term is first attested in the fourth century (the earlier term is *vehiculatio*), and is coterminous with the reorganisation of the system during the reigns of Diocletian and Constantine. Lemcke 2016, 11.

17   *Mutationes* are spaced on average 5–10km apart, while *mansiones* are on average 25km apart. At a leisurely pace this corresponds to a few hours travel between *mutationes*, and a day's travel between *mansiones*. For couriers travelling at speed, the distance between *mansiones* corresponds to a change of animals approximately every hour.

18   Lemcke 2016, 40.

19   *Cod.Theod.* 8.5.34: 'veredorum pars quarta reparatur', one fourth of horses to be replaced in a year. Mitchell 2014, 254.

It is often assumed that the *cursus publicus* simply piggy-backed on an existing network of stations and inns that were run for commercial purposes. 'The private voyager who had no access, legitimate or illegitimate, to the government post would still find himself putting up at inns and hostels that formed part of the network, because in many areas they were the only ones available.'[20] One interpretation suggests that the government granted 'contracts' to existing commercial inns who maintained a certain number of animals and provisions in readiness, in exchange for subsidies received from the state. However convenient or plausible such a solution would seem based on modern economic considerations, it does not find widespread confirmation in the sources.

Firstly, the maintenance of a *mansio* (or *mutatio*) was regarded as a *munus* – a form of public service – required of members of the curial class, and after the fourth century, from members of the provincial administration. It was an expensive and therefore not particularly desirable obligation: the role was auctioned to the lowest bidder, the station master (*manceps*) was required to be present at the station most of the time, and to supply any animals or provisions if requisitioning fell short.[21] Attempts to turn a profit seem to have involved illegal activity, such as overcharging for fodder and skimming the profits, or charging guests money for vehicle repair which was meant to be covered by state funds, or charging for animals that were not available.[22]

The legal texts from which the majority of our information derives are very clear: it is absolutely prohibited (on pain of death) to use government post-animals for private business.[23] A law of CE 395 strips even the highest senatorial rank, the *vir illustris*, of the automatic privilege of using the *cursus publicus*.[24] It was also forbidden to pay wagoners, veterinarians, or mule drivers, as they received their subsistence from the state.[25] If government animals were not immediately available at a station, travellers on the *cursus publicus* were to wait until animals were returned to the station, and not requisition animals from the fields.[26] It is difficult to construct an argument about real practice from prescriptive texts, but it is not really possible to discern a commercial system of animals and lodgings for hire operating out of the same stations as the *cursus publicus*, at least not based on the legal evidence.

---

20   Casson 1994, 189. For a similar assumption, see Matthews 2006, 62–3.
21   Auctions: Pflaum 1940, 352–6; on the role of *mancipes* in the later Empire, see especially Lemcke 2016, 61–9.
22   *Cod.Theod.* 8.6.21; 8.5.60; 6.29.2.
23   *Cod.Theod.* 8.5.10; 8.5.44.
24   *Cod.Theod.* 8.5.54.
25   *Cod.Theod.* 8.5.31.
26   *Cod.Theod.* 8.5.1.

Looking at alternative sources, like patristic writings or hagiography, does not much clarify the picture. Gregory Nazianzen described the *mansio* (*stathmos*) at Sasima as having 'dust everywhere, noise, carriages, lamentations, groans, tax-collectors, tortures and fetters; a population of total strangers and vagabonds.'[27] The inclusion of vagabonds (*planomenoi* = wanderers and deceivers) could suggest that more than just public officials congregated at the post-station (or simply presents a negative opinion of public officials). Gregory of Nyssa similarly decried 'the inns and hostelries and cities of the East present many examples of licence and of indifference to vice.'[28] Vice in the form of prostitution was readily available at the inn where St Theodore of Sykeon's mother worked, and where the holy man was born as the result of a liaison between this innkeeper and an imperial messenger.[29] This establishment is described as an inn (*pandocheion*) on the 'public highway of the imperial post'.[30] According to Olivia Remie Constable, *pandocheion* should be interpreted where it occurs as a *terminus technicus* meaning a commercial inn, distinct from either a station of the government post or a pilgrim hostel (*xenodocheion*), coded in the meaning of prefix *pan-*, 'receiving all comers'.[31] Sykeon is not listed as an official station in Galatia on either the Bordeaux Itinerary or on the Peutinger Map, so perhaps it was indeed a commercial inn rather than a *mansio*.[32] However, the only visitors it is explicitly stated to have received were 'governors and officials', not private citizens of the sort prohibited from using the *cursus publicus*. This discrepancy could be accounted for either if the inn at Sykeon was not an official *mansio*, but nonetheless popular with official travellers, or by a change occurring between the fourth and sixth century, when Sykeon could have been incorporated as an official stop, possibly at the time the bridge was built during the reign of Justinian.

---

27   Greg. Naz. *Carmina* 2.1 (*PG* 37.1059–1060).

28   Moore – Wilson 1983, 382. τῶν δὲ κατὰ τοὺς ἀνατολικοὺς τόπους πανδοχείων καὶ καταλυμάτων καὶ πόλεων πολλὴν τὴν ἄδειαν καὶ πρὸς τὸ κακὸν τὴν ἀδιαφορίαν ἐχόντων ('Epistulae', in *Gregorii Nysseni Opera Online*, ed. Jaeger, consulted online on 31 August 2016).

29   Theodore of Sykeon (*c.* 550–623) was a holy ascetic and bishop in Galatia in central Asia Minor. He was an active performer of miracles in and around Sykeon (where he had a hermitage) and Anastasioupolis (where he was bishop). He travelled several times to Constantinople, and on pilgrimage to Jerusalem and Sinai. His vita exemplifies Sykeon as a rural agrarian settlement, but with connections to major cities, and important people and events, thanks to its situation on a major imperial highway.

30   'ἡ δημοσία στράτα τοῦ βασιλικοῦ δρόμου. *Vit. Theod. Syk.*, 3.

31   Constable 2003, 11–39.

32   The site is located halfway between the *mutatio* Hyrconpotamon and the *mansio* Agania (Lagania), five kilometres from each, at the crossing of the river where a bridge was built during the reign of Justinian.

The cook at Theodore's *pandocheion* received money for his cooking, possibly to be understood as tips from grateful patrons.[33] The accounts of the fourth century traveller Theophanes also indicate that money was exchanged for food.[34] Although a permit-holder was entitled to provisions both for the animals and for himself, and for an accompanying servant, it is likely that the expenditure on food was for the remainder of his or her retinue who fell outside the stipulations of the permit. This indicates that it was possible for stationmasters to make some money from visitors, but whether stations could provide services for paying members of the public, using resources other than those made available by the state, is still not made explicit. Egeria's account uses the term *mansio* both for lodgings and as a unit of measurement, roughly equivalent to a day's travelling.[35] Should we interpret *mansio* as being used in a technical sense here? Was Egeria in fact using the stations of the imperial communications service on her journey? Did she have a permit to do so, or is this our missing evidence for mixed private and state use of the accommodations along the *cursus publicus*? It appears to me that she using the term in a more general sense for any overnight stop. The word *mansio* derives from *manere*, to stay, and the affinity of the words is demonstrated by Egeria at the crossing of the Taurus mountains: *ac sic perveniens eadem die ad mansionem quae appellatur Mansocrenas, quae est sub monte Tauro, ibi mansi.*[36] Mansocrena is in fact a stop on the *cursus publicus*, since it appears on the Bordeaux Itinerary (Mansucrinae) and is located at the Cilician Gates through which all traffic between Anatolia and the Levant would have to pass. However, it is clear that in other instances she is probably not speaking of official *mansiones*. This is suggested by her use of *mansio* to also describe her stops in the desert of southern Sinai where there is no evidence of Roman state presence, no urban *curiales* to maintain stations, and no public highway.[37]

The sources are maddeningly unclear as to whether licensed stations of the *cursus publicus* also offered legitimate accommodation to fee-paying customers. If there were no commercial side-line to the *cursus publicus*, it would

---

33   *Vit. Theod. Syk.*, 6.

34   Matthews 2006, 51–6; 66–7.

35   *E.g., It.Eg.* 17.2. 'Et hic locus [Edessa] de Ierusolima vicesima et quinta mansione est'/ 'Edessa is twenty-five staging posts from Jerusalem'. The Piacenza Pilgrim (*It. Ant. Plac.* 40) also uses *mansio* thus: 'De monte Sina in Arabia in ciuitatem, quae uocatur Abila [Aila], sunt mansiones octo.'/'From Mount Sinai to the city of Arabia called Aila is eight staging-posts.' *Mansio* as a unit of measurement also appears as a loan word in Syriac, where long journeys are measured using the term *masiōnīn*.

36   *It. Eg.* 23.7. 'Arriving that same day at the *mansio* called Mansocrenas, at the foot of the Taurus mountains, I stayed there.'

37   *It. Eg.* 6.2.

explain the state's concern over the financial burden of running it. This would also suggest that there must be a parallel strand of for-profit hostelries located at similar increments along the road as the state-run options, to provide overnight stops as well as essential food and water. Over time, the cost of the *cursus publicus* became too much for the state to bear. First the *cursus clavularis* was abolished, in the diocese of Oriens in 467/8 under Emperor Leo.[38] In effect, this meant that the transport of taxes and state goods was privatised. Among the many sins of Justinian catalogued by Procopius in the Secret History is that he dismantled the *cursus publicus* in the diocese of *Asiana*.[39]

Even though it is not entirely possible to see how the administrative networks and commercial networks of travel were intertwined in space, the stations were nonetheless important nodes of the local economy. *Mansiones* were gathering points for tax items from surrounding villages (hence Gregory Nazianzen's reference to tax collectors above).[40] At various times these taxes were either gathered in kind (where agricultural produce could be directly used for provisioning the *cursus publicus*), or where these goods could be sold to the station master in exchange for coin which was then paid as tax. Procopius mentions as a consequence of Justinian's decision to reduce the *cursus publicus* in Asia Minor, that the farmers, having nowhere to sell their crops, left them to rot in the fields.[41] The importance of inns as nodal points of the local economic landscape, intersecting with long-distance transport routes, is echoed in their importance in the social and religious landscape. This is exemplified in the *Life of St Theodore of Sykeon*, where Theodore's reputation for holy works attract many people from local villages to him. He was also able to take advantage of the long-distance connectivity to go on pilgrimages to places in Asia Minor and Jerusalem and to visit Constantinople.

Extensive though the infrastructure of the *cursus publicus* and the administrative/military communications networks was, its amenities were only available to a fairly limited subsection of the population. There were, however, a large number of secondary beneficiaries of this system, to whom we shall now turn. As we turn to the second strand, (i.e., trade) the braiding effect already becomes apparent, as it is not possible to take into account the movement of trade goods without the armature of state infrastructure. There are four ways in which these two strands interact: infrastructure, security, markets, and direct state control.

---

38   *Cod. Iust.* 12.50.22.
39   Procop. *Anecdota*, 30.
40   *Cod. Theod.* 12.6.21; 12.6.19.
41   Procop. *Anecdota*, 30.

First, there is the physical infrastructure, the roads, *etc.* that will influence the routes of trade. Second, there is the security derived from traversing roads with military garrisons which can provide protection for caravans. This can work both ways: trade routes might gravitate towards routes that are already well-traversed and protected due to their strategic importance. Alternatively, forts can be set up to guard lucrative caravan routes, especially across deserts, in places where no overt military agenda exists.[42] Third, there is the market that military garrisons (and the associated *vicus* or civilian settlement) would provide for goods. In the fourth and fifth centuries, much of the army's rations (*annona*) were acquired through taxation in kind, so the extent of the economic benefit to local populations is doubtful. At its most simplistic, the army can be regarded as a vortex into which the agricultural produce of the provinces disappeared.[43] Recently, archaeology has been challenging this bleak model, through surveys of the agricultural hinterlands of military forts, and systematic examination of pottery assemblages from excavated sites. The pottery from the fort at Dibsi Faraj on the Euphrates in Syria, for example, revealed a large amount of tablewares from Asia Minor, Cyprus, and North Africa, probably arriving at the site through commercial trade.[44] At the legionary fortress of Lejjun in Jordan, a small amount of imported tablewares like those at Dibsi Faraj was found. However, the majority of pottery was locally produced, either in the fortress itself or by local artisans.[45] This difference in the profile of the assemblages at the two sites can be explained by their different positions in the braided network systems. Dibsi Faraj, located at the crossroads of major east-west and north-south arteries, and with its riverine connections, was located at a nodal point of the administrative and civilian commercial networks. Lejjun, on the other hand, while holding a key military position on the eastern frontier was nonetheless at a distance from the main north-south road and thus less likely to see commercial traffic.

Finally, there is the direct intervention of the state in the movement of goods and people by establishing customs tolls and border crossing points customs at Leuke Kome and Aila on the Red Sea. The customs duty levied at Leuke Kome on the Red Sea in the first century was a hefty 25%; the duty levied at Aila (Iotabe) from the fourth century was 12.5%; a treaty of 561

---

42   This argument could be made in support of the Late Roman phases of originally Nabataean fort/caravanserai structures along the Petra-Gaza road. Cohen 1982, 240–7.

43   See Pollard 2000, 221–230, following the model put forward by Hopkins 1980, 101–25.

44   Harper 1975, 325; Pollard 2000, 227.

45   Parker 1987, 529; Pollard 2000, 227–8.

indicates that customs on the Roman/Persian border was 10%.[46] This was an important source of revenue for the Empire. In 408/9 a law was issued restricting cross-border trading to Artaxata in Armenia, Nisibis in Mesopotamia, and Callinicum in Syria.[47] This was just as much a means to control people (and prevent espionage) as it was to control goods.

Sacred travel has its own distinctive attributes that prevent it merging seamlessly into the networks of either administrative or mercantile travel. Primarily, the different motivation of pilgrims means that they are often interested in different destinations than the other two groups. If these destinations are a reclusive hermit's cell, then the destination could be quite remote, as the initial intention in choosing the location was isolation. At other times, the focus of worship might be determined by a natural feature, like a mountain top or a spring with healing properties, which exists independently of routes preferred by other networks. In some cases, the difficulty in accessing these sites enhances their sanctity and the spiritual profit derived from completing the pilgrimage.[48]

The sacred aspect infuses not just pilgrims' choice of destination but also the manner in which they travel. Prayer and ritual form an important part of their progress, certainly to a much greater degree than it might have been for merchants or state officials, although prayer and religiosity were part of the fabric of lived experience, including travel (thus merchants might make an offering in thanks for a profitable venture, or statesmen might travel to consult holy persons).[49] Pilgrims, however, also engage in pilgrimage with a heightened awareness of religiously appropriate behaviour, their aim is to behave with as much decorum as possible, to not undo the spiritual rewards of the act of pilgrimage by lapsing into sins of the flesh. This was often at odds with the reality of travel, where there was danger of violence and where inns were typically associated with gambling, prostitution, and other excesses. These

---

46   Leuke Kome: *Periplus Maris Erythraei*, 19. Aila: Theophanes *Anni Mundi* 5990. Jones 1964, 826–7; Mayerson 1992, 1–4. The treaty of 561 refers to customs posts as *dekautēria*, from which it is inferred that one tenth was charged in duty: Menander Protector, frag. 6.1, Pollard 2000, 216.

47   *Cod. Iust.* 4.64.4.

48   While the notion of equivalence between the length of a pilgrimage and its spiritual reward is a medieval concept, journeying into the desert was a common ascetic act in the late antique period and is in keeping with the ideals of asceticism of the time. Ascetic holy persons were admired and even emulated by those who saw and visited them, often receiving advice to act more like their models. See also the paper by Collar, this volume.

49   Maurice, the future emperor, is described as visiting Theodore of Sykeon for a blessing on his return journey to Constantinople following a successful campaign in Persia *c.* 582. *Vit. Theo. Syk.* 54. The holy man prophesies his accession to the throne.

concerns infuse the rhetoric of early church fathers; Gregory of Nyssa famously objected to pilgrimage on the grounds that it was impossible for pilgrims to maintain their spiritual purity when travel forced them to encounter the 'passions' of the real world.[50] Basil of Caesarea founded what might have been the first pilgrim hostel, known as a *xenodocheion* to differentiate it from a *pandocheion*. The purpose of this *xenodocheion* was to house strangers, and the sick, exemplifying the changing notion of hospitality as an act of Christian charity and thus of piety, differentiating it from Roman culture where hospitality was seen as an individual, rather than social, obligation.[51] Throughout the fifth and sixth centuries the development of the parallel system of Christian hospitality is evident in the construction of monasteries and pilgrim hostels, often at similar locations to where roadside amenities had already existed, as dictated by the underlying limitations on daily travel distances and need for provisions as mentioned above.

We have already seen the ways in which different strands of a braided network can exert influence on each other. Likewise, pilgrimage is both dependent on and capable of influencing these networks, despite its emphasis on the separation of space for accommodation. Like merchants, pilgrims make use of the infrastructure created and maintained by the state, and benefit from its protection. Egeria, for example, mentions staying in forts, and having an escort of soldiers, for part of her pilgrimage in the desert around Suez.[52] Pilgrimage could also influence infrastructural development: roads to Jerusalem maintained into the sixth century were doubtless improved in order to support pilgrim traffic.[53]

It is a truism that pilgrimage was a source of economic benefit to shrines and monasteries. However, often the economic exchanges taking place within the framework of pilgrimage are implicit rather than explicit due to the rhetoric of charity and piety that surrounds the practice, especially in its Christian form. Instead of a direct exchange of cash for lodgings or services, pilgrims could make gifts, especially if they had been recipients of a cure. In the *Historia Lausiaca* we hear of a monastery in Nitria (Egypt), where a guest could remain free of charge for one week, after which he was expected to contribute labour in exchange for his upkeep.[54] Pilgrims could directly purchase or make a dona-

---

50   On Pilgrimages. See Bitton-Ashkelony 2005 who argues that this rhetoric is less about objections to pilgrimage *per se*, but more about individual Church Fathers' attempt to promote their local martyrs'cults.

51   Basil. *Ep.* 94 (*PG* 32.488). See also Greg. Naz. *Or.* 43.63 (*PG* 36.577).

52   *It. Eg.* 7.2.

53   Fischer *et al.* 1996.

54   Pall. *Laus.*, 7.

tion in exchange for souvenirs: items that were endowed with the sanctity of the site or the saint who presided there, such as contact relics, *ampullae* for oil, or healing soap.[55] Such items are related to the function of the shrine as a holy place and have value in the implicit pilgrimage economy.

More direct economic activity as a result of, or concomitant with, pilgrimage is also evident. Pilgrim shrines could provide a focal point for larger scale commercial events. Commemorative days for the liturgical year, saints or martyrs' feast days attracted large crowds and inevitably became opportunities for commercial activity. Large fairs could be set up on such days. St Simeon the Elder Stylite's feast day attracted large crowds, and recent excavations have shown the extent of the commercial exchange taking place. Shops lined the ceremonial walkway up to the shrine, and the nearby village had a large market place and several inns.[56] Basil of Caesarea expressed his dismay that monks were using martyrs' festivals as opportunities to engage in trade rather than reflection through prayer.[57] Once again, pilgrimage appears to be in rhetorical conflict with the secular world in which it is nonetheless embedded.[58]

Having laid out the principle of the braided network and its applicability to the circumstances of the late antique Near East, it would be fruitful to examine a case study where the effect can be seen clearly. The Sinai Peninsula is a region where the interaction of these networks on each other is particularly clear in Late Antiquity, and where Christian pilgrimage plays a visible role in shaping communications in that period. The Sinai Peninsula is extremely arid with a narrow coastal zone on three sides. The mountainous interior consists of the waterless uplands of the Tih Plateau and the mountain district with rugged peaks separated by meandering valleys.[59] For much of human history Sinai was devoid of large-scale permanent settlement (*i.e.*, cities), occupied instead since prehistory by practitioners of pastoral nomadism similar to the present-day inhabitants, the Bedouin. Despite this, Sinai has long been of importance to outsiders, since it forms a land-bridge between Egypt, the Arabian Peninsula, and the Levant. Because it is a desert, it is easy to think of Sinai as a void, but this is not an accurate interpretation. Sinai was inhabited, and it was

---

55   For the sale of healing soap at the shrine of St Thekla at Seleucia, ch. 42 in Dagron 1978, also pp. 78–9. See also Bitton-Ashkelony 2005, 38. On pilgrim souvenirs and their place in the pilgrimage economy, see Max Ritter's contribution in this volume.

56   See especially Theodoret, *Life of St. Simeon Stylites*, 11; Sodini 2001, 253; Butler 1904, 266.

57   Basil. *Regulae fusius tractatae* 40, *PG* 31, 1020d. See also Bitton-Ashkelony 2005, 38.

58   On fairs and Christian pilgrimage, see Ritter 2018.

59   *E.g.*, Mt Sinai (Jebel Musa) elev. 2,285m, Mt Catherine (Jebel Katrina) elev. 2,629m. Mt Sinai is associated with the Biblical Mount Sinai and also with Mount Horeb (where Moses received the Law).

integrally connected with Egypt and the Levant in the Pharaonic, Hellenistic, and Nabataean periods. Even the Roman state made its presence felt before the fourth century CE. What concerns us here is the degree and geographic extent of the involvement of 'great powers' and how that was manifested in infrastructure to support interregional communications. From this it becomes clear that Christian pilgrimage provided a wholly new impetus for communications to the interior of Sinai, and that, in this case, infrastructure and trade followed where pilgrims led.

The geography is a key determining factor on the communication routes of the Sinai Peninsula. The least-cost pathways are found in the coastal areas (along the Mediterranean coast and the shores of the Gulf of Suez and the Gulf of Aqaba – the northern arms of the Red Sea). The mountains (where the peaks associated by Christians with the events of Exodus are located), are best accessed via the seasonal river valleys (wadis) that drain into the Red Sea. Historically, the primary interregional routes for communications and commerce were lateral (mainly east-west), with no need for major arteries into the interior, although pathways employed by the nomads did of course exist.

There are three known historical routes across the Sinai Peninsula (see Fig. 3.2). Firstly, there is the Mediterranean coastal route across North Sinai.[60] This route, which follows a narrow sandbank north of the swampy lagoon of Lake Bardawil, was opened up by Alexander the Great in preference to the southerly route through the desert. Greek colonies established at intervals along the sandbank served as rest-stations. This route is part of the so-called *Via Maris*, the main administrative highway through the Levant, which could be followed north to Antioch and then to Constantinople, or westward along the Mediterranean coast to Alexandria. The Pelusiac branch of the Nile also provided the access into the interior of Egypt. The route is recorded in numerous itineraries, including the travels of Theophanes and the fourth-century Peutinger Map. The *Notitia Dignitatum* of c. CE 400 indicates that the way stations along the route were protected by garrisons.[61]

A second route, probably established under the Nabataeans, ran further south and connected the Red Sea ports of Aila and Clysma. It is described on the Peutinger Map. The exact location of the stops on this route is unknown as the Peutinger Map is inconsistent: it gives a route from Elusa in the Negev to Aila ('Haila'), and the next stop is 'Phara' (distance of 50 Roman miles/ 74 km). The next stop is illegible (distance 80 miles/118km), and from there it is

---

60   See Figueras 2000.
61   *Not. Dig. Pars Secunda. In partibus Orientis*, XXVIII. Comes limitis Aegypti. Figueras 2000, 22.

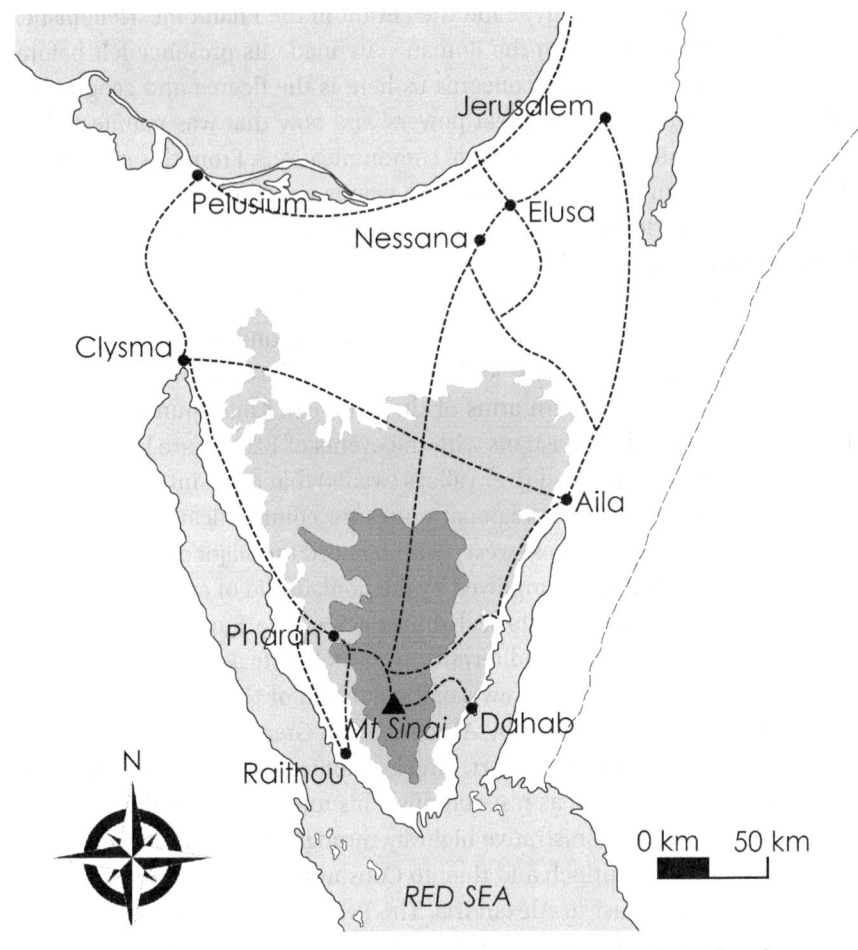

FIGURE 3.2   Sketch map of Sinai showing approximate routes (M. Whiting, based on
             U. Dahari, *Monastic settlements in South Sinai in the Byzantine period*, 13,
             Plan 2)

another 40-something Roman miles (60–70km) to Clysma. Either one rejects
the place names and accepts the distances given as correct (*c.* 250km total), in
which case the map most likely refers to the shortest route across the Peninsula
between Aila and Clysma, roughly corresponding to the Medieval pilgrimage
route (Darb al-Hajj).[62] The other interpretation is to relate the place names
to known places with similar toponyms, whereby 'Phara' would be Pharan, in
which case the map describes a more southerly route that follows the coast

---

62   K. Miller, *Itineraria romana: Römische Reisewege an der Hand der Tabula Peutingeriana*
      (Stuttgart 1916), Cols 813–814; D. Graf 1998, 110–111.

and cuts into the difficult interior, possibly passing near Mount Sinai.[63] Since the Peutinger Map combines information from sources of various dates, and itself is of indeterminate (probably fourth century) date, with a patina of (medieval?) Christianity, it is possible that the pilgrim route has been incorporated (or assumed that it included/went south of Mt Sinai). It has also been suggested that this route reflects a pre-Christian route relating to mineral extraction of copper ore and precious stones in the sandstone mountains of Southern Sinai.[64]

Finally, potential routes were provided by the narrow corridor along the coast of the peninsula between the sea and the steep interior. The maritime trade network of the Red Sea was thriving from the second century into the sixth, and had an influence on any routes that followed the southern Sinai coast, and the protection of those routes. This explains the presence of the Nabataean/Roman fortress/caravanserai on the east coast at Dahab, occupied into the late Roman period. The site has very little evidence of activity in the Byzantine period (only a few sherds), suggesting that this was not on the pilgrim route, which turned off for the interior via wadis further north.[65] Raithou on the western coast was another important port, possibly a maritime access point for material mined at Pharan. A monastery and fortress were built there by Justinian in the sixth century.

Foreign powers (e.g., the Egyptians, the Nabataeans, and the Romans) were drawn to the Sinai Peninsula for its mineral wealth, its strategic importance as a land bridge, and its entrepôts for Red Sea trade. Mineral extraction played a major role in the Egyptian presence in Sinai in the third to late second millennia BCE. This is most strongly manifested in the large temple of Serabit el Khadim at the northeast edge of the Sinai mountain range. This was a turquoise extraction site with a workers' camp as well as the large temple complex. The temple appears to have been dedicated to the Egyptian goddess Hathor and shows evidence of royal patronage. However, a local deity was also worshipped at the site, and the graffiti in the workers' camp is now interpreted as names of Sinai natives (rather than workforce conscripted from the Levant or Syria).[66]

---

63   Dahari 2000, 10.
64   Rothenberg 1980, 170. Precious stones include turquoise, and Pliny the Elder mentions the purplish stone *pharanitis* (named, he says, for the country bordering Arabia, *i.e.*, Sinai) (Plin. *Nat.* 37). Avner (2016) argues that Pharan was an important administrative centre in the Nabataean period. The Romans clearly had awareness of Sinai in the first century which may have merited its inclusion on the Peutinger Map.
65   Meshel 2000, 18–47.
66   Rothenberg 1980, 163–4.

The Nabataeans seem to have been less interested in the mineral wealth of Sinai and more interested in its potential to facilitate trade along the Red Sea.[67] A road station at the northern edge of the Sinai mountains hints at an overland route connecting the Red Sea at Dahab with the Mediterranean (possibly to avoid the 25% Roman customs duty once the Nabataean kingdom north of the Gulf of Aqaba was annexed in CE 106).[68] The oasis town of Pharan seems to have emerged as an important settlement from the first century BCE to the second century CE. The cultural influence of Nabataea is particularly evident there at the sacred sites of Jebel Serbal and Jebel Moneijah.[69] Graffiti bearing priestly titles suggest a high level of integration with Nabatean religious organisation, but the names that appear in the graffiti appear to be primarily attested in Sinai.[70] Generally, 'Nabataean' discoveries in Sinai are more indicative of local inhabitants adopting Nabataean culture than of the presence of Nabataean 'colonists'.[71]

In these examples of Egyptian and Nabataean involvement in Sinai, the braiding effect is evident. The primary need for raw materials or access routes for trade led to infrastructure investment by foreign states, along which pathways cultural elements, including artifacts and religion, were transmitted to the local people. However, direct foreign presence is not found in the mountains that would become the focus of travel to Sinai from the fourth century onward.

Roman imperial presence in Sinai likewise concentrated along the Mediterranean coast and the uppermost arms of the Red Sea. Significantly, it appears that there is no continuity of infrastructure in Southern Sinai from the Nabataean period (first century BCE to the second century CE) into Late Antiquity, i.e., the end of the third century when Sinai was formally incorporated into the province of Palaestina Tertia under Diocletian. Mining activities were still taking place, but on a scale suggestive of local activity.[72] These were not imperial mines needing routes for access and distribution, or processing facilities and provisions for a large conscripted workforce. Graffiti in Nabataean script appear to cease in the third century, at both the sacred sites and along the trade routes.[73] There is even a hiatus in the occupation of the town at Pharan: pottery evidence suggests that the site was abandoned in the second century CE

---

67   There is also some evidence that the Nabataeans were involved in the cultivation and export of dates. Negev 1977b, 73.
68   Avner 2016, 407.
69   Avner 2016.
70   Negev 1977a.
71   Negev 1977b, Meshel 2000, Avner 2016.
72   Rothenberg 1980, 170.
73   Caner 2010, 7.

and only resettled in the fourth century CE.[74] This serves to highlight the *inventio* of Sinai as a Christian pilgrimage destination as an innovation of the fourth century, not building on an earlier tradition, or existing communication routes. For example, although occasional individual Jewish travellers are attested in Sinai from the first century CE onward, there was no large-scale pre-Christian tradition of Jewish pilgrimage to the site.[75] Eusebius writing at the end of the third century describes Pharan as a *polis*, but it is not certain whether it should be interpreted as having official city status, especially given the archaeological evidence for a hiatus in settlement at that time.[76] The first bishop is attested in 400, by which time the Christian monastic presence in the area is well documented.[77]

The *Notitia Dignitatum* does not refer to any troops garrisoned in Southern Sinai, although graffiti mentioning the *Legio III Cyrenaica* found in Wadi Tuweiba near the shore of the Gulf of Aqaba demonstrates that there was a formal military presence that did extend into northeast Sinai in the Late Roman period.[78] In Egeria's account of her return from Mt Sinai to Egypt, she is accompanied by a military escort but apparently only north from Clysma (7.2, 7.4), where there was a fort and a Roman imperial presence. In Peter the Deacon's synopsis of Egeria's account, Clysma is the seat of a *logothete* charged with representing the Roman government on embassies to India.[79] By contrast, in the mountains of Sinai Egeria is accompanied by monks and clergy (5.12), and between Pharan and Clysma she is probably accompanied by Pharanite guides on camels (6.2). She refers to staging posts between Clysma and Pharan using the term *mansio* but it is unclear whether that should be read as meaning an official station of the *cursus publicus*, or even just a campsite (6.1). She describes the route through the Wadi Feinan, between Pharan and the sea, thus: 'It is all sandy desert there, and there is no road whatsoever' (6.2).[80] This supports

---

74   Grossmann *et al.* 1996, 14, 28.

75   Negev 1977b, 79; Caner 2010, 19; Hezser 2011, 75.

76   *Onomasticon*, 914/166:12. Jerome's Latin translation is *oppidum*. By contrast, Petra, which was an official *polis*, is translated as *ciuitas*.

77   Ward 2014, 92, n. 48.

78   Alt dates the inscription to the second or early third century. Alt 1935, 61–64. The *Legio III Cyrenaica* was garrisoned at Bosra in Syria, *Not. Dig. Or.* 37. See also Graf 1998, 111. The *Legio X Fretensis* was stationed at Aila after the end of the third century but is not attested in Sinai.

79   *Peter the Deacon*, 4.

80   This is unsurprising for two reasons: first, roads are usually an indication of military presence (they facilitate the movement of infantry and also construction projects prevent idleness), and second, it is impractical to build roads in the bottom of wadis due to the strength of the flash floods which would likely wash them away.

a picture of a lack of Roman official presence in Southern Sinai even into the late fourth century.

The establishing in the fourth century of Mount Sinai as a *locus sanctus* associated with the theophany of the Burning Bush, and with the revelation of the Ten Commandments, had an enormous impact on the directionality of communications in Southern Sinai. There was new emphasis on routes penetrating into the mountainous interior culminating in the very arduous ascent up Mt Sinai. This is unusual in that it means routes had to be established to a very topographically challenging area for which infrastructure for either long-distance trade or military/administrative involvement had previously not been necessary. The natural topography of Sinai means that accessing the mountainous interior is difficult. Wadi access routes flow diagonally southward to the sea, necessitating travelling some distance along the coast to find an entry point into the mountains. Instead of taking a more direct route southwest from Nessana at the edge of the Negev highlands, to the central mountains, the pilgrim route followed the southeastern route to Aila, and then followed the zone between the coast and the mountains before turning west through the wadis that cut through to Mt Sinai/Jebel Musa. These routes are indicated by rock inscriptions that include explicitly Christian graffiti, found in the wadis. There is no archaeological or epigraphic evidence of a well-travelled pilgrim route directly from Southern Palestine or the Mediterranean coast into the mountains from the north.[81] Nevertheless, the Piacenza Pilgrim did take a more direct route across the desert. He states it took ten days to reach Mt Sinai from Elusa (via the 'guesthouse of St George' near Nessana, which gives us his bearing as southwesterly, towards the Tih Plateau and not towards Aila).[82] He notes that none of his party cared to repeat the experience, however, and left via the Aila route or towards Egypt by way of Pharan and Clysma.[83] This also is the route taken by Egeria.[84] The Wadi Feiran is clearly a favourable access route, and Pharan is located at an oasis – a reliable water source that would be

---

81   'Late Roman' pottery has been found at the Nabataean road station on the Dahab-Tih Desert-Mediterranean route, but it does not appear to relate to the later pilgrimage activity. Avner 2016, 407.

82   Piacenza Pilgrim: *It. Ant. Plac.* 35–40. See Caner 2010, 12–13 on this route. The Piacenza Pilgrim does not give his exact route, the journey between Elusa and Mt Sinai is *c.* 280km as the crow flies, if such a direct route were even possible it would require a pace of 28km (or *c.* 20 Roman miles) per day to complete in 10 days, which is just feasible but does not take into account slower progress due to the terrain.

83   The Piacenza Pilgrim says it is eight staging posts to Aila (40). The Peutinger Map gives a further six stages from Aila to Elusa. If we assume one stage completed per day, it would take two weeks from Mt Sinai to Elusa via Aila, compared with the 10 days recorded by the Piacenza Pilgrim for the desert route.

84   *It. Eg.* 6.1–3; Piacenza Pilgrim: *It. Ant. Plac.* 40–1.

of vital importance to travellers in Sinai where natural water sources are rare. Apart from routes that led to water sources like Pharan, the preferred access routes were not static, but changed over time. For example, the Wadi Mujawed was isolated between the fourth and sixth centuries, though at end of the sixth century it became the access to Mt Sinai, disturbing the hermits who had isolated themselves there.[85]

The establishing of a monastery – or, rather, an agglomeration of monastic clusters – introduced a whole new way of life into Sinai, based around agricultural subsistence, to the extent that such was possible. Eremitic monks could eke out an existence, primarily from fruit orchards. Egeria describes being given fruits as *eulogiai* by the monks in Sinai.[86] Olives and some vegetables were grown, and limited wine production was possible, but barely enough for subsistence levels.[87] For ascetic monks this might be enough, but for larger populations and the influx of tourists, it was necessary to import supplies. Additionally, grain had to be imported, which, along with wine, was essential for performing the liturgy of the Eucharist. The presence at the sixth century Justinianic Basilica at the Holy Summit of Late Roman 1 amphorae – a ware produced in Northern Syria/Cyprus and used as a container for wine and olive oil – hints at this circulation (although imitation LR1 amphorae were also produced at Ayun Musa south of Clysma). The ceramic finds (amphorae and imported finewares) from Pharan also confirm extensive trade links with Egypt, the Levant, and the Mediterranean from the fifth century onward.[88] The local populations clearly benefited from the greater integration resulting from pilgrimage.

The wealth of the monastery derived from pilgrims, but this also increased the security risk. Most of the monks were outsiders drawn from around the Christian world to live in the holy place; however, it is important to remember that the region was not unpopulated, and that there is often tension between nomadic populations and sedentary ones. The estimated population of monks is 500–1000.[89] The sources are also vague about the nomadic inhabitants of Sinai, referring to them generally as 'Saracens'; they were certainly more numerous than the monks.[90] However, if tribal affiliations were as complex as

---

85   Dahari 2000, 151.

86   *It. Eg.* 3.6.

87   Dahari 2000, 161. See Shams 2014 on the discovery of a late antique/Early Islamic *qanat* irrigation system near a monastic settlement *c.* 5km west of St Catherine's.

88   Kalopissi-Verti – Panayotidi 2010, 93–7. On imitation LR1 from 'Ayun Musa, see Ballet 2001, 41–4. Pharan: Grossmann *et al.* 1996, 19–23, 28–9.

89   Caner 2010, 24; Dahari 2000, 150–2.

90   The Piacenza Pilgrim (36) reports a figure of 12,600 'Saracens' attended a pagan festival while he was on his pilgrimage, but the catchment area for this festival could have been

they are today, there were certainly different groups, some who traded with the monks and provided them with their imported goods brought via camel caravan, and those who sought these goods for themselves.[91] Theft, and kidnapping, were particular hazards of travel in Sinai.[92] Victims of raids became new martyrs, and objects of veneration in their own right, as happened at Raithou, where people from Pharan would make a pilgrimage to commemorate the martyrdom of forty monks at the hands of another tribe.[93]

Concerns about protecting the pilgrims and the monks living in the holy places also influenced decisions made about military dispositions. The garrisons placed along the *Via Maris* in Northern Sinai, and at Aila and Clysma, served as a line of protection for the more inhabited zones of Egypt and the Negev against desert raiders from the heartland of Sinai. The southern part of the peninsula was thus contained, and did not require additional garrisons. Procopius mentions that, in response to the concerns of the monks at the Monastery of the Burning Bush (later St Catherine's), Justinian built a fortification wall and installed a garrison, for precisely the strategic purpose of containing the desert tribes.[94] This is sometimes interpreted as forming part of a 'grand strategy' for the defence of the Empire.[95] This would indeed represent a considerable influence of the pilgrim network on the state network within the braided network, since provisioning a garrison would necessitate entirely new infrastructure and supply lines. However, there are many reasons to believe that Procopius may have overstated affairs, and it was unlikely that the monastery was garrisoned by soldiers. A garrison is not mentioned in the account of the wall given by Eutychius (dated to the 10th century but based on earlier sources), or even by the Piacenza Pilgrim, who visited within a decade or so of Justinian's reign. Placing troops at the monastery would also have been inconsistent with the military policy of the time, which relied decreasingly on a standing army on the desert frontiers of Palestine and Arabia, and more on local tribes to police the area and keep other, hostile, tribes in check.[96]

_____

       very large, as pilgrimage was an important feature of pre-Islamic Arab religious culture. See McCorriston 2011.

91   Ward 2014, 18.

92   Caner 2004, 142–3.

93   Shahîd 1998, 377.

94   Procop. *Aed.* 5.8.4–6.

95   *E.g.*, Huber 1980, 202: 'Emperor Justinian ordered the construction of an impressive fortified monastery, on the one hand to protect the Sinai monks against continual attacks by pre-Islamic Saracens and on the other to guard the far-flung southern flank of the immense East Roman Empire.'

96   Mayerson 1978, 33–38; Isaac 1990, 95. For a summary of the arguments pro and contra, see Ward 2014, 122–4.

This is confirmed by the account of the Piacenza Pilgrim, who does not mention a garrison, but says that 'Saracens' at Pharan were 'sent straw ... and barley from the treasury', which reflects what we know of imperial policy at the time.[97] Furthermore, garrisoning the monastery makes very little strategic sense. As we have seen, the monastery was located at a confluence of difficult routes, and easily avoided by anyone intent on accessing the imperial heartlands. Thus it is more likely that the fortified monastery was built to protect the monks and their steadily accumulating wealth, and possibly provide a refuge for hermits and pilgrims. It provided a solution to a local, albeit high-profile, problem. The fortification of the monastery does appear to have had a reciprocal impact on the number of pilgrim visitors. Intensification of pilgrim graffiti following the construction of the wall, suggesting that the greater security provided through imperial patronage and state revenues encouraged even greater numbers of pilgrims.[98]

In the Introduction to the present volume, Collar and Kristensen stress the need to look at how economics and religion, pilgrimage in particular, were linked in the ancient world. They draw on Karl Polanyi's concept of embeddedness, the idea that economics and religion are inextricable. Horden and Purcell take this one step further, arguing that 'pilgrimage was not undertaken exclusively or even principally for religious reasons' which implies a hierarchy in which religious motivations for travel are secondary to economic ones.[99] In this chapter, I have shown that in the Late Roman Empire, economics and religion are also linked to politics, insofar as decisions regarding infrastructure investment were made by political bodies (the emperor, the military, civic councils). But instead of seeing the relationship between politically, economically, and religiously motivated travel as hierarchical, whereby the infrastructure of state is primary and the economic and religious uses of that infrastructure are secondary, I see them as each having the potential to exert influence on the other. For this reason, the metaphor of 'braided networks' is particularly useful. The case of the development of Christian pilgrimage to Sinai demonstrates that arduous journeys to remote locations undertaken for purely religious reasons, to see the places of scripture, then necessitated the development of trade networks to feed the pilgrims, and the construction of state-funded fortifications to protect them. Understanding the phenomena both in isolation and in terms of their impact on each other, as the braided network metaphor allows us to

---

97 Piacenza Pilgrim: *It. Ant. Plac.* 40.

98 Negev 1977b, 77.

99 Horden – Purcell 2000, 445.

do, enables a more nuanced understanding of the multifaceted nature of life and travel in Late Antiquity.

Acknowledgements

Research for this chapter was carried out during visiting fellowships at the CBRL British Institute in Amman and the Koç University Research Center for Anatolian Civilizations (ANAMED) in Istanbul.

Bibliography

Primary Sources

Codex Justinianus, F.H. Blume and T. Kearley, trans. 2010. *Annotated Justinian Code*, http://www.uwyo.edu/lawlib/blume-justinian/ajc-edition-1/book-1.html (last accessed 21 September 2016).

Codex Theodosianus, C. Pharr, trans. 1952. *The Theodosian Code and Novels, and the Sirmondian Constitutions*. Princeton, NJ.

Life and Miracles of Saint Thekla, G. Dagron, ed. and trans. 1978. *Vie et miracles de sainte Thècle: texte grec, traduction et commentaire*, Bruxelles.

Life of Theodore of Sykeon, A.-J. Festugière, ed. and trans. 1970. *Vie de Théodore de Sykéôn*, Brussels.

Periplus Maris Erythraei, L. Casson, ed. and trans. 1989. *The Periplus Maris Erythraei: text with introduction, translation, and commentary*, Princeton, N.J.

Basil of Caesarea, *Epistulae*, J.P. Migne, ed. 1886. *Patrologia Graeca 32*, Paris.

Egeria, *Itinerarium*, J. Wilkinson, trans. 1999. *Egeria's Travels*, third edition, Warminster.

Eusebius of Caesarea, *Onomasticon*, R.S. Notley and Z. Safrai, eds. and trans. 2005. *Eusebius, Onomasticon. A Triglott Edition with Notes and Commentary*, Leiden.

Gregory of Nyssa, *On Pilgrimages*, P. Schaff, trans. 1900. *A Select Library of the Nicene and Post-Nicene Fathers of the Christian Church: Second Series. Volume 5: Gregory of Nyssa: Dogmatic Treatises, Etc.*, Oxford – New York.

Gregory Nazianzen, *Carmina de se ipso*, J.P. Migne, ed. 1857. *Patrologia Graeca 37*, Paris.

Gregory Nazianzen, *Orationes*, J.P. Migne, ed. 1865. *Patrologia Graeca 36*, Paris.

Menander Protector, R.C. Blockley, trans. 1985. *The History of Menander the Guardsman*, Liverpool.

Palladius, *Historia Lausiaca*, D.C. Butler, ed. and trans. 1898–1904. *The Lausiac History of Palladius*, Cambridge.

Piacenza Pilgrim, J. Wilkinson, trans. 2002. *Jerusalem Pilgrims Before the Crusades*, Warminster.

Pliny the Elder, *Naturalis historiae libri XXXVII*, K. Mayhoff, trans. 1897. *Naturalis histo-riae libri XXXVII*, Volume 5, Books 31–37, Leipzig.

Procopius, *De Aedeficiis*, H.B. Dewing, ed. and trans. 1971. *On Buildings*, Cambridge, MA.

Procopius, *Anecdota*, H.B. Dewing, ed. and trans. 1935. *The Anecdota or Secret History*, Cambridge, MA.

Theophanes the Confessor, *Chronographia*, C. Mango and R. Scott, trans. 1997. *The Chronicle of Theophanes Confessor: Byzantine and Near Eastern history, A.D. 284–813*, Oxford.

Secondary Sources

Alt, A. 1935. "Aus der 'Araba. II. Römische Kastelle und Straßen", *Zeitschrift des Deut-schen Palästina-Vereins* 58/1/2, 1–78.

Baedeker, K. 1876. *Palestine and Syria: Handbook for Travellers*, Leipzig.

Ballet, P. 2001. "Un atelier de potiers aux 'Sources de Moïse' ('Uyūn Mūsā)", in *Le Sinaï de la conquête arabe à nos jours*, ed. J. Mouton, Cairo, 37–50.

Bauzou, T. 1998. "'La *Via Nova*: introduction', 'Les vestiges de la Via Nova éntre Busra et 'Amman', 'La Branche de Mafraq (site de al-Fudain)', La valeur des milles romains sur la *Via Nova*: étude métrologique', 'Le système des tors associées à la *Via Nova*', 'Le segment septentrional de la *Via Nova* et le Table de Peutinger', 'Les bornes mil-liaires de la *Via Nova*: évolution du IIe au IVe siècle', 'Les inscriptions relevées sur les bornes milliaires du secteur septentrional de la Via Nova' and 'Histoire et évolution du secteur septentrional de la Via Nova: essai de synthèse historique'", in *Fouilles de Khirbet es-Samra en Jordanie*, ed. J.-P. Humbert, Turnhout, 105–255.

Bitton-Ashkelony, B. 2005. *Encountering the Sacred: The Debate on Christian Pilgrimage in Late Antiquity*, Berkeley, CA.

Browning, R.C. *et al.* 2006. "Effects of obesity and sex on the energetic cost and pre-ferred speed of walking", *Journal of Applied Physiology* 2, 390–8.

Butler, H.C. 1904. *Architecture and Other Arts (in Northern Central Syria and the Djebel Ḥaurân)*, New York.

Caner, D. 1994. "Sinai Pilgrimage and Ascetic Romance: Pseudo-Nilus' *Narrationes* in Context", in *Travel, Communication, and Geography in Late Antiquity: Sacred and Profane*, eds. L. Ellis and F. Kidner, Aldershot, 135–48.

Caner, D. *et al.* 2010. *History and Hagiography from the Late Antique Sinai: Including Translations of Pseudo-Nilus' Narrations, Ammonius' Report on the Slaughter of the Monks of Sinai and Rhaithou, and Anastasius of Sinai's Tales of the Sinai Fathers*, Liverpool.

Casson, L. 1994. *Travel in the Ancient World*, Baltimore.

Cohen, R. 1982. "New Light on the Date of the Petra-Gaza Road", *The Biblical Archaeolo-gist* 45.4, 240–7.

Collar, A. 2013. *Religious Networks in the Roman Empire: The Spread of New Ideas*, Cambridge.

Constable, O.R. 2003. *Housing the Stranger in the Mediterranean World: Lodging, Trade, and Travel in Late Antiquity and the Middle Ages*, Cambridge.

Dahari, U. 2000. *Monastic Settlements in South Sinai in the Byzantine Period: The Archaeological Remains*, Jerusalem.

Douglas, D.H. 1994. "Least-cost Path in GIS using an Accumulated Cost Surface and Slopelines", *Cartographica: The International Journal for Geographic Information and Geovisualization* 31.3, 37–51.

Fiema, Z.T. 1993. "Tuwaneh and the *Via Nova Traiana* in Southern Jordan: A Short Note on the 1992 Season", *Annual of the Department of Antiquities of Jordan* 37, 549–50.

Figueras, P. 2000. *From Gaza to Pelusium: Materials for the Historical Geography of North Sinai and Southwestern Palestine (332 BCE–640 CE)*, Beer-Sheva.

Fischer, M. *et al.* 1996. *Roman Roads in Judaea II: the Jaffa-Jerusalem Roads*, Oxford.

Graf, D.F. 1998. "Les circulations entre Syrie, Palestine, Jordanie, et Sinaï aux époques greque et romains", in *Le Sinaï durant l'antiquité et le Moyen Âge: 4000 ans d'histoire pour un désert: actes du colloque "Sinaï" qui s'est tenu à l'UNESCO du 19 au 21 septembre 1997*, eds. D. Valbelle and C. Bonnet, Paris, 107–13.

Graham, S. 2006. "Networks, Agent-based Models and the Antonine Itineraries: Implications for Roman Archaeology", *Journal of Mediterranean Archaeology* 19.1, 45–64.

Grossmann, P. *et al.* 1996. "Report on the Season in Firan – Sinai (February–March 1992)", *Byzantinische Zeitschrift* 89, 11–36.

Grossmark, T. 2006. "The Inn as a Place of Violence and Danger in Rabbinic Literature", in *Violence in Late Antiquity: Perceptions and Practices*, ed. H.A. Drake, Aldershot, 57–68.

Harper, R.P. 1975. "Excavations at Dibsi Faraj, Northern Syria, 1972–1974: A Preliminary Note on the Site and Its Monuments", *Dumbarton Oaks Papers* 29, 319–37.

Hezser, C. 2011. *Jewish Travel in Antiquity*, Tübingen.

Horden, P. and Purcell, N. 2000. *The Corrupting Sea: A Study of Mediterranean History*, Oxford.

Hopkins, K. 1980. "Taxes and Trade in the Roman Empire (200 BC–AD 400)", *Journal of Roman Studies* 70, 101–25.

Huber, P. 1980. "Monks, Pilgrims and Saracens: Sinai in Early Christian Times", in *Sinai: Pharaohs, Miners, Pilgrims and Soldiers*, eds. B. Rothenberg and H. Weyer, Washington DC, 201–11.

Hunt, E.D. 1982. *Holy Land Pilgrimage in the Later Roman Empire, AD 312–460*, Oxford.

Isaac, B.H. 1990. *The Limits of Empire: The Roman Army in the East*, Oxford.

Jones, A.H.M. 1964. *The Later Roman Empire, 284–602: A Social, Economic and Administrative Survey*, Oxford.

Kalopissi-Verti, S. and Panayotidi, M. 2010. "Excavations on the Holy Summit (Jebel Mûsâ) at Mount Sinai: Preliminary Remarks on the Justinianic Basilica", in *Approaching the Holy Mountain: Art and Liturgy at St Catherine's Monastery in the Sinai*, eds. S.E.J. Gerstel and R.S. Nelson, Turnhout, 73–106.

Kristensen, T.M. and Friese, W. eds. 2017. *Excavating Pilgrimage: Archaeological Approaches to Sacred Travel and Movement in the Ancient World*, Abingdon.

Le Guennec, M. 2018. *Aubergistes et clients. L'accueil mercantile dans l'Occident romain (IIIe s. av. J.-C.–IVe s. ap. J.-C.)*, Rome.

Lemcke, L. 2016. *Imperial Transportation and Communication from the Third to the Late Fourth Century: The Golden Age of the Cursus Publicus*, Leuven.

Llewelyn, S.R. 1994. *A Review of the Greek Inscriptions and Papyri Published in 1982–83*, North Ryde.

MacDonald, B. *et al.* 1982. "The Wadi el Hasa Survey 1981: A Preliminary Report", *Annual of the Department of Antiquities of Jordan* 26, 117–31.

Matthews, J. 2006. *The Journey of Theophanes: Travel, Business, and Daily Life in the Roman East*, New Haven.

Mayerson, P. 1978 "Procopius or Eutychius on the Construction of the Monastery at Mount Sinai: Which Is the More Reliable Source?", *Bulletin of the American Schools of Oriental Research* 230, 33–8.

Mayerson, P. 1992. "The Island of Iotabê in the Byzantine Sources: A Reprise", *Bulletin of the American Schools of Oriental Research* 287, 1–4.

McCorriston, J. 2011. *Pilgrimage and Household in the Ancient Near East*, New York.

Meshel, Z. 2000. *Sinai: Excavations and Studies*, Oxford.

Miller, K. 1916. *Itineraria Romana: Römische Reisewege an der Hand der Tabula Peutingeriana*, Stuttgart.

Mitchell, S. 2014. "Horse-Breeding for the *Cursus Publicus* in the Later Roman Empire", in *Infrastruktur und Herrschaftsorganisation im Imperium Romanum: Herrschaftsstrukturen und Herrschaftspraxis III. Akten der Tagung in Zürich 19.-20.10.2012*, ed. A. Kolb, Berlin 2014, 246–61.

Moore, W. and Wilson, H.A. trans. 1893. *Gregory of Nyssa: Dogmatic Treatises, etc., Nicene and Post-Nicene Fathers of the Christian Church 2, 5*, ed. P. Schaff, Edinburgh.

Negev, A. 1977a. "A Nabatean Sanctuary at Jebel Moneijah, Southern Sinai", *Israel Exploration Journal* 27/4, 219–31.

Negev, A. 1977b. *The Inscriptions of Wadi Haggag, Sinai*, Jerusalem.

Parker, S.T. 1987. "The Pottery", in *The Roman Frontier in Central Jordan: Interim Report on the Limes Arabicus Project, 1980–1985*, ed. S.T. Parker, Oxford, 525–653.

Pflaum, H.-G. 1940. *Essai sur le 'cursus publicus' sous le haut-empire romain*, Paris.

Pollard, N. 2000. *Soldiers, Cities, and Civilians in Roman Syria*, Ann Arbor, MI.

Ritter, M. 2018. "Panegyric Markets in the Byzantine Empire and their Role in the Byzantine Pilgrimage Economy (5th–12th Centuries)", in *Für Seelenheil und*

Lebensglück: Das byzantinische Pilgerwesen und seine Wurzeln, eds. D. Ariantzi and I. Eichner, Mainz, 367–82.

Rothenberg, B. 1980. "Turquoise, Copper and Pilgrims: Archaeology of Southern Sinai", in *Sinai: Pharaohs, Miners, Pilgrims and Soldiers,* eds. B. Rothenberg and H. Weyer, Washington DC, 137–71.

Shahîd, I. 1998. "Arab Christian Pilgrimages in the Proto-Byzantine Period (V–VII Centuries)", in *Pilgrimage and Holy Space in Late Antique Egypt,* ed. D. Frankfurter, Leiden 1998, 373–92.

Shams, A. 2014. "A Rediscovered-new 'Qanat' System in the High Mountains of Sinai Peninsula, with Levantine Reflections", *Journal of Arid Environments* 110, 69–74.

Sodini, J. 2001. "La hiérarchisation des espaces à Qal'at Sem'an", in *La sacré et son inscription dans l'espace à Byzance et en occident,* ed. M. Kaplan, Paris, 251–62.

Tobler, W. 1993. *Three Presentations on Geographical Analysis and Modeling. Non-Isotropic Geographic Modeling. Speculations on the Geometry of Geography, and Global Spatial Analysis,* Santa Barbara, CA.

Voltaggio, M. 2011. "'Xenodochia' and 'Hospitia' in Sixth-Century Jerusalem: Indicators for the Byzantine Pilgrimage to the Holy Places", *Zeitschrift des Deutschen Palästina-Vereins* 127.2, 197–210.

Ward, W.D. 2014. *Mirage of the Saracen: Christians and Nomads in the Sinai Peninsula in Late Antiquity,* Berkeley, CA.

Whiting, M. 2018 "Monastery Hostels in Late Antique Syria, Palestine and Transjordan," in *Petra – The Mountain of Aaron II: The Nabataean Sanctuary and the Byzantine Monastery,* eds. Z.T. Fiema, *et al.,* Helsinki, 108–13.

Wilkinson, J. 2002. *Jerusalem Pilgrims Before the Crusades,* Warminster.

PART 2

Communities

∵

CHAPTER 4

Gathering in the Panhellenic Sanctuary at Delphi: an Archaeological Approach

Hélène Aurigny

1 Introduction

According to Strabo (10.5.4): 'ἡ τε πανήγυρις ἐμπορικόν τι πρᾶγμά ἐστι'. (Delos): the *panegyris* is a kind of commercial thing'.[1] Gathering in sanctuaries on religious occasions has an economic dimension that ancient sources acknowledge, but which the term pilgrimage, as applied to sacred travel in antiquity, does not adequately describe. The phenomenon of the *panegyris* combined the religious with a commercial or economic event. Although scholarship has recognised this junction between religion and economy, it has received more attention recently,[2] and the economy of the sacred is at the heart of present discussions.[3] The perspective of 'sacred travel' gives us the occasion to have a fresh look at this general issue, and thinking about the 'economies of gathering' focuses on the moment when people gather in the sanctuary and the impact of this process not only on the sacred spaces, but also on the environment and even the votive practices of the pilgrims.

In this chapter, I will take the specific case of Delphi in central Greece, one of the most important Panhellenic sanctuaries of the ancient Greek world, and question the moment of gathering by taking together different kinds of sources, in order to show if and how Delphi appears as both a religious and economic hub. As I am not an economic specialist, I will treat this rich and stimulating theme from an archaeological point of view, focusing on the votive gifts to the gods. First, I examine the double dimension of the *panegyris*: the religious festival and *agora* and its modalities in Delphi. Second, I consider the impact of gathering on the development of the sanctuary. Finally, I focus on

---

1 I would like to thank very warmly Troels Myrup Kristensen and Anna Collar for their invitation to reconsider the archaeological data in Delphi following the experience of a pilgrim.
2 Dillon 1997, ch. 8. Chandezon 2000, 72; Deshours 2006, 90–2. See the introduction and Kowalzig in the present volume.
3 One can think of the question of sacred and public land, discussed in Papazarkadas 2011 for Attica. See also Rousset 2013.

the votives as consequences of gathering and as material witnesses of 'sacred travel' to Delphi and its social dimension.

2   *Panegyris* and *Agora*

2.1   *Modalities of the Panegyris at Delphi*

In the ancient Greek world, the sanctuary is the frame in which collective religious manifestations, namely *panegyreis*, regularly took place. In Delphi, those celebrations were famous and attracted a crowd of pilgrims at a Panhellenic and international level, as well as athletes and artists interested in the *agones*.[4] Because of its multiple functions, there were many reasons for visiting the sanctuary of Apollo. The oracular consultation is of course one of the main causes of travel to Delphi. While the relationships between the installation of the cult of Apollo, at the end of the ninth or at the beginning of the eighth century BCE[5] and the origins of the oracle may be controversial,[6] the oracular dimension of the sanctuary quickly attracted pilgrims. In Delphi, like in Epidauros, consulting the oracle took place throughout the year. According to Plutarch,[7] at the beginning of the site's use as an oracular sanctuary at some point during the eight century BCE,[8] the oracle could be consulted once a year, on the birthday of Apollo, the seventh day of the month of *Byzios*. However, thereafter, the oracle was consultable every month on the seventh and also on some other 'favourable' days. The oracle consultation required a preliminary sacrifice, the intercession of the authorities of the sanctuary and the 'assent' of the god.[9] Thus, the seasonality of visits to Delphi is very different from that of Olympia for instance, where the festival takes place every four years only.

Although it was possible to go to Delphi at any period of the year to offer a sacrifice to Apollo Pythios or to the numerous gods or heroes that were worshipped there, the peak visiting time at the sanctuary, since the beginning of the sixth century BCE, was the occasion of the *Pythia*, the penteteric festival that took place at the end of the summer in the second year of each *periodos*, during the month of *Boukatios* in the Delphic calendar. The Pythian games lasted about a week. Sacrifices, musical, gymnastic and horse contests attracted

---

4   Chandezon 2000, 71.

5   I keep the traditional dates, see Aurigny – Scott forthcoming.

6   Jacquemin 2017.

7   Plut. *De Pyth. Or.* 8, 398a.

8   Morgan 1990.

9   Kyriakidis 2012, 83; Roux 1976; Amandry 1950, 81–5.

many artists, athletes and pilgrims and a large audience that came to hear the announcements and proclamations after the games.[10] Questions of general interest (colonisation, honours given by different communities, political issues, *etc.*) were treated then. Many other festivals were also gradually added, giving many occasions to gather in the sanctuary.[11]

When did the fairs take place within this frame, every month or every four years? Available sources are too scarce to allow us to give a definitive answer. Moreover, the existence of the *polis* around the sanctuary, the *chôra* and the sacred land owned by Apollo means that Delphi was not a place in the open country where supply for the festivals depended solely on the fairs. On the contrary, many things were available on the spot, and cattle and instruments for the festival and the ceremonies may have been available all the year in markets in Delphi.

2.2   *Sanctified Products or Economic Votives?*

The commercial part of the *panegyris*, referred to in the inscriptions as the *agora*,[12] provided different types of products, principally slaves, cattle and luxury goods. But the commercial exchanges were not only to meet sacred demands. The economic dimension of the *panegyris* has specific forms in Delphi, and food supply was naturally one of the main issues in a sanctuary where so many people gather. We do not know much about this aspect, but an inscription, badly preserved, without provenance, presents a text determining the prices of different kinds of fish.[13] In Delphi, more than anywhere else, it could have been easy for an unscrupulous merchant to propose outrageous prices to the numerous pilgrims, coming from far away. This inscription presents indirect evidence for the existence of the fair, and an indication of the kinds of regulation the authorities may have needed to put in place, but aside from this, we know nothing more about these Delphian magistrates, the *agoranomoi*. From this perspective, it can be seen that because commodities in sacred places have in some way been 'sanctified', they suffer a considerable increase

---

10   Kyriakidis 2012, 83; Amandry 1990.

11   Bommelaer – Laroche 2015, 43–5. Some festivals, like the Septerion, Herois and Charila, were celebrated every 8 years; the Sôteria was first celebrated annually, but then became penteteric, and the Eumeneia, Attaleia, and Romaia were celebrated every year.

12   Chandezon 2000. In Delphi, the location of the *agora* is unclear: the square at the entrance of the sanctuary, called the 'Roman *agora*', may have had an economic or commercial function, but there are no known vestiges before the Roman period. See Bommelaer – Laroche 2015, 113–14. On the 'Aire' and its function, see Jacquemin, Laroche 2015 and below.

13   Vatin 1966. A similar text comes from Akraiphia in Boiotia: Vatin 1971, 95–109. For later examples of the fixing of fair prices at festival fairs, see Horster in this volume.

in price. It is also a way of understanding Strabo's comment on the *panegyris* as a 'commercial thing'.

It is difficult to assess the economic role of the *panegyris* from an archaeological point of view. Votives may help because of their particular relationships to the *agora*. In thinking about 'the economics of dedication',[14] Catherine Morgan analysed the value of the bronze votives from the eighth and seventh century BCE, at a time when they were the main consecrations at Delphi and Olympia. The votives dedicated in Delphi reflect the availability and control of metal resources: access to metal supplies was a factor in the emergence of elite power in the eighth century BCE. In Delphi, bronze tripods from Corinth, Argos and Athens too give indications of the cities that had political interests in the sanctuary, but not much information about the economic dimension of the objects. Bronze votives attest the increasing importance of Delphi as an inter-state sanctuary, which was able to attract, as early as the eighth century, objects made of metal that were not used in everyday life during this period.

Luxury bronze votives are consistent with the definition of the *panegyris* as they are exceptional objects brought or made in the sanctuary on the occasion of the Pythia; but their real economic value was neutralised by their deposition in the sanctuary. Bronze tripods have no other function than to be offerings for the god, although they refer to a symbolic value of economic power.

2.3   *Regulating the Agora*

At Delphi, the gathering of people brought economic and financial issues that had implications for the main authorities. The above-mentioned decree regulating the price of fish suggests that the authorities wanted to protect pilgrims coming to the festivals from unscrupulous merchants. In another important decree, we find that the Delphic Amphictiony imposed the Attic *tetradrachm* as the standard currency.[15] In this decree, dated to the end of the second century BCE, the Amphictiony mentions the civic and panegyric magistrates, and details the bankers who were able to operate during the *panegyris*, suggesting the existence of itinerant bankers who went to the sanctuaries during festivals. However, these kinds of decrees about monetary problems are very unusual and scholars question whether the decree addresses all Greeks, members of the Amphictionic Council, or all pilgrims coming to Delphi, in order to protect

---

14   Morgan 1990, 194–203.
15   Text inscribed on the Treasury of the Athenians: *FD* III 2, 139; *Syll.*[3] 729; Sanchez 2001, 415–20; Jacquemin – Mulliez – Rougemont 2012, no. 182.

them from dishonest money converters.[16] A late inscription (third or fourth century CE) on the Treasury of the Athenians mentioning that it was transformed into a building for changing money[17] might indicate that official spaces for money changing were needed.[18]

3　Impact on the Organisation of the Sanctuary

The gathering of people at sacred occasions has consequences for the development of the sanctuary, as spaces for gathering during the festival and ceremonies, spaces for ritual acts, and spaces for lodging were needed.

3.1　*Spaces for Gathering*

Gathering presents some difficulties at Delphi, due mainly to the mountainous situation of the sanctuary. There are no large spaces to receive a crowd of pilgrims within the sanctuary, except on the middle terrace located below the terrace of the temple. This circular place was identified in 1893 by Homolle as the 'Aire' (*Halos*),[19] known in three epigraphic texts and mentioned by Plutarch as a space for rituals and festivals.[20] This area was a rather large esplanade, which was kept empty of structures until the Hellenistic period (located between SD 317, 312, 208, 210 and 326–327 on Fig. 4.1). However, this identification has been challenged recently[21] and its function as the primitive *agora* of Delphi, where the *ecclesia* gathered, has been suggested as an alternative.[22] The 'Aire', then, could be located outside the sanctuary in a more favourable situation, where important processions would be able to form and progress.[23] Wherever the *halos* was located, it was the stage for important ceremonies, such as the

---

16　The last hypothesis proposed by O. Picard, suggests that the Technites of Athens inspired the Amphictiony to write this general decree that was very favourable to them, because they were paid by reference to the best currency of the period. Jacquemin – Mulliez – Rougemont 2012, 328.

17　Bommelaer – Laroche 2015, 161.

18　The Amphictiony was not only the authority that organised religious and economic dimension of the festivals. The city of Delphi played also an important part, but unfortunately it is very difficult to evaluate its role: Sanchez 2001, 475.

19　Homolle 1893, 613.

20　Jacquemin – Mulliez – Rougemont 2012, No. 137, 167, 168. Plut. *De def. or.* 15.

21　Jacquemin – Laroche 2014.

22　Roux 1979, 70; Jacquemin – Laroche 2014, 744–51.

23　Jacquemin – Laroche 2014, 744. The authors do not give a precise location but suggest that the esplanade outside the sanctuary, beyond the western stoa (SD 437), is a good candidate.

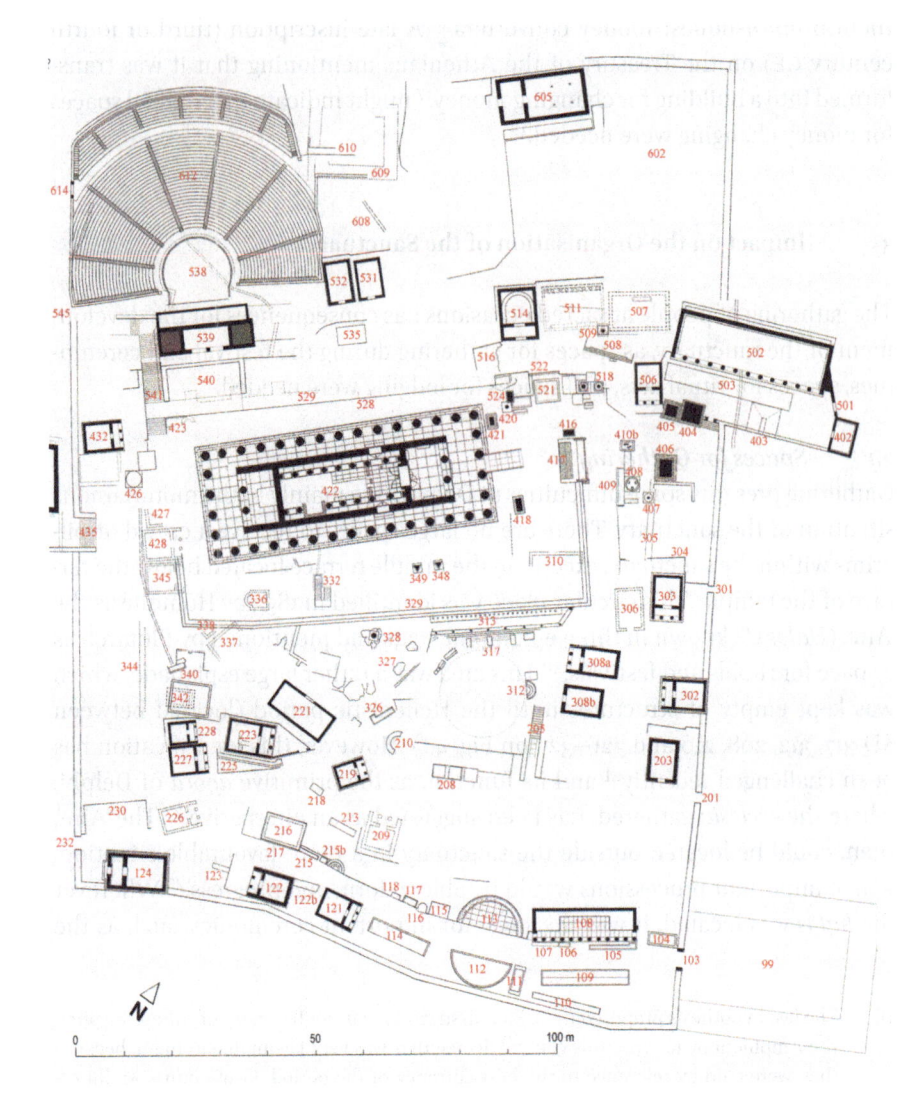

FIGURE 4.1   Map of the sanctuary of Apollo at the end of the second century CE (after
              Bommelaer – Laroche 2015, pl. V; by permission of the French School at
              Athens)

feast of the Septerion during which, according to Plutarch, a young boy, having his two parents, purified the city by setting fire to a wood construction
representing the palace of Pytho,[24] after which he ran away through the stairs,

---

24   Plut. *Quaest. Graec.* 203C; *De def. or.* dot Bommelaer – Laroche 2015, 173–5.

like Apollo did in the valley of the Tempe. This sacred 'Aire' was the point from which processions in honour of Attalos II of Pergamon began in 160/159.[25]

Space for gathering was particularly needed when sacrifices took place, especially hecatombs. The study of mass immolations in the Greek world has been addressed afresh by scholars questioning the modalities and the material of the hecatombs.[26] In Delphi, the spatial and temporal organisation of the sacrifices left scant evidence. The gathering of people and the mass sacrifices imply logistics that are now being studied inside and outside the sanctuary.[27] The location of the altar of Apollo in front of the temple of Apollo means that the space around is simply not appropriate for mass immolation (Fig. 4.1, SD 422, SD 417), and the mountainous context of the sanctuary makes it difficult to perform these rituals in the heart of the sanctuary: must we suppose that the sacrifices that made up the hecatomb were accomplished several times in sequence? The archaeological sources are too scarce to allow us to identify the exact places; but the sacrifices point to a relationship between the sanctuary and the *polis* of Delphi. Meat surplus should have been produced during the ceremonies at Delphi. Even if the Panhellenic festival attracted Greeks from everywhere, hecatombs produced a huge quantity of meat that had consequences for the alimentary practice of the city. This religious act had an economic dimension concerning not only the sanctuary but also the city.

As one would have expected, the religious life of the sanctuary was partly managed by the city of Delphi, which received regular profits and taxation. The correlation between the sanctuary and the city of Delphi is an essential part of the economic aspect of those religious ceremonies. Delphians benefitted economically from those coming to worship and consult the oracle, who had to pay, not directly for the consultation, but for key elements of the rituals conducted before a consultation was possible – the tariff was known as the *pelanos*.[28] A late fifth-century inscription, establishing a convention between Delphi and Phaselis,[29] shows the part played by the city which fixed a different price for the different cities and depending on whether or not it was an official civic or personal issue at hand. People from Phaselis had to pay seven Aeginetan drachmas and two obols for a state inquiry, four obols for a

---

25   *FD* III 3, 87–88, 207–13.

26   In Delphi: Huber 2014; Huber – Jacquemin – Laroche 2015; Ekroth 2014 with references; Pirenne-Delforge – Prescendi 2011.

27   Huber – Jacquemin – Laroche 2015.

28   The 'pelanos' is not only linked to the consultation of the oracle, but to all kind of sacrifices: Amandry 1950, 86–103, and see also Naiden, this volume.

29   *CID* I 8; Parke – Wormell 1956.32; Jacquemin – Mulliez – Rougemont 2012, no. 26, 52–53.

private one. The priests of Apollo are never mentioned, and the Delphian authorities, especially the *archon*, received the different taxes.

3.2   Spaces for Eating

The fact that no building within the Apollonion can be identified as an *hestiatorion* can be explained by the assumption that the meat was consumed within the city of Delphi. The sharing and eating of the meat is a real issue: epigraphical and archaeological sources give some evidence. The convention between the city of Delphi and Skiathos shows the religious prerogative of the civic authorities.[30] The text is dated to the first half of the fourth century BCE. It gives the tariff of the *pelanos* for the people of Skiathos, a little lower than for Phaselis,[31] and indicates that the skins rightfully belong to the Delphians. It then describes some modalities of the religious practice, and the banquet after the sacrifice. The Delphians give some privileges and commodities for the banquets to the people of Skiathos: a building called an *hestiatorion* and also wood and salt. Here it is difficult to compare the epigraphic and the archaeological data because as we have seen, there has been no *hestiatorion* yet identified archaeologically at Delphi.

However, although no official dining room is known in Delphi, the so-called 'house of the priests' in Marmaria, made of two square rooms opening on a common vestibule, corresponds to plans of *hestiatoria* known elsewhere in the Greek world.[32] Both archaeological categories of the 'priests' house' and 'hestiatoria' should be used very carefully, however. Another candidate for such a space should be mentioned, located within the Apollonion. In the northern part of the sanctuary, the Lesche of the Knidians was a place to gather and talk (Fig. 4.1, SD 605), but this rectangular building, with walls decorated with paintings, could also have been used as an *andrôn* or a *hestiatorion*.[33] Near the sanctuary, the excavations conducted by Jean-Marc Luce in the 1990s under the chariot of the Rhodians, in an area at the eastern edge of the sanctuary (Fig. 4.1, SD 406), brought to light different structures that have been called 'houses'. The 'red house', dated to the end of the seventh century BCE, with three rooms, several pieces of bronze vessels and ceramics, and located at about 15m from

---

30   Amandry 1939. Rougemont *CID* I, 13, pl. 10.4 ; Jacquemin – Mulliez – Rougemont 2012, no. 31, 68–70.

31   *CID* I 13; Parke – Wormell 1956.31–2. The Skiathos inscription also says that it costs one Aeginetan stater for 'consultation by two beans', which is the best evidence for the existence of a lot (or 'bean') oracle at Delphi.

32   The *hestiatoria* of Perachora or Aliki in Thasos: Hellmann 2006, 222–3, fig. 299 (Perachora), fig. 301 (Thasos) with references. Bommelaer – Laroche 2015, SD 44, 92–3.

33   Bommelaer – Laroche 2015, SD 605, 246, 247; Hellmann 2006, 227.

the altar, may also be interpreted as a *hestiatorion*.[34] The omphalos *phialai* discovered there[35] are very surprising in a domestic context[36] and the building would have been more convenient for a religious function. At this stage, this house was located outside the sanctuary, even if very close to the sacred space. The first *peribolos* was built exactly on this house at the beginning of the sixth century BCE.

3.3 Spaces for Lodging

A final key issue regarding the gathering of pilgrims at Delphi is their lodgings. Two different options could be chosen: camping or accommodation in the houses of the Delphians. '*Skenai*' were used both for the diners[37] and lodgings. Epigraphic evidence attests to their existence at the approaches to the sanctuary.

The amphictionic decree concerning the *stoa* of Attalos I forbids camping or making a fire inside or outside the portico.[38] The first Attalid king had built a *stoa* in the eastern part of the sanctuary of Apollo on a monumental terrace (Fig. 4.1, SD 502) and this inscription was placed on the pillar supporting a statue of the king (SD 405). Built at the boundary between the sacred space and the profane sphere, directly on the *peribolos*, the *stoa* is located at the level of the temple and the altar: it was really a choice place to gather near the heart of the sanctuary, the implication being that people had been, until this point, building fires and camping in the vicinity. However, the '*skene*' and the fire might here refer to the consumption of meat rather than camping *per se*; the fact that this amphictionic decree mentions votive offerings and a fire may suggest that sacrifices took place there.[39] Besides, it should be underlined that in this case, the Amphictiony voted for a decree that regulates behaviour within the sanctuary; the Amphictiony shares with the city of Delphi the management of the sanctuary, the city being subordinate to its authority. It is an illustration of the normal role of this collective organisation, which consisted largely in the maintenance of buildings and regulation of the frequentation of the sanctuary.

---

34   Luce 2008, 72. The location of the fireplace and the door do not correspond to the standards of the *hestiatoria* we know.

35   Luce 2008, 205–6, 212–13.

36   The plan of the building is that of a house: parallels in Luce 2008, 73.

37   Eur. *Ion* 804–807, 982, 1128–95.

38   Jacquemin – Mulliez – Rougemont 2012, no. 118, 215–216; *CID* IV, 208–210, n°85.

39   Le Guen-Pollet 1991, 163–5.

This is not the only mention of the presence of '*skenai*' at Delphi. Another amphictionic decree in honour of Mentor of Naupaktos,[40] is engraved on the east part of the polygonal wall and dates to the middle of the third century BCE. The Etolian Mentor of Naupaktos undertakes the ornamentation of the Athena Pronaia, likely meaning the panoply of the statue. The several privileges granted to the Etolian Mentor are not difficult to explain, but the right to the 'first tent', *prota skana*, raises problems of interpretation. The literary meaning might suggest only the right to camp on a privileged place.[41] But the word '*skana*', like the verb '*skenan*', in this case (as may also be the case above) refers to the banquets following the sacrifices: people used to gather under the *skenai*, temporary shelters, tents or huts. The 'first tent' may be the best place in the banquet, or the first to get the meat from the sacrifices,[42] or the tent of the greatest dignitaries in the sanctuary.[43] The exact interpretation is still debated.

We do not have much information about the accommodation of the pilgrims and visitors in Delphi, during festivals or amphictionic sessions. The lodgings of the pilgrims, at least the official ones, were in the town of Delphi. Textual evidence attests the use of several houses to welcome the official delegates. The most famous case is the house of the Thebans.[44] The city of Delphi voted a decree to resolve the situation surrounding the house where Thebans stayed during their visits to Delphi. The city of Thebes possessed a house in Delphi, but could not be the owner. The Delphian *proxenos* took care of the house. In this case, the Delphian owner, Kraton, had changed the conditions of accommodation of the Theban pilgrims, who were not satisfied with them. He built an '*oikema*' within the house, but accepted to reassign it to the accommodation of the pilgrims after their protests. In addition, we know about houses let by people of Larissa,[45] the Thessalian *hieromnemon* Kolosimmos,[46] a house of the Argive citizens,[47] and there is a reference to three houses in a decree passed by the *demos* of Andros.[48] In Delphi, the gathering of people led to original solutions: there was no *xenon*, *katagogion* or any hostel built for

---

40   Jacquemin – Mulliez – Rougemont 2012, no. 108, 198, 200.

41   Dillon 1990, 73; Sanchez 2001, 54, 475.

42   Lefèvre 1998, 232–3.

43   Jacquemin in Jacquemin – Mulliez – Rougemont 2012, 200.

44   *FD* III, 1, 357–358; Dillon 1990; Jacquemin – Mulliez – Rougemont 2012, no. 117, 213–15 with references. This case is known by three other texts: it can be dated in the middle or at the end of the third century BCE (without certainty).

45   *CID* II, 67, L. 5–6, 27.

46   *CID* II, 67–72.

47   Unpublished decree, second century BCE: *CID* IV, 56, n. 236.

48   *CID* I No. 7, 19–22.

official delegations, but once again, the city and the citizen played an important part in the welcoming of the *theoroi*.

There is no archaeological evidence to identify the houses within the town or the locations where tents were pitched.[49] The landscape in Delphi suggests that the tents would not have been near the sanctuary. It is very likely that most of the pilgrims, non-official pilgrims more exactly, camped in the plain. The first *stadion* was located there, but has not yet been discovered. The '*skenai*' could have been pitched there.[50] The presence of the pilgrims at Delphi led to other decisions of the authorities. The 'Amphictionic law of 380 BCE',[51] after the oaths taken by the *hieromnemon* and the secretary, regulates some issues about the sacred land of Apollo (lines 16–20), and enumerates the renovation works that the Amphictiony had to do before each Pythia (lines 35–41), in the sanctuaries of Apollo and Athena, but also, in the *stadion* of the plain, fountains, bridges, routes, *etc.*,[52] implying that these infrastructural features saw considerable use and needed regular upkeep.

The issue of welcoming pilgrims to Delphi forces us to go out of the sanctuary itself and to consider the broader 'Delphic complex'.[53] In a site where it is still particularly difficult to find archaeological evidence for the question of lodgings and presence of the pilgrims in the sanctuary, research conducted on the town and plain below may help to understand better the relationships between sacred and profane spheres.

Despite the fame of the sanctuary and the quantities of pilgrims that attended the festivals, it is difficult to identify specific places reserved for pilgrims. Of course, there is a lack of sources, and the absence of excavations of the surroundings of the urban settlement which could deliver important data in this field. But we must also surely note the ephemeral nature of many installations: no *hestiatorion*, no hostel or *xenon* have been identified in Delphi. It is likely that the buildings in the city, for official hosts; or temporary structures, for the masses; were used to welcome the sacred travellers.

---

49   The situation of the excavations of the town of Delphi in relation to the sanctuary has been exposed by Luce 2015.

50   The situation is different from Olympia, where the presence of the pilgrims is attested not by tent rests but by the metal rests of the chariots. They were discovered, concentrated on the south-east zone of the Altis, near the stadion and the hippodrome. A lot of fragments come from ephemeral wells where the broken chariots or wheels had been thrown away: Baitinger – Völling 2007, 162–6.

51   Jacquemin – Mulliez – Rougemont 2012, no. 27, 53–5.

52   The renovation works are detailed in another text, the list of the works attributed by contract by the Amphictiony for the Pythia. Jacquemin – Mulliez – Rougemont 2012, no. 116, 210–13.

53   Daux 1936.

4   Pilgrims and Competition through Votives

One of the most obvious consequences of the presence of pilgrims is the consecration of votive objects or votive monuments. The different materials, categories and types are closely related to the origin of the visitors and dedicators;
in a certain way, they gave material expression to the sacred travel of pilgrims
to the sanctuary.

4.1   *Bronzes and Identity*

Bronze votives provide us with the archaeological evidence for the emergence of a new cult on the slopes of the Parnassos at the end of the ninth
century BCE.[54] In Delphi, the bronze objects were offered in the middle
Geometric period village. They play a new part because of their value, but they
also indicate the presence of a dedicator. In addition, they also bear witness to
the emergence of different manners and styles reflect the gathering of people
from different cities, telling us something of their place of origin through the
votives. After the most ancient bronze tripods with 'relief-decorated' legs offered in Delphi at the end of the ninth century BCE, this phenomenon is emphasised in the second half of the eighth century BCE, when different styles
can be distinguished. Three types were offered in the sanctuary, reflecting the
growing influence of the cities and their 'elite' from the northern Peloponnese
and Attica: tripods with 'relief-decorated' legs[55] that had been offered in
Olympia since 900 BCE continue the tradition of the massive type but they
become thinner, and the leg has a Π-shape section and a decoration made of
zigzags and stripes (Fig. 4.2). Scholars have assumed that this production is
Argive.[56]

The second type has cast handles and feet decorated with a ribbed motif, like
the steps of a staircase,[57] with handles that are sometimes perforated.[58] The dimensions and the weight of some feet and handles of this category are impressive; scholars attribute the production to Corinth (Fig. 4.3).[59] The third type,
with hammered handles and feet,[60] were given engraved decoration (Fig. 4.4).

---

54   See n. 5 above.
55   Rolley 1977, 105–13; Rolley 1992.
56   Rolley 1992.
57   Rolley 1977, handles nos. 455–7, 65; feet nos. 405–10, 56–7.
58   Rolley 1977, nos. 458–67, 66–67.
59   Maass 1981, 18; Rolley 1992; Rolley 2007, 68.
60   Rolley 1977, no. 481–502, 71–75.

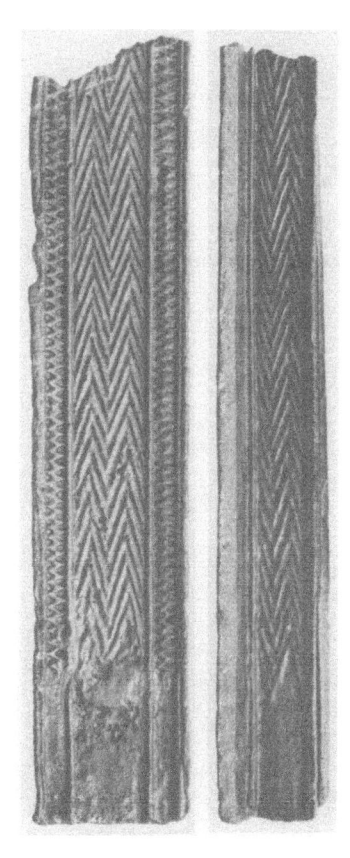

FIGURE 4.2
Bronze Tripod with "relief-decorated" legs (31 cm) (from
Rolley 1977, No. 394, pl. XXXV, by permission of the
Hellenic Ministry of Culture and Sports, Archaeological
Receipts Fund)

Feet are made of three metal ribbons put together after the decoration.[61] Many parallels in the Athenian Acropolis attest to the Attic origin of this category.[62]

Bronze tripods can be analysed not only as evidence for religious consecration, but as sources for political and social history as well. The dedication is of course an act of *eusebeia* (piety), part of a ritual gesture,[63] but is at the same time a way to show the precious objects to the whole community. More than the indication of the development of bronze trade,[64] and the importance of the people who managed it, bronze tripods refer to the origin and expression

---

61 Rolley 2007, 68.
62 Scholl 2006, 49–55, fig. 15–16; Rolley 2007, 68; Rolley 1992. Parallels have been found also in Dodona, see Raubitschek 1998.
63 On the notion of 'ritual object': Bernier-Farella – Patera 2014.
64 Morgan 1990, 195; Kiderlen 2010, 94.

FIGURE 4.3   Bronze tripod leg, decorated with a ribbed motif
                (12,5 cm) (after Rolley 1977, No. 405, pl. XXXVII; by
                permission of the Hellenic Ministry of Culture and
                Sports, Archaeological Receipts Fund)

of a civic identity. Travel to the sanctuary quickly became a political act and
the consecration of bronze tripods an expression of social status. Delphi is
one of the few sanctuaries that attracted many of those items and was a place
where elites gathered.

The dedication of weapons in particular illustrates competition through
votives. This particular category involves some peculiarities. Alongside the
tripods, bronze weapons are among the oldest votives in the sanctuary: for
instance, a Villanovan helmet from Etruria, usually dated to the first part of
the eighth century BCE (Fig. 4.5a–b). This crested helmet, decorated with incised and *repoussé* decoration of bosses, unfortunately does not have a precise

FIGURE 4.4   Bronze tripod hammered leg with engraved decoration
(10,5 cm) (after Rolley 1977, No. 483, pl. XLIX; by
permission of the Hellenic Ministry of Culture and
Sports, Archaeological Receipts Fund)

findspot in the *hieron*.[65] The artefact refers either to conflicts between Greeks
and Italians in the early period of colonisation, or to an aristocratic relationship between the Greek elite and Etruscan princes. Bronze weapons, which are
not commercial products, are not directly linked with trade and the *agorai* or
fairs that were part of the *panegyris*. They are conspicuous testimonies to the
political relationships of the pilgrims.

Finally, the offerings extend competition at the sanctuary even if the visitors
did not meet at the same time. It is therefore through the votive objects that

---

65   Kilian 1977, 427–42, fig. 1 ab, 2a; Aurigny 2016, 162, fig. 1, n. 10.

FIGURE 4.5A   Fragment of a helmet, Delphi Archaeological Museum,
               inv. 24904 (Neg. École Française d'Athènes 62078; by permission
               of the Hellenic Ministry of Culture and Sports, Archaeological
               Receipts Fund)

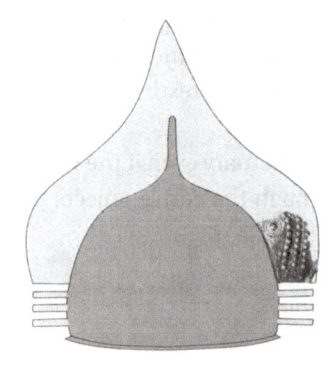

FIGURE 4.5B
Graphic reconstruction of the helmet (after Kilian 1977,
432, fig. 2; by permission of the Hellenic Ministry of
Culture and Sports, Archaeological Receipts Fund)

FIGURE 4.6   Bronze phiale, Delphi Archaeological Museum, inv. 4463, 17 cm (Neg.
École Française d'Athènes 31235; by permission of the Hellenic Ministry
of Culture and Sports, Archaeological Receipts Fund)

the gathering of the sacred visitors is concretised: they continue to compete
and to show the prestige of their dedicants after their departure.

4.2   *Overseas*

The social competition that develops through the votives is a well-known
phenomenon. Many votives in Delphi illustrate this, but some reflect the experience of the sacred journey. After the Geometric bronze tripods, Delphi received metal items of very diverse origins, 'exotic' or 'oriental' objects. Some
characteristic votives from the eighth and seventh centuries come from the
eastern Mediterranean, Anatolia (Phrygia), Cyprus, Syria, and the Levantine
coast. However we must be aware that the origin of an object, the place where
it has been produced, does not correspond systematically to the origin of the
pilgrim bringing it. We can at least say that it was early in its history, by the end
of the eighth century BCE, that Delphi received objects from certain oriental
and occidental parts of the Mediterranean.

A well-preserved incised bronze bowl is likely to come from Syria-Phoenicia
(Fig. 4.6); the main scene, which shows a siege of a city and a chariot driven by
a sphinx, has parallels there.[66] It is difficult to guess the reasons why this bowl
was offered and by whom; as this *phiale* was found near the temple of Athena

---

66   Rolley 1991, 156–7, no. 21; Aurigny 2019, 137–38, no 178, fig. 494–499.

in Marmaria, it can be assumed that it was used for cultic purposes; but no contextual data can help us to ascertain a more precise function.

The sanctuary was the place where pilgrims wanted to leave votives, in order to show to all the visitors their wealth or their external relationships. Religious and economic considerations are linked together: in the Archaic period, aristocrats are those who are committed to economic enterprises, long-distance travels and the exchange of precious gifts. So, those exotic votives give the image of those travels and of this power, politic and economic, inside the sanctuary.

4.3   *Votive Organisation within the Sanctuary*

Competition through votive dedication led to a specific votive landscape in the sanctuary of Apollo. The case of the altar zone is well known: people wanting to leave the most impressive offering chose this '*epiphanestatos topos*'.[67] But another phenomenon is worth noting. From the end of the seventh and during the sixth century BCE, the most prestigious category of votives offered to Apollo and Athena is the Treasury-house, '*thesauros*'. This building, often in marble, takes the shape of a little chapel, whether Ionic or Doric. They are noteworthy not only for their rich architectural and sculptural decoration, the precious objects they contained, but also for the fact that they were a reference for the whole community of the city, even if the dedication itself was an individual act.[68] More than thirty cities from Mainland Greece or colonial cities dedicated treasuries in Delphi, but the example of the Treasury-house of the Athenians offers an interesting case study (Fig. 4.7). The *thesauros* of a city serves as a topographical spot for the people of the city to gather. Athenians votive offerings, official texts, announcements, and so on, were made around the *thesauros* of the Athenians. The building influences the way Athenians gathered in the sanctuary, as the place where they stopped, where they met or left evidence of their presence. We even know the case of Xenophon, who sold prisoners during the expedition of the 10,000 and offered, alongside the proceeds, a gift to Apollo that he left in the treasury-house.[69] The votive was in honour of Apollo, but it was stored in the *thesauros* of the Athenians.

Strabo tells us that 'the *thesauroi* that people and kings built, where they dedicated sums of money consecrated to the god and works of art of the best

---

67   Daux 1936, 159–62: Daux uses this expression found in epigraphic texts to designate the most prominent place in the sanctuary of Apollo, the area around the altar.

68   As the Treasury of the Corinthians first offered by Cypselus: Bommelaer – Laroche 2015, SD 308, 180–1.

69   Xen. *An.* 5, 3, 4–6.

FIGURE 4.7   Treasury-house of the Athenians in the sanctuary of Apollo
PHOTO: HÉLÈNE AURIGNY

artists',[70] clearly demonstrating that the building plays the role of showcasing the power of the cities. Treasury-houses of Delphi, situated along the sacred way to the temple and altar, convey something of the picture of pilgrims gathering in the sanctuary and the Panhellenic dimension of the *hieron*.

Moreover, if the treasury-houses were used to store offerings to the deity, to which the literary texts clearly attest,[71] they could become spaces of exhibition and thus attract visitors to admire the contents of the buildings. This highlights Anne Jacquemin's observation of the function of Delphi as a 'lieu de mémoire', showing that the touristic aspect of travel to Delphi gradually increased until the Roman period,[72] when religious pilgrimage stopped. This touristic element continued to bring economic resources to the sanctuary through the visits of a different public, now coming on cultural pilgrimage.

5 Conclusion

Thinking specifically about the spaces and places of gathering in Delphi shows us how the economic and religious dimensions of the sanctuary are closely linked together; in Delphi, however, economic life did not depend only on the sanctuary, but was also related to the necessities of urban settlement. If the main sources are literary or epigraphic, archaeological data can bring something specific, especially in terms of social history and for the most ancient periods of the sanctuary. The investigation should be continued for the Archaic period, when votives were the main sources for understanding the development of the sanctuary. Considering Delphi from the perspective of sacred travel supposes a global approach: sanctuary, urban centre, circulation routes, origins of people and artefacts. The very question of gathering is also linked with the travels of the *theoroi*, the way their journeys were financed and other issues.

Gathering in the Panhellenic sanctuary at Delphi demonstrates different modalities throughout the life of the sanctuary and depending on the status of the pilgrims. But whether they were official or individual, sent by cities or whether they came for personal reasons, pilgrims gradually constructed a votive landscape that materialised the competitive dimension and the 'agonistic' spirit of the Ancient Greeks, and which survives to this day.

---

70   Str. 10, 3, 4 (C 418–419).

71   For instance Herodotus I, 14, 50–1.

72   Jacquemin 1999, 263–73.

Bibliography

Amandry, P. 1939. "Convention religieuse conclue entre Delphes et Skiathos", *Bulletin de Correspondance Hellénique* 63, 183–219.

Amandry, P. 1950. *La mantique apollinienne à Delphes: essai sur le fonctionnement de l'Oracle*, Paris.

Amandry, P. 1990. "La Fête des Pythia", Ομιλία του ξένου εταίρου κ. P. Amandry, Athens.

Aurigny, H. 2016. "Sicilian and Italic Votive Objects in the Panhellenic Sanctuary of Delphi", in *Material Culture and Identity in the Stress Field between the Mediterranean World and Central Europe*, ed. H. Baitinger, Mainz, 161–74.

Aurigny, H. 2019. *Fouilles de Delphes 5. Bronzes du haut-archaïsme. Trépieds, chaudrons et vaisselles de bronze*, Athens.

Aurigny, H. and Scott, M. 2019. "An Archaeohistorical Approach to Delphi in the Archaic Period", in *The Oxford History of the Archaic Greek World*, eds. P. Cartledge and P. Christensen, Oxford.

Baitinger, H. and Völling, T. 2007. *Werkzeug und Gerät aus Olympia*, Berlin.

Bernier-Farella, H. and Patera, I. eds. 2014. "L'objet rituel. Méthodes et concepts croisés", *Revue d'Histoire des Religions* 231.4.

Bommelaer, J.-F. and Laroche, D. 2015. *Guide de Delphes, Le site*, Paris.

Chandezon, C. 2000. "Foires et panégyries dans le monde grec classique et hellénistique", *Revue des études grecques* 113, 70–100.

Daux, G. 1936. *Pausanias à Delphes*, Paris.

Deshours, N. 2006. *Les mystères d'Andania: étude d'épigraphie et d'histoire religieuse*, Paris.

Dillon, M. 1990. "'The House of the Thebans' (FD III, 1, 357–358) and the Accommodation for Greek Pilgrims", *Zeitschrift für Papyrologie und Epigraphik* 83, 64–88.

Dillon, M. 1997. *Pilgrims and Pilgrimage in Ancient Greece*, London – New York.

Ekroth, G. 2014. "Animal Sacrifice in Antiquity", in *The Oxford Handbook of Animals in Classical Thought and Life*, ed. G.L. Campbell, Oxford, 324–54.

Hellmann, M.-C. 2006. *L'architecture grecque, 2. Architecture religieuse et funéraire*, Paris.

Homolle, T. 1893. "Institut de correspondance hellénique", *Bulletin de Correspondance Hellénique*, 611–23.

Huber, S. 2014. "Sang pour cent? Les hécatombes dans les cultes grecs", *Dossiers d'archéologie* 362, 12–5.

Huber, S., Jacquemin, A., and Laroche, D. 2015. "Sacrifices à Delphes", *Bulletin de Correspondance Hellénique*, 139–140, 775–783.

Jacquemin, A. 1999. "La fondation de l'oracle de Delphes et les fondations du temple d'Apollon", in *Quand naissent les dieux, fondation des sanctuaires antiques:*

motivations, agents, lieux, eds. S. Agusta-Boularot, S. Huber, and W. Van Andringa, Rome, 33–45.

Jacquemin, A. 1999. *Offrandes monumentales à Delphes*, Athens-Paris.

Jacquemin, A. and Laroche, D. 2014. "Un espace politique au cœur du sanctuaire de Delphes", *Comptes rendus des séances de l'Acadèmie des Inscriptions et Belles-Lettres* 2014.2, 727–53.

Jacquemin, A., Mulliez, G., and Rougemont, G. 2012. *Choix d'inscriptions de Delphes, traduites et commentées, études épigraphiques* 5, Athens.

Kiderlen, M. 2010. "Zur Chronologie griechischer Bronzedreifüße des geometrischen Typs und den Möglichkeiten einer politisch-historischen Interpretation der Fundverteilung", *Archäologischer Anzeiger* 2010/1, 91–104.

Kilian, K. 1977. "Zwei italische Kammhelme aus Griechenland", *Bulletin de Correspondance Hellénique* Suppl. 4, 429–42.

Kyriakidis, N. 2012. "Le sanctuaire d'Apollon Pythien à Delphes et les diasporas grecques, du VIIIe au IIIe s. av. J.-C. ", *Pallas* 89, 77–93.

Lefèvre, F. 1998. *L'Amphictionie pyléo-delphique: histoire et institutions*, Athens – Paris.

Le Guen-Pollet, B. 1991. *La vie religieuse dans le monde grec du Ve au IIIe siècle avant notre ère*, Toulouse.

Luce, J.-M. 2008. *Fouilles de Delphes 2.13. L'aire du Pilier des Rhodiens (fouille 1990–1992) à la frontière du profane et du sacré*, Athens-Paris.

Luce, J.-M. 2008. "Le programme ville de Delphes, Bulletin de la SFAC (XVL, 2013–2014)", *Revue Archéologique* 59, 2015/1, 145–51.

Maass, M. 1981. "Die geometrischen Dreifüsse von Olympia", *Antike Kunst* 24, 6–20.

Morgan, C. 1990. *Athletes and Oracles: The Transformation of Olympia and Delphi in the Eighth Century BC*, Cambridge.

Papazarkadas, N. 2011. *Sacred and Public Land in Ancient Athens*, Oxford.

Parke, H.W. and Wormell, D.E.W. 1956. *The Delphic Oracle*, Oxford.

Pirenne-Delforge, V. and Prescendi, F. eds. 2011. *Nourrir les dieux? Sacrifice et représentation du divin*, Liège.

Raubitschek, I.K. 1998. *Isthmia 7: The Metal Objects (1952–1989)*, Princeton.

Rolley, C. 1977. *Fouilles de Delphes 5,3. Les trépieds à cuve clouée*, Paris.

Rolley, C. 1991. "Les Bronzes", in *Guide de Delphes, le Musée*, Paris, 139–79.

Rolley, C. 1992. "Argos, Corinthe et Athènes: identité culturelle et mode de développement (IXe–VIIIe s)", in *Polydipsion Argos. Argos de la fin des palais mycéniens à la constitution de l'État classique*, ed. M. Piérart, 37–49.

Rolley, C. 2007. "Techniques, travail: la naissance des styles à l'époque géométrique", *Pallas* 73, 63–70.

Rousset, D. 2013. "Sacred Property and Public Property in the Greek City", *Journal of Hellenic Studies* 33, 113–33.

Roux, G. 1976. *Delphes, son oracle et ses dieux*, Paris.

Roux, G. 1979. *L'Amphictionie, Delphes et le temple d'Apollon au IVe siècle*, Paris.

Sanchez, P. 2001. *L'Amphictionie des Pyles et de Delphes: recherches sur son rôle historique, des origines au IIe siècle de notre ère*, Stuttgart.

Scholl, A. 2006. "Die Akropolisvotive aus dem 8. bis frühen 6. Jahrhundert v.Chr. und die Staatswerdung Athens", *Jahrbuch des Deutschen Archäologisches Instituts* 121, 1–173.

Vatin, C. 1966. "Un tarif de poissons à Delphes", *Bulletin de Correspondance Hellénique* 90, 274–80.

Vatin, C. 1971. "Le tarif des poisons d'Akraiphia", in *Inscriptions de Grèce centrale*, ed. F. Salviat and C. Vatin, Paris, 95–109.

CHAPTER 5

Hellenistic Festivals: Aspects of the Economic Impact on Cities and Sanctuaries

Marietta Horster

1 Introduction

Festivals in the ancient Greek Mediterranean were rooted in religion and often connected to a cult for a specific deity in a particular community.[1] Most such festivals (*heortai, panegyreis*)[2] existed for more than one generation, and they took place in a fixed period of time at a fixed place.[3] They had a clear, though not necessarily unique, dedication to one or more deities, and had festive elements such as processions or *pompai*, sacrifices and a sacrificial meal. Such general common elements as well as very specific parts, such as weapon-dances, specific clothing or elaborate songs for example, both followed a certain pattern in a given city.[4]

Most festivals were small and local in scale and did not last longer than one day; though some were larger, as we shall see. The core of each Greek (and later Roman) festival was the sacrifice as a communal act, often a sacrifice of animals on one or more altars.[5] The altar was the focal point during the festival, which could take place in several parts of a city and its territory, and near or far from the temple of the main deity that was to be honoured. Even festivals with associated sporting competitions, theatrical performances, music, dance, poetry and other events which were performed at more than one place in the city or sanctuary had at their cultic core the altar, which was most often within the

---

1 For several deities honoured in one festival and later additions to an established festival *e.g.* of single days in honour of a deity or a king, see Buraselis 2012. For non-community focused festivals, see Müller 2014 (rotating festival of the Boetian league) and *e.g.* Sánchez 2001, 19–20 (the involvement of the amphictiony in the Pythia festival at Delphi).
2 On terminology see Kowalzig in this volume.
3 See Iddeng 2012, 15–16 for the regular occurrence, the focal points of festivals, and for variations in both; Slater 2007, 25–34 with examples of changes in the time, period, name, and management of festivals in the Hellenistic and Roman periods.
4 Chaniotis 1995, 150; 2011.
5 The civic character is also the basis of new Panhellenic festivals in the Hellenistic period, see *e.g.* Rutherford 2013, 43–50 and Rigsby 1996, 179–279 for temples declared inviolable on the request of a city introducing a new festival. For more on sacrifice see Naiden in this volume.

boundaries of a sanctuary, and rarely outside.[6] When the festival was large or important enough to attract pilgrims from outside the celebrating civic body, often, but not always, they would become part of the sacrificing community and could take a share in the banquet of the sacrificial meat following the sacrifice itself.[7]

The more attractive a festival – for example, whether it had associated sports competitions, dance, music or theatrical performances, banquets etc. – the more necessary it was for the organising city, group or league to find good solutions to deal with all the visitors and their demands.[8] The date had an important impact on the number of visitors – the high season of harvest would not attract many pilgrims from abroad; for islands like Delos or Rhodes which relied on sea travel from the mainland and the other islands the winter period would probably not have been a good choice, either.[9] In addition there existed a calendar of well-established, large festivals which attracted hundreds, sometimes even thousands of visitors, which created a specific rhythm of festivals with wide appeal, not only for athletes.

These super-festivals were Panhellenic in scope and had been established from the Archaic period on. They did not take place every year and, because of their grandeur, tradition and incorporation into the history of many Greek states, were famous all over the Greek-speaking world and well beyond: the Olympic festival organised by Elis in honour of Zeus, the Pythian Games organised by Delphi and the Amphictyony in honour of Apollo, the Isthmia festival organised by Corinth in honour of Poseidon, and the Nemea for Zeus and Heracles organised by Kleonai or Argos.

Following the Classical period, the number of festivals increased all over the Greek-speaking world for a number of reasons, in which the agonistic festivals were the exception, though not rare.[10] Apart from the four great Panhellenic

---

6   For libations, animals (*thusia*) and other kinds of sacrifices on altars as the core of religious rituals in Greek cults, see Hermary *et al.* 2004, esp. 60–4. Naiden 2013, 33 asks 'what does it mean to please a god' and answers in his book that it needs an apt offering (sacrifice, votive) for the god to accept what an individual or the community requests in his/its prayer. See Horster 2010 and Iddeng 2012, 19 for modern concepts of sacred space, and for a specific example of cults in Demetrias and Thessaly, Kravaritou 2016.

7   For public meals in a cultic setting, see Bruit *et al.* 2004; Schmitt Pantel 2012 gives a general historiographical overview. The integrating role of sacrificial meals for larger communities and cities is discussed by Naiden 2012 and for women by Schmitt Pantel 2011.

8   For festivals of leagues in the Hellenistic period, see *e.g.* Knoepfler 2010 and Müller 2014 (Boeotia), Horster 2013 (Ionia), Mackil 2013, 147–236 (Greek Koina).

9   For travel seasons in the Mediterranean, see Casson 1971, 270–3.

10   Invitations by public envoys had been known in the Classical period for the Pythia at Delphi, the Asclepieia at Epidauros and the Heraia at Argos; three hundred years later,

festivals mentioned above and some festivities organised by leagues of several cities or by cult groups which could in some cases gain recognition at a civic level as well,[11] most of these festivals were, as already stated, an expression of a civic community's aim to praise a deity, a god or goddess, a hero or – from the Hellenistic period more often – a ruling king. In these cases, therefore, neither official delegations from across the Greek world nor individual pilgrims from abroad formed part of such festivals, but instead the participants consisted of the community of or communities within a Greek *polis*.

The following pages outline the main features of Greek festivals and some of the reasons why these religious[12] events became an important medium for Hellenistic interstate diplomacy, not only because of the envoys and sacred delegations involved. This will be followed by a short description of the various participating groups and finally the presentation of some aspects of the economic impact of festivals and pilgrimage on cities and sanctuaries.

2   Civic Interests in Festivals: International Visibility and Networking

During the Hellenistic period the number of festivals increased dramatically for various reasons, of which the economic impact on the organising cities and sanctuaries does not seem to have been of importance in this expansion.[13] The main and most self-evident explanation for a city to be interested in organising a new international festival was likely political. It is probable that cities did everything to get a foot in the door of the newly organised political order of the Greek world: after Alexander's death in 323 BCE, the establishment of several

---

fifteen festivals used the system of official delegations inviting the Greek world, Perlman 2000, 22. See also below, note 13.

11   On cult organisations and their festivals which usually were reduced to the members of the association as participants, see Aneziri 2003.

12   In the last decades, the term 'religion' or 'religious' was often replaced by 'cult' or 'cultic' to underline the ritual aspects of the devotion in a cult as its organised form and to avoid any resemblance with the alleged Christian (or *e.g.* Jewish, Muslim) notions of 'belief' and 'piety'. The historiography of the recent 'religious' terms-avoidance tendency is sketched by Mili 2015, 4–6.

13   See above note 10. A list of 28 new Panhellenic festivals attested between 250 and 100 is collected by Parker 2004, 18–22 in a chronological overview. The many local festivals, those of the leagues and perhaps those of the kings without Panhellenic approval are not included in the list. Chaniotis 1995, 164–8 presents a list of c. 130 known festivals, which had been introduced in the Hellenistic period and were not installed to honour kings and the royal families; see Archibald 2011, 60–1; Wiemer 2009 and below note 55 for the kings' presentation of wealth and power by the means of festivals and processions.

strong dynasties in the eastern Mediterranean had consequences not only for those regions and cities in the respective king's realm, but for the free cities and leagues as well. The role of diplomacy increased, and communication and exchange were necessary to establish and conserve the international network of Greek cities. The length of cultic traditions, the age of a sanctuary and of its cult image were one of the valued currencies in the economics of diplomatic rhetoric (of which Pausanias' stories are a pale reflection); the benefactions and support of a city to other Greeks cities constituted another.[14]

In any case, the endless wars and smaller conflicts of the Hellenistic period would have had an impact on 'the regular course of religious life and the celebration of festivals'.[15] To keep the gods benevolent and to maintain their protection, sacrifices and offerings had to continue whatever the circumstances and threats, and festivals offered the opportunity to single out the commitment of specific communities. Putting on expensive festivals was not a way out of such difficulties and conflicts, but they were an established part of interstate diplomacy and thus may have been seen as a way to reduce the risk of war – by intense networking and by raising the status and prestige of the festival and its organising city.[16]

State-organised pilgrimage was thus one means to intensify interstate communications and international exchange. Kent Rigsby elucidated the Hellenistic phenomenon of the spread of declarations, admissions and grants of *asylia* (inviolability and legal immunity guaranteeing protection to a supplicant – *hikesia*) for a sanctuary during a festival period, of *ekecheiria* (sacred truce) for the official embassies and the individual visitors to the international festivals and crucially, of territorial inviolability to a city and its territory.[17] Until the late first century BCE and the consolidation of Roman domination in the East, *asylia* continued to be an important tool of the expression of religious esteem, interstate diplomacy and regional policy. However, such diplomatic activity was costly, even before the festivals took place.

---

14   On diplomatic rhetoric see Erskine 2002; for the relevance of the age of a cult and the history of a sanctuary, see Deshours 2011, 14.

15   Chaniotis 2005, 156.

16   Van Nijf – Williamson 2016 for the networking aspect.

17   Rigsby 1996 on asylia. For other means of diplomacy of cities, leagues and kings in the Hellenistic age, see *e.g.* Ager 1996, 3–35; Erskine 2002; Giovannini 2007, 92–7.

3   Pilgrims and Pilgrimage

To launch their international festival, the Magnesians in Ionia invested considerably in manpower and money in the year 208 BCE.[18] In their quest to have the new festival accepted, they sent out *theoroi* – sacred ambassadors – to announce it – and we know of sixty responses that the Magnesians received from all over the Mediterranean. Robert Parker assumes that some thirty more, now lost, were on public display as inscriptions at the agora, while more than a hundred cities (perhaps less important, small in size, later in accepting the festival?) are simply said to have 'voted in the same way'.[19]

Even if one calculates only for c. 100 cities which responded to Magnesia's request, this would mean that several (at least twenty) teams of *theoroi* left Magnesia in spring and travelled for several months across the Mediterranean in a bid to gain supporters for the new Artemis festival, its entitlement to international quasi-Panhellenic status and recognition for their *asylia*-inviolability claim.[20] In this case, the quest for recognition was at the same time the invitation to the first celebration, with contests conferring an honour similar to Delphi and other such festivals, that is, with garland-crowns instead of prizes.[21]

In the corpus of letters from Magnesia, one letter of a Hellenistic king addresses economic aspects as well: King Attalos I of Pergamon happily accepted the Magnesian festival as garlanded and isopyhtian – similar to the Pythia-festival at Delphi in its honours – recommended its acceptance to the cities under his rule, and declared that he had not only sacrificed an *aparche* (a first-fruit offering) at Pergamon in honour of Artemis Leukophryene, but was also willing to support the festival. Such a promise of support probably included sending a *theoria* (a sacred embassy) to the festival and competitions at Magnesia. Perhaps he also planned to make gifts and donations, such as money for a sacrifice, grain or oil, as attested by generous kings for other cities and festivals,[22] but the inscription is broken just after the lines with Attalos'

---

18   Slater – Summa 2006, 277 speak of the Magnesian's 'costly effort'.

19   Parker 2004, 9 argues that the thirty cities had the available space on the perimeter wall.

20   Parker 2004, 10. There were probably twenty attested teams of two or three, Rigsby 1996, 181. For attested number of envoys announcing other festivals, see Rutherford 2013, 156–7; van Nijf – Williamson 2016, 11–12 for the example of the Stratonikeia/Lagina–network by such delegations. Perlman 2000, 30–4 presents the historiographic discussion on the function of the names of toponyms in the lists of the envoys (*theoroi, theorodokoi*).

21   For the *stephanos* (crowns of foliage) as a mark of the Panhellenic contests in Magnesia instead of costly prizes for the athletic competitions, see Slater – Summa 2006.

22   Royal grants for festivals are known for example in Delphi by Eumenes II Soter, *FD* III 3. 237–9; Bringmann – von Steuben 1995, 148–52 no. 93 (160–159 BCE), by Attalos II Philadelphos, *LSCG* 80; Bringmann – von Steuben 1995, 154–8 no. 94 (160 BCE), and in

promise and we can make out no specifics. One of the most generous royal benefactions would have been to exempt the market that took place during the festival from taxes (*tele*).[23]

It might baffle the modern reader to classify the two ambassadors mentioned in king Attalos' letter as pilgrims. The modern words pilgrim and pilgrimage convey a Christian (or Buddhist, Muslim etc.) notion, and therefore do not fit exactly into 'pagan' antiquity.[24] Most of the Greek and Roman participants in a festival should not be classified as seeking an individual spiritual experience except in the case of mystery cults with its initiation rituals. We rarely hear of travel to a sanctuary as part of a kind of penance. However, the word may be used for the antique cultural practice of 'any journey undertaken for religious reasons, whether by an individual or a group'.[25] The religious motive of such travel was conspicuously visible, as the members of the sacred delegations, the animals they had with them, the carriages and ships for their transport – were all decorated with garlands (at least, this is what literary evidence and a few depictions would have us believe).[26] It is not known whether it was common practice for individual pilgrims to follow this custom, too, although travelling athletes and artists are supposed to have been marked out by their attire. Clothing and garlands might sometimes have had a protective value against religiously scrupulous robbers and pirates,[27] if such a species existed. Some scholars assume that most people did not keep the necessary animals for

---

Didyma by Eumenes II Soter, *I. Didyma* 488; Bringmann – von Steuben 1995, 353–6 no. 286 (160/58 BCE).

23   Chandezon 2000, 85–92; Migeotte 2014, 117. In 214/3 BCE, the city of Sardis established the festival Laodikeia, in honour of Laodike, wife of king Antiochos III for which the king granted tax exemption (*SEG* 36.1087; Bringmann – von Steuben 1995, 298–300 no. 260). Heraclea on the Latmos received a letter of Zeuxis (c. 196–193 BCE), a representative of king Antiochos III, granting the city a tax exemption during their festival, a privilege that had already been granted to Heraclea before: Bringmann – von Steuben 1995, 363–6 no. 296.

24   Dillon 1997, xv–xvi with arguments why, though different in meaning and scope, he retains the terms; *cf.* Rutherford 2013, 12. The use of the terms 'pilgrim' and 'pilgrimage' in the context of 'pagan' antiquity is criticised as inappropriate by Schlesier 2000, 144–5 with note 2. She prefers to speak of 'kultisch geprägte Reisen' (cult-inspired travelling); but see above note 12 on the well argued (but going too far) preference of the terms 'cult' and 'cultic' rather than any term connected to religion. Scullion 2007, esp. 111 qualifies it a 'misleading' term as the Greeks did not 'clearly distinguished secular from sacred.' See also the introduction to the present volume.

25   Rutherford 2013, 12.

26   Rutherford 2013, 174–5.

27   Dillon 1997, 32–4; travelling in times of war (in the Classical period) and pilgrims and officials in danger (with examples of the Classical and Hellenistic eras), *ib.* 38–59. On piracy during the Hellenistic period, see Chaniotis 2005, 8–9; 12; 119 and *passim*.

draft and private travel,[28] and most probably walked, with some hiring draft animals.[29] But irrespective of ownership, at least wealthy pilgrims probably decorated the animals in a similar manner to those of the state ambassadors.

The official and private participants, groups and individuals may be classified by two main directions of movement: the one *from* the festival-city or community itself: the *theoroi*, sacred delegates sent by the inviting city or (less often) a sanctuary to other cities, kings or leagues; and the other, as a consequence, *to* the festival and into the city and its territory: *theoroi*, sent by the invited cities to some of the festivals, and, in the case of the few outstanding international Panhellenic festivals we know of, delegations from all over the Greek-speaking world. Paula Perlman's study of the *theorodokoi*, the hosts for the delegates, demonstrated that there was indeed a huge network of official sacred delegations: in the surviving list of the hosts of delegates to Delphi, hundreds of city names are attested which cover the region between Syria (two cities) and Sicily (seventeen).[30] According to Ian Rutherford, the rising number of festivals during the Hellenistic period led to an increase in the theoric missions per year, which 'must have doubled or tripled in the second half of the third century'.[31] However, we have no proof that all the cities that recognised the newly organised festivals, those with a change in status of a festival and/or the cities' *asylia* request actually participated in every celebration of the new festivals and continued at the same time to visit established festivals as before.

Other individuals and groups of travellers would come from outside the city: other delegations than the standard *theoroi* of foreign cities seem to have regularly sent envoys to fulfil sacred obligations. In addition, athletes, musicians and other artists from abroad as well as those from inside the city took part in the competitions of the festival.[32] Choruses, athletes and others from the city would also participate in the competition. Craftsmen and traders, both from the city and the vicinity (and a few from further away) would provide the city and sanctuary with the necessary instalments and had a primary interest in the market activities accompanying the festivals. The possibility to profit from

---

28   Archibald 2013, 20.

29   For the idea of walking as part of the pilgrim's experience, see Collar in the present volume; on travel by land, André – Baslez 1993, 404–8; Dillon 1997, 34–8.

30   Parker 2004, 10 gives the number of 330 cities.

31   Rutherford 2013, 46.

32   Ebert 1972 with a collection of epigrams honouring the winners in gymnic and hippic competitions; Scullion 2002 on dramatic performances in festivals outside Athens (Cyrene, Delphi, Argos, Dodona etc.); Aneziri 2007 for the involvement of travelling members of artist's associations (Dionysiac *technites*) in the organisation of musical and dramatic festivals.

the gathering of a large number of people would attract some to a festival as long as income and expense would yield a positive balance, especially if there were no taxes and customs duties on import during the festival.[33] In addition, we hear of many serious injuries at sporting events, so medical specialists from inside and outside the city were needed as well.[34] Finally, participants from the organising city included active personnel, priests and magistrates, citizens and also inhabitants without civic rights, some of whom made up the bulk of the spectators as well.

Leopold Migeotte and others have examined the evidence (usually epigraphic) for the funding of city and league festivals in the Hellenistic period.[35] The systematic compilation elucidates that the many variations and combinations were adapted to local contexts.[36] Apart from public funds and sacred money, the necessary means for the festival were provided by individual citizens. Some took over offices and duties (liturgies) at their own expense, others donated money either as a one-time benefaction or as a permanent foundation with a specific aim (i.e. to pay for the sacrificial animals at a given day of a festival). There were many costs: the repairs and cleaning of the sanctuary, the sending of sacred envoys if it was a supra-regional festival, the awards for the victorious choruses, musicians and athletes and the sacrifices for the deities: all these parts of a festival had to be arranged for and someone had to pay for it. It is difficult to calculate the immediate revenue that the visitors and tradesmen would have generated and their overall economic contribution. Therefore, some of the evidence concerning sacrifices and a list of some of the many other important economic aspects of such festivals for the inviting city

---

33   Des Bouvrie 2004, 237 speaks of the 'search for profit', *cf. ib.* 240 markets and fairs at festivals; Feyel 2006 has analysed the presence of craftsmen in sanctuaries according to the inventories and a few other epigraphic sources; many came from outside, however, the documentation does not allow us to extract those working in the context of specific festivities. Archibald 2011, 53–5 for artisans and *passim* for various professions and their economic incentives to travel. At the *Aktias*-festival of the Acarnanians installed in 216 BCE, the taxes on import and export (a *pentekoste* 50ths – 2%) and the sales taxes were collected by the organising city of Amorgos which kept 50% and gave the other half to the league, *cf.* Habicht 1957 and Migeotte 2010, 131–2.

34   *E.g.* Poliakoff 1987, 93–4 on injuries and physicians. Dillon 1997, 221–7: Regulations for athletes sometimes mention fines for competitors in case of misconduct (bribery and unfair behaviour).

35   *E.g.* Habicht 1957 for the *Aktias* festival at Anaktorion; Bruneau 1970, 260–4 for the *Poseidia* on Delos; Migeotte 2010 gives an overview over some of the festivals at Amorgos, Anaktorion, Bargylia, Delos, Iasos, Ilion, Tanagra.

36   Migeotte 2010, 138–43.

and its sanctuaries, from travel expenses to markets and fairs, are presented in the next section.[37]

4   The Costs and Gains of a Festival

A festival had to be magnificent to attract as many foreign visitors as possible and there are many economic aspects connected to sanctuaries and festivals to consider, however, there is not space to deal with all aspects here. Excepting the long-established famous Panhellenic festivals mentioned above, even those with international recognition and a quasi-Panhellenic status had only a regional catchment area.[38] One reason was that travelling was expensive and sometimes perilous, not only in the case of sea travel.[39] In addition, most people were not able to afford to leave the area where they worked and lived for more than one or two days. The travel itself was therefore the first of the economic implications of an international festival for the inviting city as well as for the visitor travelling from afar. We will then examine sacrifice, the housing of the pilgrims and the market of the festival (*panegyris*).[40]

4.1   *Travel Expenses*
The city organising the festival sent out invitations through *theoroi*. At least half a year before the festival, these envoys travelled, often in teams of three, to other cities to inform them of the event, the date and to invite them to participate.[41] The city receiving the envoys appointed citizens as *theorodokoi*,

---

37   A collection of papers with the focus on the costs and financing of the competitions as part of these festivals is provided by Le Guen 2010.

38   On regional catchment areas see des Bouvrie 2004, 241; van Nijf – Williamson 2016, 2–3; Rutherford 2013, 56–66 differentiates between a) international festivals with dominating regional delegations, b) local and regional festivals with exchange of delegations, and c) leagues' festivals.

39   For dangers of travel, see Casson 1974, 72–4; Dillon 1997, 27–59. For the invocation of gods, the reassuring presence and relevance of the protecting deities while travelling, see Muir 2011 *inter alia* with references for fixed sites on the roads like herms, 36–9; for portable shrines, 39–41.

40   Chankowski 2011, esp. 159–63 deals with the sanctuaries' influence on the market by their demand of building material, metals, animals etc., the efforts of the officials to obtain the best price for their demands, the consumers of sacrifices, and all other financial and economic exchanges in the realm of the sanctuary.

41   Rutherford 2013, 156 most often three of such groups; *ib.*, 77 Kos had at least eight teams, Magnesia at least sixteen delegations. For the invitations to participate in Magnesia (Artemis festival) and Pergamon (Nikephoria festival), the delegations had been sent one year in advance.

who received these official visitors and hosted them with lodging and banquets. Sometimes, but not often, the travelling *theoroi* received a small daily allowance from their hometown's treasury.[42] The resident *theorodokoi* were usually wealthy people, who would be able and willing to entertain international visitors in their house. At least in Delphi, these hosts received money from public funds for the welcoming sacrifice and a few other expenses.[43]

4.2 Sacrifices

At every level of the festival the supplies and arrangements connected to the sacrifices were of primary religious importance. They were both an expense and a source of income. For example, in Cyrene, an inscription details the income and expenditures of the sanctuaries in a given year (c. 335 BCE) documented by the magistrates (*damiourgoi*): 'for the sacrifice, to the Bear for maintenance, to Artemis *Katagoris* for the ceremonies, to the priestess of Athena for maintenance, (to? the) *periaktriai*? for the adornment, to each of the three tragic choruses an ox, ... to the aulos player, ... the sacrificer, the guards, illumination for Iatros towards the evening; for the preparation of the thighs of the oxen ... Total expenditure for the year, sacrifices included, 20,669 drachmas, two obols and 7/10.'[44] It is sacrifice and the other expenditures for festivals in honour of Apollo, Artemis and Athena that dominate the list.[45]

In many inscriptions we hear of libations financed by the city, and animals bought with money from civic or sacred funds. For the organisation of the *Poseidonia* festival on Delos, the *hieropoioi* received money from public and sacred funds for the sacrificial animals and their fodder. The money for the sacrifices of the *Itonia* festival in honour of Athena on Amorgos, which was paid for by the cities of Arkesine and Minoa in the third and second centuries BCE, was taken from the sacred money of the celebrated goddess.[46] The supply of sacrificial animals for the period of the festival had to be guaranteed. As the sacrifice and the sacrificial meal lay at the centre of the communal religious experience, this was an important point in all festivals and a serious

---

42 Perlman, 2000, 48–9.

43 Perlman 2000, 49–50 with reference to the Delphic *Theorodikai* lists as presented in fig. 5 (*ib.*, 52–5) with column VI indicating the one who pays.

44 *SEG* 9. 13; 48. 2052, *cf.* Ceccarelli – Milanezi 2007 with a translation, cited above; the concern of the festival officials for all their expenses is presented in these texts.

45 Ceccarelli – Milanezi 2007, 204–10 for the prizes: two more lists of similar content have also survived. The oxen-sacrifices were prizes for the choruses, and because of the thighs mentioned, were eaten together.

46 See *inter alia* from Delos *ID* 401 (190 BCE), 445 (178 BCE) and *IG* XII 7.22, 24, 33 etc. from Arkesine, *cf.* Migeotte 2010, 130–1.

effort in logistics and organisation was needed. An early first century BCE regulation of Andania in Messenia informs us that:

> Concerning the Supplying of Sacrificial Animals: After their appointment, the sacred men, having advertised, are to contract out the supplying of sacrificial animals which must be sacrificed and presented in the Mysteries and those (sacrificial animals) for the purifications, contracting out, whether it seems expedient for all the animals to be on the same contract or on separate contracts, to the one who offers to take the least sum. It is necessary to supply the following: two white lambs before the beginning of the Mysteries, a ram of healthy complexion for the purification, and three little pigs when one purifies in the theater, one hundred lambs on behalf of the first-time initiates, and in the procession, a pregnant sow for Demeter, a two-year old young pig for the Great Gods, a ram for Hermes, a boar for Apollo Karneios, and a sheep for Hagna. And the contractor, having provided guarantors to the sacred men, must take the funds and present very holy, pure, whole animals and show them to the sacred men ten days before the Mysteries. The sacred men are to put a mark on those approved, and the contractor must present the marked ones. If he does not present them for the scrutiny, the sacred men must exact from the guarantors the amount plus half, and they themselves must supply the animals and from the extracted funds recover the resulting expenditure for the animals.[47]

Similar to the examples from Delos and Amorgos, these animals were paid for by the sanctuary funds, parts of which were given to it by the civic treasurer.[48] A different solution was found in the late second century BCE by the city of Bargylia in Karia.[49] Probably due to the lack of public and/or sacred money, the community created a competitive setting in which the wealthy paid for the oxen and cows needed for the sacrifices at the festival in honour of Artemis. Every selected citizen, metic, and magistrate received 100 drachma as a kind of seed money, and when all the animals were to be presented, they were examined and publicly ranked according to beauty and purity.

Apart from municipal, federal, sacred and private funding, many documents from all over Greece, the Aegean islands and Asia Minor demonstrate

---

47   Lines 65–73, translation by Gawlinski 2012: 79; 81; commentary by Deshours 2006, 87; 130–3 and Gawlinksi 2012, 164–76.

48   For the keeping of 'sacred' animals by a sanctuary, see Isager 1992.

49   *SEG* 50. 1101, *cf.* Migeotte 2010, 135.

that festival participants had to provide sacrificial animals as well. Some pilgrims brought the sacrificial animals from their hometown to the sanctuary, and others bought them on site, probably from individual traders. In addition, it seems as if some sacred delegations had taken with them not only the expected *aparche* – the first fruits gift, but that such delegations also brought votives to donate to the deity of the sanctuary, most probably on the occasion of a festival. Apart from an inventory list in Delphi, just one rare, non-Hellenistic find from a shipwreck at Mahdia in Tunisia provided information on this issue. It is a decree of the Athenian people about the offerings and dedications the *theoroi* should take with them on their way to the oracle of Ammon in Egypt in 363/2 BCE.[50] Another Athenian inscription, an inventory from the mid-fourth century, mentions votives dedicated by one or more *theoroi* who had obviously made an offering when he or they had come home from (this) one (or another) mission to this sanctuary of Ammon in Egypt.[51]

As it seems, official delegates and (most?) individual pilgrims took sacrifices with them and perhaps also votives to the festival, and after their return they were also thankful to the gods of their hometown.[52] This practice is attested in the early fourth century BCE (or even earlier) – an inscription from the sanctuary of Athena Alea of Tegea in Arcadia details that during the festival of Tripanagorsis, Tegean citizens and the civic officials appointed for the administration of the sanctuary and the festival had the privilege to graze a restricted number of sacred animals on the land belonging to the sanctuary, whereas the animals of visitors were allowed to rest and graze only for one day and one night. For a longer stay the pilgrim had to pay one drachma per day for a cow or a pig and one obol for a goat or a sheep.[53] During the last three days of the festivals, the responsible Tegean *hierothyte* was allowed to graze an unrestricted number of animals – most probably because on those days the most important rituals with animal sacrifices took place.

---

50 *SEG* 21.241 (now Tunis).

51 *IG* II² 1642, *SEG* 21.562, reprinted and translated in Rutherford 2013, 382–5 (no. C4): lines 9–10 An[other phiale on which is inscribed: / Ath]enian *theoroi* who [took this gold [to Ammon?]; lines 13–14 An[other on which is written: / ...] of Athens having performed a *theoria*, w[eight ...], followed by lines 14–15 [Another of silver, on which is inscri]bed *theoroi* from Athe[ns in the archonship of ... / who brought the gol]d to Ammon ....

52 In the early third century, Kallias of Sphettos, who financed a theoria to Alexandria in Egypt, was honoured in an Athenian decree; inter alia it is mentioned that the delegation brought back with them gifts made by Ptolemy for the Panathenaia festival, *SEG* 28.60, lines 66–70 (see Rutherford 2013, 120 and translation App. D 2).

53 *IG* V 2.3 = *LSCG* 67, Isager 1992, 15–6; Horster 2010, 131. We also know of sacred cattle belonging to sanctuaries as attested in Locris and Delos, however, it is difficult to trace their use in detail. For the Tegean inscription, see Kristensen in the present volume.

In 102/1 BCE king Nikomedes II donated thirty slaves to the sanctuary of Apollo and the city of Delphi, most of whom were used as herdsmen for the sacred animals.[54] Although the Greek cult of the royal dynasty in Egypt was somewhat unusual in some respects, they kept the main Greek features of individual sacrifices combined with collective sacrifices, and joined individual ways of participating with public arrangement of the main rituals and ceremonies. For the festival in honour of the deified queen Arsinoe, people living in the deme itself (where the procession passed by?) were supposed to put an altar of sand in front of their houses and offer sacrifice, whereas those – at least those of some standing and wealth – living in the hinterland or at a greater distance, were supposed to travel to Alexandria to attend the festival and to take with them animals for the sacrifices.[55] But this was not a standard regulation for all ruler cults with festivals, and no such obligation is known from civic festivities. However, civic institutions had a wide range of options for how to receive as many animals and sacrifices as possible without paying for all of them or with only a small contribution. In Delphi, for example, delegates and individual pilgrims had to pay for each sacrifice – and this sacrifice was a precondition for everything they wanted to participate in.[56] In addition, in the Hellenistic period, the so-called *pelanos*, a sacrificial cake the visitor could bring, was substituted by a fee the pilgrim had to pay to the sanctuary official.[57]

Other rules concerned the use of the sacrificial meat after the sacrifices. At Didyma near Miletos with its festival in honour of Apollo, the sacrificial meat had to be consumed in a tent set up for this purpose. It was, however, allowed to take it away, but in this case one had to pay for the meat in order to prevent participants from making private profit by selling publicly funded food.[58] *Mageiroi*, sacrificial butchers and cooks involved in such rituals, could also have been paid for their duties by the cities, as in the case of a sacrifice for Demeter Chloé at Mykonos around 200 BCE. Here, the *mageiros* would receive two units of barley-flour and three of wine as a compensation for his duties.[59] In many other cases, the priest or other personnel sacrificing for individuals or

---

54   *SGDI* II 4. 2738; Bringmann – von Steuben 1995, 161–3. Berthiaume 1982, 33 dates the text to 92/1 BCE (and highlights the sacrificial butcher slave, mentioned in line 22).

55   Caneva 2012 for the *Arsinoeia* festival at Alexandria; *cf.* Wiemer 2009 on the splendour of the festivals organised and paid for by the Hellenistic kings which differed in its representational substance from the civic festivals including those which were installed to honour a king.

56   For such regulations at Andros, see Aurigny in the present volume.

57   Delphi: *CID* 1.1; 1.13 etc., *cf.* Migeotte 2014, 300–1; festival *Metroia* at Amorgos, *ib.* 200–1 with note 333. For fees *etc.*, see Naiden in the present volume.

58   *LSAM* 54, *cf.* Dillon 1997, 216.

59   *LSCG* 96, lines 11–15, *cf.* Berthiaume 1982, 28.

groups received a part of the meat or the hide.[60] He or she could either keep it or sell it, as in Didyma. The decoration of the altar or altars where all this took place was often paid for by the sacred or civic funds, as were all the elements that embellished the procession: the musicians, chorus, rarely dancers, sometimes animals or whatever else was appropriate to the specific occasion connected to the myth of the deity or the history of the city and its sanctuary.[61] However, some cities made these expenses a financial obligation for the liturgies involved in the organisation of these festival parts (*choregia, agonothesia* etc.) as it is the case for some Athenian festivals of the Hellenistic period and the Delian *Apollonia*.[62] We have only few hints to such civic duties for a festival and almost nothing about the costs involved.

However, the responsible civic or federal institutions had to manage all the rituals and accoutrements and could not rely on the individual citizens and pilgrims and their spontaneous decisions. They had to provide a festival of high standards, and could set up rules for participation fees, sacrifices, taxes or dues for services etc. for the participating residents and the pilgrims.

4.3 Housing and Other Supplies for Pilgrims

There were different options for housing pilgrims. In the sanctuary of Apollo Karneios of Andania, where the mysteries of the Great Gods took place, tents were allowed to be pitched (*IG* V 1, 1390, l. 34–41) within a marked area:

> Concerning tents: The sacred men must not allow anyone to have a tent in a rectangle greater than thirty feet or to put skins or hangings around the tents, and, in the area that the sacred men mark off, no one of those who are not sacred men is to have a tent. And they must not allow any uninitiated person into the place which they marked off [for the tents]. And they must also place lustral basins (there). And they must also write down from what one must be pure and what one must not have to enter.[63]

However it is clear that only a limited number of pilgrims, the initiates, could put up their tents in the convenient area of the main festival site, the sanctuary.

---

60 *E.g.* connected to the funding of the festivals of the *Apollonia* and *Poseidia* on Delos see Migeotte 2010, 128–30.

61 Rutherford 2013, 243–4 with three ambiguous examples from Delphi, Priene, and Palaikastro on Crete. Commemorative festivals are seen as one specific characteristic of Hellenistic expressions of religion by Chaniotis 1991 and Dunand 2003, 105–6 including those in honour of the kings.

62 Migeotte 2010, 141–2 with more examples and references.

63 Translation by Gawlinski 2012, 73 with commentary 143–8.

The uninitiated were not allowed to spend the night in the sanctuary, either having to pitch a tent outside the *temenos* or look for a *xeneon*, a hostelry, or a private room in the city.[64] The costs of renting a room during the festival may have been higher than average, but we have no data, only anecdotes attesting the practice of letting private rooms. Other texts also mention tents, for example the *skenai* (tents) at a Boiotian sanctuary that were let to visitors, as the inscribed list of revenues indicates.[65] Official delegations were usually hosted by their *theorodokai*, and wealthy individual pilgrims may have been welcomed by the *proxenoi* of their respective city, if there were any.

After the main sacrifice, many festivals held a common sacrificial meal for all or at least many participants. However, although this was perhaps enough meat for a day, it was not enough food for all participants of the festival.[66] The 100 lambs mentioned in Andania were reserved for the initiation ritual. Far more animals, like the often-mentioned hecatomb (100 oxen) were needed to give many people a share of the cooked meat after the gods had received their part.[67] For special participants, the priests and magistrates of the organising city, selected citizens, winners of the athletic contests and artistic competitions, probably the *theoroi* of the official delegations and other important persons, there existed banquet-rooms in some of the sanctuaries or the adjacent cities, for example, a *hestiatorion* for the victors of the Olympic Games in Elis (Paus. 5.15.12).[68] For the Delian festival *Posideia*, the largest amount of money that was given to the *hieropoioi* for expenditure was that for the food and wine at the banquets – even more than for the sacrifices.[69]

All other pilgrims had to organise and pay for their own food during their stay. These expenses could be reduced if the city or one of the responsible

---

64 The earliest known *xeneon* dates to ca. 500 BCE and is attested on an inscribed bronze from Olympia, Siewert 2002, *cf.* Rutherford 2013, 31. For housing, see Marasco 1978, 114–21 and Dillon 1997, 209–11; Rutherford 2013, 2 and with a review of Greek and Roman housing for guests and travellers, see André – Baslez 1993, 449–66.

65 *Cf.* Dillon 1997, 216.

66 Naiden 2012 for the difficulties in calculating the animals (and meat) necessary to give at least small portions to a large crowd of people.

67 Rhodes – Osborne 2003, 403 estimate that 20,000 participants of the Panathenaia festival (in the fifth century) were provided with meat of sacrificed animals. Diod. Sic. 18.8.5 writes of more than 20,000 people gathered at the festival of the Olympic Games in the year 324. Modern authors have calculated numbers of participants at festivals by the seat numbers in theatres and the number of spectators a stadium might have held (often with differing results for the respective monuments). The numbers of pilgrims and participants was probably most often several hundreds to some few thousands.

68 For public dining and sacrificial meals, see Schmitt Pantel 1992 and 2012; for a discussion and evidence for archaeological remains of such dining-rooms, *cf.* Rutherford 2013, 31–2.

69 Migeotte 2010, 130 with references.

magistrates made special arrangements for the food supply, as is attested for example in one inscribed decree of the *synhedrion* of the league of Ilion dated to the third century BCE. This honorific decree was passed for an *agoranomos* of Parion appointed especially for the *Panathenaia*, because he had taken care of the provision of grain, so that "the participants could buy grain at an affordable price, and in addition he looked after all the other goods and arranged for a physician who took care of sick persons during the festival".[70]

Comfort, sufficient supplies and security were part of the attractiveness of festivals in combination with the rituals and the cultic splendour.[71] Accordingly, appointed officials ensured the water supply for ritual purity as well as for drinking and cleaning. One paragraph of the law of Andania mentioned above deals with the *agoranomos'* responsibility for the quality and quantity of the water during the festival, 'so that during the time of the *panegyris* no one damages the sluice of the channels or anything else is constructed in the sanctuary for the sake of water, and so that the water runs ... and no one hinders those using it.'[72] The festival's *agoranomos* had to ensure that the entrance fee for bathing was kept low, and that enough firewood, fresh water and oil was available for a small fee or gratis. In Andania, a communal bathtub ensured that both the initiated and uninitiated pilgrims could clean themselves.[73] Moreover, those who did not behave properly, or who destroyed or disturbed the water supply had to pay a fine. Such fines probably amounted to a rather large income for the city or sanctuary, for example, athletes could be fined for misconduct, especially bribery, but also for unsportsmanlike conduct, such as breaking an opponent's fingers in wrestling, as seen in an early inscription at Olympia.[74]

---

70   *I. Ilion* 3.

71   Chankowski 2005 stresses however, that processions and the overall civic festival-arrangements differed only in details. For the festivals arranged by the kings and their officials, see note 54.

72   *IG* v 1, 1390. l. 103–106, trans. Gawlinski 2012, 87.

73   *IG* v 1, 1390 l. 106–111 (trans. Gawlinski 2012, 87; 89) deal with regulations for ointments and bathing: 'The *agoranomos* must take care that those wanting to manage the bath in the sanctuary do not charge the bathers more than two *chalkoi* and supply fire and a temperate communal bathtub and temperate water to those washing themselves down ...'. In her commentary (pp. 219–26) Gawlinski 2012 presents other such regulations (with references) and discusses the different solutions the civic institutions found for water supply and the bathing opportunities of pilgrims at religious festivals.

74   For fines as an income for the sanctuary, see Horster 2011, 201–3; Dillon 1997, 224–45 with examples for bribery; 278 with note 117 (Olympia).

4.4   *The Panegyris*

However, in terms of the economic impact on the city and the sanctuary, all the fees, fines, single sacrifices, offerings and gifts, housing and catering, pale by comparison with the festivals which were accompanied by fairs and markets. A *panegyris* was a general name for any religious festival, but it was often used to denote the commercial activities, especially the transactions at the *agora* (market) or near the sanctuary.[75] Some festivals were exempted from taxes and fees, and such exemptions, *ateleia*, could be granted by a king or by the organising city itself.[76] More often, however, cities preferred not to renounce fiscal profits, but rather to control the prices of goods during the festival.[77]

In the Andania law, market stands were not charged for, there were no price limits on the products on offer, and traders could sell their merchandise day and night.[78] There was an enormous variety of rules and regulations concerning trade activities and supplies of crafts and services during many Greek religious festivals, most known to us through inscriptions published in the respective city or sanctuary. In Andania and at other places, the traders were explicitly warned to be honest and to use weights and measures which corresponded exactly to the Andania standards set up by the demos. If inspections detected fraud, the fine was twenty drachmas, a high sum. In Eleusis a public slave is attested in an inscription dated to around 100 BCE, who was responsible for the control of the weights and measures during the festival of the Great Mysteries.[79] In the third-century honorific decree for an *agoranomos*

---

75   De Ligt 1993, 35–9, followed by Dillon 1997, 214–7.

76   Such exemptions are attested but rarely, Chandezon 2007, 291 and Migeotte 2014, 118 with references. The city would in these cases abstain from customs and taxes, on the other hand such an *ateleia* would make the fair and the festival more attractive and would increase the prestige of the city, and even more the income of citizens, inhabitants and sanctuary.

77   Migeotte 1997, 39–43; 2006; ²2007, 122–44; Gabrielsen 2011, 235–8.

78   Lines 99–103 deal with the market: 'Concerning the Agora: The sacred men must appoint a place in which all things will be sold. The *agoranomos* for the city must take care that the sellers sell things unadulterated and pure and use weights and measures that coincide with the public ones, but he must not fix the price at which they must sell, and no one is to set the time or charge the sellers anything for the space. Those who do not sell as written, he must scourge if they are slaves, but fine twenty drachmas if they are free men. And the judgement must be in the presence of the sacred men.' Gawlinski 2012, 87 (translation), *ib.* 214–19 (commentary with many examples from other festivals in Greece and Asia Minor).

79   Dillon 1997, 215 referring to *IG* II² 1013 = *IE* 237, lines 45–49. The market at Eleusis (including the measures and weights used) was supervised by the hierophant and appointed men, *cf.* Clinton 2005–2008: 278 *ad* 237 with a short commentary.

of the *Panathenia*-festival at Ilion mentioned above,[80] he was honoured *inter alia* because he had looked after the goods on offer carefully, something that was also part of the long list of duties of the responsible sacred and civic officials in other cities. This was already a prescribed duty of the *hieromnamones* at the festival of Panagorsis at Tegea, fixed in the early fourth century BCE.[81] The Tegean *damiourgoi*, the superior magistrates of the city, were responsible for the overall organisation of the festival. Markets connected to such festivals needed thorough inspection and supervision: The comic author Menander mentions in one of his plays dice-playing, thieves and entertainments as part of a religious festival-market.[82] Similar details for the market at Olympia date to the Imperial period.[83] Money exchange at fixed conversion rates and its supervision was also an important part of a well organised fair, and is attested in Delphi and at a few other places.[84] The methodological difficulties to understand the mechanisms of such commercial gatherings near or in sanctuaries and connected to festivals are connected to the scarcity of written evidence and the archaeological evidence.[85]

5 Conclusion

Security and safe lodging, sufficient supply of water and food, medical care, entertainment and attractive trade merchandise at acceptable prices were aspects of religious festival in the Hellenistic period, which was supposed to attract masses of sacred delegations, participants in competitions and individual pilgrims. In reality, there could be enormous differences in the standards of comfort and provision for the festival. It seems that some could afford to perform rather badly – this is Matthew Dillon's characterisation of the conditions at Olympia – whereas others, like Eleusis and Andania seem to have been very attentive and invested in manpower and amenities to attract pilgrims from all over the Greek world.

---

80   See above note 70.

81   See above note 52.

82   Menander Fragment 481 (ed. Th. Kock, *Comicorum atticorum fragmenta*, vol. 3, Leipzig 1888).

83   Dillon 1997, 215 with further references.

84   *E.g. FD* III 2.139 (= *Syll.*[3] 729), *cf.* Dillon 1997, 276 with note 72.

85   Some aspects of these difficulties are discussed by Andreau 2002 although with a focus on the Roman fairs and markets. For some durable installments of 'shops', with or without consumption of food and beverages in or near sanctuaries, see Thür – Taeuber 1978 on *IG* XII 6/1, 169 (second half of the third century BCE) regulating the leasing conditions of four shops in the Samian sanctuary of Hera.

As concerns 'experience economy', there are lively descriptions of the inter-actions and feelings of participants at festivals in literary sources of the classi-cal period and of the Imperial period connected to more or less romantic love stories.[86] Similar 'real' stories and their diffusion may have added to the re-nown of festivals as matchmakers. In addition, the experience of getting to the sanctuary, taking part in the event, watching or taking part in the procession and finally getting home again may have been fuelled by expectations at all parts of the pilgrimage. Some pilgrims may have been looking for a short love affair, others were hoping for recovery of an illness. We can safely assume that the pilgrims' narrations of such important stimuli and emotional sensations added to the fame of a festival and led to a short-time increase of the num-ber of participants. But there is no 'evidence' for such an economic impact, nor do we know how often in the real world healing and recovery was suc-cessful, and emotional success stories were common. The famous Epidaurian *iamata* inscriptions of the late fourth century BCE with 70 reports of healing had been the results of a successful pilgrimage but not in the context of a festi-val.[87] However, 'experience economy' will probably be a good guide for further analyses of the impact of the souvenir trade in the broadened and changed appearance of festival landscape of the Hellenistic period.

Another non-economic aspect certainly had a great influence on the po-litical and economic success of the Hellenistic festivals: inter-state diplomacy and networking resulting in stronger ties and trust between cities, leagues and kings. Although an exact calculation of the economic benefits for sanctuary and city is not possible, it is plausible that the increase in the number of fes-tivals in the Hellenistic period as well as the attested increase in the details of dispositions and regulations, including those for the financial aspects of such festivals, would not make sense if the calculations for the festival did not pay off. However, such an accounting should not only include the economic as-pects, but also the gain in religious prestige as an important asset for political reputation and international standing in the Hellenistic period.[88]

---

86   The beautiful and young Anthia meets her Habrocomes at the Artemis festival in Roman
      Ephesos (Xen. *Ephes.* 1.2, written probably in the second century CE).
87   *IG* IV² 1, 121–4.
88   For the Hellenistic expressions of religion as partly different from the Classical period but
      not less 'religious', see Dunand 2003.

Bibliography

Ager, S. 1996. *Interstate Arbitration in the Greek World, 337–90 BC*, Berkeley, CA.

André, J.-M. and Baslez, M.-F. 1993. *Voyager dans l'antiquité*, Paris.

Andreau, J. 2002. "Markets, fairs and monetary loans: cultural history and economic history in Roman Italy and Hellenistic Greece", in *Money, Labour and Land. Approaches to the economies of ancient Greece*, eds. P. Cartledge, E.E. Cohen, and L. Foxhall, London, 113–29.

Aneziri, S. 2003. *Die Vereine der dionysischen Techniten im Kontext der hellenistischen Gesellschaft. Untersuchungen zur Geschichte, Organisation und Wirkung der hellenistischen Technitenvereine*, Stuttgart.

Aneziri, S. 2007. "The Organisation of Music Contests in the Hellenistic Period and Artists' Participation. An Attempt at Classification", in *The Greek Theatre and Festivals. Documentary Studies*, ed. P. Wilson, Oxford, 67–84.

Archibald, Z.H. 2011. "Mobility and Innovation in Hellenistic Economies: The Causes and Consequences of Human Traffic", in *The Economies of Hellenistic Societies, Third to First Centuries BC*, eds. Z.H. Archibald, J.K. Davies, and V. Gabrielsen, Oxford, 42–65.

Archibald, Z.H. 2013. *Ancient Economies of the Northern Aegean: Fifth to First Centuries BC*, Oxford.

Berthiaume, G. 1982. *Les rôles du mágeiros. Étude sur al boucherie, la cuisine et le sacrifice dans la Grèce ancienne*, Leiden.

des Bouvrie, S. 2004. "The Pilgrimage to Olympia. Settings and Sentiments", in *Celebrations. Selected Papers and Discussions from the Tenth Anniversary Symposion on the Norwegian Institute at Athens, 12–16 May 1999*, Bergen, 237–74.

Bringmann, K. and von Steuben, H. 1995. *Schenkungen hellenistischer Herrscher an griechische Städte und Heiligtümer. Vol. 1, Zeugnisse und Kommentare*, Berlin.

Bruit, L. *et al.* 2004. "Le banquet en Grèce", in *ThesCRA*, vol. 2, 218–50.

Bruneau, Ph. 1970. *Recherches sur les cultes de Délos à l'époque hellénistique et a l'époque imperial*, Paris.

Buraselis, K. 2012. "The Coordination and Combination of Traditional Civic and Ruler Cult Festivals in the Hellenistic and Roman East", in *Greek and Roman Festivals: Content, Meaning, and Practice*, eds. J. Rasmus Brandt and J.W. Iddeng, Oxford, 247–58.

Caneva, S.G. 2012. "Queens and Rulers Cults in Early Hellenism: Festivals, Administration, and Ideology", *Kernos* 25, 75–101.

Casson, L. 1971. *Ships and Seamanship in the Ancient World*, Princeton, NJ.

Casson, L. 1974. *Travel in the Ancient World*, London.

Ceccarelli, P. and Milanezi, S. 2007. "Dithyramb, Tragedy – and Cyrene", in *Greek Theatre and Festivals. Documentary Studies*, ed. P. Wilson, Oxford, 185–214.

Chandezon, C. 2000, "Foires et panégyries dans le monde grec", *Revue des études grecques* 113, 70–100.

Chandezon, C. 2007. "Foires et panégyries dans le monde grec classique et hellénistique", in *Économie et Société en Grèce ancienne (478–88 av. J.-C.)*, eds. P. Brulé, J. Oulhen, and F. Prost, Rennes, 277–302.

Chaniotis, A. 1991. "Gedenktage der Griechen. Ihre Bedeutung für das Geschichtsbewußtsein griechischer Poleis", in *Das Fest und das Heilige. Religiöse Kontrapunkte zur Alltagswelt*, ed. J. Assmann, Gütersloh, 123–45.

Chaniotis, A. 1995. "Sich selbst feiern? Städtische Feste des Hellenismus im Spannungsfeld von Religion und Politik", in *Stadtbild und Bürgerbild im Hellenismus*, eds. M. Wörrle and P. Zanker, München, 147–72.

Chaniotis, A. 2005. *War in the Hellenistic World. A Social and Cultural History*, Malden, MA.

Chaniotis, A. 2011. "Greek Festivals and Contests: Definition and General Characteristics", in *ThesCRA VII: Festival and Contests*, eds. A. Hermary and B. Jaeger, Los Angeles, 4–43.

Chankowski, A.S. 2005. "Processions et cérémonies d'accueil: une image de la cité de la basse époque hellénistique?", in *Citoyenneté et participation a la basse époque hellénistique*, eds. P. Fröhlich and C. Müller, Geneva, 185–206.

Chankowski, A.S. 2011. "Divine Financiers: Cults as Consumers and Generators of Value", in *The Economies of Hellenistic Societies, Third to First Centuries BC*, eds. Z. Archiblad, J.K. Davies, and V. Gabrielsen, Oxford, 142–65.

Clinton, K. 2005–2008. *Eleusis. The Inscriptions on Stone: Documents of the Sanctuary of the Two Goddesses and Public Documents of the Deme*, 2 vols., Athens.

De Ligt, L. 1993. *Fairs and Markets in the Roman Empire. Economic and Social Aspects of Periodic Trade in a Pre-Industrial Society*, Amsterdam.

Deshours, N. 2006. *Les Mystères d'Andania. Étude d'épigraphie et d'histoire religieuse*, Bordeaux.

Deshours, N. 2011. *L'été indien de la religion civique : études sur les cultes civiques dans le monde égéen à l'époque hellénistique tardive*, Bordeaux.

Dillon, M. 1997. *Pilgrims and Pilgrimage in Ancient Greece*, London.

Dunand, F. 2003. "Fêtes et reveil religieux dans les cites grecques à l'époque hellénistique", in *Dieux, fêtes, sacré dans la Grèce et la Rome antique. Actes du Colloque tenu à Luxembourg du 24 au 26 octobre 1999*, eds. A. Motte and C.-M. Ternes, Turnhout, 101–12.

Ebert, J. 1972. *Griechische Epigramme auf Sieger an gymnischen und hippischen Agonen*, Berlin.

Erskine, A. 2002. "'O brother where art thou?' Tales of Kinship and Diplomacy", in *The Hellenistic World: New Perspectives*, ed. D. Ogden, Swansea, 97–117.

Feyel, C. 2006. *Les artisans dans les sanctuaires grecs aux époques classique et hellénistique à travers la documentation financière de Grèce*, Athens.

Gabrielsen, V. 2011. "Profitable Partnership: Monopolies, Traders, Kings and Cities", in *The Economies of Hellenistic Societies, Third to First Centuries BC*, eds. Z.H. Archibald, J.K. Davies, and V. Gabrielsen, Oxford, 216–50.

Gawlinski, L. 2012. *The Sacred Law of Andania: A New Text with Commentary*, Berlin.

Giovannini, A. 2007. *Les relations entre états dans la Grèce antique: du temps d'Homère à l'intervention romaine (ca. 700–200 av. J.-C.)*, Stuttgart.

Habicht, C. 1957. "Eine Urkunde des akarnanischen Bundes", *Hermes* 85, 86–122; 501–4.

Hermary, A. *et al.* 2004. "Les sacrifices dans le monde grec", in *ThesCRA* Vol. 1, Los Angeles, 60–134.

Horster, M. 2010. "Religious Landscape and Sacred Ground: Relationships between Space and Cult in the Greek World", *Revue de l'histoire des religions* 227, 435–458.

Horster, M. 2011. "Dionysus-cults: The Economic Aspects", in *A Different God? Dionysos and Ancient Polytheism*, ed. R. Schlesinger, Berlin, 61–85.

Horster, M. 2013. "Priene: Civic Priests and Koinon-Priesthoods in the Hellenistic Period", in *Cities & Priests. Cult Personnel in Asia Minor and the Aegean Islands from the Hellenistic to the Imperial Period*, eds. M. Horster and A. Klöckner, Berlin, 177–208.

Iddeng, J.W. 2012. "What is a Graeco-Roman Festival. A Polythetic Approach", in *Greek and Roman Festivals: Content, Meaning, and Practice*, eds. J. Rasmus Brandt and J.W. Iddeng, Oxford, 11–37.

Isager, S. 1992. "Sacred Animals in Classical and Hellenistic Greece", in *Economics of Cult, Proceedings of the Uppsala Symposium 1990*, eds. T. Linders and B. Alroth, Uppsala, 15–9.

Knoepfler, D. 2010. "Louis Robert en sa forge: ébauche d'un mémoire resté inédit sur l'histoire controversée de deux concours grecs, les *Trophônia* et les *Basileia* à Lébadée", *Comptes rendus de l'Académie des Inscriptions et Belles-Lettres*, 1421–62.

Kravaritou, S. 2016. "Sacred Space and the Politics of Multiculturalism in Demetrias (Thessaly)", in *Hellenistic Sanctuaries between Greece and Rome*, eds. M. Melfi and O. Bobou, Oxford, 128–51.

Le Guen, B. 2010. *L'argent dans les concours du monde grec. Actes du colloque international Saint-Denis et Paris, 5–6 décembre 2008*, Saint-Denis.

Mackil, E. 2013. *Creating a Common Polity. Religion, Economy and Politics in the Making of the Greek Koinon*, Berkeley, CA.

Marasco, G. 1978. *I viaggi nella Grecia antica*, Rome.

Migeotte, F. 1997. "Le contrôle de prix dans les cités grecques", in *Prix et formations dans les économies antiques*, eds. J. Andreau, P. Briant, and R. Descat, St-Bertrand-de-Comminges, 33–52.

Migeotte, F. 2006. "Les interventions des cités grecques dans l'économie à la période hellénistique", in *Approches de l'économie hellénistique*, ed. R. Descat, Saint-Bertrand-de-Comminges, 387–96.

Migeotte, F. 2007. *L'économie des cités antique de l'archaïsme au Haut-empire romain*, Paris.

Migeotte, F. 2010. "Les financement des concours dans les cités hellénistique: Essai de typologie", in *L'argent dans les concours du monde grec*, ed. B. Le Guen, Saint-Denis, 127–43.

Migeotte, F. 2014. *Les finances des cités grecques aux périodes classique et hellénistique*, Paris.

Mili, M. 2015. *Religion and Society in Ancient Thessaly*, Oxford.

Muir, S. 2011. "Religion on the Road in Ancient Greece and Rome", in *Travel and Religion in Antiquity*, ed. P.A. Harland, Waterloo, 29–47.

Müller, C. 2014. "A *Koinon* after 146? Reflections on the Political and Institutional Situation of Boeotia in the Late Hellenistic Period", in *The Epigraphy and History of Boetia: New Finds, New Prospects*, ed. N. Papazarkadas, Leiden, 119–46.

Naiden, F. 2012. "Blessèd are the Parasites", in *Greek and Roman Animal Sacrifice. Ancient Victims, Modern Observers*, eds. C.A. Faraone and F.S. Naiden, Cambridge, 55–83.

Naiden, F. 2013. *Smoke Signals for the Gods: Ancient Greek Sacrifice from the Archaic through Roman Periods*, Oxford.

van Nijf, O.M. and Williamson, C.G. 2016. "Connecting the Greeks: Festival Networks in the Hellenistic World", in *Athletics in the Hellenistic World*, eds. C. Mann, S. Remijssen, and S. Scharff, Stuttgart, 43–71.

Parker, R. 2004. "New 'Panhellenic' Festivals in Hellenistic Greece", in *Mobility and Travel in the Mediterranean from Antiquity to the Middle Ages*, eds. R. Schlesier and U. Zellmann, Münster, 9–22.

Perlman, P. 2000. *City and Sanctuary in Ancient Greece: The Theorodokia in the Peloponnese*, Göttingen.

Poliakoff, M.B. 1987. *Combat Sports in the Ancient World. Competition, Violence, and Culture*, New Haven.

Rhodes, P. and Osborne, R. 2003. *Greek Historical Inscriptions: 404–323 BC*, Oxford.

Rigsby, K.J. 1996. *Asylia. Territorial Inviolability in the Hellenistic World*, Berkeley, CA.

Rutherford, I. 2013. *State Pilgrims and Sacred Observers in Ancient Greece. A Study of Theōriā and Theōroi*, Cambridge.

Sánchez, P. 2001. *L'Amphictionie des Pyles et des Delphes. Recherches sur son rôle historique, des origines au IIᵉ siècle de notre ère*, Stuttgart.

Schlesier, R. 2000. "Menschen und Götter unterwegs: Rituale und Reise in der griechischen Antike", in *Gegenwelten zu den Kulturen Griechenlands und Roms in der Antike*, ed. T. Hölscher, München, 129–57.

Schmitt Pantel, P. 1992. *La cité au banquet. Histoire des repas publics dans les cités grecques*, Rome.

Schmitt Pantel, P. 2011. "Dionysos, the Banquet and Gender", in *A Different God? Dionysos and Ancient Polytheism*, ed. R. Schlesinger, Berlin, 119–136.

Schmitt Pantel, P. 2012. "Les banquets des cités grecques: bilan historiographique", *Dialogues d'historie ancienne. Suppl.* 7, 73–93.

Scullion, S. 2002. "Nothing to do with Dionysos", *Classical Quarterly* 52, 102–37.

Scullion, S. 2007. "Pilgrimage and Greek Religion: Sacred and Secular in the Pagan Polis", in *Pilgrimage in Graeco-Roman and Early Christian Antiquity: Seeing the Gods*, eds. J. Elsner and I. Rutherford, Oxford, 111–30.

Siewert, H. 2002. "Die wissenschaftsgeschichtliche Bedeutung der Bronze-Urkunden aus Olympia. Mit der Erstedition einer frühen Thearodokie-Urkunde als Beispiel", in *Olympia 1875–2000. 125 Jahre deutsche Ausgrabungen. Internationales Symposium Berlin 9.–11. November 2000*, ed. H. Kyrieleis, Mainz, 359–70.

Slater, W. 2007. "Deconstructing Festivals", in *Greek Theatre and Festivals. Documentary Studies*, ed. P. Wilson, Oxford, 21–47.

Slater, W.J. and Summa, D. 2006. "Crowns at Magnesia", *Greek, Roman and Byzantine Studies* 46, 275–99.

Thür, G. and Taeuber, H. 1978. "Prozessrechlicher Kommentar zur 'Krämerinschrift' aus Samos", in *Anzeiger der Österreichischen Akademie der Wissenschaften, phil.-hist. Kl.* 155, 205–25.

Wiemer, H.-U. 2009. "Bild der Polis oder Bild des Königs? Zur Repräsentationsfunktion städtischer Fest im Hellenismus", in *Stadtbilder im Hellenismus*, ed. M. Matthaei and M. Zimmermann, Berlin, 116–30.

CHAPTER 6

Housing Pilgrims in Late Antiquity: Patrons, Buildings, and Services

Robin M. Jensen

1   Introduction

While early Christian communities were generally expected to provide hospitality to travelling members of their community, this was particularly true for religious pilgrims *en route* to Rome and sites in the Holy Land as well as those travelling to other shrines, such as the tomb of St. Felix at Nola or the complex dedicated to St. Crispina at Theveste. In addition to overnight lodgings, these accommodations might also provide meals, baths, stables, horses or donkeys for hire, guides, and basic provisions for the road. This gave rise to a specialised service industry, which often was overseen by monastic communities or local bishops. This chapter considers the textual and archaeological evidence for this aspect of the economy of pilgrimage.

In early 426 CE, probably just after the Feast of Epiphany, Augustine preached a sermon in which he discussed various ways that members of his clergy disposed of their worldly possessions upon joining his monastic circle at Hippo Regius.[1] Although these men were expected to share all things in common, reserving nothing for their personal use, some had complicated arrangements that allowed them to continue to support dependent family members or domestic servants. Others had ongoing investments whose proceeds were transferred to the church. Among exemplary individuals, Augustine mentions two whom he had charged with constructing buildings for ecclesial functions. One, the deacon Heraclius, had constructed a martyrium to house some recently received relics of St. Stephen and apparently had dedicated his personal capital to this project.[2] The other, Leporius, accepted the task of establishing a monastery, a garden, and a basilica dedicated to the Eight Martyrs.[3] Leporius, the son and heir of a distinguished family, renounced his inheritance when he joined

---

1   August. *Serm.* 356. PL 39: 1577.
2   August. *Serm.* 356.7. A trefoil structure abutting the surviving remains of a basilica in Hippo might be the site of this shrine.
3   These eight martyrs were unnamed and remain anonymous.

the community. Initially, Augustine charged the newly penniless Leporius to build an accommodation for housing strangers (*xenodochium*), using money given to the church for that specific purpose. Yet, almost as soon as he began construction, he received additional funds from generous congregants who he describes as 'devout people who desired to have their works recorded in heaven' (*religiosi desiderantes opera sua in caelo scribi*).[4]

Evidently this targeted collection raised enough money to allow Leporius to build not only a guesthouse but also a basilica, even leaving some funds left over. Leporius began his project by using a portion of the initial donations to buy a house that he intended to demolish in order to recycle its building materials. However, when he received the necessary raw materials from another generous source, he decided instead to rent out the house and donate the income to the church.[5] Thus, Leporius, the impoverished monk, had financial oversight of a guesthouse, a basilica dedicated to the 'Eight Martyrs,' and a rented property. Unfortunately, although the site of Hippo Regius' Christian quarter has significant archeological remains, the site of the basilica of the Eight Martyrs has not been identified nor is there any trace of Leporius' *xenodochium*.

Members of the clergy built both of these structures during Augustine's episcopate and by his urging. Augustine, like his contemporaries, would have regarded the building of churches, shrines, and guesthouses as a Christian form of traditional Roman *munera* – private benefactions to the city, often in the form of temples, games, or other public works. As he explains in his sermon, by their generous contributions to Leporius' projects, donors would have a means of transferring their treasure to heaven, where their good deeds would be recorded. In this instance, rather than a single, rich benefactor, many individuals evidently made gifts, perhaps some of them rather modest.[6] Leporius' building of a guesthouse might be linked with his construction of a basilica dedicated to the Eight Martyrs, but it seems even more likely that the *xenodochium* was intended to house the influx of out-of-town visitors to Heraclius' martyrium and its precious relics of St. Stephen.

Augustine's prompting of wealthy members of his flock to assist in basilica construction is unsurprising, but his assigning one of his clergy to build a guesthouse, likely intended to provide for visitors to St. Stephen's shrine, suggests his change of mind about the benefits of making a pilgrimage.[7] Earlier

---

4   August. *Serm.* 356.10.

5   *Ibid.*

6   In another case, Augustine praises a congregation of relatively poor folk for coming together to build themselves a church. See *Serm.* 107a.9.

7   Augustine's ambivalence is most expressed in *De cura pro mortuis gerenda.* 16.20, where Augustine muses that the saint's power is not necessarily linked to his/her tomb or relics.

in his career, Augustine attached little value to undertaking long, arduous journeys to Holy Land sites or pilgrimage elsewhere – *e.g.*, Rome.[8] However, sometime around the year 424 CE, a portion of St. Stephen's remains (in the form of dust) had arrived in Hippo from Jerusalem and in 425 CE Augustine preached a sermon to celebrate their installation in Heraclius' new shrine and even wrote four lines of verse to be set up within it.[9] Soon, he was acclaiming the miracles wrought there, although carefully giving the credit to the saint's intercession for God's mercy.[10] Augustine thus not only encouraged Heraclius to construct a shrine to house the visitors who came to seek the saint's aid, he expressed unwavering conviction in the relics' healing power. Before long, their reputation attracted a significant number of out-of-town visitors who would require temporary housing. Augustine asserted that in only the short time since it had arrived and been enshrined, Stephen's dust had produced at least seventy recorded miracles and probably many more of which he had no knowledge. Among them were a sister and brother from Cappadocia who stayed two weeks in Hippo seeking a cure for palsy.[11]

Annual commemorations of martyrs' deaths customarily were held at the site where the martyr's body was buried. The vigil services were often celebratory gatherings that included feasting, drinking wine, dancing, and singing, although the clergy made regular efforts to curb these indecorous activities and substitute solemn Eucharistic services. Documentary evidence shows that, in Hippo, a feast for a sainted former bishop, Leontius, was the focus for a rowdy festival.[12] This prompted criticism from a Manichee who claimed that Christians were behaving no better than pagan Romans. This moved Augustine to try to convince the community to forego a banquet for an extended service of readings, psalms, and sermons.[13] The community objected, claiming that their practice was no different from those held in Rome at the shrine of St. Peter. Augustine, defended his innovation by comparing them to the poorly behaving Donatist congregation down the road and appealed to his congregation's aspirations to practice more respectful forms of

---

      Earlier in this treatise he questions the value of *burial ad sanctos* – *De cura pro mortuis gerenda* 4–5.

8   Bitton-Ashkelony 2005, 106–8 (and see following discussion related to Augustine's evaluation of holy space and martyrs' relics).

9   August. *Serm.* 318, 319.7.

10   August. *Serm.* 322, 323–324, (miracles at the shrine).

11   August. *De civ. D.* 22.8; and *Serm.* 322 and 323.

12   Burns – Jensen 2014, 535–6.

13   August. *Faust.* 20.4, 21.

worship.[14] A similar transition took place in Carthage, where there were two shrines of St. Cyprian – one at the place where he was executed known as the Table of Cyprian (Mensa Cypriani) and one at the site of his burial known as the Mappalia or the Memoria Cypriani. In the Council of Carthage held in 397 CE, the gathered bishops voted to restrict dining in churches, with the exception of feeding and housing visiting clerics.[15]

2 Hospitality for Pilgrims in Early Christian Documents

The attraction of Stephen's relics must have had an impact on Hippo's economy. As in other, more long-standing pilgrimage destinations, travellers needed places to sleep, eat, bathe, stable their mounts (if they had them), hire horses or donkeys (if they did not), and renew basic provisions for the road. In some instances they also needed guides. Presumably, this gave rise to a specialised service industry, which often were overseen by monastic communities or, as in the case of Hippo, a local bishop. The importance of these resting and refuelling stops is indicated by the simple fact that the term 'mansio' was used to indicate the length of a day's journey (from one 'house' to the next). For example, the Pilgrim Egeria explains to her readers that it is twenty-five mansiones from Jerusalem to Edessa.[16]

Providing hospitality to travelling members of their community was enjoined upon Christians from early days. The first-century document, the Didache, gives instructions for receiving itinerant teachers, apostles, and prophets as well as anyone who comes in the name of the Lord. It does, however, specify that while the faithful should take in and assist wayfarers, anyone who stays longer than three days should either be put to work or be regarded as a fraud.[17] Similarly, Justin Martyr's First Apology, written in the latter half of the second century states that the Christian community cares for orphans, widows, prisoners, and any strangers sojourning among them.[18] St. Paul refers to apostles carrying letters of recommendation when on the road (1 Cor. 3.2) and, by Egeria's time, it seems that travellers were typically expected to carry such letters from their bishops – so called 'pacifical letters' – in order to obtain hospitality and admission to communion. The Council of Antioch in 341 con-

---

14   August. *Ep.* 29.9–11.
15   *Breviarium Hipponense 29.*
16   Egeria, *Itinerarium pereginatio.* 17.2. This is noted in Hunt 1984, 58.
17   *Didache,* 11–13.
18   Justin, *Apol.* 67.

tained a canon specifying these letters and is similar to an earlier instruction in the church order known as the *Apostolic Canons*, which refers particularly to receiving foreign bishops, deacons, and presbyters.[19]

Olivia Remie Constable's 2003 monograph, *Housing the Stranger in the Mediterranean World: Lodging, Trade, and Travel in Late Antiquity and the Middle Ages* attends to many of the issues regarding ancient travellers. The first chapter surveys the existence of hostelries and inns in various geographic regions. Constable notes that the Greek term *pandocheion* (literally: 'a place that receives all comers') appears in the Gospel of Luke's story of the Good Samaritan (10.34) and is usually translated into English as 'inn.' Constable adds that *pandocheion* has no clear cognate in Latin. When Jerome compiled his Latin Bible he chose the word *stabulum* for the place the Good Samaritan brought his rescued victim. Jerome's choice is odd, since this connotes something lowlier – a stall, a rustic cottage, or even a brothel. Although the Greek *pandochieon* can be translated simply as a place for receiving strangers, it also tended to suggest a place of 'ill repute,' even though that does not seem implied in the narrative.[20]

By contrast, Luke's nativity narrative specifies that no room could be found for Joseph and Mary in the *katalyma*, a term which denotes a kind of guesthouse (literally = 'a place to rest'). In this instance, Jerome used the Latin word *diversorium* (literally a place for turning aside) where *stabulum* might have been apt. In one of his letters, however, Jerome uses the word *xenodochium* for the inn in the nativity story – clearly a Greek loan word – and the very term that Augustine uses for the structure he asked Leporius to construct in Hippo.[21]

Ancient travellers had a variety of options for lodging places, some of them clearly more perilous or uncomfortable than others. Many could stay with friends or acquaintances but, lacking social or official hospitality networks, most would have had to resort to an inn of some kind. What Latin speakers typically called *diversoria* or *hospitia*, and Greeks called *xenodochia* or *pandocheia*, were not always safe or sanitary. They could range from fairly well-equipped establishments with clean, private, and comfortable rooms to rougher places where one might share a room or even a bed with strangers and risk being robbed or eaten up by bedbugs. Most offered hot meals, some provided stables for vehicles and draft animals, even a change of mount or a

---

19   Council of Antioch, *Canons*. 7; *Apostolic Canons* 34 (*Apostolic Constitutions* 8.47.34).

20   Constable 2003, 11–18.

21   Jer. *Ep.* 66.11. Augustine also uses the word in *In Evang. Iohan.* 97.4 in reference to the apostles' founding of hospices and monasteries in Antioch: *in antiochia enim primum post adscensionem domini appellati sunt discipuli christiani, sicut legitur in actibus apostolorum; et xenodochia et monasteria postea sunt appellata nouis nominibus ....*

blacksmith if needed. Services also included procuring local guides or prosti-
tutes. Baths were an unusual luxury; travellers usually availed themselves of
the local public facilities.[22]

For those of modest means, travel was thus an arduous undertaking, even
though the good Roman roads must have made the journey somewhat easier,
at least along the major routes. Christian pilgrims might be especially wary
of the dangers inherent in lodging houses. Around the year 379 CE, in a letter titled, 'Concerning those who are travelling to Jerusalem,' Gregory of Nyssa
specifically warned monks and consecrated virgins against pilgrimages largely
because of the difficulties and temptations they would face staying in hostels
that could not offer them separate quarters. Noting that the necessities of a
journey are bound to break down scruples, Gregory particularly singles out the
inns and hostelries that were characterised by licentious behaviour and indifference to vice, asking 'how will it be possible for one passing through such
smoke to escape without smarting eyes ... how will it be possible to thread
without infection such seats of contagion?'[23]

Some scholars have argued that Gregory's admonition primarily was motivated by his desire to discourage pilgrimage abroad. In this same letter he
displays this attitude generally; it was not specific directed to monks or nuns.
Rather, he wished everyone to stay closer to home and patronise the local
shrines; some of them, like Augustine's *xenodochium* in Hippo, constructed
under the patronage of the bishop himself. According to Vasiliki Limberis,
Gregory tried to deter pilgrimage at least in some part in order to encourage
visits to the sacred sites in his region, perhaps fostering a competitive sense
of regional pride.[24] Limberis goes on to note that Gregory had even extended
himself personally and financially to build a shrine to honour the forty martyrs
and was deeply involved in the construction of the structures, down to keeping
track of the bricks, mortar, and marble columns. Given this situation, it appears that church authorities, especially bishops like Augustine, saw it as both
their duty and privilege to found establishments that would draw pilgrims, and
with it most likely housing that could particularly cater to religious travellers
who desired safe and reputable accommodations.

For example, in a poem probably written around the year 397 CE, Paulinus
of Nola describes accommodations for the countless guests streaming to
the shrine of St. Felix, especially for the celebration of that saint's feast day
(January 14). He notes that their devotion to the saint overcame the difficulties

---

22   See Casson 1994, 197–218.
23   Greg. Nyss. *Ep.* 2.5–7, trans. Moore – Wilson 1893, 382 (here called 'On Pilgrimages').
24   Limberis 2011, 31.

of the journey and then comments that the city of Nola was nearly bursting at its seams with visitors, but somehow managed to find room for them all.[25] A few years later he describes the newly built facilities for guests in a second story, above porticoes surrounding the complex's central courtyard. These, he says, were intended for guests more interested in prayer than in drink.[26] To some extent they replaced two little privately-owned huts that had formerly served as pilgrims' lodgings. According to Paulinus, these rustic huts were an eyesore and moreover obscured the view of the other, lovelier, buildings. They even blocked the light from the main basilica door. Thus, Paulinus sought to demolish them. Although he promised that the new facilities would afford excellent views of the shrine, the landlord and his guests absolutely refused to budge and he feared a brawl. Then one night, a random spark kindled a fire and consumed one of the cottages, while sparing the second and – miraculously – the other buildings in the complex. The first was damaged beyond repair, forcing the landlord to undertake to demolish it by his own labour. Admiring his new buildings, Paulinus hastens to credit this prodigy to St. Felix and that saint's desire that his shrine should be a place of both beauty and decorum.[27]

Aristocratic bishops like Paulinus probably could rely on the hospitality of their brother bishops or wealthy friends when travelling and were thus able to avoid the rowdy crowds and immoral behaviours. However, when Paulinus was in Rome, where he had many friends, he apparently stayed in a *hospitium*.[28] In a letter to his friend Severus, Paulinus commends him for making his house into a hospice, filling it house with travellers and the poor, living as a servant rather than as a *paterfamilias*.[29]

Travelling clerics were actually restricted from entering or lodging in certain places and thus must have depended on the kindness of their colleagues. Various church orders, concerned about maintaining the appearance of clerical decorum, expressly forbade them even to enter taverns unless absolutely necessary.[30] Possibly for this reason or perhaps out of a concern for propriety, legislation also limited overnight stays in churches to visiting clergy.[31]

As in the case of Paulinus' friend Severus, the earliest evidence for the establishment of Christian guest facilities demonstrates the role of wealthy individuals over against ecclesial structures. In a letter, written around 397 CE,

---

25   Paul. Nol. *Carmina* 14.44, 71–88.
26   Paul. Nol. *Carmina* 27.395–405.
27   Paul. Nol. *Carmina* 28.
28   Paul. Nol. *Epistulae* 17.2.
29   Paul. Nol. *Epistulae* 24.3.
30   *Apostolic Canons* 54 (*Apostolic Constitutions* 8.47.54).
31   *Breviarium Hipponense* 26.

consoling the Christian aristocrat Pammachius on the loss of his wife, Paulina, Jerome commends him for founding a *xenodochium* at Portus, comparing him to Abraham, who extended hospitality to his three angelic visitors.[32] In a letter eulogising Fabiola, a pious and wealthy Roman matron and penitent, Jerome adds she was Pammachius' partner in this venture and adds that the two (Pammachius and Fabiola) had started out by competing with one another in demonstrations of this particular type of charity but eventually joined forces so that harmony overcame rivalry and an even better outcome was achieved.[33] The resulting facility welcomed travellers on landing as well as those embarking to distant places. Jerome explains that Fabiola and Pammachius not only welcomed the destitute but also offered free lodging to those with some means.

Following the example of Fabiola and Pammachius, Jerome decided – along with Paula – to build a guesthouse (*diversorium*) for his Bethlehem monastery. Their motive, he says, was that if Joseph and Mary returned, the Holy Family would find a better welcome.[34] According to Jerome, when Paula first visited Jerusalem, she chose to stay in a humble cell in a Bethlehem hospice rather than in the grander lodgings of her family friend, the Proconsul of Palestine.[35] For her part, Melania the Elder (along with Rufinus) also established both a *xenodochium* and a monastery on the Mount of Olives, where they welcomed strangers (including monks, bishops, and other dignitaries) arriving to Jerusalem in fulfilment of a vow.[36]

Despite the generosity of the upper classes, the surge in the number of pilgrims in the fourth and early fifth century must have created a pressing need for church-sponsored housing as well as other kinds of arrangements. Other textual references to early Christian hostels are plentiful. The fourth-century Bordeaux pilgrim organised his itinerary according to the availability of both staging posts (*mutationes*) and inns (*mansiones*). The late sixth-century (ca. 570s CE) Piacenza pilgrim refers to *xenodochia* eight times. He describes the basilica of St. Mary in Jerusalem as having a large congregation of monks and guesthouses for men and women as well as a hospital with more than

---

32 Jer. *Ep.* 66.11. Dey 2008, 407, argues that the text of *Ep.* 66 does not suggest lodging was offered, but only food to unspecified recipients in the style of Abraham's hospitality (Gen. 18). This is hard to sustain on the basis of both of Jerome's letters, as well as his use of the word *xenodochium*, which clearly meant places for housing (not merely feeding) guests.

33 Jer. *Ep.* 77.10.

34 Jer. *Ep.* 66.14, 108.14 (*donec exstrueret cellulas, ac monasteria, et diversorium peregrinorum juxta viam conderet mansions, in qua Maria et Joseph hospitium no invenerant ...*).

35 Jer. Ep. 108.9.

36 Palladius, *Laus. Hist.* 46.6; 54.2. Also see Jer. *Ep.* 39.5.4–5. On the role of women as patrons of hostels see Whiting 2014, 73–83.

3000 beds and two inns for traellers at Surandala, on the road from Succoth to Migdol.[37]

This reference raises the question of whether pilgrims were often also invalids. In at least one instance the pilgrim explicitly says that those coming for healing (at the Baths of Elijah) were fed and lodged at public expense.[38] Thus, whatever they were called – *xenodochia*, *diversoria*, or *hospitia* – these guest houses seem to have been places that typically offered free accommodations to all kinds of travellers: from invalids seeking healing to able-bodied pilgrims, and perhaps even merchants and others. Moreover, lodgings appear to have been offered to poor and rich alike. Some were likely founded by wealthy individuals like Pammachius, Fabiola, Paula, and Melania, while others, like that established by Leporius, required donations from many members of a community.[39]

Although wealthy lay folk like Jerome and Melania could establish guesthouses or put up visiting dignitaries in their own villas, they also founded monasteries for housing more ordinary pilgrims. Over time, welcoming travellers seems to have become a special ministry of monasteries.[40] Egeria reports staying the night with some monks on Mt. Sinai and with a holy bishop in Arabia.[41] The Piacenza Pilgrim mentions two guesthouses at the large monastery of St. John by the Jordan and a great congregation of monks at Jerusalem's basilica of St. Mary with guesthouses for both men and women.[42] This might have presented problems for monks who preferred more seclusion and their hospitality must have been occasionally abused. Palladius noted that the monks at Nitria restricted their guests to a week's stay. If they wished to stay longer – even as much as two or three years – they would be put to work.[43] Local churches also appear to have had problems with boorish guests. One of the canons from

---

37   Piacenza Pilgrim: *It. Ant. Plac.* 23, 41.

38   Piacenza Pilgrim: *It. Ant. Plac.* 7 (baths of Elijah for lepers, meals at public expense), 9, 12, 13, 23, 35, 41 (two references). The Council of Chalcedon, *Canons* 10, seems to suggest that churches had a variety of dependencies: martyria (*martyria*), almshouses (*ptochia*), and hostels (*xenodochia*).

39   Noted above, August. *Serm.* 356.10; see also Constable 2003, 11–13, 17.

40   For Rome in the early Middle Ages, see Dey 2008, who argues that the term *xenodochium* specifically referred to a charitable institution – feeding and housing the poor and sick but not actually poor pilgrims – by the eighth or ninth century. He also maintains that the word for pilgrimage inns is more commonly "*hospitalis*" and quotes Leo III (795–816) in support.

41   Egeria, *Itinerarium pereginatio* 3.1; 9.1.

42   Piacenza Pilgrim: *It. Ant. Plac.* 12, 23: *xenodochia virorum ac mulierum susceptio peregrinorum mensas innumerabiles.*

43   Palladius, *Laus. Hist.* 7. Evidence for a guesthouse as well as stables and a chapel has been found at the sixth-century monastery in Ma'aleh Adummim, east of Jerusalem. See Tsafrir 1989, 1753 – cited by Dietz 2005, 148–9.

the council of Nîmes (394/6) sought to curb those who took advantage of free housing by presenting themselves as pilgrims.[44]

The Piacenza pilgrim also refers to sites with nothing more than a church and a couple of inns (presumably run by secular proprietors).[45] Even where large monastic establishments existed, space must have been at a premium at certain times of the year, and some of the masses of pilgrims that would have arrived at places like Jerusalem during Holy Week must have had to find other accommodations.[46] This might have included sleeping in tents, or even in the open air. Additionally, shrines in inhabited towns and villages would have relied on the local residents to supply food for meals, not to mention other basic services for road-weary travellers: caring for their animals, organising tour guides, staffing the bath facilities, renewing essential supplies, or laundering and repairing their garments. While each site could have been like an operating campground, caring for the needs of the visitors would have generated a significant tourist industry.

3   Archaeological Evidence for Pilgrims' Guesthouses

This kind of base camp is known in various places in the early Christian world. One such well-known pilgrimage staging area is Deir Sem'an (ancient Telanissos – Fig. 6.1). This small town was also the site of the Simeon Stylites' monastery. Once his column became a major pilgrim attraction, the village of Deir Sem'an, which lay at the beginning of the *via sacra* that led up to the main shrine of Qal'at Sem'an, experienced an economic boom. Based on surviving inscriptions, Deir Sem'an had at least two large lodging houses (*pandocheia*), built in the late 470s CE, and were probably operated by one or more of three monasteries. Archaeological remains reveal that both were long, rectangular structures. One was considerably larger than the other, and had two (or possibly three) stories and was able to accommodate a fairly large number of guests. It had exterior porticoes and a large central, interior room. The smaller *pandocheion* was possibly a place for where wealthier clients and their extended parties could occupy the entire space, thus not having to mingle with

---

44   Council of Nîmes, *Canons* 5, text in SC 241, 128: *Additum aetiam est, ut, quia multi, sub specie peregrinationis, de ecclesiarum conlatione luxuriant, victura (victuaria) non omnibus detur (dentur); unusquisque voluntarium, non indictum habeat de hac praestatione judicium.*

45   Piacenza Pilgrim: *It. Ant. Plac.* 41, and see 13 – an inn in the house of Rahab.

46   By the sixth century *xenodochia* were attached to most of the major pilgrimage sites in Jerusalem, see Hunt 1984, 64, fn. 66.

FIGURE 6.1   Pandocheion, Deir Sem'an
               PHOTO: TROELS MYRUP KRISTENSEN

less affluent travellers. Each building's ground floor also appears to have had stables for the guests' horses.[47]

Constable comments upon other guesthouses nearby, one at Kafr Nabū, built at the beginning of the sixth century, which, she suggests, may have been patronised by travellers *en route* to Deir Sem'an. The bishop of Constantina in the northern Syrian province of Osrhoene founded another.[48] Although Constable notes the difficulties inherent in definitely identifying various building as inns and not simply large private houses, she cites the existence of several stories, numerous rooms, external porticoes, multiple doors and windows, and stables with many feeding troughs as features that archaeologists have used to label them as such.

Similar facilities were constructed at the shrine of St. Menas (Abu Mena), a day's journey into the Mar'yut desert, about forty-five kilometres west of Alexandria. Although a pilgrimage centre from at least the mid-fourth century, the site was greatly expanded in the fifth and sixth centuries, largely under imperial patronage. In addition to an elaborate basilica, baptistery, and martyr church, were rooms for sleeping, baths, kitchens, bakeries, libraries, a refectory,

---

47   See Constable 2003, 30 citing Butler 1920, Vol. 2, Sec. B, 268–78. Also see Strube 1996, 59, 69, 73.
48   Constable 2003, 31.

and stables for the guests' animals. A place also renowned for miraculous healings, it included an area for incubation. The large influx of travellers prompted the building of a small village near the site, consisting of local workers who served their needs.[49]

The churches and the baptistery are situated on the south side of the complex, while rather grand *xenodochia* were constructed to the northwest, directly off the main courtyard of the complex. Additional, more humble guest quarters were built a bit further to the north. Like the hostels in Deir Sem'an, those at Abu Mena featured small rooms arranged around a large inner courtyard. They were of two kinds, however, as the less grand lodging was constructed with a single story rather than two or three and had only a few large rooms that faced into one or two peristyle courts and outward from exceptionally wide porticoes. According to Peter Grossmann, this may have been a *xenodochium* intended for more humble guests who may have shared a room or possibly bedded down in the porticoes. He adds that one of the two peristyles may have been reserved for men, the other for women and children.[50]

Only traces of other evidence for early western, non-Roman *xenodochia* exist apart from Pammachius' and Fabiola's facility in Portus, Paulinus's at Nola, or Augustine's reference to the *xenodochium* established by Leporius. Moreover, very little actual archaeological evidence has come to light that could give us a clear picture of how they might have been constructed or where they were precisely situated *vis a vis* the church or shrine. Some scholars, however, have identified a late fourth- or early fifth-century structure at the African site of Theveste as a guesthouse for visitors to the shrine of St. Crispina.

The ancient city of Theveste (modern Tébessa) lies in the Merdja plain in the southern part of the Roman province of Africa Proconsularis, a part of Numidia until Diocletian incorporated it into the Proconsular province. Advantageously situated, it was connected to Carthage by a highway built during the reign of Hadrian (c. 123 CE) and was a prosperous urban hub for the grain and olive trade. It became a temporary headquarters of the Third Augustan Legion, probably under Vespasian. Trajan settled a colony of veterans there, but the garrison was moved to Lambaesis in two stages, the first under Titus, and then at the start of Trajan's reign.[51]

Theveste's most remarkable landmark is its enormous and elaborate pilgrimage complex (Fig. 6.2). Perhaps a convincing demonstration that characteristically Christian civic munificence focused on building churches, shrines, and hostels rather than theatres and temples, this complex was being

---

49   Grossmann 2015, 281–302.
50   *Ibid.* 287.
51   Lepelley 1977, 186–8.

FIGURE 6.2   Theveste/Tébessa. Overview of pilgrimage basilica dedicated to St. Crispina
                PHOTO: ROBIN M. JENSEN

constructed around the same time as other town leaders were donating funds
to repair their amphitheatre.[52] The existence of this monumental structure,
erected simultaneously with expansion and renovation of other public buildings suggests not only a significant number of wealthy townsfolk, but also busy
and prosperous construction trades.

Although no inscriptions specifically name her, the pilgrimage site now
usually is identified as a shrine to St. Crispina, a Roman matron from nearby
Taoura (modern Thagura), who was martyred in Theveste around the year 304,
during the Diocletianic persecution. According to the *Passio Sanctae Crispina*,
she repeatedly refused to sacrifice to the Roman gods and so was beheaded.
The text makes a brief mention of some companions who died with her but
does not name them.[53] Her widespread fame is evident from the fact that
Augustine mentioned her in several sermons, once as an instance of a married
woman achieving sainthood and at least twice on her feast day (December 5).[54]

----

52   *Ibid.*; see also Brown 2012, 335.
53   *Actae Sanctae Crispinae*, trans. Musurillo 1972, 302–309.
54   August. *Serm.* 286.2; 354.4; and *Enarrationes in Psalmos* 120.13, 15; 137. 3, 14, 17. Also *Serm.*
        Morin 2 (313G), 2.

The site was first excavated in the 1850s, and originally presumed to be a large monastic establishment. However, its most thorough, modern investigator, Jürgen Christern, persuasively identified it as a pilgrimage centre, built over a twenty-five year period in the late fourth century.[55] Located in a cemetery area about 600 yards northeast of the modern city on the road to Ammaedara (Haidra), Christern concluded that a small shrine was initially constructed over the site of Crispina's martyrdom and which housed a reliquary urn and a sarcophagus. A decade or so later, a certain deacon, Novellus, added a mosaic pavement recording the names of seven other martyrs. Gradually this was surrounded by additional burials *ad sanctos*.[56] The reliquary, containing bits of bone and teeth that plausibly were Crispina's, apparently prompted the construction of the enormous basilica in the latter part of the century.[57]

One of the features that the Theveste pilgrimage shrine appears to share with sites like Deir Sem'an or the martyrium of Abu Mena is its lodgings for pilgrims. This site has a large structure that Christern and others believe was used as an inn as well as stables for travellers' horses. Hitching posts and feeding troughs (or possibly troughs for distribution of other goods) have been identified, adjacent to and below what are presumed to have been guest rooms (Fig. 6.3).[58] Dining facilities could have been situated within this space, or across the way in another large structure. Assuming the hostel had as many as fifty rooms, it could have held between 100 and 150 guests.

In addition to this simple dormitory, along the exterior wall of the basilica were twenty-four cell-like chambers. Each had a locking door. Although these may have been monks' quarters, they also may have served as storage rooms or special quarters reserved for privileged dignitaries.[59] Even if all available rooms were used for housing visitors to the shrine (and they slept three or four to a room), the total number of guests could not have been much more than 250 or so. At peak season or at the feast of St. Crispina, others must have had to camp within the enclosure walls or find accommodations elsewhere in the city.

---

55 Christern 1976. Christern dates the building campaign of the basilica and trefoil martyrium to c. 400 (between 395–420).

56 A number of epitaphs of clergy at the site appear to date to the mid fourth century.

57 Christern 1976, 112. The basilica was set up on a podium and approached by a flight of thirteen steps. Its *quadratum populi* was 720 square metres, thus potentially accommodating as many as 2,000 congregants. Archaeologists believe the large rectangular lower area featured four large pools of water separated by walkways.

58 *Ibid.* 90, 303. A smaller stable appears to be across the central passage. Some archaeologists have expressed doubts about these supposed stables, noting that the holes identified for reins appear to date from a much later time.

59 *Ibid.* 85–90.

FIGURE 6.3   Theveste/Tébessa. Possible stables and guest chambers (as interpreted by
Christern)
PHOTO: ROBIN M. JENSEN

Compared especially with Egypt and Syria, the western African provinces were not home to many large or geographically extensive monasteries, it therefore seems likely that Theveste's facilities were, like the foundations in Hippo, constructed with significant donations of money from wealthy citizens (clergy and lay) and a great deal of local labour. At the same time, the influx of pilgrims would have contributed significantly to the local economy, buying provisions for themselves and their mounts. Those who could not secure lodgings within the complex itself would have had to find rooms elsewhere in the city.

4   Xenodochia in the Later Fifth Century and Beyond

Pilgrimage centres in Africa were significantly expanded after the Byzantine reconquest in the 530s CE. This is particularly true of the extramural churches of Carthage, which were greatly expanded during the sixth century. Among these are the basilica complexes today known as Damous el Karita and Bir Ftouha which were significantly rebuilt with dramatic features like a subterranean rotunda (Damous el Karita) or an immense baptistery with a cruciform font

(Bir Ftouha).[60] The intramural Vandal-era basilica of Bir Messaouda was also reoriented during this period and extended by transforming the original nave into a broad transept and the addition of two flanking structures: a subterranean martyr crypt and a baptistery.[61] Although all three of these structures were clearly designed to attract and facilitate pilgrims' visits, none of them apparently included any obvious provision for housing pilgrims. According to Susan Stevens, writing about Bir Ftouha, travellers might have been lodged in a nearby set of structures that may have been an earlier, small basilica or shrine complex. She notes that this area continued to have some residential use through the early Middle Ages and, as such, has some parallels to Abu Mena, which similarly featured a medieval settlement into the 11th century.[62] By contrast to the pilgrimage centres in Carthage, lodgings for pilgrims were mentioned in a papyrus fragment found at the desert city of Nessana in Palaestina Tertia. Dated to the late Byzantine era, it bore the name 'The House of Abu Joseph, Son of Douhahos' and is described as having two storeys that accommodated ninety-six bedmats and a walled yard to stable animals.[63]

The most useful evidence for later western *xenodochia* comes from Rome. Rome, more than any other western city, was a major pilgrimage destination from the fourth century onwards. Constantine's basilicas, built over pre-existing shrines for Peter and Paul, were a contributing factor, as well as Pope Damasus' efforts to make the tombs of saints in the catacombs more accessible and attractive. To the extent that can it be known, it seems that Rome's Christian aristocracts (rather than monastic communities) were – as elsewhere – the primary benefactors of guest houses, both in their founding and maintenance over time. Gregory the Great mentions houses funded prior to the Gothic sack by two Roman noble families, the *xenodochium Anichoriorum* (from the gens Anicia), likely located on the Campus Martius and the *xenodochium a Valeris* (of the gens Valeria), which is more difficult to locate. Both of these facilities probably were constructed in the late fourth or early fifth century.[64]

Patronage also began to shift during the later fifth century. Surviving written sources indicate that by that time, Rome's guesthouses, like those at Nola or Hippo Regius, had begun to be established by the bishop. The *Liber Pontificalis* reports that Pope Symmachus (498–514 CE) established three houses for the

---

60   On these two basilicas see Stevens *et al.* 2005; Dolenz – Baldus 2001.
61   See Miles – Greenslade 2018.
62   Stevens *et al.* 2005, 571.
63   Kraemer 1958, 27, mentioned in Wilkinson 2002, 32.
64   Discussed by Santangeli Valenzani 2014, 69–88, esp. 71. Also Santangeli Valenzani 1996–
      1997, 203–26.

poor in Rome: at the basilicas of St. Peter, St. Paul, and St. Lawrence.[65] While they were expressly designated as poorhouses, their situation, immediately adjacent to three great pilgrimage churches suggests that one of their primary functions was to shelter and feed paying guests. One exception to this developing role for papal patronage was the richly endowed hospice on the Via Lata founded by the Byzantine general Belasarius, who likely used funds from his successful campaigns to recover southern Italy for Justinian.[66] By the end of the eighth century, almost two dozen of these facilities existed in Rome, most of them established and managed by the reigning bishop, who would appoint supervisors to oversee them.[67]

As Debra Birch has acknowledged, it is difficult to distinguish from textual sources alone whether there was a difference between guesthouses for pilgrims or hospitals that took in and cared for the sick.[68] Already by the fourth century, the Cappadocian bishop and monastic founder Basil of Caesarea had made the care of the sick part of his monks' vocation.[69] The monks at the shrine of Abu Mena also must have cared for the sick who came to that place specifically for healing. It appears that, by the early sixth century, buildings perhaps originally built as inns for pilgrims or even ordinary travellers had begun to be more identified as places that took in and cared for the sick, the poor, orphans or the elderly. This transition from inn to infirmary may have been due in part to monastic communities' performance of charitable works but could also have been by caused the simple fact that many pilgrims would have been invalids seeking cures, making the distinction between a guesthouse and a hospital somewhat blurred in any case. Birch calls attention to the *Liber Diurnus*, an anonymous collection of standard epistolary formulae drawn up by the papal chancery in the late seventh- or early eighth century. Among its entries are the duties of the manager of a *xenodochium*, which included being prepared to take in and care for the sick and the impoverished, to provide medical care, and to call in doctors if necessary.[70] Thus, the guests at one of these guest houses could vary between the destitute, the sick, foreigners, and pilgrims.

Hendrik Dey argues that the church became the primary provider of care for the needy in the course of the fifth and sixth centuries, primarily due to the disappearance of the traditional forms of civic charity, including (but not

---

65   *Liber Pontificalis* 1.263 (Pope Symmachus). The text reads, *pauperibus habitacula construxit*.
66   *Liber Pontificalis* 1.296 (Pope Vigilius), discussed in Santangeli Valenzani 2014, 74.
67   See *Liber Pontificalis* (Leo III, Gregory III, Stephen II, Hadrian I).
68   Birch 1998, 126–7.
69   Greg. Naz. Epist. *Or.* 43.63.
70   Birch 1998, 127. See also Dey 2008, 405–6.

limited to) the *annona*, which distributed food to all citizens and not only to the poor.[71] He points out, however, that while Roman documents typically call establishments meant to serve the poor, *diaconiae* rather than *xenodochia*, and that these two terms typically mean different things through the eighth century, the distinctions are not so clear in practice and that both terms could refer to charitable institutions.[72] What does seem to emerge by the ninth century is the term, *hospitale*, primarily to designate a place that housed foreigners and perhaps also the poor.[73] Thus, a word that in English has mainly come to mean a place that cares for the sick, originally designated a place for housing the stranger.

In conclusion, it is important to consider the impact of large pilgrimage attractions on the local economy generally, although short of additional documentary evidence, we can only surmise that residents of cities that hosted them, like Rome, Jerusalem, Deir Sem'an, Theveste, or Hippo, must have developed a service industry to care for travellers. It further seems likely that some of these shrines were specifically constructed in order to draw these visitors and the revenue they provided to those residents, not to mention those engaged in building and maintaining the buildings and grounds. It even may be that these were consciously developed in competition with other centres. For example, the Theveste shrine may have rivalled the Donatist centre (and pilgrimage site) at Timgad.[74] Augustine may have been eager to establish a major attraction in his St. Stephen memorial at Hippo as a response to Donatist claims for the particular patronage of native, African, martyrs, by promoting the universal proto-martyr as more powerful than a local saint. And a good guesthouse to go along with a newly constructed martyrium would have aided his effort.

Bibliography

Birch, D.J. 1998. *Pilgrimage to Rome in the Middle Ages: Continuity and Change*, Woodbridge.

Bitton-Ashkelony, B. 2005. *Encountering the Sacred: The Debate on Christian Pilgrimage in Late Antiquity*, Berkeley, CA.

Brown, P.L. 2012. *Through the Eye of the Needle*, Princeton, NJ.

---

71 Dey 2008, 399–400.
72 *Ibid.* 404–5.
73 *Ibid.* 408.
74 Suggested by Frend 1996, 364.

Burns, J.P. and Jensen, R.M. 2014. *Christianity in Roman Africa: The Development of Its Practices and Beliefs*, Grand Rapids.

Butler, H.C. 1920. *Early Churches in Syria*. Vol. 2, Sec. B, *Architecture, Northern Syria*, Leiden.

Casson, L. 1994. *Travel in the Ancient World*, Baltimore.

Christern, J. 1976. *Das frühchristliche Pilgerheiligtum von Tebessa*, Wiesbaden.

Constable, O.R. 2003. *Housing the Stranger in the Mediterranean World: Lodging, Trade, and Travel in Late Antiquity and the Middle Ages*, Cambridge.

Dey, H. 2008. "*Diaconiae, Xenodochia, Hospitalia* and Monasteries: 'Social Security' and the Meaning of Monasticism in Early Medieval Rome", *Early Medieval Europe* 16.4, 398–422.

Dietz, M. 2005. *Wandering Monks, Virgins, and Pilgrims: Ascetic Travel in the Mediterranean World, A.D. 300–800*, University Park, PA.

Dolenz, H. and Baldus, H. 2001. *Damous-el Karita: Die österreichisch-tunesischen Ausgrabungen der Jahre 1990 und 1997 im Saalbau und der Memoria des pilgerheiligtums Damous-el-Karita in Karthago*, Vienna.

Frend, W. 1996. *The Archaeology of Early Christianity: A History*, Minneapolis.

Grossmann, P. 2015. "The Pilgrimage Center of Abû Mînâ", in *Pilgrimage and Holy Space in Late Antique Egypt*, ed. D. Frankfurter, Leiden, 281–302.

Hunt, E.D. 1984. *Holy Land Pilgrimage in the Later Roman Empire AD 312–420*, Oxford.

Kraemer, C.J. 1958. *Excavations at Nessana, vol. 3 (Non-Literary Papyri)*, Princeton, NJ.

Lepelley, C. 1977. *Les Cites de l'Afrique romaine au Bas-Empire, etude d'histoire municipal 2*. Turnhout.

Limberis, V. 2011. *Architects of Piety: The Cappadocian Fathers and the Cult of the Martyrs*, Oxford.

Miles, R. and Greenslade, S. 2018. *The Bir Messaouda Bailica: Pilgrimage and the Transformation of an Urban Landscape in Sixth Century AD Carthage*, London.

Moore, W. and Wilson, H.A. trans. 1893. *Gregory of Nyssa: Dogmatic Treatises, etc., Nicene and Post-Nicene Fathers of the Christian Church 2, 5*, ed. P. Schaff, Edinburgh.

Musurillo, H. trans. 1972. *The Acts of the Christian Martyrs*, Oxford.

Santangeli Valenzani, R. 1996–1997. "Pellegrini, senatori e papi: gli xenodochia a Roma tra il V e il IX secolo", *Rivista dell'Istituto nazionale di archeologia e storia dell'arte* 3rd ser. 19–20, 203–26.

Santangeli Valenzani, R. 2014. "Hosting Foreigners in Early Medieval Rome: from *xenodochia* to *scholae peregrinorum*", in *England and Rome in the Early Middle Ages*, ed. F. Tinti, Turnhout, 69–88.

Stevens, S. *et al.* 2005. *Bir Ftouha: A Pilgrimage Church Complex at Carthage*, Portsmouth, RI.

Strube, C. 1996. *Die "Toten Städte", Stadt und Land in nordsyrien während der Spätantike*, Mainz.

Tsafrir, Y. 1989. "Christian Archaeology in Israel in Recent Years," in *Actes du XIe congress international d'archéologie chrétienne. Lyon, Vienne, Grenoble, Genève, Aoste (21–28) September 1986*, Rome, 1737–70.

Whiting, M. 2014. "Asceticism and Hospitality as Patronage in the Late Antique Holy Land: The Examples of Paula and Melania the Elder," in *Female Founders in Byzantium and Beyond*, eds. L. Theis, M. Mullett, and M. Grünbart, Vienna, 73–83.

Wilkinson, J. 2002. *Jerusalem Pilgrims Before the Crusades*, Oxford.

PART 3

Transactions

∴

CHAPTER 7

The Monetisation of Sacrifice

F. S. Naiden

This paper asks how Greek worshippers, especially pilgrims, experienced two common but overlooked types of sacrificial offerings. The first is an offering or first fruits presented either by the worshipper or on his behalf and then promptly consumed or eliminated. Unlike most offerings, however, it is purchased, sold, or accompanied by payment of a fee; in effect, it is a commodity. The second type requires the expenditure of money, too, but not a purchase or a fee. Instead, the worshipper provides a fund for offerings, dedications, and shrine repairs. In effect, the offering has been commuted. As the term 'first fruits' implies, these offerings may be either animal or vegetal.

In regard to both commodities and funds this paper asks the elementary question of what the worshipper did and how he understood it. To answer the first question, several examples of types of offering appear. To answer the second question, more examples appear, but these additional examples all involve words designating commutation, especially *pelanos, aparchē*, and *dermatikon*. Long familiar to scholars of shrine finance and to those interested in the origin of coinage, beginning with Georg Simmel and Bernhard Laum, these words are important for this paper as evidence for the phenomenology of Greek sacrificial practice.[1]

The worshipper's money, and his experiences with his money, are a neglected subject in the much traversed field of sacrifice. The leading recent writers on sacrifice, Walter Burkert, Jean-Pierre Vernant, and Marcel Detienne, concern themselves only with offerings that were not purchased or accompanied by a fee, in other words, only with offerings *en nature*, and they also avoid the subject of commutation. Purchases, fees, and commutation are topics left to numismatists and economic historians, among whom only Sitta von Reden has written as much as a chapter about Greek religious attitudes towards money. She thinks that spending money on sacrifice and other religious practices was 'problematic' because a tyrant's or a foreigner's or a criminal's money might be as good as the money of people in high standing.[2] Richard Seaford

---

1   Simmel 1978; Laum 1924; further bibliography: Parise 1984.
2   Money as an 'ideology': von Reden 1997, 176, following Kurke 1995. The chapter: 2010, 156–86. At 2010, 160–61 von Reden briefly notices the 'cross-over' between payments in cash and offerings in kind.

studied money as an expression of an ideology, but only by way of giving a new explanation for the origin of coinage.[3] Outside Classics, only a few scholars have written about religious ritual and commodities. Within Classics, the most useful short notice on sacrificial commodities and commutation remains that of Martin Nilsson in *GGR*.[4]

1   Types of Offerings

Greek sacred calendars contain hundreds of prices to be paid for victims. In cities, butchers bought victims for their patrons, as shown by Menander and Plautus. (The *polis* used official cattle-buyers, the *Boōnai*.[5]) Yet buying also went on in the countryside amongst the poor. A provision in a fourth-century cult calendar from the little town of Thebes at the foot of Mount Mykale reveals this feature of country life. The regulation tells shepherds to:

> Bring to Hermes the *koureion* of wool suitable for sacrifice. Each shepherd shall draw on his own herd. It is not permissible for him to buy the *koureion*.[6]

As Jacques Labarbe explained, the *koureion* was an offering made at the season of wool-shearing. Shepherds had been buying the wool, or the shrine issuing this regulation feared they might, and so the shrine forbade these purchases. The regulation says that the shepherds must make several offerings in kind, but they are not so poor or so isolated that they cannot spend money on religion.

First fruits were sold rather than bought; a rural example appears in Xenophon's *Anabasis*. The narrator says that he has established a rural shrine to Artemis, and he announces the following rule:

---

3   Seaford 2004, esp. 48–68, 102–25.
4   The general issue: Appadurai 1986, esp. 3–64, and van Binsbergen – Geschiere 2005, esp. 319–368. Nilsson: *GGR* 1.76 with refs.
5   Butchers: Men. *Dys.* 393, Plaut. *Aul.* 280–1. Calendars: Erchia (*LSCG* 18), Marathon *tetrapolis* (*LSCG* 20a), Marathon deme (*LSCG* 20b), Salaminioi (*LSCG Supp.* 19).
6   *I Priene* 216.12–5 = *LSAM* 39.12–5:

     φέρειν δὲ
κούρειον τῶι Ἑρμῆι ἔριφον θύσιμον
ἀπ᾽ ἑκάστου αἰπολίου ἐκ τοῦ ἑαυτοῦ,
πριάμενον δὲ μὴ ἐξεῖναι,

     κούρειον: Labarbe 1953, 366–7.

> Let the person holding and receiving the tithe from shrine lands use it to make a sacrifice every year and let him maintain the temple using any remaining income.[7]

Although part of the tithe was used to make sacrifices *en nature*, part was sold to realise 'the remaining income'. Although Xenophon does not use the most common Greek word for first fruits, *aparchai*, the word he uses instead, *dekatē*, is synonymous. Xenophon's shrine, a miniature version of the shrine of Ephesian Artemis located near Olympia, was no ordinary affair. His financial arrangements, though, were unproblematic. Some 500 years later, a shrine founder in Ithaca copied them word for word.[8]

Farmers sometimes sold tithes or other *aparchai* to buy dedications. In the early fifth century, a woman named Philea, in charge of produce from a farm probably in the deme of Athmon, set up a marble pillar on the Athenian acropolis:

> Philea, the daughter of Chaerodemus of Athmon, dedicated to Athena a tithe of the produce of the land.[9]

In all likelihood, Philea spent part of the tithe on the pillar. Comparable to a farmer's selling a tithe of produce for the purpose of making a dedication was a fisherman's selling a tithe of his catch to commission a statue, as in this Attic inscription of the same date:

7 Xen. *An.* 5.3.13. 'Use it to make a sacrifice': Casabona 1966, 99–100.
8 *IG* ix.1 654 = *LSCG* 86:
  ἱερὸς ὁ χῶρος τῆς
  Ἀρτέμιδος. τὸν ἔ-
  χοντα καὶ καρπού-
  μενο[ν] τὴν μὲν δε-
  κάτην καταθύειν ἑ-
  κάστου ἔτους, ἐκ δὲ τοῦ-
  περιττοῦ τὸν ναὸν ἐ-
  πισκευά[ζ]ειν·
  Sokolowski with refs. canvassed the possibility there was no shrine founded, but only a copy made by an admirer of Xenophon.
9 *IG* i³ 800 = *DAA* 191:
  τἀθηναίαι
  δεκάτην
  χοριόω
  Ἀθμονόθεν
  Χαιρεδέμο Φιλέα.
  Χαιρεδέμο<ς>: Kirchner, positing two dedicators.

Naulochus dedicated this *korē* as an *aparchē* of the catch provided to him by the lord of the sea with the golden trident.[10]

Groups of fishermen would cooperate in making bigger dedications, such as the bronze bulls dedicated by Korkyran fishermen as a tithe for their catch of tuna.

Whether fish or produce, first fruits sold for dedications resembled other *aparchai* that were sold for this purpose. These *aparchai* ranged from military plunder to craftsmen's wares and authors' writings.[11] Selling first fruits in the same way as these varied items had the effect of commercialising or secularising first fruits. Yet there was a subtle difference between most sales and selling a tithe. Most sales were final. Selling a tithe did not put an end to the worshipper's obligation to his god, and so one sale implied another.

Just as offerings could be bought, and first fruits could be sold, leftovers could be sold, for example, fleeces. After Posidonios of Halikarnassos obtained an oracle about honouring several gods, he gave the following instructions to local officials called *epimēnioi*:

> After the *epimēnioi* put aside enough meat for the diners and their wives, they should cut the rest of the meat into equal pieces and assign one piece to each person present or absent, keep the heads and feet for themselves, and sell the fleeces among the *thiasos* and on the next day give an account before the assembly....[12]

---

10   *IG* i³ 828 = *DAA* 229:
    [τέ]νδε κόρεν ἀ[ν]έθεκεν ἀπαρχὲν
    [Ναύ(?)]λοχος ἄγρας : / ἓν οἱ ποντομέδ-
    [ον χρ]υσοτρία[ι]ν' ἔπορεν.
    ['Ισό] : Hoffmann.
    Korkyran bronze bulls: Paus. 5.27.9, 10.9.3–4. Other *aparchai en nature* : *SEG* 53.630a. 15–16.
11   Jim 2015, 130–203, a survey updating Rouse 1902, 39–95.
12   *I Halikarnassos* 188.45.40–6 = *LSAM* 72.40–6:
    τὰ δὲ λοιπὰ κρέα οἱ
    ἐπιμήνιοι, ἀφελόντες ἱκανὰ τοῖς δειπνοῦσιν καὶ
    γυναιξίν, μερίδας ποησάντωσαν ἴσας καὶ ἀποδόντω-
    σαν ἑκάστωι μερίδα τῶν τε παρόντων καὶ τῶν ἀπόντων,
    τὰς δὲ κεφαλὰς καὶ τοὺς πόδας αὐτοὶ ἐχόντων, τὰ δὲ
    κώιδια πωλούντων ἐν τῶι θιάσωι καὶ τῆι δευτέραι
    λόγον ἀπο<δ>όντωσαν πρὸ τοῦ δήμου....
    Fleeces reserved for a priest, and thus not immediately monetised: *Priene* 116.6.

The fleeces mentioned in this third-century inscription perhaps were sold at a local butchers' market such as are attested for Athens, Corinth, and Alexandria.[13]

Many regulations refer to sacrificial fees; often the fees are higher for the sacrifice of large animals. A list of fees that were to be paid into collection boxes appears in Gabriele Kaminski study of *thēsauroi*. For example, a worshipper in the Asklepieion in Pergamon in the second century CE would make preliminary offerings and then:

> Must sacrifice a suckling pig on the altar of the Asklepieion and put the right leg and the *splanchna* on a table. He must put three obols in the collection box and in the evening set up three breads in the shape of navels, two on the outside altar to Tyche and Mnemosyne.[14]

This fee allowed the worshipper to incubate as well as sacrifice. If there was no collection box, as was true at some shrines without temples or other buildings, the worshipper could throw his fee into a spring, where a nymph would receive it and then let priests surreptitiously collect it.[15]

Fees are sometimes harder to identify than purchases or sales. In these difficult instances, the context is so sparse we cannot tell whether a payment is a fee or some other expense. If the *polis* imposed and received the fee, it may be regarded as a tax; if the priest of the shrine received it, it may be regarded as an emolument. Another difficulty is that the words *aparchē* and *pelanos* sometimes mean 'fee' rather than 'offering'. Often it is clear which it is, but not always. In some cases, the worshipper pays a fee to participate in a ritual such as initiation. These rituals are not examples of sacrifice, but they include sacrifices, and so the ritual and sacrifice overlap.[16]

---

13 Meat markets in these cities: Naiden 2013, 247 with n. 82.
14 *IvP* III 161a.6–10:
   ταῦτα δὲ ποήσας θυέτω χοῖρον γαλαθηνὸν ν
   [τῶι Ἀσκλ]ηπιῶι ἐπὶ τοῦ βωμοῦ καὶ τραπεζούσθω σκέλος δεξ[ι]-
   [ὸν καὶ σπ]λάγχνα. ἐμβαλλέτω δὲ εἰς τὸν θησαυρὸν ὀβολοὺς τρεῖ[ς].
   [εἰς δὲ τὴ]ν ἑσπέραν ἐπιβαλλέ[σ]θω πόπανα τρία ἐννεόμφαλα,
   [τούτων μὲ]ν δύο ἐπὶ τὴν ἔξω θυμέλην Τύχηι καὶ Μνημοσύνηι,
   As Habicht ad loc. says, it is not clear whether the three obols cover all the sacrificial costs involved.
15 Paus. 1.34.4 (Oropus).
16 *Aparchai* that are fees or taxes: *LSCG* 88, *LSCG Supp.* 72, *SEG* 50.766.10–13. Fee: Pafford 2006, 44. Tax: Sokolowski 1954, 163. Conceding that fees were sometimes charged, Sokolowski held they were temporary. *Pelanos* as a fee: *IG* xii 7.237 (Amorgos). *SEG* 11.33.11–2 (Argos) lacks the context needed to explain the *pelanos* indicated on the base for this dedication.

This evidence for fees, and for sacrificial sales and purchases – in a word, for commodities – has come from various places in the Classical and Hellenistic periods. Most of it concerns individual worshippers. Over the course of some three centuries, these individuals experienced a partial redefinition of the rite of animal and vegetal sacrifice. Never monetised in Homer, this rite had now been monetised to some degree. How did this change affect the sacrificial norms familiar to us from the work of Burkert and of Vernant and Detienne? In my book on sacrifice, I quoted the following passages describing these norms, and I now revisit them. First, Burkert:

> The peculiar form of Greek sacrificial ritual [is that]… together on the same level, men and women stand about the altar, experience and bring death, honor the immortals, and in eating affirm life in its conditionality: it is the solidarity of mortals in the face of immortals.

Next, Detienne:

> The ritual marks equality before the meat.[17]

How well do these norms mix with commodities, fees, and collection boxes? Is a religious commodity a problematic manifestation of an ideology, as with van Reden and Seaford?

Some of the norms in Burkert and Detienne mix well with the business of commodities and collection boxes. Fees do not change what happens after they are paid, and the gods do not object to receiving money. Some do not mix well. Spending money does not put worshippers around the altar, 'experiencing death'. Instead it puts them around the collection box, dropping coins, or in the marketplace, bargaining. The marketplace makes people with spending money equal in a way, but it does not make them 'equal before the meat', and it does not make them identical. They 'stand together', but not in a spirit of 'solidarity'. Spending money is mundane, not problematic, a convenience and not a manifestation of some large scheme of thought such as an ideology.

Initiation fees: *IG* i³ 6, which is so fragmentary that sacrifices as part of initiation cannot be pinpointed. Marriage fee: SEG 11.482 (an *aparchē* for the *thēsauros* of Aphrodite). The sacrifice that might be provided by paying the fee: Hesych. s.v. προτέλεια.

17   Burkert 1985, 58; Vernant – Detienne 1989, 13. A longer statement of this view: Zaidman – Schmitt Pantel 1992, 49–52 (*isonomia*), 76–90 (citizenship), 131–47 (festivals).

2   Commuting Offerings and Establishing Sacred Funds

After this short survey of sacred commodities come the topics of commuting offerings and establishing sacred funds. For these topics, the main collective worshipper, the *polis*, is more important than before, and the worshipper's situation is more complicated. Before, he either made a sacrifice *en nature*, or he bought or sold offerings, or paid a fee. Now he has three choices – *en nature*, purchase or the like, or commutation and contribution to a fund.

First, a simple example. The second-century regulation from Pergamon that provides for a collection box for fees also provides for offerings of the third kind, funds established by commutation. The relevant words are:

Let them put *ta iatra* in the collection box [using] Phokian coins.[18]

Ta iatra were thank offerings made *en nature* to Asclepius. Now worshippers make them in the form of money. Similarly, the portion of a sacrifice given to a priest could be commuted, and then was called *apometra*. There are several more or less secure examples.[19]

Now a complex example from Kos, where sacrifices made by some seamen were commuted at some point late in the second century BCE. At the start of the century, the *polis* required shipmasters to make sacrifices. A resolution of 196–5 BCE says,

Likewise let merchants and shipmasters who set sail from the polis accomplish sacrifices and if they don't sacrifice as provided in writing, let them be punished and owe a fine of ten drachmas to the priestess. She has the right to act against them as provided by law.[20]

---

18   *IvP* III 161a.31–2:

ἐμβαλέτωσαν δὲ ν?
[εἰς τὸν θησ]αυρὸν τοῦ Ἀσκληπιοῦ τὰ ἴατρα Φωκαῖδα τῶι Ἀπό[λ]-
[λωνι καὶ Φ]ωκαῖδα τῶι Ἀσκληπιῶι...

Gold instead of first fruits at Delos: Str. 6.264c, Plut. *De pyth. or.* 401f.

19   Commutation of priestly share of a sacrifice to a money payment, provided that the *apometra* are coin, and the recipient is a priestess: *IG* i³ 250, as at Pafford 2006, 34–37 following Sokolowski 1954, 155. More *apometra* alleged to be coin paid in lieu of a priestly portion: Loomis 1998, 76–87. Loomis, however, does not distinguish between this kind of monetary compensation and an annual fee, such as at *IG* i³ 36.4–8

20   *IG* xii 4.1.302a.21–7 (= *Iscr. Di Cos* ED 178.21–27):
ὁμοίως δὲ καὶ ἀκολούθως τοῖς
προκεκυρωμένοις συντελῶντι τὰς θυσίας τοί {ς} τε
ἔμποροι {ς} καὶ τοὶ {ς} ναύκλαροι {ς} τοὶ {ς} ὁρμώμενοι {ς} ἐκ τᾶς π-

The goddess involved is Aphrodite Pontia, the patroness of sailors. The phrase 'accomplish sacrifices' means to be responsible for them, and it probably means attending them, even if it does not mean performing them. (To use Marcel Mauss's term, it probably refers to the *sacrifiant*.)

Later in the same century, or perhaps at the start of the next, the polis allowed some shipmasters to commute their offerings:

> Fishermen who fish outside the city and shipmasters who sail around the region shall also give as an offering five drachmae annually per ship.[21]

Lines elsewhere in the inscription make it clear that these worshippers should put their money in a collection box in the shrine. Annual payments have either replaced sacrifices or been added to them.

Unlike the earlier regulation, this one does not deal with any and all shipmasters, but only those who sail 'around the region', in other words, in coastwise trade or cabotage. Why were their sacrifices commuted, but not the sacrifices of traders on the high seas? The answer perhaps is ability to pay. Coastwise ships sailed frequently, as did fishermen, but earned comparatively little on each voyage, and so the polis demanded a small sum from them. At five drachmae per year for 30 voyages or more, the cost per voyage was less than an obol. Ships engaged in foreign trade probably sailed less often, but earned more per voyage, and so the polis did not offer them this bargain. It expected them to 'accomplish sacrifices' as before.

In Pergamon and on Kos, some authority ordered the commutation of offerings. Elsewhere, worshippers sometimes volunteered to pay money rather than make offerings. According to Plutarch, the Athenians called such contributions *epidōseis*, and the public sometimes pressured those volunteering to pay them.[22] On Rhodes in the second century BCE, the volunteers took pride in their contributions, and erected a stele in their own honour:

ὅλιος· ὅσσοι κα μὴ θύσωντι ὡς γέγραπται, ἐπιτίμιόν τε
αὐτοῖς ἔστω, καὶ ὀφειλόντω ἐπιτίμιον τᾶ<ι> ἱερείαι δραχμὰς
δέκα, ἁ δὲ πρᾶξις ἔστω αὐτᾶι καθάπερ ἐγ δίκας.

21   *IG* xii 4.1.319.27–9 (= *SEG* 50.766.27–9):

                        διδόντω δὲ ἐς ἀπαρχὰν καὶ τοὶ
ἁλιεῖς τοὶ ὁρμόμενοι ἐκ τᾶς πόλιος καὶ τοὶ ναύκλαροι τοὶ πλέοντες
περὶ τὰν χώραν καθ' ἕκαστον πλοῖον τοῦ ἐνιαυτοῦ δραχμὰς πέντε·
Cabotage: N. Purcell apud Parker – Obbink 2000, 443–444.

22   *Epidōseis* as at Plu. *Phoc.* 9.1–2: Πρὸς δὲ θυσίαν τινὰ τῶν Ἀθηναίων αἰτούντων ἐπιδόσεις, καὶ
τῶν ἄλλων ἐπιδιδόντων, κληθεὶς πολλάκις ἔφη· 'τούτους αἰτεῖτε τοὺς πλουσίους· ἐγὼ δ' αἰσχυνοί-
μην ἄν, εἰ τούτῳ μὴ ἀποδιδοὺς ὑμῖν ἐπι<δι>δοίην', δείξας Καλλικλέα τὸν δανειστήν.

The people choosing to augment the honours for the gods and for the Panathenaic festival undertook to make gifts of money to build cisterns and installations for sacrificial banquets held by demes:

> The deme Arioi, 50 (drachmas);
> Critobulus the son of Aristombrotides,
> also on behalf of his wife Nicaina and his sons
> Aristombrotides and Nausippus, 100 (drachmas)....[23]

These subscribers wished to fund dining during the Panathenaia. Migeotte, the most recent editor of this inscription, estimates fifteen lines are missing, and so, if the other donors gave comparable sums, the total may have reached one or two thousand drachmas, or up to 1/3 of a talent. This considerable sum suggests that the subscription valuably supplemented inadequate public funds. Like the regulations on Kos, the Kamarina subscription reflected donors' ability to pay.

In this case, the subscribers paid for sacrificial banquets. In many other cases, they paid other costs that were at a farther remove from an act of sacrifice, such as temple repairs. The various purposes served by subscriptions elicits a feature of money payments that is not apparent in Pergamon and Kos, but surely was found there as well as here. Unlike contributions in kind, contributions of money were fungible. Rather than support a ritual, the worshipper could support a cult; besides providing a benefit for himself and others standing at Burkert's imaginary altar, he could support a community.

---

23   *Tit. Cam.* 159 = Migeotte 1992, #43.1–12:
     τοίδε προαιρούμενοι ἐπαύξειν
     τάς τε τῶν θεῶν τιμὰς καὶ τὰν
     πανάγυριν τῶν Παναθηναίων
     ἐπαγγείλαντο δώσειν χρήματα
     δωρεὰν εἰς τὰν κατασκευὰν τῶν
     χρηστηρίων καὶ τῶν ἐλύτρων καὶ
     εἰς τὰν ἑστίασιν τῶν δάμων
     Ἀρίων ὁ δᾶμος ν′
     Κριτόβουλος Ἀριστομβροτίδα
     καὶ ὑπὲρ τᾶς γυναικὸς
     Νικαίνας καὶ ὑπὲρ τῶν υἱῶν
     Ἀριστομβροτίδα καὶ Ναυσίππου ρ′

3   Formal Commutation of Sacrifice: Three Terms

The three examples above do not involve any terms meaning 'commutation'
or 'fund'. Elsewhere, terms meaning 'commutation' or 'fund' do appear, but
they may be deceptive, for they do not always mean the same thing. Three
terms are noteworthy. *Pelanos* can designate the commutation of a vegetal
sacrifice, and the resulting fund of money, or it can designate an offering in
kind or a purchased offering, or, rarely, a fee. As an offering in kind, *pelanos*
means 'cake', but in some authors it means a thick, flowing offering, and, by
extension, flowing blood, as when Orestes slaughters victims in the *Libation
Bearers* and Aeschylus speaks of the blood spilled at Plataea. A *pelanos* might
thus be poured rather than burned. Pollux says all gods receive *pelanoi*.[24] The
flexibility of this word in literary sources anticipates the varied meanings that
it has in inscriptions. *Aparchē* is a fluid term, too. It can designate commutation as well as first fruits that may or may not be sold, and it may designate a
fee. *Dermatikon* designates another fund. Paul Stengel and Pierre Amandry are
among the scholars who have analysed these terms.[25]

3.1   *Pelanos*

The original meaning of *pelanos* persisted throughout the Classical and
Hellenistic periods, and throughout Greece. In the third century, the deme of
Rhamnous praised a local benefactor for offering cakes to the gods and heroes,
and in Rhodes in the first century the mourners at a grave erected a stele describing how they threw cakes into fire to honour the Muses. At Selinous, in the
early 400s, a worshipped dedicated an altar for burning *pelanoi*.[26]

About the same time, if not earlier, another meaning of *pelanos* appears at
Delphi. This, the second meaning, is a sum of money for buying a *pelanos*. In
a regulation dating to 425, Delphi told pilgrims from Andros what the *pelanos*
would cost. This instruction appears among half a dozen others: Delphic officials must receive the hides of sacrificial victims, the pilgrims would receive
free meals the first day, and after that would pay an Aeginetan obol a day for
food, and Delphi would reciprocate by sacrificing for them an animal worth
more than half the money collected. Next, the regulations says,

---

24   Amandry 1950, 87–88, giving literary sources including A. *Ch.* 87, 92, *Pers.* 816, and
       Poll. 6.76. *Pelanoi* only as cakes: Suda s.v. πελανοί.
25   Eitrem 1915, 276; Ziehen 1937; Stengel 1894 and Stengel 1923, 66–7; Amandry 1950, 88–99.
26   *Demos Rhamnous* 11.6; Hiller von Gaertringen 1912, 230,1 (Rhodes); *SEG* 12.411 (Selinous).

Certain select costs: For each hecatomb, the *pelanos* costs four obols, the services of the priest cost six, and the entry fee for foreigners costs two.[27]

This *pelanos* is cheap, and so is another, reported in Attica. Sacrificial regulations for the Attic Salaminioi, posted in 363/2, require:

As for whatever sacrifices the Salaminioi made using rent money, they should make them according to custom. Each of the two groups should contribute half for all the sacrifices. To the priests and priestesses they should give the perquisites provided in writing. To the priest of Heracles they should give a priestly perquisite of thirty drachmas. For the *pelanos*, they should give three drachmas.[28]

The cake, like the other items, would be provided at some number of sacrifices, and so the sum of three drachmas is appropriate. The regulation mentions the cake because the price had been misunderstood or had changed, and needed to be clarified.

About a generation earlier, around 400, Delphi set not one but two prices for *pelanoi*. In a regulation for pilgrims from Phaselis:

The Delphians decree that the Phaselitans pay seven Delphic drachmae and two obols for the *pelanos* for a communal sacrifice, and four obols for the *pelanos* for a personal sacrifice.[29]

---

27 *CID* 1.7.24–8:

ὑπ-

ἀρχέτō δὲ τὰ ἐξαίρετα· π[ε]-
[λ]ανὸς τέσσαρας, μεταξέ[ν]-
[ι]α δύο, ἱερēι' ἕξ ἀπὸ τῆς ἑ[κ]-
[ατ]όμβης ἑκάστ[η]ς

28 *Agora XIX Leases* L.4a.24–31:

ὅσα δὲ ἀπὸ τῆς μισθώσεως ἔ-
θυον Σαλαμίνιοι παρὰ σφῶν αὐτῶν θύειν κατὰ τὰ
†ἥμυσυ ἑκατέρος συμβαλλομένος εἰς ἅ-
παντα τὰ ἱερά· τοῖς δὲ ἱερεῦσι καὶ ταῖς ἱερείαι-
ς ἀποδιδόναι τὰ γέρα τὰ γεγραμμένα· τῶι δὲ τ δὲ τ Ἡρ-
ακλέος ἱερεῖ ἱερεώσυνα ΔΔΔ δραχμάς· εἰς πελανὸν δὲ ╫╫╫ δραχμάς·

29 *CID* 1.8:

ἅδε Δελφοῖς Φασēλίτας τὸν
πελανὸν διδόμεν· τὸ<δ> δαμόσιον ἑπτὰ δραχμὰς δελφίδες ð-
ύ' ὀ<δ>ελός, τὸν δὲ ἴδιον, τέτορε-

The *pelanos* payment for the personal sacrifice is once again cheap. The payment for the communal sacrifice is not. The reason is not likely to be that the cost of the cake or cakes at a communal sacrifice is eleven times greater than the cost for a personal sacrifice. Delphi may want the polis of Phaselis to pay according to its ability, and it may also want Phaselis to subsidise other religious activities by paying a premium. Phaselis is buying cakes, like all the worshippers so far, but it also may be spending its money in a different way, as a subvention for activities that Phaselitans may never participate in.

A *pelanos* that is a subvention reappears in an agreement between Delphi and Sciathos of about the same date:

> The Delphians have granted privileged access to the oracle and exemp-tion from all obligation save the *pelanos*. The *pelanos* for the community is an Aeginetan stater, and the *pelanos* for an individual is two obols.[30]

John Davies called this *pelanos* a fee.[31] For the individual, no: he or she is pay-ing two obols for a cake. The community, though, is paying a fee, or, as I would prefer to say, a subvention. In this same inscription, Delphi grants *ateleia* from all costs but the *pelanos*, confirming that it was an obligatory payment.

In Athens in the late 400s, the *pelanos* became a large subvention. The occa-sion for this shift was the collection of first fruits for the *Proerōsia* at Eleusis. In 422, perhaps, the Athenians invited states that were not their allies to contrib-ute to these sacrifices. This inscription, unlike those quoted so far, describes at some length both a *pelanos* subvention and the sale of first fruits:

ς ὀδελός· Τιμοδίκō κα̣ὶ Ἱϲτι<α>ί̣-
ō θεαρόντōν· Ἐρύλō ἄρχο̞ϲ̣.

30   *CID* 1.13.5–15:

ἔ[δ]ωκαν προμαν-
τεί[α]ν καὶ ἀτέλει-
αν πά̣[ντ]ω̞ν νόσφι π-
ελαν[ō]· πελανὸν δ[ὲ]
τὸν μ[ὲν] δαμόσιο̞ν
ϲτατῆ[ρ]α αἰγιναῖ-
ον τὸν [δ]ὲ ἴδιον δύ-
ο ὀδελώ· ἐς τὸ δέρμ-
α τὸ δαμόσιον δύο
ὀδελ[ώ], τὸ δὲ ἴδιον
ὀδελόν·

31   A fee: Davies 2001, 120. At 118, Davies coins the phrase, 'sacrifice *en nature*'.

Let the council notify all other Greek cities, so far as that seems possible, and say that that Athens is not ordering them to contribute first fruits as Athens and the allies do, but is encouraging them to do so, if they wish, according to custom and according to the oracle from Delphi. If any city brings a contribution, let the *hieropoioi* receive it in the same way [as it would receive contributions from allies]. Let the *hieropoioi* sacrifice from the *pelanos* fund as the Eumolpidae advise. From the money got by the sale of the barley and wheat let them sacrifice a *trittoia* starting with a gilded ox to each of the two goddesses ... and let the *hieropoioi* together with the council sell the rest of the barley and wheat and set up dedications to the two goddesses.[32]

The words 'from the pelanos fund', or *apo tou pelanou*, designate a fund that will not provide cakes, but instead will provide whatever the priestly experts advise. This is a sacrificial offering that has been commuted. The grain from the allies will partly be sold, and this is a sale of first fruits. The inscription does not say so, but the source of the *pelanos* fund is the contribution made by the foreign cities, which will be spent in three ways: as advised by experts, on sacrifices, and on dedications. The act of sacrifice has become less important than the cult as a whole.[33]

An account of first fruits at Eleusis in 328 gives further information about the first fruits, while using *pelanos* twice. In one instance, it refers to a sum of money paid to a tribal priest.[34] The subvention provides an emolument.

---

32   *IG* i³ 78.31–44:

ἐπαγγέλλεν δὲ τὲν βολὲν καὶ τêσι ἄλλεσι πόλεσιν [τ]ê[σι] hε-
[λ]λενικêσιν ἁπάσεσι, hόποι ἂν δοκêι αὐτêι δυνατὸν ἔναι, λ[έγο]ν-
τας μὲν κατὰ hὰ Ἀθεναῖοι ἀπάρχονται καὶ οἱ χσύμμαχοι, ἐκέ[νοι]-
[ς] δὲ μὲ ἐπιτάττοντας, κελεύσοντας δὲ ἀπάρχεσθαι, ἐὰν βόλονται,
[κ]ατὰ πάτρια καὶ τὲν μαντείαν τὲν ἐγ Δελφôν. παραδέχεσθαι δ-
ὲ καὶ παρὰ τούτον τôν πόλεον ἐάν τις ἀπάγει τὸς hιεροποιὸς κατὰ ταὐτά. θύεν δὲ ἀπὸ μὲν τô πελανô καθότι ἂν Εὐμολπίδαι [ἐχσhε]-
[γô]νται, τρίττοιαν δὲ βόαρχον χρυσόκερον τοῖν θεοῖν hεκα[τέρ]-
[αι ἀ]πὸ τôν κριθôν καὶ τôν πυρôν καὶ τôι Τριπτολέμοι καὶ τôι [θε]-
ôι καὶ τêι θεâι καὶ τôι Εὐβόλοι hιερεῖον hεκάστοι τέλεον καὶ
τêι Ἀθεναίαι βôν χρυσόκερον· τὰς δὲ ἄλλας κριθὰς καὶ πυρὸς ἀπ-
οδομένος τὸς hιεροποιὸς μετὰ τêς βολês ἀναθέματα ἀνατιθέν-
αι τοῖν θεοῖν.

The doubtful date: Jim 2015, 208–209 with refs. The *pelanos* as a cake, not a fund: Clinton 2010, 3, ignoring the genitive.

33   Clinton 2010, 4, notes that in some years leftover money was kept in reserve, and thus available for various purposes.

34   *I Eleusis* 177.419–20.

In the other instance, the *pelanos* is a cake, but perhaps one funded by selling grain. The context is the allotment of the first fruits:

> The total in barley was 1,108 *medimnoi* and 42 and one half *choinikes* ... of this, the *prokōnia* for the two goddesses was one *medimnos*, and for the *pelanos* for the *hieropoioi* appointed by the council there were 16 *medimnoi* less three *choinikes*.... The total in wheat was 86 *medimnoi* and 10 and one half *choinikes*, of which the *prokōnia* for the two goddesses was one *medimnos*, and for the *pelanos* for the *hieropoioi* there were 10 *medimnoi*.[35]

In this text, all three kinds of sacrificial offering appear. One *pelanos* is a cake, the first fruits are commodities to be sold, and the other *pelanos* is a subvention.

3.2   *Aparchai*

With the documents of 439 and 422, we come to the next term, *aparchai*. Both documents show that *aparchai* could be sold, and that the proceeds could be turned into a fund. Examples of Athenian *aparchai* that were *en nature* also appear.[36] For example, Priene told its *theōroi* to bring Athens *aparchai*, meaning grain, and also to make sacrifices. These offerings were a vegetal counterpart to the bulls sent to the Panathenaia by Athenian subjects.[37]

Greek sources mention one kind of individual who, like a *polis*, presents first fruits in kind and also commutes offerings. Surprisingly, these are hunters. They gave Artemis first fruits such as a hide or some other part of the quarry, but in the second century CE Arrian reports that hunters could commute these offerings. The Celts in this passage live in Galatia:

---

35   *I Eleusis* 177.408–10, 412–14:
   κεφάλαιον κριθῶν μέδιμνοι ΧΗΓΙΙΙ ἡμιεκτεῖα τέτταρα δύο χοίνικες· ἀπὸ τούτων εἰς
   [π]ροκώνια τοῖν θεοῖν μέδιμνος, εἰς τὸν πελανὸν ἱεροποιοῖς ἐγ βουλῆς ἑκκαίδεκα μέδιμνοι τρι-
   ῶν χοινίκων ἀπολείποντες· ...
                        πυρῶν κεφάλαιον μέδιμνοι ᴾΔΔΔ[ΓΙ]
   δέκα ἡμιεκτεῖα χοῖνιξ· ἀπὸ τούτων εἰς <προκώνια> τοῖν θεοῖν μέδιμνος καὶ <εἰς τὸν πελανὸν>
   ἱεροποιοῖς ἐγ βουλῆς
   Δ μέδιμνοι.
   The *pelanos* not sold: Clinton 2005, 12 n. 25.
36   Amount of money available in the fund known as the *aparchē* in 400s: *IG* i³ 386.4–387.4–5.
37   First fruits in kind: *I Priene* 5; so also *IG* i³ 34.41–3, 71.56–8 (cattle sent to the Athenian Panathenaia).

> Some Celts have the custom of making a yearly sacrifice to Artemis, and they present her a collection box. If they catch a rabbit they put in two obols; if a fox, a drachma ... for a deer, four drachmas.[38]

Arrian distinguishes this yearly sacrifice from occasional sacrifices made after a kill. He implies that all hunters make the occasional sacrifices, but only the Galatians Celts add an annual, monetary contribution. In Galatia as in Pergamon, the goddess has a collection box.

By the end of the Classical period, the winners at Greek games somewhat resembled these hunters, except they received two kinds of rewards rather than make two kinds of offerings. At the leading games, the rewards in kind were items such as laurels and olive branches, and money was a reward of a second type. Solon, for example, ordered that Athens pay money to all Olympic victors. If Barclay Head was right, Syracuse paid coins to victors.[39] The contrast between money and rewards in kind replaced an earlier situation, in which winners received valuables such as silver.

3.3   *Dermatikon*

The next term to consider, *dermatikon*, returns us to Athenian civic sacrifices. It was an all-purpose religious fund sustained by the sale of the hides of victims slaughtered in communal sacrifices. Whereas some leftovers were eaten, and others were sold and eaten afterwards, the most valuable leftover, the hide, was sold and effectively liquidated by being converted into a fund.[40] The physical fact of the hides disappeared from the shrine's ledger, the same as the barley and wheat at Eleusis, and turned into money.

In other parts of the field of ancient Greek sacrifice, the term *dermatikon* has played a large and controversial role – for example, in calculating Athenian sacrificial expenditures.[41] In this paper, it has a small and simple role to play. The *dermatikon* is neither an offering of an animal hide nor a way to buy one. Instead it designates a sacrificial fund, like the two words *aparchai* and *pelanos*.

---

38   Arr. *Cyn.* 34: Κελτῶν δὲ ἔστιν οἷς νόμος καὶ ἐνιαύσια θύειν τῇ Ἀρτέμιδι, οἳ δὲ καὶ θησαυρὸν ἀποδεικνύουσιν τῇ θεῷ. καὶ ἐπὶ μὲν λαγωῷ ἁλόντι δύ' ὀβολὼ ἐμβάλλουσιν ἐς τὸν θησαυρόν, ἐπὶ δὲ ἀλώπεκι δραχμήν,..... ἐπὶ δὲ δορκάδι τέσσαρας δραχμάς,...

39   Plut. *Sol.* 23.3. Coins: Head 1911, 76. Sceptical. Fischer-Bossert 1992, discussing this and other evidence.

40   *Dermatikon*: Rosivach 1994, 48–65. A rare example of a sacrificial fine paid in kind: *I Cret.* II 9.

41   Expenditures: Rosivach 1994; von Reden 2010, 166–7; Naiden 2013, 272–3 with refs.

4   A Silent Innovation

Why should the Athenians have taken words that meant 'cake', 'first fruits', and 'hide' and given them the meaning 'sacred money'? Lest we give an answer that refers to Athens alone, and not to the rest of Greece, we should remember that the other Greeks made similar use of words related to sacrifice. On Crete, some fines were paid in cauldrons, which were sacrificial accoutrements, and in tripods, which originally were perhaps stands for boiling sacrificial meat. Cauldrons and tripods used for this purpose were not money in every sense, but they were money in one sense, which is a means of payment. Similarly, the obscure word *phthoïs* meant either 'sacrificial cake' or 'small gold bar'. The familiar word *obeliskos* meant 'spit' and later 'obol' (and for this reason became the subject of more than a century of scholarly speculation and dispute).[42] Greeks habitually gave a monetary meaning to sacrificial terms.

In contrast, only one term for 'sacred money' refers to money alone, rather than referring to sacrifice *en nature* and to some fund or kind of payment. This term, *eparchē*, differs from *aparchē*. At Oropos it means a fee, at Eleusis a fund, at Delphi a voluntary contribution, in Boeotia a stipend. At Athens it means a levy and a store of money for use on Delos. It never refers to first fruits (although *epargmata* does).[43]

When worshippers began to use money – say, around 525 – they did not put into words the change that was occurring.[44] The word for a new fund was the word for a familiar cake, and the word for another new fund was the word for first fruits. The word for a third fund was an adjective derived from the noun for animal hides. There was no word for commutation, and no word or phrase for 'sacred funds' as opposed to sacred property. Rather than inspire the invention of coinage, sacrifice apparently continued as though coinage had not been invented. As Simmel said, a kind of 'religious social unity.... became active ... through money'.[45]

Why did this silent innovation occur? It let worshippers and shrine administrators keep accounts and increase revenue. Burkert and Vernant, and recent writers like von Reden and Seaford, do not conceive of Greek worshippers as thinking in such plain, practical terms. Yet they did think in these terms. Yes,

---

42   Cauldrons: *I Cret.* iv 1. Tripods: *I Cret.* iv 8a–d, with speculation at Papalexandrou 2005. Φθοῖς: *LSJ* s.v. 1, 3. Speculation and dispute about spits: see nn. 1–2.

43   *Eparchai* at Oropus: *Epigr. tou Oropou* 177.20–22. Eleusis: *I Eleusis* 177.183, 263. Delphi: *CID* 2.102. Boeotia: Bizard 1903, no. 9.9. Athens: *IG* ii² 1215.13–16, *IG* i³ 130.7, 18. *Epargmata*: *IG* xii.3 436 = *LSCG* 134. A general interpretation, with refs: Petropoulou 1981.

44   A date implied by *CID* 1, 9, discussed by Picard 2005, 61–5.

45   Simmel 1978, 187.

the vocabulary was *en nature*, but so is some contemporary monetary vocabulary. An American or Englishman owning stock does not have to own cattle, and if he owns bonds he does not have to – and legally is not allowed to – own bondmen, or slaves.

Instead of drawing conclusions from word roots, a bad habit as old as antiquity, we should try to pinpoint the effect of commutation, purchase, sale, and fees. This effect was subtle but broad. Ritual mattered less, and the cult as a whole mattered more. Ritual did go on. The physical facts remained what they had been, except that thanks to economic growth they became more extensive. The context for the ritual changed. Monetisation linked ritual to other aspects of the cult, and linked the cult and everything in it to payments of money. Seaford, who was right about the impact of money on Greek thought, could have added that money made an impact on Greek religion. And not just Greek religion in the narrow sense: once the Greeks began to worship Egyptian gods, they set up collection boxes for them, too.

The collection box symbolised this new context. As Kaminski shows, it sometimes stood near the altar. Figures 7.1–7.3 present her drawings of the Asclepieion at Corinth, the Serapeion at Delos, and the cult room for Artemis at Messene. Square and built of stone, many of these boxes looked like altars, as at Figure 7.4, her drawing of the collection box in the temple of the Egyptian gods on Thera, and Figure 7.5, her reconstruction of the box in the marketplace on Thasos. This resemblance is appropriate. The business done at the altar depended partly on the business done at the collection box. No source says how brisk the business at the collection box was, but boxes were surely emptied regularly.[46]

Besides dictating amounts, an obvious task, inscriptions about collection boxes say that priests made sure worshippers put their payments in the collection box and used legal tender.[47] They specify collection dates and order officials to report irregularities.[48] Some officials commemorated their services by dedicating a box.[49] The encouragement or pressure to pay was considerable, aside from any fear of divine disapproval of scofflaws.[50]

---

46   *IG* xii 4.1.302a.16–17. To add to Kominski's catalogue: *SEG* 41.182 (Athens, Aphrodite Urania, early third century; *SEG* 51.1066 (Cos, around 100 BCE). *Thēsauroi* in healing cults: Melpi 1998–2000.

47   Amounts: *SEG* 32.415–6, combining *LSCG* 35 and *IG* viii 235. Police work: *Epigr. Tou Oropou* 277.9–13, 23–4. (The same collection box: Lupu 2005 #9.4–5). Summary of the priest's police powers: 14–20.

48   Schedules: *IG* xii 4.1.302a.16–17. Irregularities: *LSCG* 70.33–9.

49   *SEG* 48.1075 with refs. Dedicating the platform beneath the box: *SEG* 42.855.

50   *LSCG Supp.* 72.2–5.

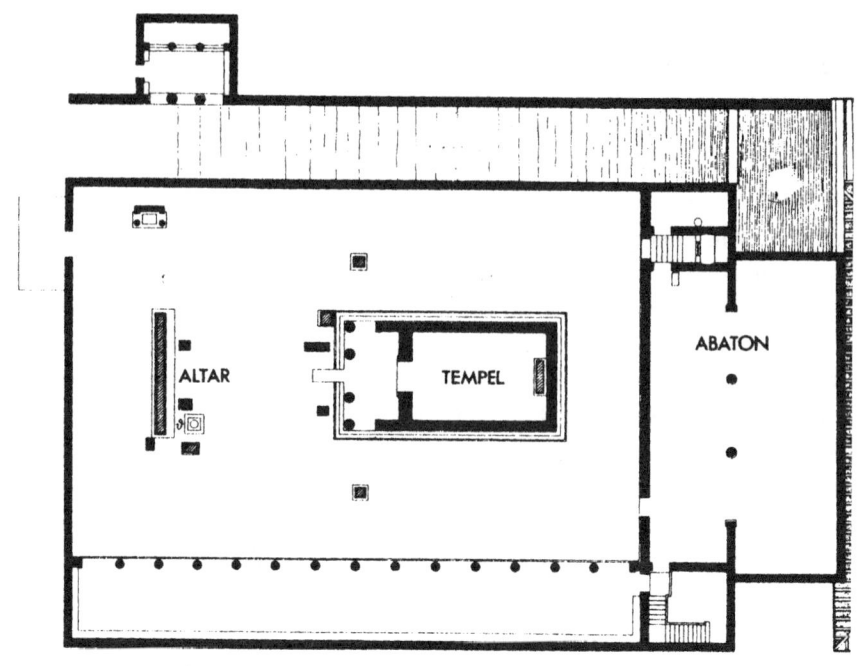

FIGURE 7.1   Asclepieion at Corinth. *Thesauros*: θ below altar. Temple 15 m. long (after
                    Kaminski 1991, 115)

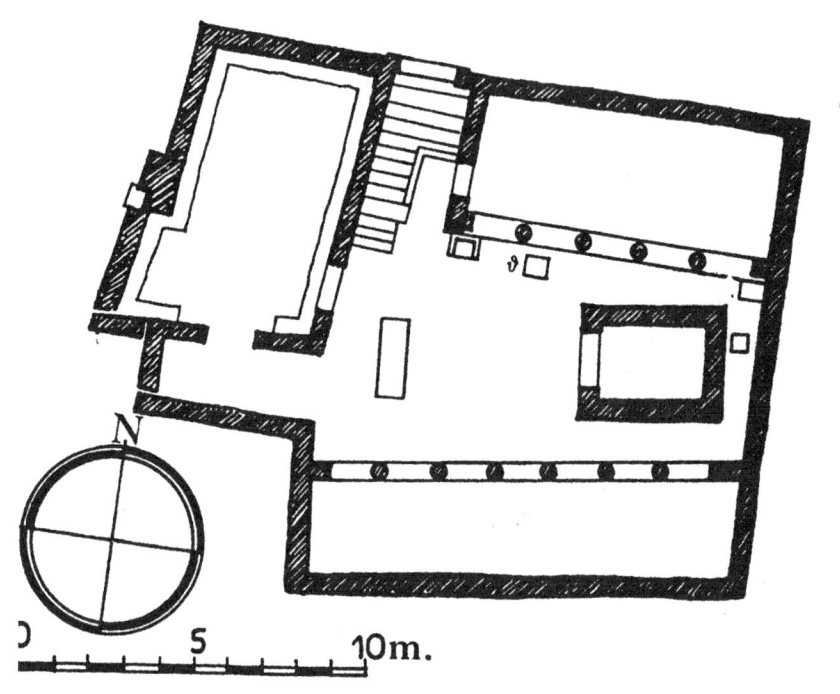

FIGURE 7.2   Serapeion at Delos. *Thesauros*: θ above and between altar and cella (after
                    Kaminski 1991, 116)

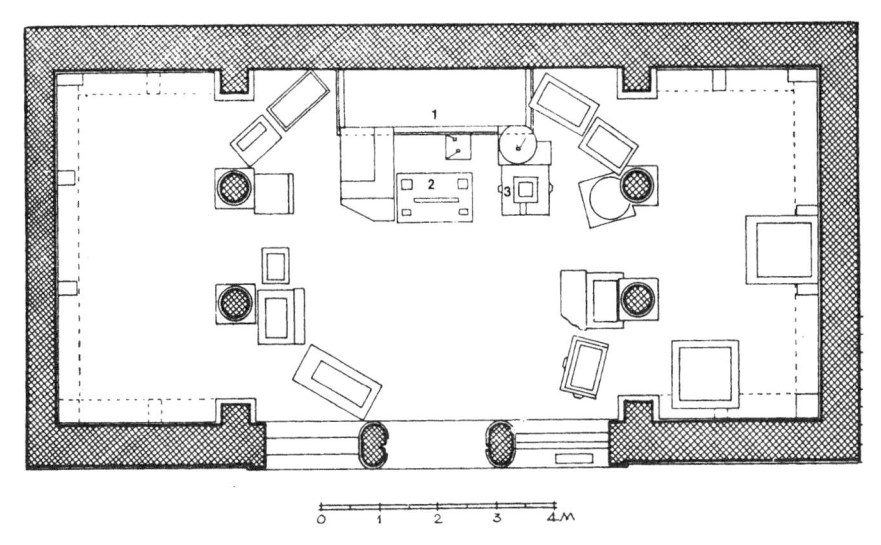

FIGURE 7.3   The cult room for Artemis at Messene. *Thesauros*: no. 3 beside *trapeza* (after Kaminski 1991, 116)

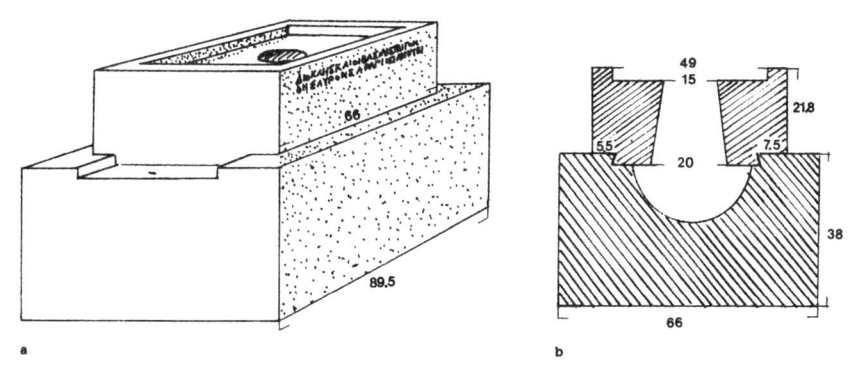

FIGURE 7.4   *Thesauros* in the temple of the Egyptian gods, Thera. Size in cm. The inscription (*IG* xii.3 443), reads, Διοκλῆς καὶ οἱ Βασι[λ]ισταὶ τὸν / θησαυρὸν Σαράπι Ἴσι Ἀνούβι (after Kaminski 1991, 96).

Pilgrims were perhaps especially sure to pay. They were strangers, and in particular they were strangers who used money in lieu of the animal victims and other offerings which they could not make in kind. The monetisation and regulation of sacrifice were even more convenient for them than for others.

The collection box is noteworthy in another, visual way. Before the invention of money, a *thesaurus* was a temple treasury containing precious items. Afterwards, it continued to be that, but it could also be a strongbox containing coins. A Greek shrine might now have one house or box for the god, one

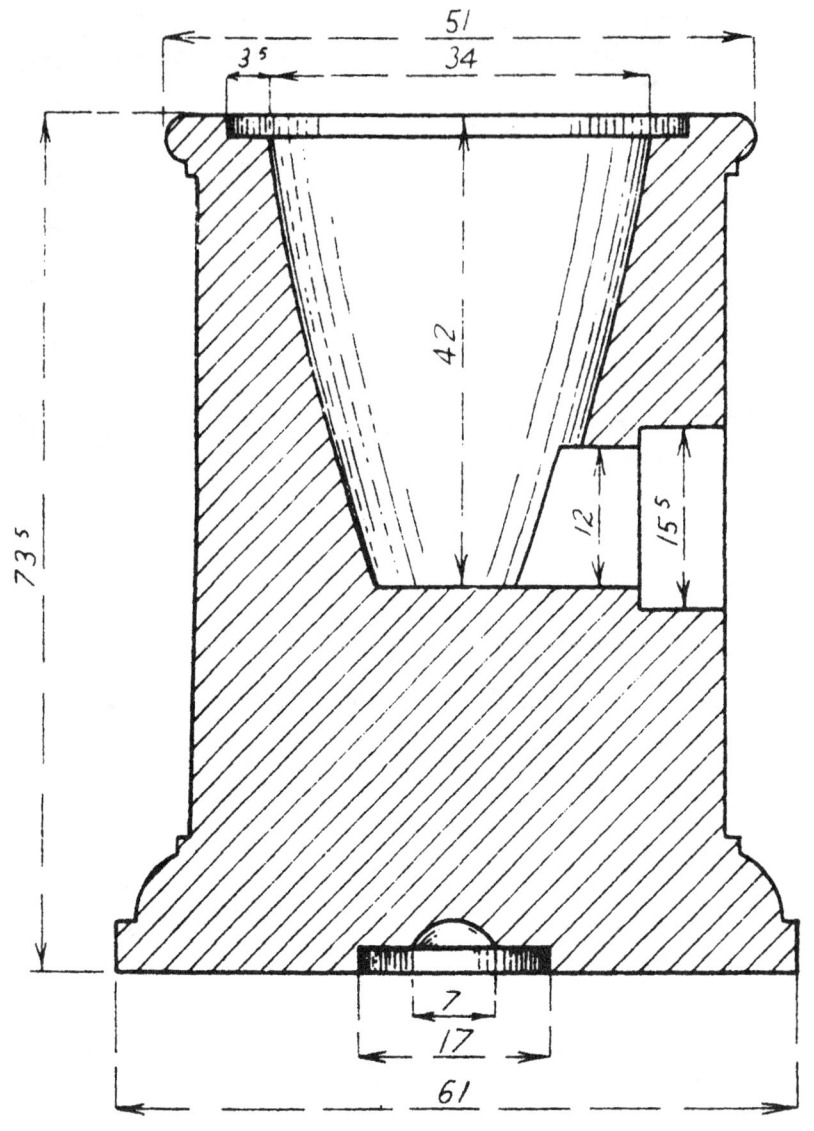

FIGURE 7.5   *Thesauros* in the centre of the agora on Thasos. Size in cm (after
Kaminski 1991, 164)

or more for precious items, and one for cash. Even in the countryside outside
little Thebes at Mykale, a cash box would be handy.

If we return again to the views of Burkert, and of Vernant and Detienne, we
can make a further criticism of these writers: Burkert should add a collection
box to his prototypical scene of sacrifice and the French authors should put a

box in the agora of their democratic *polis*. By the same token, the ideological aspect of the introduction of money should be revised to allow for a theological aspect: the gods have their say, which is to be paid in full and on time.

The Greeks did not invent the practice of putting gods in houses, and they did not invent altars or sacrifices. They did, however, invent the collection box. This invention stuck. Christians have collection boxes or plates, Jews have charity boxes, and Muslims, especially in Western countries, have donation boxes placed in mosques on Fridays before prayers. A Greek precedent sometimes turns up where neither scholars nor believers would think to look for it.

5 Ancient and Modern Collection Boxes

This chapter concludes with a postscript comparing the ancient collection box and the collection box or plate in modern Christianity. Neither box nor plate could have existed unless many worshippers or parishioners had money to spare. That would suggest that some worshippers or parishioners were prosperous. In Greece they spent their own money on priesthoods and other kinds of religious benefactions, and in modern Christianity they made charitable donations.

Ancient payments, though, differed from modern ones on three counts. Many ancient payments were compulsory, including both fees and subventions. Modern payments are always voluntary. (The compulsory Christian tithe was mostly medieval, not modern, and it was seldom paid in money.) Next, ancient payments were always specified, whether by law or in a public record of payments made as part of a subscription. Modern payments put in a plate might be guessed, but no public record is made, and larger donations are seldom commemorated by stating the exact amount. The modern donor, especially of millions, is squeamish about amounts, but the much poorer ancient subscriber was not.

A third difference concerns sacrifice in particular. Ancient payments sometimes were for performing a particular act of sacrifice. Modern, Christian payment are never for performing a particular mass that the payer of the money would attend, and modern payments are never for anything so carnal as food and drink.

Differences about sacrifice also involves the use of contributions in kind. Both paganism and Christianity allowed for these contributions. The difference between the two religions lay in the relations between contributions and the sacrificial act. In paganism, the worshipper contributed offerings. In Christianity, Christ made the offering, not the worshipper, and so the worshipper contributed in another way, by making donations for the cult. Finally, the sacred meal differed. The pagan meal was sacrificial. Medieval Christians ate festive meals in or next to churches, just as pagans ate in shrines, but these meals were not sacrificial.[51]

In sum, ancient payments were enjoined by law, were often publicised, and were minutely recorded. Modern payments were encouraged by fear of public disapproval, were less publicised, and were seldom recorded. In modern times, the role of money has been, to return to von Reden's word, 'problematic'. Some donors were unwelcome, and some did not wish to be known; a desire for fame or a good reputation competed with fear of the reaction of a hostile public. The Christian virtue of modesty did not always sit well with the civic virtue of munificence. In ancient Greece, the donor felt no fear of public criticism, and notions of modesty did not complicate widespread, traditional acceptance of euergetism.

The monetisation of sacrifice, eptitomised by the introduction of collection boxes, would not have occurred without the widespread use of coins, not just by the rich, but by the poor. In this respect, monetisation equalised worshippers, giving the rich a motive to distinguish themselves through euergetism. This response, in turn, strengthened one kind of religious and social inequality. Although all collection boxes were much alike, all donations were not. This truism holds good for both ancient and later worship.

Two famous remarks about the modern rich illuminate this subject. The American novelist F. Scott Fitzgerald observed, 'The rich are different'. Ernest Hemingway answered, 'Yes, they have more money'. In his own way, each writer is right. The paradox of money is that it equalises yet discriminates.

Bibliography

Amandry, P. 1950. *La mantique apollonienne à Delphes*, Paris.

Appadurai, A. ed. 1986. *The Social Life of Things: Commodities in Cultural Perspective*, Cambridge.

van Binsbergen, W. and Geschiere, P. eds. 2005. *Commodification: Things, Agencies and Identities (The Social Life of Things Revisited)*, Münster.

Bizard, L. 1920. "Fouilles du Ptoion (1903). Inscriptions II", *Bulletin de Correspondance Hellénique* 44, 227–62.

---

51   Animal offerings and thus meals in churches: Kovalchuk 2008. Ascetics criticised these meals (Caesarius of Arles, sermon 55, CCSL 103.240–44).

Burkert, W. 1983. *Homo Necans: The Anthropology of Ancient Greek Sacrificial Ritual and Myth*, trans. P. Bing, Berkeley, CA.

Burkert, W. 1985. *Greek Religion*, trans. J. Raffan, Cambridge, MA.

Casabona, J. 1966. *Recherches sur le vocabulaire des sacrifices en Grèce des origines à la fin de l'époque classique*, Aix-en-Provence.

Clinton, K. 2010. "The Eleusinian Aparche in Practice: 329/8 B.C.", in *Sanctuaries and Cults of Demeter in the Ancient Greek World*, eds. I. Leventi and C. Mitsopoulou, Volos, 1–15.

Davies, J. 2001. "Temples, Credit, and the Circulation of Money", in *Money and its Uses in the Ancient Greek World*, eds. A. Meadows and K. Shipton, Oxford, 117–29.

Eitrem, S. 1915. *Opferritus und Voropfer der Griechen und Römer*, Christiana.

Fischer-Bossert, W. 1992. "ΑΘΛΑ", *Archäologischer Anzeiger* 1992.1, 39–60.

Head, B. 1911. *Historia Nummorum*, Oxford.

Hiller von Gaertringen, F. 1912. "Arideikes und Hieronymos von Rhodos", *Bulletin de Correspondance Héllenique* 36, 230–9.

Jim, T. 2015. *Sharing with the Gods: Aparchai and Dekatai in Ancient Greece*, Oxford.

Kaminski, G. 1991. "*Thesauros*. Untersuchungen zum antiken Opferstock", *Jahrbuch des deutschen archölogischen Instituts* 106, 63–181.

Kovalchuk, K. 2008. "The Encaenia of St. Sophia: Animal Sacrifice in a Christian Context", *Scrinium* 4, 161–203.

Kurke, L. 1995. "Herodotos and the Language of Metals", *Helios* 22, 36–64.

Labarbe, J. 1953. "L'Age correspondant au sacrifice du κούρειον et les données historiques du sixième discours d'Isée", *Bulletin de la Classe des Lettres de l 'Academie Royale de Belgique* 39, 358–94.

Laum, B. 1924. *Heiliges Geld*, Tübingen.

Loomis, W. 1998. *Wages, Welfare Costs and Inflation in Classical Athens*, Ann Arbor.

Lupu, E. 2005. *Greek Sacred Law. A Collection of New Documents*, Leiden.

Melfi, M. 1998–2000. "Il vano del thesauros nel santuario di Asclepio a Lebena", *Annali di Archeologie e Storia Antica* 40–42, 251–314.

Migeotte, L. 1992. *Les souscriptions publiques dans les cités grecques*, Geneva.

Naiden, F.S. 2013. *Smoke Signals for the Gods: Greek Sacrifice in the Archaic through Roman Periods*, Oxford.

Pafford, I. 2006. *Cult Fees and the Ritual of Money in Greek Sanctuaries of the Classical and Hellenistic Period*, unpublished PhD dissertation, Berkeley, CA.

Papalexandrou, N. 2005. *The Visual Poetics of Power: Warriors, Youths, and Tripods in Early Greece*, Lanham, MD.

Parise, N. 1984. "Sacrificio e misura del valore nella Grecia antica", *Studi STORICI* 25.4, 913–23.

Parker, R. and Obbink, D. 2000. "Sale of Priesthoods on Cos, I", *Chiron* 30, 415–50.

Petropoulou, A. 1981. "The *Eparche* Documents of the Early Oracle at Oropus", *Greek, Roman and Byzantine Studies* 22, 39–63.

Picard, O. 2005. "Les χρήματα d'Apollon et les débuts de la monnaie à Delphes", *Topoi* 12/3, 55–68.

von Reden, S. 1997. "Money, Law, and Exchange: Coinage in the Greek Polis", *Journal of Hellenic Studies* 67, 154–76.

von Reden, S. 2010. *Money in Classical Antiquity*, Cambridge.

Rosivach, V. 1994. *Athenian Public Sacrifices in the Fourth Century*, Atlanta.

Rouse, W. 1902. *Greek Votive Offerings*, Cambridge.

Seaford, R. 2004. *Money and the Early Greek Mind: Homer, Philosophy, Tragedy*, Cambridge.

Simmel, G. 1978. *The Philosophy of Money*, trans. T. Bottomore and D. Frisby, London.

Sokolowski, F. 1954. "Fees and Taxes in Greek Cults", *Harvard Theological Review* 47, 153–64.

Stengel, P. 1894. "Aparchai", *RE* 1, 2666–28.

Stengel, P. 1923. *Griechische Opferbräuche*, Berlin.

Vernant, J.-P. and Detienne, M. eds. 1989 *Cuisine of Sacrifice among the Greeks*, trans. P. Wissing, Chicago.

Zaidman, L.-B. and Schmitt Pantel, P. 1992. *Religion in the Ancient Greek City*, trans. P. Cartledge, Cambridge.

Ziehen, L. 1937. "Pelanos", *RE* 19, 246–8.

CHAPTER 8

'What Will You Give Me?': Narratives of Religious Exchange

Esther Eidinow

1 Introduction: Dynamics of *Do ut Des*

The quotation that heads this chapter is from the Epidaurian *iamata* (A8) and is a question posed by the god Asklepios to one Euphanes, a boy from Epidauros who suffered, we are told, from stone. The boy slept in the sanctuary there and 'it seemed to him the god came to him and said "What will you give me if I should make you well?" The boy replied "Ten dice?" and the god laughing said that he would 'make it stop' (which may mean the pain or the stone), and the account concludes happily, 'When day came, he left well.'[1] I start with this story because it provides an example of a narrative concerning divine-mortal interaction (one of a number found in the *iamata*), in which an exchange takes place: divine power or knowledge in return for a material object of value to the giver. This chapter focuses on the idea of gift exchange (both material and metaphysical) to contribute to the theme of sacred economies.

The Greeks themselves were well aware of the paradigms of exchange that underpinned – in various ways – their religious practices, in terms of interactions between both mortals, and mortals and divinities. Among them was the crucial concept of *charis*, which William Furley takes as a description of the beneficence that the worshipper/giver requested in the future, rather than in the moment of worship/giving itself.[2] In relations between mortals and gods, *charis* created a link between the metaphysical and the mundane; it was an abstract quality that emerged from a very human process of trade involving material objects. As Plato, slightly tongue in cheek, reminds Euthyphro, in the dialogue of that name, piety is an *emporike techne* (a 'trading skill'). Plato notes that we give the gods honour and praise and *charis*; the gods are gratified (they are, as it were '*charis*-ed' from these transactions).[3] Even if such an explicit

---

1 Trans. LiDonnici 1995. Edelstein – Edelstein 1945 (i), 223.
2 Furley 2010, 155; *cf.* Day 2010, 232–3, who sees it as generated in a (repeatable) 'now', which merges past, present and future encounters with the god. See Parker 1998, 109 for the way in which the term came to acquire the meaning 'gratitude'.
3 Pl. *Euthphr.* 15a and 14c–15b.

analysis of *charis* is rare in our sources, epigraphic evidence suggests that most ancient people treated their interactions with the gods as rooted in a relationship of expectant exchange. The language of numerous *ex-votos* indicates a widely shared narrative in which one side gave to please the other, and felt justified in asking that something be given in return.

But although, at first sight, this paradigm of exchange seems to have been common and straightforward – *do ut des* – its underlying nature was likely to have been more intricate in a number of dimensions. Recent research on the significance of the gift draws our attention to the complex social dynamics that comprise the giving and receiving of gifts and the related network of emergent meanings.[4] The giving of a gift is an assertion of identities about both giver and recipient: as Schwartz notes, '… to accept a gift is to accept (at least in part) an identity, and to reject a gift is to reject a definition of oneself'.[5] Moreover, the implications of this interaction may reach well beyond the momentary response of giver and recipient, and not only for those immediately involved. As an example, research on the 'biographies' of gifts of aid following a tsunami in Sri Lanka in 2003 reveals the dynamics of their meaning – and its manipulation. The authors of the research show how, in this context, 'the altruistic gift implied by the humanitarian discourse … inevitably collides with divergent discourses, practices, and expectations associated with 'gift' when it enters a local domain.'[6] As this demonstrates, the meanings attributed to a gift may be shaped by 'divergent gift rationales' as different actors, at different social levels, employ diverse 'strategies to negotiate, bend, or circumvent the contradictions' between them.[7] Such an example concerns the network of relations of meaning between gift, giver and recipient, and, as it illustrates, these are likely to diverge according to the specific cultural context in which the gift-giving takes place. In the case of divine and mortal interactions, however, a further set of questions must be raised because of the nature of those involved: if one player in a relationship of exchange in fact does not exist, how does that affect how we understand the emergent network of meanings and its manipulation?

This chapter sets out to explore the dynamics of mortal/divine reciprocity in ancient Greek religion, suggesting that the paradigm of exchange in this context is one that we not only trace through narratives that have survived in our sources, but that also itself crucially comprised stories – and, importantly, co-existing and competing stories. This chapter focuses on the creation

---

4   I have explored these dynamics in more detail in Eidinow 2015b, 143–4 (see also Eidinow 2016, 205–32) in the context of analysis of mortal and divine *phthonos*.

5   Schwartz 1967, 3.

6   Korf *et al.* 2010, 61.

7   Korf *et al.* 2010, 71.

of narratives at both the individual and the social level – and the relationships between the two. At the level of the individual, it employs a relational sociological approach to establish how interpersonal relationships create meaning through the development of individual and social narratives (in the next section) and how this may bear on our conceptual approach to ancient Greek religion. As noted above, individual narratives shape and are shaped by social narratives, and this chapter will then – in the third section – examine some of the ways in which such narratives about divine/mortal exchange were communicated and instantiated, and how this may shape our perception of ancient Greek ritual phenomena.

But this process of relational story-telling is not to be understood only as a descriptive process; it is also creative. Mirroring the dynamic of gift-giving, the development of a narrative is also itself the construction of a relationship that defines the individuals involved and their roles. Like gift-giving, it is likely to comprise different rationales, producing multiple stories. Focusing on contexts of oracular consultation and healing, the fourth section of this chapter will examine how the multiple narratives that describe sanctuary activities, in turn, generated diverse social roles not only for worshippers, but also for the gods they worshipped. This returns the chapter to the theme of the ontological status of the divine in these relationships of exchange, and the question of the development of a relationship of exchange in which one player does not exist. To explore these questions, in the fifth section, this chapter uses theory of mind to examine the role of narratives of gift-giving in the generation of the divine, before drawing some overall conclusions about 'Narratives, Networks, and the Generation of the Sacred'.

2 Negotiating Narratives and Networks

Individuals exist in networks of relations; those relations between individuals create meaning and identity, and vice versa, and they constitute, and are constituted by, stories. In making this argument, I am drawing on the work of Harrison White, who argues that all interaction is driven by uncertainty, which prompts individuals to establish 'footing' and to try to gain 'control' in social contexts.[8] In the process of that struggle, individuals tell stories, thus defining both their identities and their relations to each other. White's extensive work – and the development of that work by his students and collaborators – analyses the scope and operation of a network in both space and time, revealing how

---

8 See further Eidinow 2011a.

meaning is developed not only through those first dyadic interrelations but 'across a mesh of interrelations'; such a network develops a story set that not only multiplies meanings, but also allows for what he describes as 'explainings away' that 'reaffirm context'. In this way, a network can be said to emerge almost intermittently, as individuals interact in particular ways in particular domains, and in doing so, 'switch' between different identities, generating fresh meanings – and building the network.[9]

Looking at ancient society as a network of narrativised relations between individuals may help to nuance our approach to ancient Greek religious activities in particular. Specifically, it may further develop the current concept of 'embeddedness', which draws on a paradigm of exchange borrowed from economic research and focuses on social institutions.[10] Introducing instead the key role of interactions between individuals, rather than (or than only) social structures, has the potential to offer a more nuanced understanding of the individual dynamics involved.[11] If, as White has argued, such networks are crucially created by narratives, then a picture of ancient Greek religion emerges as comprising a network of individuals in which relational ties were developed through narratives that emerged in the formation of identities (and vice versa). The process of 'embedding' may also be clarified: these relationships could be negotiated, denied, or become a focus of competition; in turn, they would also create expectations that governed the development of new relationships.[12]

This approach does not mean that we abandon the level of the social group in favour only of myriad emergent relationships among individuals: our own experiences, let alone the theories of sociologists, demonstrate that both individual and group activity is shaped by more broadly shared ideas, and comes to achieve stable patterns of activity. Interpersonal relationships are shaped by self-descriptions that draw on public narratives, and these draw on background knowledge: scripts, frames, schemata, which allow us to make inferences in complex situations – to evaluate and act, interpret the past and plan for the future.[13] In turn, within society a certain level of stability is achieved

---

9   White *et al.* 2007, 50; Godart – White 2010, 567–71.
10   See Parker 1986 for the borrowing of the idea of embedded religion from economic approaches.
11   The development of the idea of embeddedness as comprising a network of individual relations is already current in economic research: see Granovetter 1985. I have developed this idea at greater length in Eidinow 2015a and so keep my remarks here brief.
12   Fuhse 2009, 54: 'the definitions of identities and relationships emerge in the course of transactions. The expectations embodied in these definitions in turn guide future transactions. To be more precise: Every transaction is laden with meaning. And the meaning structure of a network exists only as embodied in transactions'.
13   See Eidinow 2011b for use of cultural models in a context of Greek religion.

through the bedding-in of social institutions. White includes this in his theory of relationality, and argues that social institutions are sustained by the emergence of shared story-sets – he calls them 'rhetorics' – which make a particular institution explicit.[14] We can use this to describe the behaviours of exchange in discussion here: it was the rhetorics of reciprocity, the shared stories about giving and receiving gifts to and from the gods, which established the concept of *charis* and helped to sustain the social institutions of dedication/worship. Using the setting of a sanctuary as a case study, the focus of the next section is on the process of this instantiation of social meanings and their communication through various media, including embodied information, creating a variety of 'sanctuary narratives'.

3   Sanctuaries and 'Sanctuary Narratives'

There is a widely held general idea of what an ancient Greek sanctuary comprised. James Whitley describes this – and the problems with it: 'The image we have of the Classical Greek sanctuary – Delphi springs to mind – is of a temple and altar standing alone in rural Arcadia'. He goes on: 'No amount of scholarly effort will entirely erase this popular, Romantic misconception, which owes more to Western painting than it does to Greek reality. It is a picture the Greeks themselves would not have recognised. This is not because Greeks were insensitive to landscape and place – far from it. It is rather because sanctuaries were a part of the everyday. Sanctuaries, from simple altars to impressive temples, can be found in almost every public space.'[15]

But although Whitley challenges the way we make a sanctuary extraordinary, his response still focuses on material evidence – buildings, walls, offerings – as comprising the key elements of a sanctuary, although as the quoted passage itself acknowledges, this is not really a reliable index. More recent developments have added the body in movement. As Beate Dignas has suggested, we can get some sense of the individual and embodied interaction of individual and sacred space through ritual from other sources: the Sacred Journal inscription from Epidauros, for example, is an account, albeit unusual, of the ritual activity that shaped the sanctuary experience.[16] And, as Ioannis Mylonopoulos

---

14   White 2008, 171.
15   Whitley 2001, 294. The Greeks had their own preconceptions (as van Straten observes, 1992, 264–5, when the Greeks portrayed themselves in votive offerings they tended to include votive sculpture 'of a more or less monumental nature'; in contrast, the 'majority of votive offerings depicted by vase painters are pinakes').
16   Epidauros, *LSS* 25, see Dignas 2007, 163.

has suggested, we can also consider the role of contextual dynamics, such as 'violent interaction, social transformation, peaceful cultural communication, migrational waves, the introduction of new cults, the mobility of ethnic and religious groups, ideological and political factors, and rivalry between cult places' as factors that help shape a space over time.[17]

These are, indeed, all important elements in the creation of a sanctuary, but they still focus primarily on phenomenological aspects, such as buildings and activities. They overlook the ways in which a space and its meaning is created not, or not only, by the fact of the edifices erected or the rituals conducted, but specifically in the way that those who inhabit the space give it meaning.[18] In contrast, Hubert Cancik's examination of the nature of 'sacred landscape' in Roman religion brings objects (natural and man-made) together not only with ritual, but also, in turn, with perceptual experiences.[19] He argues that the sacred landscape may be 'conceived of as a "text", composed by natural, artificial, and religious signs according to rules, which direct sight, perception, movement'; this is, in effect, 'a materialized memory of society' and is 'a phenomenon of "long duration".'[20]

In what follows, I want to build on this approach and consider how social and individual cognitive processes may have prompted phenomenological and ideological factors to come together in a meaningful system, such that shared ideas were embodied in physical actions and objects, in the creation of a 'sacred' space – and vice versa. Whether constructed by a social group – a polis or deme – or by an individual, a sanctuary achieved its status as a *temenos* because it was marked off as separate by a community of interest, which might be drawn together by a variety of different factors, *e.g.*, common citizenship or shared devotion.[21] My aim here is to reflect on sanctuaries as phenomena developed within relational networks – and not just mortal networks – which were expressed in different kinds of 'sanctuary narratives'.

The mortal owner(s) of a sanctuary was only a custodian; the consecrated land belonged to the gods. As Albert Schachter says, 'a sanctuary is a place where a person or people expects to come into contact with a supernatural

---

17   Mylonopoulos 2008.

18   As Hdt. 8. 144.2 reminds us.

19   Cancik 1985–1986.

20   Cancik 1985–1986, 260. See also Bodenhamer 2015 on the relationship between narrative, perceptions of space and place, and social interaction, and how the recent 'spatial turn' may enable a process of 'deep mapping' of heritage and culture.

21   See Purvis 2003, 12. At the most basic level, the division of space is important – a *temenos* is a separate space/marked off – the creation of boundaries in both mortal and divine realms: it is the first thing done when a sanctuary is created.

force or being ... the basic activity at a sanctuary was the establishment of contact with a deity for the benefit of the worshipper, which might range anywhere from the averting of divine anger to the granting of a divine favour.'[22] Such a meeting could be marked in a variety of different ways – it could for example, involve the setting up of an altar – and, as we will see with our final example, below, it was, often, already a moment marked by narratives.[23]

More commonly, however, we identify the site of a sanctuary nowadays by the remains of its votive offerings. A well-known inscription from Athens, which allows the priest to move the votive offerings blocking view of the cult statue, suggests the possible multiplicity of these objects.[24] Once within the sanctuary, these would become the property of the god and were never removed from the *temenos*. In this way they were marked by the relationship with the divine, and were, in turn, a marker of that relationship with the divine.[25] So Folkert van Straten describes votive offerings as constituting 'a sort of permanent link between the worshipper and his god.'[26]

It is worth dwelling on the nature of that link: the material presence of the offering was obviously crucial, but so was the meaning it conveyed. Votive offerings were sources of stories, insofar as they revealed to observers the existence of a particular relationship between mortal and divinity. In a sanctuary, this could occur directly, in the details of specific inscriptions; but objects could also convey their stories in other ways. Thus, as Harriet Flower has argued, Herodotus probably based key parts of his Lydian *logos* on stories related to the dedications made by Kroisos at Delphi.[27] As she points out, 'It is not hard to imagine that Herodotus was only one among many visitors to Delphi who asked about the origins of these remarkable objects'.[28] Building on this, it is likely that there were stories about other objects dedicated at Delphi;[29] and that at most sanctuaries, visitors would discuss the stories – both historical

---

22 Schachter 1992, 56.

23 Olympia's altar provides perhaps the best example of this: comprising bones and ash from hundreds of years of sacrifices to the god Zeus, we know it gradually grew to an enormous height (over 22ft, that is 7m or so, when Pausanias saw it; Paus. 5.13.9).

24 *LSCG* 43 (Athens): further evidence for problems in the sanctuary created by too many votives: *LSS* 107 (Rhodes) and 123 (Miletus); see also Pl. *Leg.* 909e–910a.

25 They might be discarded and/or used for landfill, or melted down to create new cult paraphernalia, but these changes must be ratified; see *IG* II³ 1, 445 ll. 24–51 and *IG* II³ 1, 1154. See discussion in Dignas 2007, 168.

26 Van Straten 1992, 274.

27 Flower 2013, 131.

28 Flower 2013, 140.

29 For example, Herodotus (Hdt. 2.135.4) tells us about the spits of iron that the *hetaera* Rhodopis dedicated there.

and mythical – connected to particular objects.[30] Literary sources provide examples of characters discussing both the content and the context of particular offerings: for example, the chorus members in Euripides' *Ion* tell each other the stories of the images they see as they come into the sanctuary at Delphi. In Herondas' fourth mime, the conversation of Phile and Kynno as they look over the dedications in the Asklepios sanctuary on Kos reminds us of the real-world information that may have remained attached to such objects. Phile admires the statues and then asks her friend to tell her who made them and who dedicated them – both of which details Kynno supplies.[31]

These passages show how objects could instantiate narratives about relationships between gods and mortals. As the examples suggest, these narratives (and the relationships they described) were not static, but were likely to develop – told in different ways by different audiences, who would bring their own interpersonal experiences to bear on their telling.[32] In turn, the presence of these objects and the narratives associated with them were also likely to create and shape further relational ties between both gods and mortals, and between mortals and mortals. As a brief example, consider the competitive aspect of votive offerings and how they were likely to provide a prompt for others to act – to submit a more impressive dedication for example, or give thanks for individual success.[33] Each offering was an instantiation of a relationship between mortal and god, with a narrative to be shared.

If we look at a sanctuary in this light, then it becomes not just an assemblage of dedications, but a knot of multiple current and past narratives about individuals and communities, and their relationships with the divine. These 'sanctuary narratives' were many and various: there were those that were associated with the space itself and/or the establishment of the sanctuary; there were mythological stories represented on buildings or on votive offerings; moreover, the rituals conducted within the sanctuary might also articulate mythological and/or historical events. As an example of this multiplicity, we can consider the Samian Heraion: founded where the goddess was born, its location was evoked, and explained, by the story of her birth and marriage to Zeus; its rituals (such as the festival of the Tonaia) commemorated key physical objects of the sanctuary (the statue of Hera and the Lygos tree), while also referring back to the founding of the temple, and looking forward to the fertility of

---

30   Herodotus use of priests as a source of information in book 2 (on Egypt) perhaps provides
     a model of their role elsewhere.
31   Eur. *Ion* 184–232; Herondas *Mime* 4.21–25.
32   See Fuhse 2009, 61.
33   See Snodgrass 1989–90, 293.

the celebrants.[34] Further stories could be found from among the sanctuary's myriad votives: not only the more monumental (such as the statues offered by Amasis, as reported by Herodotus, or the excavated larger-than-life *kouros*), or the exotic (among them an Egyptian ivory carving of a lion from Ramessid Egypt, and the bronze relief on a forehead piece of a war-chariot horse dedicated by Syrian ruler Hazael of Basan);[35] but also the myriad wooden objects, including miniature ships;[36] rock crystals; and pine cones.[37] The little ships are alluded to in a fragment of the local historian Leon of Samos, and it has been suggested that some of these objects may have memorialised epiphanies of Hera in foreign places.[38]

These narratives were likely to be multiple and dynamic. Even in the case of narratives that were more broadly shared – such as those concerning the foundation of the sanctuary itself – the evidence suggests that accounts varied and developed as they were told. The Samian Heraion again provides an example: Pausanias tells us that 'some say that the sanctuary of Hera in Samos was established by those who sailed in the Argo, and that these brought the image from Argos. But the Samians themselves hold that the goddess was born in the island by the side of the river Imbrasos under the willow that even in my time grew in the Heraion.'[39] Analysis of the evidence for local sacred histories provides some insight into at least one of the ways in which such variations may have developed: votives were used as points of reference around which writers compiled different kinds of material, including literary histories and priests' records, intertwining local myths with the master narratives of Homer and Herodotus (to fill out 'missing' information).[40] These offer a final illustration of the ways in which narratives could be used to describe relationships between mortals and gods, but they also offer a useful initial example of the ways in which all these narratives also *created* relationships between mortals and gods; the next section turns to this aspect in more detail.

---

34   Menodotus of Samos, 541 F 1 (= Athen. 15.672a–674b).

35   Kouros: Hdt. 2.182.1, see Kyreleis 1993, 119–120, fig. 7.16, p. 121. Lion: Inv. no. E133, see Kyreleis 1993, 114 and fig. 7.12, 116. Forehead piece: late ninth century BCE; Inv. no. B 2579, see Kyreleis 1993, 115–6, and fig. 7.15, 119.

36   The miniature ships of which c. 40 had been found in 1993 (Kyreleis 1993, 217, suggesting hundreds more had been dedicated) are about 40cm in length and fairly abstract in shape; Kyreleis (1988, 217 and 1993, 212) suggests that they were not from individual sailors but had a symbolic meaning of some kind.

37   Kyreleis 1988.

38   Leon of Samos *FGrH* 540 F1; Chaniotis 1988, 308 E16; as also Dillery 2005, 513.

39   Paus. 7.4.4. It seems likely that the surviving fragment of the historian Leon of Samos may allude to these contested stories; see also Diod. Sic. 5.62–63.

40   Dillery 2005, 505–26.

4   Delphic Stories: Narratives That Conflict

If we are looking for narratives structured by a paradigm of exchange between mortal and god, those from oracular and healing sanctuaries are usefully explicit: gods were portrayed as possessing a precious resource of information that mortal visitors were seeking and were grateful to receive. But, as above, this is not to imply that this produced a single, simple type of narrative, which provided a straightforward model of exchange. As an example of the potential complexity of sanctuary narratives, the stories about Delphi portray it as playing a variety of roles for different individuals and communities. In doing so, they evoke a variety of potential and actual relationships between the sanctuary and its god, and mortals, that are diverse, nuanced, and even contradictory.[41]

Thus, as Pindar notes, Delphi was described as a *pandokos naos* – a sanctuary that 'receives all'.[42] Yet, we know there were certain prerequisites for those who wanted to consult the oracle. To begin with, the Delphians reserved initial consultations for themselves and then allocated further consultations by precedence and lot.[43] Some narratives seem to allude to these requirements: the account of how *promanteia* was given to Kroisos after his extraordinary beneficence to the sanctuary seems to suggest that extravagant gifts were required in order to win this status.[44] The story of the Alcmaeonids' lavish expenditure at the sanctuary – and the resulting series of anti-Peisistratid oracular pronouncements it produced – suggests that it was not only the order of consultation which might be considered as susceptible, but even the content of resulting oracles.[45]

---

41   Just as an example, in the case of Delphi, its marginal position made it ideal for the resolution of community problems as *poleis* developed in the eighth century, but it was also a location for the displays of elite power, which, in that context, could no longer continue in those *poleis* (see Morgan 1990, 19–21, 183–4).

42   Pind. *Pyth.* 8.61–2: Neer 2003, 136 traces the ideological origins of this idea; Kurke (2011) emphasises the way this message is undermined by the reality of the financial costs of visiting the sanctuary.

43   As Kurke notes 2011, 57–8; on *promanteia*, see Amandry 1950, 113–14; Roux 1976, 76–8.

44   Hdt. 1.54.

45   Hdt. 5.66.1.

But even a straightforward consultation was far from cheap, from the *pelanos* that had to be offered on the main altar;[46] to unspecific taxes;[47] to the sacrifices within the sanctuary.[48] This is not to say that other sanctuaries did not have equivalent charges;[49] but, as Leslie Kurke has argued, the reputation for Delphic expense seems to have been complemented by a reputation for greed among the Delphians, according to the allusions made by later proverbs.[50] As inscriptions and literary sources indicate, the Delphians took a cut of the sacrifice for themselves.[51] Further evidence gives a glimpse of how that particular activity may have been regarded by some: for example, Callimachus compares a swarm of men to 'flies about a goatherd, or wasps from the ground, or the Delphians returning from a sacrifice';[52] and Kurke has argued for the ways in which the story of Aesop censures this reputed greed as part of a larger critique of elitist privileges at Delphi.[53] Finally, it is possible that the god himself was not considered immune to similar criticisms. The story of Aesop can be seen to parody and challenge Apollo's mantic authority, while some proverbs may also allude to his rapacity.[54] As we might expect, any

---

46 Eur. *Ion* 226–9. See arrangements between Delphi and Phaselis *CID* 8 (fifth century), and an agreement with Skiathos *CID* 13 (fourth century; Amandry 1939, 184 and 1950, 245, no. 16) in which the costs were much cheaper. It may be that the price had dropped in the time between the two treaties or that Skiathos was simply deemed to be a poorer state (see Parke – Wormell 1956(1), 32; Dillon 1997, 168). See also the chapter by Naiden in this volume.

47 Alluded to in *Syll.*[3] 548, which also mentions the key role of the Delphic *proxenos* in performing preliminary sacrifice (see discussion Mack 2015, 69; and Roux 1976, 82–6).

48 *Plut. De* def. or. 435b–c and *437a–b*. Amandry 1950, 104–14. That there may have been a sacrifice to Athena as well is suggested by Aristid. *Athena* 2.14 (vol. 1, p. 23 Dindorf): Roux 1976, 85 offers further possible epigraphic evidence (*e.g.*, see Bousquet 1956, 588, also published *LSCG* 42 and *SEG* 16.326) but it is not convincing.

49 For a brief overview see Dillon 1997, 167–8.

50 See Kurke 2011, 56–7. Proverbs: 'When you sacrifice at Delphi you'll have to buy meat' (Plut. *Quaest. Conv.* 709a); 'Delphic knife' is glossed as 'taking one share of the sacrificial victims, and [then] exacting another share for the knife' (von Leutsch – Schneidewin 1839, 393, no. 94 = Zenobius 147; briefer version at L-S 2, p. 155, Macarius 3.22). A further proverb (von Leutsch – Schneidewin 1839, 393, *App. Prov.* 1 no. 95) *Delphoisi thusas autos ou phagei kreas* is glossed as 'for those who spend a great deal of money but get no enjoyment from it. Since it used to happen that those sacrificing at Delphi, because of the number of people received at the hearth/participating in the feast, themselves got no taste [of the sacrifice]'.

51 *Hom. Hymn Ap.* 532–9; see also Schol. ad Ar. *Vesp.* 1446, and *P.Oxy.* 1800 with Kurke 2011, 71–4

52 Call. frag. 191.26–8 (trans. Trypanis *et al.*).

53 Kurke 2011, 53–95.

54 *Vita* G, ch. 33; see Kurke 2011, 61. 'Without bronze, Phoebus doesn't prophesy', see Kurke 2011, 71 who observes that the text includes the gloss 'this signifies the power of gifts'.

implied charges here are more ambiguous. As Kurke points out, these points of apparent criticism are also characteristics of the god that we find in ostensibly eulogistic narratives: the *Homeric Hymn to Hermes* also tells us that Apollo is the god 'who loves booty'.[55]

These multiple narratives still evoke a *techne emporike*, a science of giving and receiving, as Plato suggests, but they also complicate any straightforward model of exchange, and generate a range of potential roles and identities for mortal and god. Herodotus' account of the consultation made at Delphi by Kroisos provides a useful illustration. Despite his lavish offerings, Kroisos was not successful: his gifts were no help against the future that fate already had in store for him. The most he could obtain was some divine sympathy and a small delay arranged by a god. In effect, his story disrupts the straightforward paradigm of *charis* – as his own comment indicates when he describes the gods as *acharistoi*.[56] If, as discussed earlier, a relationship gives meaning to an exchange or gift, and vice versa, then this story models the unequal and uncertain nature of the relationship between mortals and the unseen powers that direct their lives. Apollo is described as having values and motivations different from those of Croesus, which lead in turn to very different goals, and profoundly different outcomes from those expected. The unequal nature of this relationship is reflected in the form and content of the narrative, which, like many narratives about oracular consultation, includes a riddle. The narrative about this gift exchange evokes a relationship that is uncertain, unreliable, and fundamentally asymmetrical: mortal and immortal are portrayed as imbalanced not only in the sense of the god's cognitive powers and powers to grant gifts, but also in much broader cosmological terms.

As these examples suggest, the multiplicity of narratives about reciprocity that existed at a sanctuary were, on the one hand, descriptive, insofar as they evoked the variety of perceptions of the nature of divine/mortal relations. But these stories were also generative, that is, in the telling, they also created those relations. And this, finally, brings us to the question of how we understand the relational paradigm and the narratives that invoke it when one player in the relationship does not actually exist – to be explored in the next section.

---

55   Kurke 2011, 79–80 on *Hom. Hymn Herm.* 335; See also Richardson (2010 ad ll. 176–81) on this theme in the poem, drawing attention to 335, 494–5, 549; and for this theme and the reputation for greed of the Delphic priests, to *Hom. Hymn Ap.* 535–7, 540–3nn. and Hom. *Il.* 9. 404–5.

56   Hdt. 1.90.4.

5   Divine Minds: Narratives That Create

I want to approach this question through theory of mind (ToM), so-called because it involves an individual imputing mental states to herself and others.[57]
At a basic level, I suggest, ancient sources offer us evidence for ToM among our
subjects with regard to gods. Votive offerings, for example, do not only suggest
the mental states of those who brought them, but indicate that those individuals, in turn, were attributing states of mind to divinities. They indicate an
assumption that the divinity had knowledge, likes or dislikes, and, above all,
intention; that a god could be swayed by the provision of a gift, responding to
the institution of *charis*.[58] As this chapter has demonstrated, the narratives
recounted about these objects confirm this analysis – but they also reveal a
more advanced ToM.

Take, for example, a visitor to the sanctuary of Asklepios who read the story of
Euphanes, described at the beginning of this chapter. That narrative describes
a character who both exhibits and demonstrates ToM: by going to the sanctuary he can be said to exhibit a purposeful state of mind; in turn, by offering his
dice to the god, he demonstrates some understanding or assumption about the
mental state of the god whom he is addressing. A visitor to the sanctuary who
understood the story in this way would be exhibiting both ToM and second-
order ToM. But the story of Euphanes as told in the *iamata* offers another level
of recursiveness. Asklepios' laughter on receiving the answer 'ten dice' from
Euphanes, also suggests that Euphanes, when he offered the gift, understood
that the god would hold a particular understanding of Euphanes' state of mind
in that moment. So, a visitor to the sanctuary who read this story is being led
through a number of levels of theory of mind: the narrative suggests, first,
Euphanes' own mental states of purpose and knowledge; second, Euphanes'
assumption regarding Asklepios' mental states of knowledge and purpose; and,
third, Euphanes' understanding regarding Asklepios' empathy and purpose
concerning Euphanes' own state of mind.[59] Thus we see how this narrative – and
others like it – described and instantiated a relational tie of *charis* between worshipper and worshipped, which established basic social roles. But in addition,
the details of the story also provided a model for worshippers to think about
the inner mental states of everyone involved – not only other worshippers,

---

57   Premack – Woodruff 1978.

58   Perner – Wimmer 1985.

59   It can be argued that by making this observation, I am demonstrating fourth-order ToM:
      that is, I am expressing an understanding of the states of mind of my historical subjects
      concerning the mental state of Euphanes, *etc.*

but also the presumed mental state of the god or goddess. In this way, sanctuary narratives, perhaps especially those that described transactions, provided a link with the divine; but, in addition to, or rather alongside, these processes, they were also responsible for engendering the divine in the first place.

6   Conclusion: Narratives, Networks, and the Generation of the Sacred

This chapter has set out to examine divine-mortal interactions in which an exchange takes place, where divine power or knowledge is sought in return for a material object of value to the giver. These interactions created relational ties between individuals and/or groups and divinities, and such relations were generated, sustained and expressed through stories or other narratives that were communicated in a range of ways through various media, including embodied information. From this perspective, a sanctuary, a sacred space, can be described as instantiating a 'knot' of stories about divine-mortal interactions. 'Sanctuary narratives' might be realised through various media, from a material and semi-permanent form, like a building; to a material and more temporary form, like a votive; to a more ephemeral form, such as a ritual. Individual stories shaped, and were shaped by, broader social narratives that helped to support social institutions: stories multiplied, some might reinforce each other's meanings, others might undermine and subvert them.

This model of the individual's role in developing broader social institutions and their narratives, and vice versa, helps to nuance our current model of 'embedded' religion, revealing the individual relational ties of action and meaning which it comprised. But not only does it elaborate the more performative aspects of religious practice, it also helps to illuminate the creation of the concepts that nurtured them. Analysis of sample narratives, and their inferences for theory of mind, suggests that it is through the network of individual relationships, and the concomitant exchange of narratives – which were in turn narratives of exchange – that conceptions of divinity itself were generated. With this point, we return to the story with which we started, and the healing of Euphanes at Epidauros. As we have seen, this narrative prompts a series of inferences about the inner mental world not only of Euphanes, but also of the god. Thus, when the god is depicted as asking Euphanes 'What will you give me if I should make you well?', what the god receives is not, or not only, dice, but, implicitly, the gift of existence.

Bibliography

Amandry, P. 1939. "Convention religieuse conclue entre Delphes et Skiathos", *Bulletin de Correspondance Héllenique* 63, 183–219.

Amandry, P. 1950. *La mantique apollinienne à Delphes. Essai sur le fonctionnement de l'oracle*, Paris.

Bodenhamer, J. 2015. "Narrating Space and Place," in *Deep Maps and Spatial Narratives*, eds. J. Bodenhamer, J. Corrigan, and T.M. Harris, Bloomington, IN, 7–27.

Bousquet, J. 1956. "Inscriptions de Delphes", *Bulletin de Correspondance Héllenique* 80, 579–83.

Cancik, H. 1985-6. "Rome as Sacred Landscape: Varro and the End of Republican Religion in Rome", *Visible Religion* 4.5, 250–65.

Chaniotis, A. 1988. *Historie und Historiker in den griechischen Inschriften: Epigraphische Beiträge zur griechischen Historiographie*, Stuttgart.

Day, J. 2010. *Archaic Greek Epigram and Dedication: Representation and Reperformance*, Cambridge.

Dignas, B. 2007. "A Day in the Life of a Greek Sanctuary", in *A Companion to Greek Religion*, ed. D. Ogden, Oxford, 163–77.

Dillery, J. 2005. "Greek Sacred History", *American Journal of Philology* 126.4, 505–26.

Dillon, M. 1997. *Pilgrims and Pilgrimage in Ancient Greece*, London.

Eidinow, E. 2011a. "Networks and Narratives: A Model for Ancient Greek Religion", *Kernos* 21, 9–38.

Eidinow, E. 2011b. *Fate, Luck and Fortune. Antiquity and its Legacy*, London.

Eidinow, E. 2015a. "Embedded ... and Embodied", in *Communities and Networks in the Ancient Greek World*, eds. C. Taylor and K. Vlassopoulos, Oxford, 54–79.

Eidinow, E. 2015b. *Envy, Poison, and Death: Women on Trial in Classical Athens*, Oxford.

Eidinow, E. 2016. "Popular Theologies: The Gift of Divine Envy", in *Theologies of Ancient Greek Religion*, eds. E. Eidinow, J. Kindt, and R. Osborne, Cambridge, 205–32.

Flower, H. 2013 [1991] "Herodotus and Delphic Traditions about Croesus", in *Herodotus: Volume 1: Herodotus and the Narrative of the Past*, ed. R.V. Munson, Oxford, 124–53.

Fuhse, J. 2009. "The Meaning Structure of Social Networks", *Sociological Theory* 27.1, 51–73.

Furley, W.D. 2010. "Life in a Line: A Reading of Dedicatory Epigrams", in *Archaic and Classical Greek Epigram*, eds. M. Baumbach, A. Petrovic, and I. Petrovic, Cambridge, 151–66.

Godart, F.C. and White, H.C. 2010. "Switchings under Uncertainty: The Coming and Becoming of Meanings", *Poetics* 38.6, 567–86.

Granovetter, M. 1985. "Economic Action and Social Structure: The Problem of Embeddedness", *American Journal of Sociology* 91.3, 481–510.

Korf, B. *et al.* 2010. "The Gift of Disaster: The Commodification of Good Intentions in Post-Tsunami Sri Lanka", *Disasters* 34 Suppl 1, 60–77.

Kurke, L. 2011. *Aesopic Conversations: Popular Tradition, Cultural Dialogue, and the Invention of Greek Prose. Martin Classical Lectures*, Princeton – Oxford.

Kyrieleis, H. 1988. "Offerings of the 'Common Man' in the Heraion at Samos", in *Early Greek Cult Practice, Proceedings of the Fifth International Symposium at the Swedish Institute at Athens*, eds. R. Hagg, N. Marinatos, and G. Nordquist, Stockholm, 215–21.

Kyrieleis, H. 1993. "The Heraion at Samos", in *Greek Sanctuaries: New Approaches*, eds. R. Hagg and N. Marinatos, London, 99–122.

von Leutsch, E. and Schneidewin, F.W. 1839. *Corpus Paroemiographorum Graecorum*, Göttingen.

LiDonnici, L.R. 1995. *The Epidaurian Miracle Inscriptions: Text, Translation and Commentary*, Atlanta.

Mack, W. 2015. *Proxeny and Polis: Institutional Networks in the Ancient Greek World*, Oxford.

Morgan, C. 1990. *Athletes and Oracles: The Transformation of Olympia and Delphi in the Eighth Century*, Cambridge.

Mylonopoulos, I. 2008. "The Dynamics of Ritual Space in the Hellenistic and Roman East", *Kernos* [Online] 21: DOI: http://dx.doi.org/10.4000/kernos.1601.

Neer, R. 2003. "Framing the Gift: The Siphnian Treasury at Delphi and the Politics of Public Art", in *The Cultures Within Ancient Greek Culture: Contact, Conflict, Collaboration*, eds. C. Dougherty and L. Kurke, Cambridge, 129–49.

Parke, H.W. and Wormell, D.E.W. 1956. *The Delphic Oracle*, Oxford.

Parker, R. 1986. "Greek Religion", in *The Oxford History of Greece and the Hellenistic World*, eds. J. Boardman, J. Griffin, and O. Murray, Oxford, 306–29.

Parker, R. 1998. "Pleasing Thighs: Reciprocity in Greek Religion", in *Reciprocity in Ancient Greece*, eds. C. Gill, N. Postlethwaite, and R. Seaford, Oxford, 105–26.

Perner, J. and Wimmer, H. 1985. "'John Thinks That Mary Thinks That …' Attribution of Second-order Beliefs by 5–10 Year Old Children", *Journal of Experimental Child Psychology* 39, 437–471.

Premack, D. and Woodruff, G. 1978. "Does the Chimpanzee Have a Theory of Mind?", *Behavioral and Brain Sciences* 1.4, 515–26.

Purvis, A. 2003. *Singular Dedications: Founders and Innovators of Private Cults in Classical Greece*, London.

Richardson, N. 2010. *Three Homeric Hymns: To Apollo, Hermes, and Aphrodite. Hymns 3, 4, and 5*, Cambridge – New York.

Roux, G. 1976. *Son oracle et ses dieux*, Paris.

Schachter, A. 1992. "Policy, Cult and the Placing of Greek Sanctuaries", in *Le sanctuaire grec*, ed. A. Schachter, Geneva, 1–64.

Schwartz, B. 1967. "The Psychology of the Gift", *American Journal of Sociology* 73.1, 1–11.

Snodgrass, A. 1989–90. "The Economics of Dedication at Greek Sanctuaries", in *Atti del Convegno internazionale Anathema: regime delle offerte e vita dei santuari nel Mediterraneo antico, Roma, 15–18 giugno 1989*, eds. G. Bartoloni, G. Colonna, and C. Grottanelli, Rome, 287–94.

van Straten, F. 1992. "Votives and Votaries in Greek Sanctuaries", in *Le sanctuaire grec*, ed. A. Schachter, Geneva, 247–90.

Trypanis, C.A., Gelzer, T., and Whitman, C.H. ed. and trans. 1989. *Callimachus: Aetia, Iambi, Hecale and Other Fragments. Musaeus: Hero and Leander*, Cambridge, MA.

White, H.C. 2008. *Identity and Control. How Social Formations Emerge*, Princeton, NJ.

White, H.C. *et al.* 2007. "Networks and Styles and Switching", *Soziale Systeme* 13.1/2, 543–55.

Whitley, J. 2001. *The Archaeology of Ancient Greece*, Cambridge.

CHAPTER 9

Space, Exchange and the Embedded Economies of Greek Sanctuaries

Troels Myrup Kristensen

1 Introduction

Maps of ancient Greek sanctuaries typically feature large quantities of empty, white space.[1] These spaces designate the seemingly open, unoccupied areas that are located between standard architectural features, such as temples, altars, theatres and votive monuments. These areas are sometimes labelled as part of a *temenos*, a term that signifies 'divine real estate' and that was theoretically always separated from the outside, secular world by a clearly defined *peribolos* wall.[2] Yet, in spite of scholarly interest in the semantic developments of the term *temenos* and the recent spatial turn in the study of Greek religion, the multifaceted uses of the open spaces themselves are rarely given much serious discussion, indicative of the extent to which most archaeological approaches to sacred space still tend to privilege monumentality and permanence over more ephemeral phenomena.[3] This blind spot in the archaeological field of vision is a useful starting point for the present chapter, which aims to identify some of the material footprints of economic exchange in Greek sanctuaries that are likely to have occupied a considerable proportion of the open spaces of the *temenos*, in close correlation with the ebbs and flows of the ritual calendar.[4]

Studies of economic exchange in relation to sanctuaries generally tend to adopt a macro-scale view, looking at interregional trade networks, long-range imports and (by extension) mobility on a scale that takes us far beyond the

---

1 For archaeological critiques of the map, see Lock 2000. For an attempt to fill (some of) the blanks on maps of Greek sanctuaries in terms of their function, see Connelly 2012.
2 Bergqvist 1967.
3 The discipline of classical archaeology is not alone in this neglect. Bille – Sørensen 2016 have recently pointed out that archaeologists in general should study architecture as assemblages rather than as discrete entities. On space and Greek sanctuaries, see also Alcock – Osborne 1994; Scott 2010; Agelidis 2017 and Kristensen 2018.
4 The related question of production has attracted considerable interest among archaeologists, *e.g.* Linders – Alroth 1992.

spaces of the sanctuaries themselves, or alternatively focus exclusively on specific classes of objects, such as pottery.[5] In contrast, this chapter is less concerned with how individual objects got to sanctuaries than with where they were bought and sold within them. The chapter therefore considers the micro-scale of economic exchange *inside* sanctuaries, and the temporary, ephemeral uses of space during the festival markets (*panegyreis*) that are known from a variety of sources. It begins by establishing the general significance and typology of festival markets, then presents an overview of some individual markets as known from inscriptions, and finally turns to an archaeologically grounded discussion of the spaces of economic exchange in sanctuaries. I argue that such discussions, although complicated by the poor state of the evidence in addition to the usual problems of interpretation, are necessary to fill in the blanks in our understanding of the embedded economies of Greek sanctuaries as well as the uses of their sacred spaces more broadly.

2   Greek Pilgrimage in the Marketplace

Many ancient sanctuaries took advantage of the commercial opportunities offered by pilgrimage and organised markets and fairs in conjunction with festivals and other religious gatherings (see Kowalzig, this volume).[6] While these forms of exchange are sometimes described by scholars as peripheral phenomena, or as functional spin-offs of religious gatherings, they were clearly fundamental in bringing both people and goods together through the entangled occasions of pilgrimage and trade.[7] Divine protection was useful to encourage trade and even consumer protection, as in the case of Rome's Forum Boarium where exchange took place under Hercules' supervision.[8] Festival markets have also been linked to other social and political developments in the ancient world, such as the rise of urbanism. The site of Lucus Feroniae, located north of Rome, hosted an annual fair for both the Sabines and the Latins in honour of the goddess Feronia and later grew into a proper urban settlement, and is sometimes seen as a model case for the transition of a sanctuary fair

---

5   For recent examples, see the papers in Kistler *et al.* 2015.
6   On the Greek sacred economy, see Linders – Alroth 1992; Dillon 1997, 214–17; Horster 2011; Horden – Purcell 2000, 434; Bresson 2016, 237–9 For comparative Roman material, refer to MacMullen 1970; de Ligt 1993; Morcillo 2013. On the modern context, see Reader 2014.
7   In her recent discussion of Greek festivals, Synnøve des Bouvrie notes that markets existed at the outer limits of such gatherings (2012, 62). For spin-offs, see Iddeng 2012, 19.
8   Potts 2015, 114–15.

into a town.[9] The number of *panegyreis* grew during the Hellenistic period, especially in Asia Minor, and the potential for profit has been interpreted as a key motivation for cities to introduce and promote these new festivals (see Horster, this volume).[10] Some ancient *panegyreis* furthermore proved remarkably resilient throughout periods of significant social, economic and religious change. Thus, at the sanctuary at Mamre in Palestine, sacred travel and commerce went hand in hand into Late Antiquity, seemingly pursued by pagans, Christians and Jews alike.[11]

More broadly, in the history of sacred travel, separating trade from pilgrimage is often not meaningful or even helpful, as the two phenomena are so closely connected. This association between sacred travel and economic exchange has a very long history, especially in the Near East. In her study of pilgrimage as it developed on the Arabian Peninsula from the pre-Islamic period onwards, Joy McCorriston suggests that one of the key attributes of pilgrimage was its facilitation of economic exchange through the bringing together of different communities.[12] McCorriston likens such markets to 'the constitution of a temporary society of different ethnic or cultural groups',[13] emphasising the multicultural, multi-ethnic and ephemeral dimensions that we also see in Lucus Feroniae and Mamre. The phrase 'braided network', suggested by Marlena Whiting in this volume as one way of describing the joint development of travel for religious, economic and political reasons, may be particularly apt in this context. Trade/pilgrimage can be seen as one kind of braided network enabling exchange between various spheres of production, such as urban and rural economies, as well as between different ethnic and social groups (a point that is further explored below in a case study of a Syrian sanctuary). In the Greek world, Delos, the holy island of Apollo and Artemis, and one of the most important *emporia* in the Mediterranean, is also evidence of the fact that trade and religion go hand in hand (see Padilla Peralta, this volume).[14]

---

9   Dion. Hal. 3.32; Taylor 1920; Edlund 1987, 87; Morcillo 2013, 250–7. The grove was turned into a colony during the reign of Augustus.

10   See Dillon 1997, 217, for a critique. For recent work on festivals, see Brandt – Iddeng 2012.

11   Burkert 2012, 40–2; Drbal 2017.

12   McCorriston 2011, 52; also see McCorriston 2017.

13   McCorriston 2011, 52.

14   Strabo tells us that the festival of Apollo and Leto included a fair (10.5.4; and see de Ligt 1993, 253).

TABLE 9.1   De Ligt's typology of fairs and markets in pre-industrial societies (based on de Ligt 1993, 15).

Type	Duration	Catchment area	Volume of goods	Type of transaction
Local	Limited (1–2 days)	Small (< 50 km)	Low	Direct from trader to consumer
Regional	1–2 weeks	Up to 300 km	Medium	Large-scale and specialised
Interregional	3–8 weeks	Very large	High	Long-range and luxury goods

Although it is a reasonable assumption that all major gatherings at sanctuaries would have attracted some level of commercial activity, it is useful to break this down further. In his book *Fairs and Markets in the Roman Empire*, Luuk de Ligt presents a typology of the different markets associated with sanctuaries in the pre-industrial age which is also helpful in terms of understanding the Greek context (Table 9.1).[15] De Ligt considers three sizes of fairs, ranging from local to interregional, each defined by duration, catchment, the volume of goods exchanged, and the type of transaction involved (whether goods were sold directly by the producer to the consumer, or whether they passed through more intricate networks of exchange before reaching the place of the transaction). Reconstructing such networks in archaeological terms is notoriously difficult, as is evident from discussions of *exotica* in early Greek sanctuaries, such as the Heraia of Samos and Perachora.[16] For instance, how many stages did Egyptian ivories or Phoenician scarabs pass through before reaching a sanctuary in the Aegean or on the Greek mainland?

Mobility is a key factor in all of these three types of markets. For instance, de Ligt defines the catchment of a local fair to be less than 50 km, whereas a regional market may attract people from a distance of up to 300 km, and the interregional area extends even further than that.[17] Attempts have been made to define the catchment areas of individual Greek sanctuaries, often based on epigraphic evidence such as lists of *theoroi* and *theorodokoi* that are known from a number of sites, but these present significant interpretive challenges.[18]

---

15   De Ligt 1993, 15.
16   On Samos, see Kyrieleis 1993; and see Kristensen 2012b.
17   De Ligt 1993, 15.
18   Rutherford 2013, 9. On Samothracian lists, see also Dimitrova 2008.

For example, we may ask how representative such epigraphic snapshots of connectivity really are. The processes through which particular delegations and institutions were documented in the medium of stone inscriptions are indeed poorly understood; as are the relationships between the social and political institution of *theoria* on the one hand, and economic networks on the other. Archaeological attempts to define catchment and questions of mobility present similar problems to those outlined above in relation to the type of exchange involved.[19]

De Ligt qualifies his typology of fairs and markets in a way that helps us to think more broadly about the types of evidence that we are looking for. The simplest type of market, which he calls the 'festival-connected food market', offered only the bare necessities for pilgrims, such as food and water.[20] Although this type of food market is predominantly accessible only indirectly, by means of the pottery that was used to prepare and serve food and drinks, recent zoo-archaeological evidence provides important information about the complexity involved in catering for sanctuary feasting practices, such as the more than 3,500 fish bones representing more than 19 families that were uncovered in the sanctuary of Poseidon at Kalaureia on the island of Poros.[21] Fishing equipment was discovered in a building immediately outside the *temenos*, suggesting that it may have been used for a commercial operation based around the sanctuary.

In many sanctuaries, supplies for ritual activities were available, including sacrificial animals, figurines and a selection of other votive offerings in terracotta or metal, often produced in the vicinity of or even within the sanctuary itself and intended for consumption on site. De Ligt refers to these items as the essential components of the 'accessory festal market'. In light of the non-permanent nature of most religious gatherings, most of the needs of this particular type of market could have been met by travelling craftsmen.[22] However, when sanctuaries and their markets grew, new opportunities emerged. In the case of Olympia, evidence of on-site votive production, including mis-castings and debris, has indeed been interpreted as an indication of the sanctuary's growing popularity and importance after 700 BCE.[23]

Finally, de Ligt reserves the term 'genuine fairs' for 'low-frequency commercial gatherings held at regularly spaced intervals and involving the distribution

---

19   For such an approach to the evidence from Delphi, see Jacquemin 1999. See also Aurigny, this volume.

20   De Ligt 1993, 14–15.

21   See Mylona 2015 on the fish bones and related finds from building 1.

22   Morgan 1990, 39–43.

23   On the production of votives at Olympia, see the discussion by Morgan 1990, 35–9.

of merchandise not destined for consumption on the spot'.[24] This final type focuses on the position of more important sanctuaries as hubs in broader economic networks, from which pilgrims bought goods to take home with them that may or may not have had a specifically religious meaning. Souvenirs have attracted substantial interest as a discrete type of object in studies of late antique Christianity, whereas in earlier periods it may be very difficult to conclude that particular groups of material artefacts originated in specific sanctuaries and were associated with pilgrimages.[25] Some other classes of goods that were sold in Greek sanctuaries, such as slaves and cattle, were clearly not intended for consumption on the spot. Pausanias, for example, describes both of these goods as being on sale in the market of a sanctuary of Isis in Phocis.[26] Difficult as it is to see a slave as a fitting souvenir of a pilgrimage, it is worth remembering that Delos was not only the sacred island of Apollo and Artemis but also home to one of the largest slave markets in the Mediterranean. Although these types of goods presumably would have taken up substantial space within any given sanctuary, they are typically invisible in the archaeological record.

De Ligt's typologies of pre-industrial festival markets constitute a useful starting point, but they are insufficient to fill in the blanks on our archaeological maps, or even to assess the lived experience of sanctuary markets and how they worked in spatial terms.[27] To do so, it is helpful to look at contemporary ethnographic examples of pilgrimage fairs.[28] Although they do not make it possible to reconstruct the precise character of individual markets in the past, such fairs are at least useful analogies for further probing, as Kowalzig also explores further in her contribution to this volume.

Ethnographic examples of pilgrimage fairs range in character from being transient and ephemeral to being fixed or at least semi-permanent. A particularly evocative example is the Star Snow or Quyllurit'i Festival in Peru, which has taken place every year since the late 18th century between Ascension Day and Corpus Christi, and which is the topic of a major study by the anthropologist Michael Sallnow.[29] In characteristically syncretic fashion, this pilgrimage festival combines Catholic elements with a pre-Christian celebration of the stars. Organised by a special brotherhood in the Sinakara Valley in the Cusco

---

24 De Ligt 1993, 15, my emphasis. He uses 'markets' and 'fairs' synonymously.

25 Kristensen 2012a. And see Ritter, this volume.

26 Paus. 10.32.13–5 (Tithorea); and see de Ligt – de Neeves 1986, 404. He also tells us of merchants setting up small stalls made of reeds and other readily available materials.

27 For an archaeologically grounded perspective on Roman markets, see Holleran 2012.

28 Garraty – Stark 2010 cover further comparative perspectives.

29 Sallnow 1987; and see the recent *BBC News* feature: http://www.bbc.com/news/magazine -32888643 (accessed 22 October 2019).

region of the Andes Mountains, some 4,700 m above sea level, it is attended today by more than 10,000 pilgrims, who cross some extraordinarily difficult terrain to get there. The location high up in the mountains is tied to the origins of the festival: it is supposed to be the site of a miracle in which the image of Christ appeared on a boulder. This Peruvian festival is a particularly revealing case for us, as the temporary and ephemeral nature of the pilgrimage belies the sophistication of the whole enterprise. Some of the items that are transported all the way up the mountain include live fish transported in large barrels of water; but there is also a broad range of more portable goods such as counterfeit 1,000-dollar bills that are seen as bringing future wealth.[30] The Star Snow Festival is a useful reminder that pilgrimage fairs are not always the first steps in a chain of urban evolution that ultimately leads to a more permanent settlement, as in the case of Lucus Feroniae.

Closer to the ancient Greek context are modern-day feasts for patron saints (*panighiria*) at rural churches on the sparsely populated peninsula of Methana, which have been discussed in recent ethno-archaeological work by Hamish Forbes, and are similarly ephemeral in their nature and organisation.[31] On these occasions, what are usually empty spaces become central locations with people from all over Methana gathering to participate in religious ceremonies, to socialise and to purchase goods such as wool and other agricultural products, amounting to what de Ligt calls a 'genuine fair'.

Other contemporary fairs at pilgrimage sites do take on a more permanent, settled form. The new Coptic monastery at Abu Mena, located some 45 km outside Alexandria and in close proximity to the ruined late-antique pilgrimage complex dedicated to St. Menas, is one such instance.[32] Housed in metal-roofed stalls, this is where merchants sell products which are often branded with imagery related to Menas, such as two camels, to visitors when they arrive (Fig. 9.1). The products sold include olives, shampoo and other household products, presumably merchandise that was destined for consumption outside the sanctuary context (Fig. 9.2). In this case, the stalls are permanent fixtures, although they were built using simple materials, whereas the level of activity clearly depend on which day in the liturgical calendar the pilgrims happen to visit. Abu Mena presents a model of the sanctuary market in which the distinction between the permanent and the periodic is more fluid than de Ligt allows for in his approach to pre-industrial sanctuary markets. What is a festival-connected food market on one day may be a genuine market on

---

30   On the organisation of the festival market, see Sallnow 1987, 216.

31   Forbes 2007, 358–74.

32   For an overview, see Grossmann 1998.

FIGURE 9.1   Market stall in the new Coptic monastery at Abu Mena
PHOTO: TROELS MYRUP KRISTENSEN

FIGURE 9.2   Shampoo and other products for sale in the new Coptic monastery at
Abu Mena
PHOTO: TROELS MYRUP KRISTENSEN

FIGURE 9.3   Souvenirs for sale near the House of the Virgin Mary at Bülbüldağı near
              Ephesos
              PHOTO: TROELS MYRUP KRISTENSEN

another, and vice versa. At the House of the Virgin Mary at Bülbüldağı near
Ephesos, a major pilgrimage site since the 19th century, there are also semi-
permanent stalls that conveniently flank the road leading up to the central
part of the sanctuary.[33] The goods on offer here are more of the souvenir variety, such as plastic figurines and snow globes depicting the Virgin Mary, bottled
holy water, and a range of archaeologically-themed trinkets (Fig. 9.3). This site
clearly belongs in de Ligt's category of the festal accessory market, even though
the volume of pilgrims is very high during the summer and the catchment area
is effectively global, as is evident from the multitude of languages that can be
heard when visiting.

3   Marketplaces in Greek Sanctuaries, I: Epigraphy

Whereas the preceding section covered the issue of economic exchange in
sanctuaries first in abstract and then in indirect terms (by means of typology and comparison respectively), this section presents a short overview of

---

33   Kristensen 2012a, 73–4; Pülz 2012, 252–4; Yasin 2012.

the epigraphic evidence that sheds light on specific markets held at individual Greek sanctuaries, including important information about their organisation.[34]

The earliest inscription relating to a sanctuary market dates to the early fourth century BCE and comes from the temple of Athena Alea at Tegea.[35] It mentions a public official (the *hieromnamon*) who was in charge of 'everything relating to the merchandise', although it is less clear whether this can be regarded as a true market or simply as a festival-accessory market.[36] More detailed regulations for a sanctuary market are found in the so-called 'Sacred Law' of the Messenian mystery cult of Andania, dating to 91 BCE.[37] These mysteries took place in a sacred grove located 16 km from Messene. City and sanctuary were linked by an annual procession.[38] The two large blocks that display the Sacred Law, reused in a church after their discovery in 1858, present very detailed regulations for both sacred and profane aspects of the mysteries.[39] For instance, they tell of special sandals, which, arguably, were part of the ritual requirements for entry into the mystery cult at one level, but which stimulated a particular type of production and exchange related to the festival at another level.[40] The inscriptions also inform us of the *hieroi*, presumably a board of sacred men responsible for deciding the location of a market, specifically called an *agora*, which here must mean a temporary marketplace rather than a permanent one.[41] The implication of this passage is that the location could alternate from year to year, although it is not clear why this was the case, nor which criteria the *hieroi* may have applied when choosing a location. The inscription further stipulates that the *agoranomos* is entrusted with making sure that all sellers use weights and measures, suggesting that tourists and pilgrims were potentially subject to all kinds of tricks and scams – just as they are today.[42] It is also important to point out that economic exchange was actively encouraged, as no charges or restrictions on the use of space were imposed on traders.

---

34   This evidence has been compiled and discussed in some detail by de Ligt 1993, and, more recently, Chandezon 2003.

35   *LSCG* 67; de Ligt – de Neeves 1986, 404; de Ligt 1993, Appendix I.D., 245–246; Chandezon 2003, 33–40; and see comments in Harris – Carbon 2015, 18.

36   The same inscription may also refer to land owned by the sanctuary. On sacred land in Athens, see Papazarkadas 2011.

37   For recent critique of the concept of sacred laws, see Carbon – Pirenne-Delforge 2012.

38   Gawlinski 2012, 49–58; Friese 2017; Nielsen 2017, 39–42; Clinton 2019, Appendix.

39   Gawlinski 2012, 60–3.

40   Dillon 1997, 214

41   Gawlinski suggests that the regulations for the institution of the *hieroi* were inscribed on a different stone (2012, 102). On the use of *agora* as a periodic market, see de Ligt 1993, 40–1. And see Horster, this volume.

42   Gawlinski 2012, 99–103, and for commentary see Gawlinski 2012, 214–9.

Although stalls are not specifically mentioned in the case of Andania, they were probably temporary structures, perhaps similar to those of the Star Snow Festival.[43] Unfortunately, we have no archaeological evidence from Andania that would allow us to locate the market within a particular physical setting in the sanctuary.[44]

The epigraphic record offers evidence of more permanent structures than those we have to imagine at Andania. Excavations in the Heraion on Samos have uncovered a remarkable inscription dating to the mid-third century BCE that presents a charter for shopkeepers (*kapeloi*) in the sanctuary.[45] The charter essentially monopolises trade in the sanctuary to the lessees of four individual shops. If anyone else set up shop, they were to be fined. The shops on Samos were open all year round, thus offering a rather different model of exchange than the types of periodic markets known from Andania, and perhaps looked something like those observed at modern Abu Mena. Inscribed measuring tables, such as those found in the mystery sanctuary at Eleusis, are probably also associated with markets of a similar scale and permanence.[46]

4   Marketplaces in Greek Sanctuaries, II: Archaeology

Scholarship has mostly refrained from contextualising the epigraphic evidence discussed above within the topography of individual sanctuaries, often because the relevant inscriptions have been found in secondary contexts and rarely indicate specific areas for the placement of stalls and other marketplace features. The inscriptions are indeed generally silent or unspecific about the exact locations of marketplaces. Similar efforts to identify slave markets in the archaeological record have received intensive criticism, with one scholar going so far as to denounce them as nothing more than 'archaeological fictions'.[47] Although there clearly are substantial methodological obstacles involved in this endeavour, the two final sections of this chapter attempt to move forward and address some specific spaces for economic exchange in selected Greek sanctuaries in more detail. I argue that this is an essential undertaking if we want to understand the social and economic practices that have produced the blanks on archaeological maps of sanctuaries that were outlined in the

---

43   Pausanias on such makeshift booths: 10.32.13–5.
44   Friese 2017.
45   Shipley 1987, 216–17; Dillon 1997, 216–17; Lupu 2009, 285–97.
46   For examples: De Ligt 1993, 253; Clinton 2005, 207, no. 179, 261, no. 237; 2008, 23.
47   Trümper 2009.

introduction to this chapter. The present section presents some general observations, whereas the following section focuses on one sanctuary that has yield-
ed a combination of epigraphic and archaeological sources, making it possible
at least to propose the specific location of its festival market.

As pointed out in the introduction, classical archaeology has focused traditionally on monumental architecture. But evidence of a variety of ephemeral constructs such as marketplaces does exist, even though they were related
mostly to urban spaces rather than to sanctuaries.[48] Humble inscriptions specifying where exchange and production were located have been identified, for
example, in recent work on late antique cities.[49] Even without textual aids,
archaeological scrutiny of the physical surfaces of public spaces has revealed
evidence of the transient usage of space, including various kinds of formal economic exchange. For instance, a close study of the paved surfaces of the Upper
Agora at Sagalassos has revealed evidence of market stalls, making it possible
to reconstruct a rich picture of commercial life across several centuries in the
city.[50] This evidence mostly consists of holes for erecting temporary stalls selling goods in what was a busy urban thoroughfare, and thus a favourable place
to set up shop. It is generally only in such crowded everyday spaces that one
can expect to find deliberate attempts at regulation involving inscriptions or
demarcations of areas for specific purposes, such as a market.

Evidence of stalls in sanctuaries has only been found very rarely, for instance
in the sanctuary of Demeter and Kore at Corinth (Fig. 9.4). The excavators have
suggested that a series of postholes found here was intended for the erection of
temporary stalls during busy festival days, although it is unclear which goods
they would have offered to visitors.[51] These postholes were concentrated in an
area west of the steps that run through the central part of the sanctuary, in an
area that would have attracted substantial numbers of people at 'peak times'
in the sacred calendar. The shops were also conveniently placed close to the
steps that made it easier to enter and leave the sanctuary and its many dining
rooms, indicating that they may have catered for on-site consumption. Near
the stalls, a *horos* stone was found, indicating concern to separate sacred and
profane spaces, a matter of considerable importance in all ancient sanctuaries,
and something which was also noted in the Andanian inscription.

---

48 For example, see papers in Chankowski – Karvonis 2012, focusing particularly on com
  mercial aspects of the *agora*.

49 Lavan 2012a, 338–40; 2012b, 333–4.

50 Lavan 2012b, 328–32.

51 Bookidis – Stroud 1997, 201; pls. 23–4a–b. Also noted by Gawlinski 2012, 215.

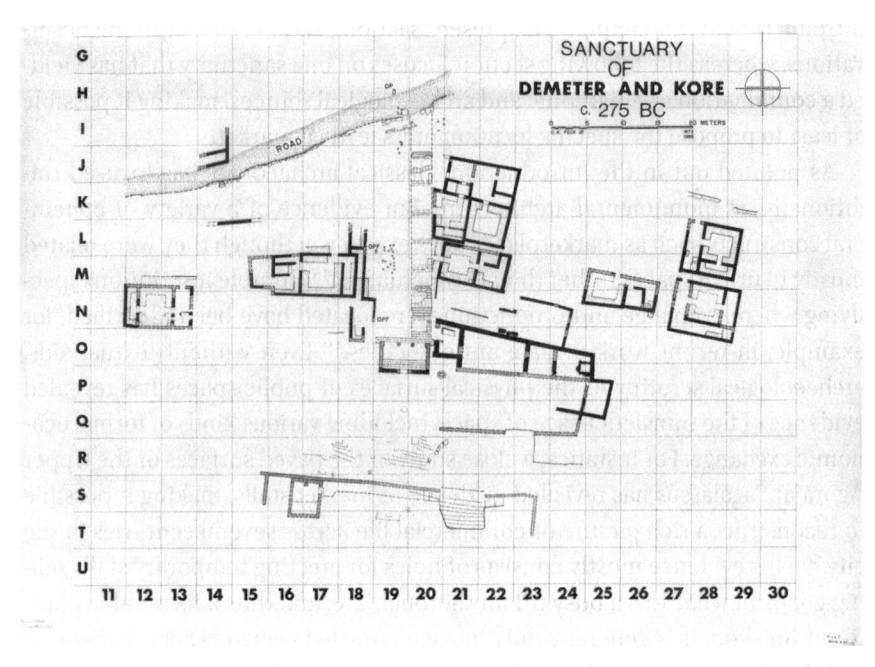

FIGURE 9.4   Sanctuary of Demeter and Kore, Corinth. Note the concentration of postholes
west of the central steps, possibly used to erect stalls (after Bookidis and
Stroud 1997, plan 5, artist: D. Peck, courtesy of the American School of
Classical Studies at Athens, Corinth Excavations).

Although the Corinthian evidence is admittedly rather meagre, it does provide
some rough criteria that could help us to locate further examples of marketplaces in other sanctuaries, and specifically to consider how patterns of movement and evidence of temporary stalls may be linked to exchange in various
contexts. More generally, we would expect festival markets to be located in
close proximity to the *temenos* (as is indeed evident from the sanctuary of
Demeter and Kore),[52] in order to attract the most pilgrims – although it is a
moot point exactly how closely demarcations between sacred and profane
spaces were observed. The necessity of placing a *horos* stone in the Corinthian
sanctuary may be taken to suggest that the separation was not always easy
to maintain, especially in a crowded space on busy festival days. Indeed, any
available space where pilgrims congregated before, during or after religious activities would have allowed merchants to engage in small-scale exchange if the

---

52   Gawlinski 2012, 215, observing that at the very least, markets were held on land owned or
controlled by the sanctuary. And also see Chandezon 2000, 96–8.

opportunity presented itself.[53] In the case of Andania, the use of the specific term *agora* suggests that there would have been an area set aside specifically for commercial activities; whereas on Samos the shops were placed within the sanctuary proper.[54] We can thus imagine a relatively broad range of configurations of marketplaces that would have had to take several factors into account, including the natural environment, other aspects of the sanctuary's topography, local traditions, cultic requirements, and the opportunities afforded by particular situations in the ritual calendar. Further complicating the circumstances (and once again emphasising the ephemerality of the enterprise as a whole), the Andanian inscription emphasises that the location could change from year to year.

Genuine, regional and interregional markets would have required considerable space, much greater than that available in the Corinthian sanctuary of Demeter and Kore, which would have accommodated only the kind of festal accessory market defined by de Ligt. This would have been especially true in cases where goods which demanded more space were sold, such as slaves and cattle. Apart from space, major fairs would also have depended on adequate natural features and resources, in particular access to spring water, which would have been essential for the development of a festival fair into a genuine market.[55] The Law of Andania includes detailed regulations about the maintenance of a fountain and the statue that adorns it, although here such arrangements also served the festival as a whole, and not the *agora* exclusively.[56] This requirement has more to do with the selection of a particular site than with specific requirements for a market space. Relatively flat, open spaces would have been preferable in terms of transporting goods that were put on sale, but would have been difficult to come by in mountainous sanctuaries such as Delphi.

5   Freeport Baitokaike

The final part of this chapter focuses on one particular sanctuary and its associated market, the sanctuary of Zeus Baitokaike, which is located in the mountains of Syria, some 750 m above sea level, close to the modern village

---

53   As described in late antique sources, see Kristensen 2017, 235.
54   It is not unlikely that no general rules are possible, as the separation of spaces within sanctuaries was probably not as neat as a structuralist would like.
55   Horden – Purcell 2000, 433.
56   Gawlinski 2012, 82–3 (l. 84–9), 194–9 (commentary). Sacrifices were also to take place at the fountain.

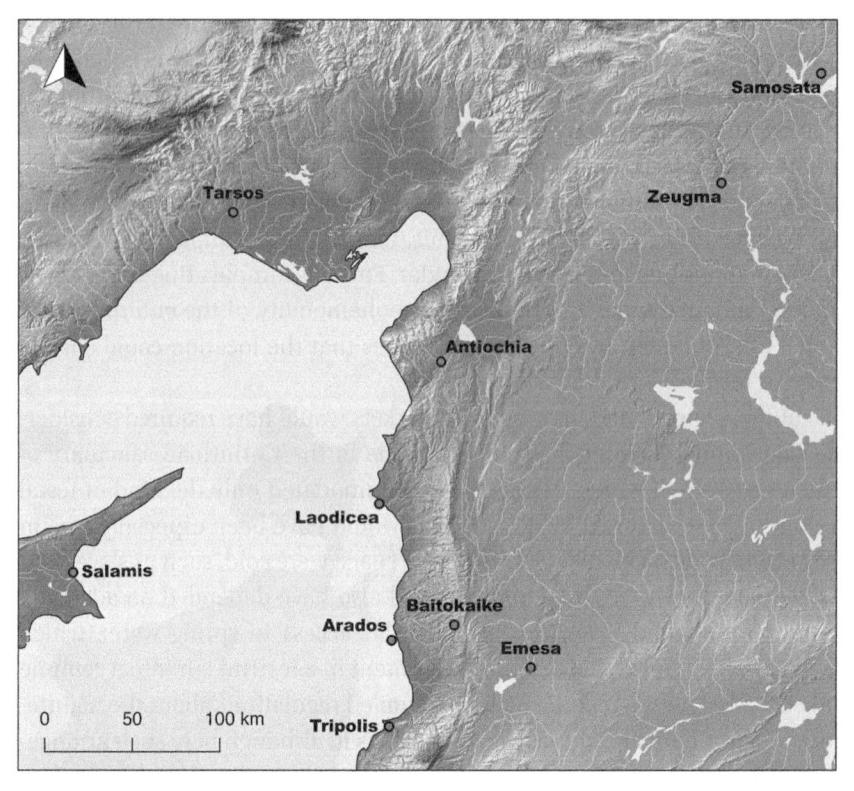

FIGURE 9.5   Location of the sanctuary of Zeus Baitokaike
                MAP BY NIELS BARGFELDT

of Hosn Suleiman (Fig. 9.5).[57] Because of its relative isolation and the fact that there was no adjacent urban settlement with the means to fund a sanctuary of this size, scholars have debated how Baitokaike fitted into the region's political landscape. Although some have argued that Baitokaike was a federal sanctuary, others have proposed that it belonged to the island city of Arados (modern Arwad), located 3 km off the Syrian coast. What is clear is that most of its visitors travelled for considerable distances to reach the sanctuary.

The sanctuary of Zeus Baitokaike is situated beside a spring that certainly added to its appeal in mercantile terms, as the easy access to water made it a convenient and appealing place for groups to congregate. In his recent work on the archaeology of the sanctuary, Klaus Freyberger has emphasised the

---

57   Dignas 2002, 7484 and 156ff. On the basic archaeology, Krencker – Zschietzschmann 1938, 65–101; Taf. 31–51 remains key. Also see Burns 1992, 130–2; Steinsapir 2005, 31–45; Freyberger 2004; 2009. On the political context, see Butcher 2003, 352.

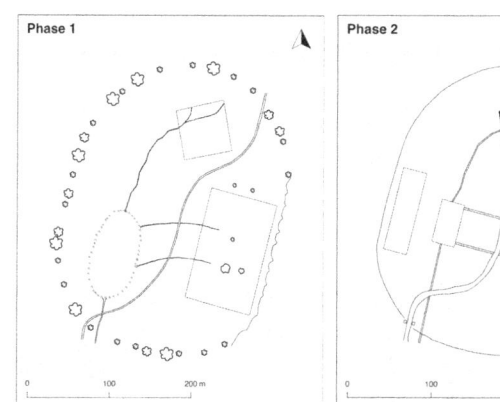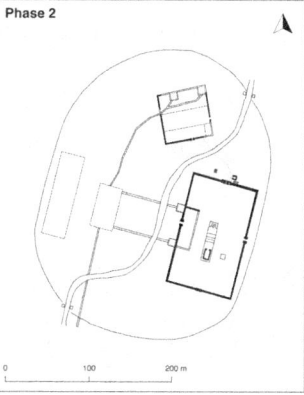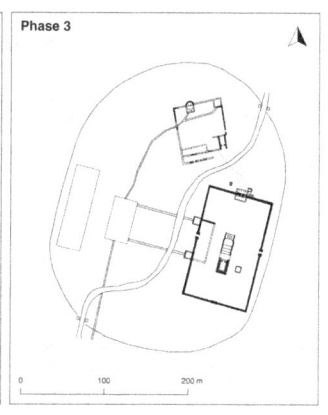

FIGURE 9.6A–C Development of the sanctuary of Zeus Baitokaike, as reconstructed by
Klaus Freyberger
MAP BY NIELS BARGFELDT, AFTER FREYBERGER 2009, PLAN 4–6

purported healing powers of the sanctuary's water as one of the key features
that attracted pilgrims to this place and thus as part of a long history of attributing sacred qualities to springs.[58] He reconstructs the earliest phase of
Baitokaike, possibly going as far back as the Bronze or Iron Ages, as a natural sanctuary of which the spring, the landscape and possibly also *baityloi*
were integral elements (Fig. 9.6a). The sanctuary was monumentalised in the
third century BCE with the construction of a temple and two large enclosures made of gigantic stone blocks (Fig. 9.6b). Both were dedicated to Zeus
Ouranios, but must have had distinctive functions within the cult. Water was
channelled from the spring to both enclosures through underground pipes.
Then, in the second century CE, a new temple and a larger propylon were built
in the large enclosure, and a small ante-temple was constructed in the smaller
enclosure (Fig. 9.6c).[59] The imperial cult appears to have been introduced to
the sanctuary at this time, although the overall design of the sanctuary remained the same. In Late Antiquity, a basilica church was built in the small
enclosure (known locally as *ed-Der*, meaning 'the monastery').[60] Olive presses
found in the area of the sanctuary indicate that agricultural production took

58 Freyberger 2009; and see papers in Harmanşah 2014.
59 Freyberger 2009, 270, Plan 4; 279 (first phase); 270, Plan 5; 279–280 (second phase); 271,
Plan 6; 280–282 (third phase).
60 Freyberger 2009, 269, Plan 3; 282.

place in its immediate vicinity.[61] A relief from the sanctuary depicts a man carrying *amphorae*, perhaps indicating that wine would also have been sold here.[62]

One of the many remarkable features of the sanctuary of Zeus Baitokaike is a rich epigraphic dossier that is preserved on its walls, and which dates from the Hellenistic period to the mid-third century CE. The inscriptions relate to the organisation of the sanctuary, its sacred land, and, importantly for our purposes, the regulation of its market, and have been discussed at some length by Beate Dignas in her *Economy of the Sacred in Hellenistic and Roman Asia Minor*.[63] The earliest document records the letter of a Seleucid king (Antiochus, although it is unclear to which king of that name it refers), granting a series of rights to Baitokaike, including ownership of the small village close to the sanctuary and the right to hold twice-monthly markets on the 15th and 30th of the month (following the Seleucid calendar).[64] As in the case of Andania, these were exempt from tax, thus encouraging trade and keeping outside interests at bay. The profits were reserved for funding monthly sacrifices and for endowing the priesthood, thus feeding directly into the sacred economy of the sanctuary. The inscription also hints at the networks of exchange in which the sanctuary was enmeshed, concluding that 'it will now be necessary to write to those that normally receive notice so that things may be carried out as indicated'.

A later document in the dossier from Baitokaike dates to the Augustan period, and also concerns the sanctuary's market. It insists on the independence of the sanctuary in relation to an unnamed city (possibly Arados), again granting it exemption from taxation and other privileges. For our purposes, what is interesting is the evidence of the transport of goods up to the sanctuary over a considerable distance from its *chora*, the extent of which has been debated. We are also told that slaves and other animals were sold in the sanctuary's market, which as noted above would have required considerable space to accommodate. Other goods that may have been sold in the sanctuary include agricultural products and other perishable materials.[65] Two later documents in the dossier have been dated to the middle of the third century CE, implying that the history of the festival market stretches across at least 500 years. Following de Ligt's typology, it seems probable that the sanctuary of Baitokaike hosted a genuine market of a local or regional scale occurring frequently at fortnightly

61   Freyberger 2009, 284.
62   Freyberger 2004, 36–7, Abb. 8.
63   Dignas 2002.
64   Dignas 2002, 77; Freyberger 2004, 31–5.
65   Freyberger 2009, 283.

intervals. I suggest that this kind of permanence and regularity further blurs distinctions between trade and pilgrimage, to an extent that again confirms that we cannot really to speak of one without the other.

Closer scrutiny of the layout of the sanctuary of Baitokaike suggests some basic but revealing observations relating to the location of its market. First, the area within the large enclosing wall is vast, measuring 134 by 85 m, that is, more than 11,000 m², slightly larger than a football field. This space could accommodate very large groups of people and, as I shall propose below, possibly also goods traded between the different communities that frequented Baitokaike's market. Secondly, the communal sense of a gathering was accentuated by the enclosure's four gates, one at each compass point, adding a powerful theatrical element to the act of entering.[66] The decoration and forms of the gates bear witness to a hierarchy suggested by their different degrees of elaboration. The northern approach was most elaborately adorned by a 15 m wide propylon and three gateways (and it was also chosen as the location of the largest inscription in the dossier). The western and eastern approaches have slightly scaled-down propylaea, whereas the southern approach has the simplest example.

Where would the market of Baitokaike, known in such rich detail from the inscriptions, have been located? The answer to this question is that the marketplace was not necessarily static throughout the sanctuary's long history. In the earliest phase, when there was no monumental architecture, any area in the vicinity of the spring would have provided an adequate space for a fair. From the Hellenistic period onwards, when the sanctuary had become monumentalised, at least three possible locations are possible. The first option is that the market may have been located outside the two enclosures and beside the spring. Given that the terrain slopes down to the east, the area around the spring would have provided a large open space in which both cattle and slaves could have been kept. A road ran between the two enclosures,[67] and it is likely that this area would have been attractive for selling goods of the festal accessory type. The disadvantage of this location is that the large open area would have been relatively difficult to regulate.

The second possibility, suggested recently by Freyberger, is that the market was located in the small enclosure.[68] As this enclosure was not adorned with any major building until the second century CE, for a substantial part of its history it would have provided a large, suitable space for a market selling both

66   Freyberger 2004, 16–22.
67   Freyberger 2009, 284.
68   Freyberger 2004, 35–6; 2009, 283–4.

slaves and cattle. The walls would have restricted movement into and out of the market, clearly separating commercial from religious activities.

However, it is worth noting that the monumental inscription that documents (and advertises) the bi-weekly market was placed on the propylon of the northern gate to the large enclosure, rather than the small enclosure. While challenging clear-cut conceptions of sacred space but in line with the evidence from the Corinthian sanctuary of Demeter and Kore, this could suggest that a third location of the marketplace is possible, specifically *inside* the large enclosure. As already noted, the dimensions of this enclosure are vast, providing ample room for the temporary provision of stalls and other market features. And the colossal wall around the enclosure would have been useful for regulating access in and out. This certainly would have been beneficial in ritual terms, but it also made sense in terms of keeping the goods on display secure and, importantly in this case, determining which goods were tax-free. As we have seen, this was a major concern in the inscriptions, which show that there were persistent tensions between the sanctuary and an unnamed city, perhaps Arados, whose officials subjected traders and worshippers to requisition, taxation, exaction and reclamation, according to the dossier. If this interpretation of the large enclosure as not only a sacred place but also a multi-functional space of religious and economic transaction is accepted, the massive walls of the enclosure embodied not only the power of Zeus Baitokaike, but also the commercial opportunities offered by Freeport Baitokaike.

6   Conclusions

This chapter has ended on a speculative note, and it may be prudent to return to some of the broader implications of the preceding discussions. First, it is abundantly clear that the blank spaces that are so common on topographical maps of Greek sanctuaries would not have been empty, but rather offered a range of possibilities for economic exchange. This is not only suggested by literary evidence, but also confirmed by the epigraphic evidence of markets at a wide range of Greek sanctuaries, and the sparser archaeological evidence of various marketplaces. Open areas in sanctuaries served as multi-purpose spaces that were essential to the way in which ancient sanctuaries worked and integral to the pilgrims' experience when they moved through them, particularly during festivals and other large-scale gatherings. Second, there are methodological implications arising from this chapter: the study of sanctuary markets would be advanced if more micro-scale archaeological investigations of the spaces and surfaces in sanctuaries were undertaken and published. Such investigations would hopefully allow us to identify more evidence of transient use, such as market stalls, temporary workshops and so on. Such work would be a great help in efforts to understand the embedded economies of Greek sanctuaries. Third, the observations offered above have implications related to our use of terminology. In the context of ancient Greece and Rome, several scholars have insisted that the use of the term 'pilgrimage' introduces dangerous anachronisms, whereas 'trade' is seen as a concept essentially free of ideology or preconceptions of social structure. One way out of this conundrum is to broaden our definitions and to see sanctuaries as various focal points in multi-spectral networks of sacred travel. As McCorriston observes in relation to the Arabian Peninsula, trade was an integral component of pilgrimage, and separating the two phenomena is not productive. In her words, 'Pilgrimage ... reifies ... mobility with ideological justification of economical practice.'[69] This point is indeed central to the interpretation of the sanctuary of Zeus Baitokaike offered here.

Bibliography

Agelidis, S. 2017. "The 'Spatial Turn' in Ancient Greek Festival Research. Venues of the Athenian City Dionysia and the Great Panathenaia *Pompai*", in *Theoretical Approaches to the Archaeology of Ancient Greece. Manipulating Material Culture*, ed. L. Nevett, Ann Arbor, 230–45.

Alcock, S.E. and Osborne, R. eds. 1994. *Placing the Gods: Sanctuaries and Sacred Space in Ancient Greece*, Oxford.

Bergqvist, B. 1967. *The Archaic Greek Temenos. A Study of Structure and Function*, Lund.

Bille, M. and Sørensen, T.F. 2016. "Into the Fog of Architecture", in *Elements of Architecture. Assembling Archaeology, Atmosphere and the Performance of Building Spaces*, eds. M. Bille and T.F. Sørensen, London, 1–29.

Bookidis, N. and Stroud, R. 1997. *Corinth 18.3. The Sanctuary of Demeter and Kore. Topography and Architecture*, Princeton, NJ.

des Bouvrie, S. 2012. "Greek Festivals and the Ritual Process. An Inquiry into the Olympia-cum-Heraia and the Great Dionysia", in *Greek and Roman Festivals. Content, Meaning, and Practice*, eds. J.R. Brandt and J.W. Iddeng, Oxford, 53–93.

Brandt, J.R. and Iddeng, J.W. eds. 2012. *Greek and Roman Festivals. Content, Meaning, and Practice*, Oxford.

Bresson, A. 2016. *The Making of the Ancient Greek Economy. Institutions, Markets, and Growth in the City-States*, Princeton, NJ.

---

69 McCorriston 2011, 51.

Burkert, W. 2012. "Ancient Views on Festivals. A Case of Near Eastern Mediterranean Koine", in *Greek and Roman Festivals. Content, Meaning, and Practice*, eds. J.R. Brandt and J.W. Iddeng, Oxford, 39–51.

Burns, R. 1992. *Monuments of Syria. An Historical Guide*, London.

Butcher, K. 2003. *Roman Syria and the Near East*, London.

Carbon, J.-M. and Pirenne-Delforge, V. 2012. "Beyond Greek 'Sacred Laws'", *Kernos* 25, 163–82.

Chandezon, C. 2000. "Foires et panégyries dans le monde grec classique et hellénistique", *Revue des Études Grecques* 113, 70–100.

Chandezon, C. 2003. *L'élevage en Grèce (fin Ve-fin Ier s. a.C.). L'apport des sources épigraphiques*, Bordeaux.

Chankowski, V. and Karvonis, P. eds. 2012. *Tout vendre, tour acheter. Structures et équipments des marches antiques. Actes du colloque d'Athènes, 16–19 Juin 2009*, Paris.

Clinton, K. 2005. *Eleusis. The Inscriptions on Stone. Documents of the Sanctuary of the Two Goddesses and Public Documents of the Deme. Volume IA: Text*, Athens.

Clinton, K. 2008. *Eleusis. The Inscriptions on Stone. Documents of the Sanctuary of the Two Goddesses and Public Documents of the Deme. Volume II: Commentary*, Athens.

Clinton, K. 2019. "Journeys to the Eleusinian Mysteria (with an Appendix on the Procession at the Andanian Mysteria)", in *Ascending and Descending the Acropolis. Movement in Athenian Religion*, eds. W. Friese, S. Handberg, and T.M. Kristensen, Aarhus, 161–78.

Connelly, J.B. 2012. "Ritual Movement through Greek Sacred Space. Towards an Archaeology of Performance", in *Ritual Dynamics in the Ancient Mediterranean. Agency, Emotion, Gender, Representation*, ed. A. Chaniotis, Stuttgart, 313–46.

De Ligt, L. 1993. *Fairs and Markets in the Roman Empire. Economic and Social Aspects of Periodic Trade in a Pre-Industrial Society*, Amsterdam.

De Ligt, L. and de Neeve, P.W. 1986. "Ancient Periodic Markets: Festivals and Fairs", *Athenaeum* 66, 391–416.

Dignas, B. 2002. *Economy of the Sacred in Hellenistic and Roman Asia Minor*, Oxford.

Dillon, M. 1997. *Pilgrims and Pilgrimage in Ancient Greece*, London.

Dimitrova, N.M. 2008. *Theoroi and Initiates in Samothrace. The Epigraphical Evidence*, Princeton, NJ.

Drbal, V. 2017. "Pilgrimage and Multi-religious Worship: Palestinian Mamre in Late Antiquity", in *Excavating Pilgrimage. Archaeological Approaches to Sacred Travel and Movement in the Ancient World*, eds. T.M. Kristensen and W. Friese, Abingdon, 245–62.

Edlund, I.E.M. 1987. *The Gods and the Place. The Location and Function of Sanctuaries in the Countryside of Etruria and Magna Graecia (700–400 B.C.)*, Göteborg.

Forbes, H. 2007. *Meaning and Identity in a Greek Landscape. An Archaeological Ethnography*, Cambridge.

Freyberger, K.S. 2004. "Das Heiligtum in Hössn Soleiman (Baitokaike): Religion und Handel im syrischen Küstengebirge in hellenistischer und römischer Zeit", *Damaszener Mitteilungen* 14, 13–40.

Freyberger, K.S. 2009. "Das Heiligtum in Baitokaike (Hössn Soleiman): Chronologie, Funktion und Bedeutung", *Archäologischer Anzeiger* 2009.2, 265–92.

Friese, W. 2017. "Of Piety, Gender and Ritual Space. An Archaeological Approach to Women's Sacred Travel in Greece", in *Excavating Pilgrimage. Archaeological Approaches to Sacred Travel and Movement in the Ancient World*, eds. T.M. Kristensen and W. Friese, Abingdon, 43–66.

Garraty, C.P. and Stark, B.L. eds. 2010. *Archaeological Approaches to Market Exchange in Ancient Societies*, Boulder, CO.

Gawlinski, L. 2012. *The Sacred Law of Andania. A New Text with Commentary*, Berlin.

Grossmann, P. 1998. "The Pilgrimage Center of Abû Mînâ", in *Pilgrimage and Holy Space in Late Antiquity Egypt*, ed. D. Frankfurter, Leiden, 281–302.

Harmanşah, Ö. ed. 2014. *Of Rocks and Water. Towards an Archaeology of Place*, Oxford.

Harris, E. and Carbon, J-M. 2015. "The Documents in Sokolowski's *Lois sacrées des cites grecques* (*LSCG*)", *Kernos* 28: DOI: http://dx.doi.org/10.4000/kernos.2373.

Holleran, C. 2012. *Shopping in Ancient Rome. The Retail Trade in the Late Republic and the Principate*, Oxford.

Horden, P. and Purcell, N. 2000. *The Corrupting Sea: A Study of Mediterranean History*, Oxford.

Horster, M. 2011. "Cults of Dionysos: Economic Aspects", in *A Different God? Dionysos and Ancient Polytheism*, ed. R. Schlesier, Berlin, 61–84.

Iddeng, J.W. 2012. "What is a Graeco-Roman Festival? A Polythetic Approach", in *Greek and Roman Festivals. Content, Meaning, and Practice*, eds. J.R. Brandt and J.W. Iddeng, Oxford, 11–37.

Jacquemin, A. 1999. *Offrandes monumentales à Delphes*, Athens.

Kistler, E. *et al.* eds. 2015. *Sanctuaries and the Power of Consumption. Networking and the Formation of Elites in the Archaic Western Mediterranean World*, Wiesbaden.

Krencker, D. and Zschietzschmann, W. 1938. *Römische Tempel in Syrien*, 2 vols., Berlin.

Kristensen, T.M. 2012a. "The Material Culture of Roman and Early Christian Pilgrimage: An Introduction", *HEROM* 1, 67–78.

Kristensen, T.M. 2012b. "Textiles, Tattoos and the Representation of Pilgrimage in the Roman and Early Christian Periods", *HEROM* 1, 107–34.

Kristensen, T.M. 2017. "Excavating Meriamlik: Sacred Space and Economy in Late Antique Pilgrimage", in *Excavating Pilgrimage. Archaeological Approaches to Sacred Travel and Movement in the Ancient World*, eds. T.M. Kristensen and W. Friese, Abingdon, 224–44.

Kristensen, T.M. 2018. "Mobile Situations: *Exedrae* as Stages of Gathering in Greek Sanctuaries", *World Archaeology* 50.1, 86–99.

Kyrieleis, H. 1993. "The Heraion at Samos", in *Greek Sanctuaries. New Approaches*, eds. N. Marinatos and R. Hägg, London, 125–53.

Lavan, L. 2012a. "From *polis* to *emporion*? Retail and Regulation in the Late Antique City", in *Trade and Markets in Byzantium*, ed. C. Morrison, Washington, DC, 333–78.

Lavan, L. 2012b. "The Agorai of Sagalassos in Late Antiquity: An Interpretive Study", *Late Antique Archaeology* 9, 289–353.

Linders, T. and Alroth, B. eds. 1992. *Economics of Cult in the Ancient Greek World*, Uppsala.

Lock, G. ed. 2000. *Beyond the Map. Archaeology and Spatial Technologies*, Amsterdam.

Lupu, E. 2009. *Greek Sacred Law. A Collection of New Documents*, second edition, Leiden.

MacMullen, R. 1970. "Market-Days in the Roman Empire", *Phoenix* 24.4, 333–41.

McCorriston, J. 2011. *Pilgrimage and Household in the Ancient Near East*, Cambridge.

McCorriston, J. 2017. "Inter-cultural Pilgrimage, Identity, and the Axial Age in the Ancient Near East", in *Excavating Pilgrimage. Archaeological Approaches to Sacred Travel and Movement in the Ancient World*, eds. T.M. Kristensen and W. Friese, Abingdon, 11–27.

Morcillo, M.G. 2013. "Trade and Sacred Places: Fairs, Markets and Exchange in Ancient Italic Sanctuaries", in *Religiöse Vielfalt und soziale Integration. Die Bedeutung der Religion für die kulturelle Identität und politische Stabilität im republikanischen Italien*, eds. M. Jehne, B. Linke, and J. Rüpke, Heidelberg, 236–74.

Morgan, C. 1990. *Athletes and Oracles. The Transformation of Olympia and Delphi in the Eighth Century BC*, Cambridge.

Mylona, D. 2015. "From Fish Bones to Fisherman: Views from the Sanctuary of Poseidon at Kalaureia", in *Classical Archaeology in Context. Theory and Practice in Excavation in the Greek World*, eds. D.C. Haggis and C.M. Antonaccio, Berlin, 385–418.

Nielsen, I. 2017. "Collective Mysteries and Greek Pilgrimage. The Cases of Eleusis, Thebes and Andania", in *Excavating Pilgrimage. Archaeological Approaches to Sacred Travel and Movement in the Ancient World*, eds. T.M. Kristensen and W. Friese, Abingdon, 28–46.

Papazarkadas, N. 2011. *Sacred and Public Land in Ancient Athens*, Oxford.

Potts, C. 2015. *Religious Architecture in Latium and Etruria, c. 900–500 BC*, Oxford.

Pülz, A. 2012. "Archaeological Evidence of Christian Pilgrimage in Ephesus", *HEROM* 1, 225–60.

Reader, I. 2014. *Pilgrimage in the Marketplace*, Abingdon.

Rutherford, I. 2013. *State Pilgrims and Sacred Observers in Ancient Greece. A Study of Theoria and Theoroi*, Cambridge.

Sallnow, M.J. 1987. *Pilgrims of the Andres. Regional Cults in Cusco*, Washington DC.

Scott, M.C. 2010. *Delphi and Olympia. The Spatial Politics of Philhellenism in the Archaic and Classical Periods*, Cambridge.

Shipley, G.J. 1987. *A History of Samos 800–188 BC*, Oxford.

Taylor, L.R. 1920. "The Site of Lucus Feroniae," *Journal of Roman Studies* 10, 29–36.

Trümper, M. 2009. *Graeco-Roman Slave Markets. Fact or Fiction?*, Oxford.

Steinsapir, A.I. 2005. *Rural Sanctuaries in Roman Syria. The Creation of a Sacred Landscape*, Oxford.

Yasin, A.M. 2012. "Response: Materializing the Study of Late Antique Pilgrimage", *HEROM* 1, 261–75.

CHAPTER 10

Pricing Salvation: Visitation, Donation and the Monastic Economies in Late Antique and Early Islamic Egypt

Louise Blanke

1   Introduction

This chapter examines the role played by visitation in the economies of Egypt's monasteries over the *longue durée*.[1] It argues that while late antique monasteries relied on a myriad of different types of income, the socio-political changes in the early Islamic period (e.g. increased land tax (*kharaj*), the introduction of the poll tax (*jizyah*) and the gradually declining size of Egypt's Christian population) may have caused monasteries to become increasingly dependent on the economic exchange associated with visitation.

I will maintain a distinction between the related but distinct processes of visitation and pilgrimage. I use the term visitation to account for the recurring short-distance visits that were orientated towards consumption of spiritual services at local shrines in churches and monasteries. These services included, but were not limited to, celebration of feast days, participation in the liturgical calendar and also fulfilment of vows. The outcome of the visits were blessings (material or immaterial) and prayers. Pilgrimage, in my definition, was often long-distance, episodic and targeted at the commemoration of a saint or relic. Some monasteries accommodated both visitation and pilgrimage.

I start by outlining Egypt's late antique monastic landscape followed by an introduction to the chapter's four archaeological case-studies. These sections

---

1   I began writing this chapter while I was a postdoctoral researcher at the project *The Emergence of Sacred Travel: Experience, Economy and Connectivity in Ancient Mediterranean Pilgrimage* (directed by Troels Myrup Kristensen) at Aarhus University. It was completed while I held a Carlsberg International Postdoctoral Fellowship at University of Oxford, a Junior Research Fellowship at Wolfson College and was a Research Associate at the Khalili Research Centre. I am most grateful to these institutions for supporting my research. Also heartfelt thanks to Stephen J. Davis and to the Yale Monastic Archaeology Project for supporting my research at the White Monastery. Many thanks to Anna Collar and Troels Myrup Kristensen for inviting me to contribute to this volume and to Stephen J. Davis, Annet Den Haan, Gillian Pyke, Luke Treadwell and Brill's anonymous reviewer for their insightful and rewarding comments.

---

are followed by an overview of the late antique monastic economies and a discussion of the factors that caused the monasteries' economic circumstances to change in the early Islamic periods. My case-studies are examined in order to show how different monasteries facilitated visitation within their built environments. The chapter concludes with a discussion of the economic exchange that derived from visitation.

2   The Monastic Landscapes of Late Antique Egypt

The past decades have seen a fundamental change in the scholarly approach to Egypt's monastic landscapes. This development has been driven by advances in the study of Coptic and Arabic papyrology and by investigations of the archaeological remains of monasteries.[2]

The traditional approach to Egyptian monasticism saw the institutionalised *coenobitic* communities and the more loosely organised *eremitic* and *semi-eremitic* societies as the main expressions of the monastic movement. Recent research has nuanced this picture and underlined the complexity and diversity of not only the monasteries' internal organisation, but also their geographical settings and economic realities. In view of these developments, James Goehring has argued that we should consider late antique Egyptian monasticism as a 'complex continuum from the fully solitary monk to the fully communal monk.'[3] At one end of the spectrum was the monastic living alone in the desert or within a community of hermits leading solitary lives, but under the leadership of an abbot with a shared economic foundation and a weekly mass and communal meal.[4] The archetypical examples of these monastic communities are found, for example, in Kellia and in the Wadi Natrun. Monastic foundations were established at both these locations in the first half of the fourth century.[5]

At the other end of the spectrum were the fully communal monks organised within federated monastic foundations. The origins of these *coenobitic* communities are ascribed to St. Pachomius (CE 292–348). He was a soldier in the Roman army, who converted to Christianity during his service and organised his monasteries with inspiration from the strict military hierarchies.[6] Daily life

---

2   Wipszycka 2011, 162. For diversity within monastic settlements, see also Brooks Hedstrom 2007; 2017; Gascou 1991, 1639; Goehring 1986, 245–50; Goehring 2007, 392.
3   Goehring 1992, 53.
4   Grossmann 2002, 246–7.
5   Grossmann 2002, 246–7; Wipszycka 2013, 118.
6   Layton 2014, 6–9.

in a *coenobitic* monastery was rule-bound, hierarchical and highly regulated: the monastics shared all daily activities including prayer, work, eating and sleeping.[7] The physical expression of the *coenobitic* monasteries comprised a walled settlement with a single gate, a church, workshops, cells or dormitories and a refectory. In the fourth century, a federation of monasteries led by Pachomius developed on the east side of the Nile some 80km north of Thebes and soon spread through large parts of Upper Egypt comprising nine monasteries at the time of Pachomius' death.[8] The remains of the Pachomian monasteries have not been preserved, and today the White Monastery stands as Egypt's best example of a late antique *coenobium*.[9] As I will demonstrate below in the section on Egypt's monastic economies, the economic potential of some *coenobitic* communities far exceeded that of other types of monasteries.

2.1   *Four Case Studies*

In my discussion of the economic role of visitation to monasteries, I refer to textual material from a range of sites located throughout Egypt but I draw on archaeological remains from four monastic case-studies. These are Kellia, Deir al-Bala'izah, The White Monastery (Deir Anba Shenoute) and Deir Anba Hadra (Fig. 10.1). These monasteries are located in Egypt's Western Desert: all but Kellia are walled communities but only the White Monastery can securely be defined as *coenobitic*. The case studies were not selected to be representative of the full spectrum of Egyptian monasticism, but were chosen as they represent different geographical as well as temporal manifestations of monastic practice and they serve as good archaeological examples for the architectural manifestation of visitation. Below follows a brief overview of the history and archaeology of each site.

Kellia is perhaps the most famous monastic site in Egypt featuring prominently in fourth and fifth century travelogues and hagiographies, such as Rufinus' *Historia Monachorum* and Palladius' *Lausiac History*.[10] The site is located west of the Nile Delta, some 40 km from Alexandria. A story in *The Sayings of the Desert Fathers* reports that it was founded in the first half of the fourth century by a monk called Ammon from the nearby monastic settlement at Nitria and archaeological remains suggests that it was largely abandoned

---

7   See Layton 2002; 2007; 2014 for comprehensive overviews of life in a *coenobitic* monastery.
8   Rousseau 1985.
9   Goehring 2008; Layton 2014, 14–34.
10   Palladius *Historia Monachorum*, Clarke 1918; Rufinus *Lausiac History*, Szkilnik 1993.

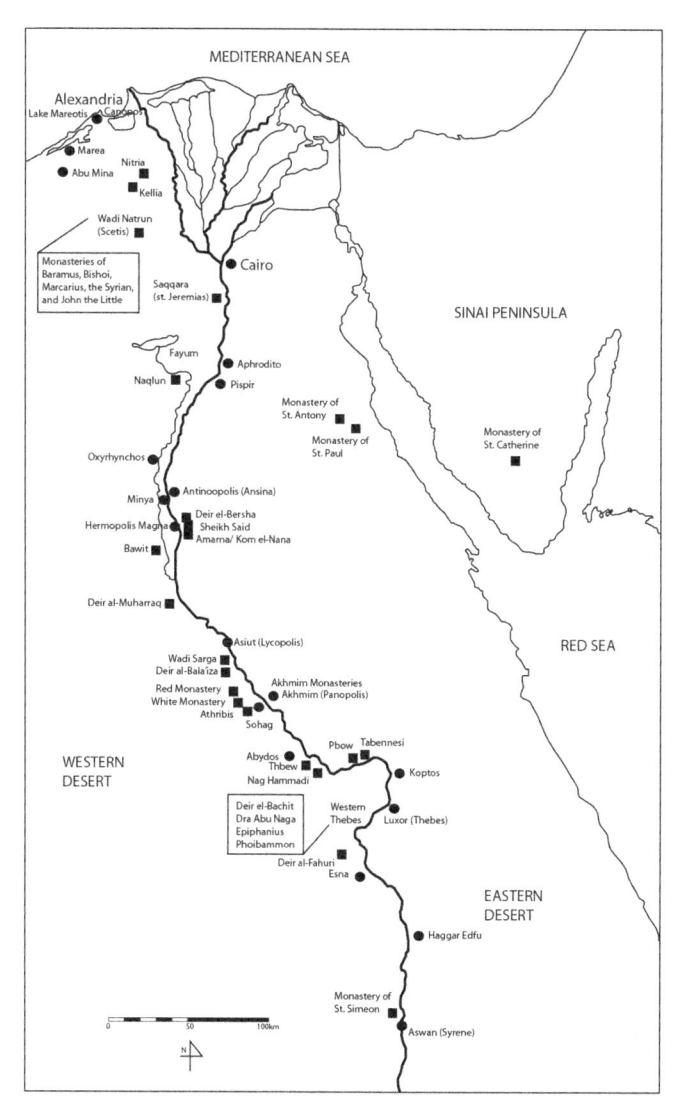

FIGURE 10.1   Map of Egypt showing location of monasteries that are
discussed in the chapter.
BY MAP BY LOUISE BLANKE

by the ninth century.[11] Since 1964, French, Swiss and Egyptian missions have surveyed and excavated the site.[12] These missions have documented an astonishing monastic landscape formed by clusters of monastic dwellings extending across an area of 125km^2 and comprising more than 1500 dwellings in seventeen distinct groups.

Despite their large numbers and geographical spread, the archaeological remains of dwellings dating to the sixth and seventh centuries show a surprising uniformity in their size and organisation. The average dwelling is demarcated by a rectangular wall taking up some 25m by 35m. The residential section itself is usually located in the northwest corner and comprises a bedroom, a room with painted decoration that has been interpreted as an oratory (or prayer room), a workroom, a guestroom, a kitchen and also a bedroom (and sometimes a second oratory) for a disciple or servant. In some dwellings, a latrine is found in the opposite corner of the courtyard from the residential section while additional rooms for residents or visitors are found along the north or south enclosure wall.

Deir al-Bala'izah (henceforth Bala'izah) is located on the edge of the cultivated land, some 20km from the modern city of Assiut (Fig. 10.2). An archive of papyri found on site suggests, according to Poul E. Kahle, an occupational history from the fifth to the eighth or ninth century.[13] Bala'izah was partly excavated by William Matthew Flinders Petrie in the early 20th century and surveyed by a German team in the 1980s.[14] The site is centred on a quarry, which was converted into a church. The mountains serve as the settlement's western limit, while the northern, eastern and southern parts of the site are demarcated by a wall. The total intra-mural complex occupies some 15,000m^2. The monastery was accessed through a gate in the south wall. The area within the wall is heavily built up with remains of mud brick buildings preserved in two stories. Among these buildings, Peter Grossmann has identified a refectory, a church and an extra-mural guesthouse, although the purpose of most of the monastery's structures remains obscure.

The White Monastery is located some 20km south of Bala'izah and c. 5km east of the modern city of Sohag. A fragmentary chronicle that is now preserved in the National Library of Naples recounts how a monk named Pgol from the Pachomian federation founded the monastery in the middle of the

---

11   For summaries of the archaeology of Kellia, see, for example, Coquin *et al.* 1991; Patrich 2004, 414–21; Wipszycka 2009, 206–12. For *The Sayings of the Desert Fathers*, see Ward 1975, 8.

12   See, for example, Daumas – Guillaumont – Garcin 1969; Kasser 1983; 1984.

13   Kahle 1954. See also Gonis 2004.

14   Grossmann 1993; Petrie 1907.

FIGURE 10.2   The archaeological remains of Deir al-Bala'izah. View towards west
                PHOTO: AUTHOR

fourth century.[15] The White Monastery is famous for the prolific writings of its third abbot, Shenoute, who was a zealous anti-pagan and an instrumental figure in the flourishing of the monastic movement.[16] Shenoute's textual corpus was transmitted as compilations of *Canons* (rules) and *Sermons*.[17] Through his writings, Shenoute became a renowned monastic figure in contemporary Egypt and from the sixth century onwards, he was venerated as the monastery's patron saint.[18] The archaeological remains of the ancient monastery were excavated by Petrie in the early 20th century; by the Egyptian Supreme Council of Antiquities from the 1980s and since 2005, North American missions have studied and excavated the site.[19]

During Shenoute's lifetime, the White Monastery was the leading partner of three federated communities and among the largest walled monasteries in

---

15   Layton 2014, 14–19; Emmel – Layton 2016.
16   See, for example, articles in Gabra – Takla 2008.
17   Emmel 2004.
18   Blanke 2017.
19   See, for example, Blanke 2019; Brooks Hedstrom – Bolman 2012; Davis 2010; Grossmann
      et al. 2004; 2009; Petrie 1908.

Egypt. The *intra-mural* site comprises a densely built environment that took up some 77,500 m² and in the monastery's heyday it could have housed 500 monks or more.[20] The monastery also included hermitages in the nearby desert as well as extensive *extra-mural* landholdings.[21] The archaeological remains suggest that it prospered well into the eighth century, but in the ninth century, it gradually began to diminish in size. By the fifteenth century, the monastery was described, by the Arab historian Taqi al-Din al-Maqrizi (1364–1442), as largely abandoned with only the church still standing.[22] However, a Christian community continued to utilise the church (for habitation) well into the 20th century.

My fourth case study is Deir Anba Hadra, which is located on the edge of the desert about 1km from the Nile opposite the modern city of Aswan (ancient Syene) and the settlement on the island of Elephantine (Fig. 10.3 and Fig. 10.5). Although the monastery's origin remains obscure, the surviving architectural remains date to the tenth century. Tombstones from a nearby cemetery suggest some monastic activities already from the sixth century onwards.[23] Several projects have examined the monastery over the past two centuries. It was surveyed in the late 19th century by, among others, Gaston Maspero and in the early 20th century by George Somers Clarke and Ugo Monneret de Villard.[24] Since 2013, a German mission has carried out key-hole excavations combined with an epigraphic survey and studies of the architectural remains.[25]

The monastery is among the better-preserved medieval monastic complexes in Egypt. It is compact and fortress-like in its form, with entrances at its east and west sides. It takes up some 15.000m² that are divided between three heavily built-up storeys. The lower part of the complex comprised a church and facilities for visitors, while the upper parts of the monastery contains facilities for the resident monastics, such as a living quarter, a refectory and an area for food production and storage.

The following sections provide a brief survey of the late antique monastic economies during the transition to the Islamic period and discuss the factors that caused the monasteries' financial situation to change. Using examples from the four archaeological case studies as well as from textual sources pertaining to these and to other monastic sites in Egypt, it frames the

---

20   Blanke 2019.

21   Leipoldt 1903, 95–6. See also Blanke 2019.

22   Wüstenfeld 1847, 96.

23   Munier 1930–1931; Timm 1984–2007, 666.

24   Maspero 1906; Monneret de Villard 1927; Somers Clarke 1912.

25   Publications are still forthcoming.

FIGURE 10.3   The archaeological remains of the Monastery of Anba Hadra. View towards
south
PHOTO: AUTHOR

circumstances within which visitation came to play an increasing role in the
monasteries' economic lives.

3   Egypt's Monastic Economies

Until recently, scholars of late antique Egypt looked to literary sources as the
key evidence for monasteries' economic circumstances. Texts, such as *The
Saying of the Desert Fathers* described productive work, not as a revenue-
producing activity, but as a part of the ascetic lifestyle and as a meditative
practice accompanied by prayer.[26] According to these sources, monasteries
produced goods such as baskets and ropes that could be sold or exchanged
and combined with charitable donations, providing the economic basis for
the survival of the monastics. For this reason, influential scholars such as
Arnold H.M. Jones, saw the monasteries as an economic and social drain on
society. Jones described in his book on *The Later Roman Empire*, a 'huge army
of clergy and monks' as 'idle mouths, living upon offerings, endowments and
state subsidies.'[27] They were described as sterile in a strictly economic sense.

26   Ward 1975.
27   Jones 1973, 933.

More recent studies using both documentary and archaeological evidence have established a very different economic reality.[28] Ewa Wipszycka's synthetic work on documentary papyri, for example, has been instrumental in changing the scholarly view on monastic wealth.[29] Wipszycka has demonstrated that although the economies of Egypt's monasteries varied enormously, it is possible to reconstruct a picture of some monasteries as important landowners, producers and consumers of goods as well as significant contributors to the regional economy.[30]

The textual sources associated with the White Monastery, for example, suggest that it was an economic powerhouse, which may have been comparable in organisation and wealth to some of late antique Egypt's great estates. In the fifth century, the monastery owned landholdings amounting to 50 km^2 in a patchwork of properties, which were located as much as 70 km from the main site.[31] The White Monastery was probably exceptional in the scale of its possession and should not be considered as representative for the average monastic economy. However, that monastic landownership was common is clear from several documentary papyri. A sixth-century cadastre from Aphrodito, for example, reveals that one third of all taxable land in the regions of Hermopolis Magna and Antinoopolis belonged to monasteries (including the White Monastery).[32]

How did such landholdings come into the possession of monasteries in the first place? It is not possible to reconstruct a complete picture of any monastery's economic life, but in the case of the White Monastery, offerings, donations and the transfer of monks' properties seem to have been three important avenues through which the monastery expanded its territory and wealth.

Shenoute's *Canons* reveals that the White Monastery required the aspiring monastic to give up all property before becoming a full member of the community.[33] While the Pachomian *coenobitic* communities allowed this property to be passed on to relatives, the White Monastery under Shenoute's rule required the novice to transfer all property to the monastic administration within three months of joining the community. Once belonging to the monastery, the property could not be reclaimed should the monastic choose to leave monastic life. The property transferred could consist of money, houses, land or farm animals and would actively contribute to the wealth of the

---

28   See also Brown 2016 who revisits the literary sources.
29   See, for example, Wipszycka 1972; 1999; 2009; 2011.
30   For a general discussion of labour in Egyptian monasteries, see Brown 2016.
31   Leipoldt 1903, 95–6; Kuhn 1954, 37.
32   Gascou 2008; MacCoull 2011.
33   Layton 2007, 60.

FIGURE 10.4   Overview of the fifth century White Monastery church. View towards
               northeast
               PHOTO: AUTHOR

community, thus making the recruitment of new monks a profitable endeavour for the monastery.[34]

Gifts in the form of land, houses, money or objects to monasteries are well
documented in, for example, papyri from Antinoe and Aphrodito: an example
is a sixth-century testament that records the donation of landed property and
livestock.[35] Two of the more extravagant examples of donations are the entire
Monastery of Tbew, which was gifted to the Pachomian foundation by the father of a monk named Patronios, possibly as part of the political negotiations
of the foundation's leadership following Pachomius' death – Patronios was the
immediate successor of Pachomius.[36] The other example is the church of the
White Monastery, which, according to an inscription on a door lintel, was funded by a local Christian dignitary referred to as Caesarius, son of Candidianus
(Fig. 10.4).[37]

---

34   Wipszycka 2011, 166.
35   Wipszycka 2011, 167–8.
36   Rosseau 1985, 74.
37   Grossmann *et al.* 2009, 169.

Given the size of the White Monastery's landholdings, agrarian production of cash crops, oil and probably several other products would have been important surplus-generating activities. The production of luxury items, such as books, and everyday goods, such as linen, rope, baskets and sacks, are well attested in the textual record and would have contributed towards a regular income for the monastery.[38]

From the sixth century onwards, both textual and archaeological sources suggest that visitation began to play an increasingly important role in the monasteries' economic life.[39] Whereas beforehand most monasteries had been named according to their proximity to a settlement or a topographical feature, some communities now changed their names to associate themselves with a patron saint.[40] A papyrus, for example, refers to the Monastery of St. Shenoute in the year 567, which is the earliest record of Shenoute as the White Monastery's patron saint.[41] This process, which has been described by Arietta Papaconstantinou as the monasticisation of the cult of saints also entailed obtaining relics for the monasteries.[42] The archaeological remains of monasteries, such as Kellia, reveal a gradual modification to the built environment to accommodate visitors and to give them access to some aspects of the monasteries' ritual lives.

Late Antiquity and the early Islamic period was also a time when many hagiographies were written, some of them in monasteries. There is a general consensus among scholars today that they often served to promote the cult of saints and more specifically, the cult sites and their local economies.[43] As such, hagiographies from the sixth and seventh centuries onwards are, according to Papaconstantinou, filled with stories of gifts and donations often following an account of a miracle performed by the patron saint.[44]

However, the Islamic conquest (639–641) led to a gradual shift in the organisation of the monasteries' economic situation and their role within contemporary society.[45] Our principal written evidence concerning Egypt's Christian communities in the early Islamic period derives from the documentary papyri and from a literary source known as *The History of the Patriarchs of Alexandria*,

---

38   Layton 2007, 49. See also Blanke 2019.
39   Papaconstantinou 2007.
40   Papaconstantinou 2007, 356–7.
41   Zereteli – Jernstedt 1925–1935, vol. 3, 48.
42   Papaconstantinou 2007, 358.
43   Papaconstantinou 2012, 84.
44   Papaconstantinou 2012, 76.
45   For an overview of Egypt in the early Islamic period, see Kennedy 1998; Sijpesteijn 2006; 2009.

which comprises a number of hagiographical entries of various dates and origins that were first compiled into a collected work in the eleventh century.[46] Both *The History* and the papyri suggest that Egypt's monastic communities flourished during the first 50 years of Muslim rule.[47] Petra Sijpesteijn has noted that the conquest did not adversely affect the monasteries' landholdings as the new rulers were mainly concerned with maintaining Egypt's agricultural productivity.[48] While at first, it seems to have been business as usual for most monasteries, the sources point to a change in the early eighth century. The caliphs Abd al-Malik (r. 685–705) and his son al-Walid (r. 705–715) introduced centralising administrative changes, which led to a gradual change in Egypt's ethnic and religious demography and introduced new fiscal burdens for Egypt's monastic communities.[49]

The History of the Patriarchs of Alexandria recounts how in 705 CE, a new poll-tax was introduced, which required each monastic to pay an annual sum of one dinar.[50] The new taxes were accompanied by a gradual decline in the size of the monasteries' landholdings thus leading to a reduction in the monasteries' agricultural output. *The History* states that the heavy taxation continued well into the ninth century and the documentary sources confirm that it took its toll on Egypt's monastic communities.[51]

The archives from the Monastery of Apollo at Bawit and from Bala'izah are particularly important for our understanding of the new economic reality. Receipts from Bala'izah reveal that taxes on the monastery were indeed substantial. The monastery frequently had to borrow money, sometimes from its own members and in a single year, it paid a tax of 88 dinars.[52] Importantly, the toll of paying the monastery's taxes fell on the superior, which is why, according to Kahle, Apa Ammone, who was a wealthy monk, was elected to lead the community at Bala'izah.[53] Kahle interpreted the situation at Bala'izah as representative of a wider development and suggested the disappearance of many monasteries in the eight century was a direct consequence of the heavy taxation.[54] Documentary papyri from Bawit also suggests a

---

46   Seybold 1912.
47   Booth 2013; Sijpesteijn 2006; 2009.
48   Sijpesteijn 2006; 2009, 126.
49   Sijpesteijn 2009, 126.
50   Swanson 2010, 16.
51   Egypt's non-monastic population was also affected by the new taxes. Thirteen anti-tax riots are documented between 767 and 832 (Swanson 2010, 31).
52   Kahle 1954, 41–5. For a discussion of land-tax (*kharaj*) paid at Bala'izah, see Gonis 2004.
53   Kahle 1954, 42.
54   Kahle 1954, 42.

change in attitude towards monastic finances and the personal wealth of the monastics.[55] From these sources, we learn that monastics were permitted to own land, livestock, houses, workshops and possibly money even after they joined the congregation.[56] The property could be leased out or continue as a source of income for the monastic throughout his or her ascetic life. The property could also be bequeathed in a will to a family member or to the monastery.[57] The Bawit papyri further reveals that the monastery would lease land to its own monks, thereby providing an income for both the monastery and for the monks.[58]

To the best of our knowledge, the monastics at the White Monastery were not permitted any personal property. The monastic rules discussed above are ascribed to the fifth-century abbot, Shenoute, but were copied continuously into the twelfth century, perhaps suggesting that they were still in place during the Early Islamic period. This would mean that the expense of the taxes would fall upon the monastery's administration. The large population of monks – up to 500 – would have resulted in an additional annual tax of the same amount as the number of monks.

Although we do not have the documentary sources to back this claim, the archaeological remains of the White Monastery's built environment confirm a gradual alteration in the size and wealth of the monastic community. The archaeological remains suggest that the monastery flourished into the eighth century, but by the ninth century, a marked shift took place. Graveyards and waste disposal, which had previously been confined to the *extra-mural* spaces were placed in areas that had previously been taken up by buildings. While building activities continued at the monastery, the materials used were no longer stone and fired bricks, but cheaper mud bricks. These two tell-tale signs reveal that the number of monks at the monastery was shrinking (fewer monks needed less space) and that the finances available to the monastery's administration were decreasing.[59]

The new fiscal pressure on the White Monastery is further alluded to in the Upper Egyptian calendar of saints (*The Synaxarion*) in the entry relating to Apa Seth, who was the leader of the White Monastery in the first half of the eighth century. The entry tells us that Apa Seth's feast day was on 29 Tubah (23rd January). On this day, he was commemorated for his piety, ascetic

55 Boud'hors *et al.* 2009; Clackson 2008 (Bawit); Wipszycka 2011, 183 (Western Thebes).
56 Wipszycka 2011, 163.
57 Wipszycka 2011, 163.
58 Richter 2009.
59 For a more elaborate description of this development, see Blanke 2019.

practice, humility and monastic teachings as well as his success in persuading the Muslim authorities not to impose new taxes on the monastery.[60]

Another miraculous story derives from *The History of the Patriarchs* and recounts a visit to the White Monastery around 740 by al-Qasim ibn Ubaydallah, who was Egypt's financial director during the reign of the Caliph Hisham (r. 724–743). The story recounts how al-Qasim visited the monastery accompanied by his troops and his favourite mistress and insisted on entering the church on horseback.[61] An old monk pleaded with al-Qasim not to "enter with such pride into the house of God, above all in the company of this woman; for never from the beginning has any woman entered into this church!"[62] Al-Qasim ignored his plea and entered the church without dismounting, which according to the account, led to the death of his mistress, whose horse fell to the ground, both horse and rider dying instantly. The story ends with al-Qasim donating 400 *dinars* to the monastery as an offering and later adding another 300 *dinars* when thirty of his men attempted to steal a chest, which belonged to the monastery.

The historicity of the account is questionable and the reason behind al-Qasim's provocative act may reflect contemporary problematic relations between Muslims and Christians in Egypt rather than an actual situation, but it can also be read as an expression of the Coptic anxiety about the ever-present threat of tax demand, here represented by none other than the financial director in person.

The size of Egypt's Christian community seems to have declined consistently from the late 8th or early 9th century onwards. According to *The History of the Patriarchs*, the Umayyad Caliph Umar II (r. 717–720) encouraged conversion to Islam with the promise of exemption from the poll tax, a trend that continued throughout the Umayyad period (661–750) and later under Abbasid rule (750–973).[63] In the long run, both taxation – including land and poll-tax – and an increasing rate of conversion, especially in the 9th century, adversely affected the monasteries' potential for growth and led to a reduction in their landholdings and building activities.

Despite adversity, the history of the White Monastery is not only one of decline and abandonment, but also of resilience and survival. The monastery shrank in size and numbers, but maintained an economic profile. The monastery ensured its long-term survival by establishing networks in which

---

60   Swanson 2016, 196.

61   Seybold 1912, 204.

62   Abu Salih the Armenian 1895, 238.

63   Swanson 2010, 19–31.

people from nearby towns and villages took part in the monastery's religious life in a way that far exceeded any previous involvement from the extramural community.

It is inevitably somewhat speculative to link an increase in monastic investment in visitation with the new fiscal pressures. However, that visitation remained important well into the Islamic period is clear from the prolific production of hagiographies, from the continuously developing narrative tradition of the Holy Family's flight to Egypt and most importantly for this chapter, from the archaeological remains.[64] A statement ascribed to the Alexandrian Patriarch Yusab I (831–849) identifies the economic importance of visitation. According to *The History of the Patriarchs*, Yusab I encouraged the construction of pilgrimage sites as an income-generating activity for the church.[65]

The following sections explore the archaeological remains of visitation. It serves to demonstrate how monasteries gradually incorporated visitation into their built environments and how the practice in some monasteries increased through time.

4   An Archaeology of Visitation

At many monasteries, accommodation was a key facility provided to visitors and one that is traceable in both textual and archaeological sources. Lucas Schachner has collected literary references from the fourth to the eighth centuries that refer to guesthouses.[66] Schachner identified eight named monasteries and a single anonymous community in Thebaid. The named sites include monasteries in Pbow and Tabennesse (fourth century), the White Monastery (fourth/fifth century), Nitria (fourth century), Kellia (fourth century), Deir Apa Dios (sixth century), Deir Apa Apollos (sixth century) and Deir Anba Samuil (seventh century).

According to Schachner, the textual sources suggest that the normal arrangement included provision in individual or collective guest-rooms located near the gate. We learn, for example, from the monastic rules of Pachomius that visitors could stay in a designated house that was located outside the monastery's enclosure wall, while Shenoute, the fifth-century leader of the

---

64   Gabra *et al.* 2001.
65   Swanson 2010, 30.
66   Schachner 2005.

White Monastery federation, stated that visitors could remain in the monastery's gatehouse for up to two days.[67]

The evidence in the archaeological record is scarce, as guesthouses have been identified in the physical remains of only three monastic settlements: at Kellia, Bala'izah and Deir Anba Hadra. The scarcity of guesthouses in the archaeological record does not necessarily mean that only few monasteries had guesthouses, but is more likely to reflect the choices made by past archaeological missions to focus on *intra-mural* settlements and especially on monumental structures such as churches and shrines.[68]

At Bala'izah, a building identified by the excavators as a guesthouse is located immediately south of the main gate.[69] The ground floor consists of at least nine rooms that are organised around a central hallway with remains of two staircases leading to an upper storey.[70] The structure was well-built and constructed from good quality mud bricks – the same material that made up the remaining part of the settlement. The nature of visitation at Bala'izah is not clear – we cannot say whether the visitors were prospective novices, traders, relatives of the monastic or pilgrims who came to seek the advice or blessings from the monastics or partake in the monastic liturgies. Regardless of the nature of the visitation, the investment in the construction of a guesthouse suggests that visitors were an important and consistent part of the monastic life. The mud bricks used to construct the guesthouse were of good quality, manufactured in the Nile Valley and transported into the desert and up a steep slope to reach their destination.[71] The construction of a two-story building would further have required builders with an expertise in brick-work.

The inclusion of visitation within a monastic environment is better documented from the archaeology of Kellia. Textual sources suggest that visits to Kellia in the fourth and fifth century were performed by travelling monks from monastic communities in, for example, Palestine, who remained at Kellia for periods ranging between a few days to several years. Some of the more famous travellers include Jerome and Paula.[72] These visitors were likely hosted within the monastic dwellings and their presence does not seem to have left any traces in the archaeological record.

From the sixth century onwards, visitation is traceable within Kellia's physical remains. Archaeological investigations of the site have shown how some

---

67   Layton 2007, 49–50.
68   On such absences in the archaeological record, see also Kristensen, this volume.
69   Grossmann 2002, fig. 147.
70   Grossmann 1993, 194–6.
71   On the economy of the production of mud brick, see Kemp 2000.
72   Frank 2000, 6.

dwellings were gradually expanded from smaller houses intended for the use of one or two monks in the fifth century to larger structures in which audience halls were constructed alongside accommodation that was perhaps intended for visitors.

Perhaps the best example of the transition from *ad hoc* visitation to a more institutionalised practice is found at Kellia in a cluster of more than 50 dwellings known as Qusur Hegeila.[73] Between the fifth and the eighth century, two small adjoining structures (defined by the excavators as Kom 39 and 40) gradually grew into one large structure over the course of ten architectural phases. These phases are described in detail by Elzbieta Makowiecka.[74] During the fourth phase, a martyrium that housed relics within a small shrine was established in the complex's northeast corner and a kitchen and guesthouse were built in the new southern part of the complex. A continuous occupation of the dwelling was achieved by using the complex's former south wall to maintain the privacy of the monastics from the intrusion of visitors. The growing popularity of visitation to this particular complex is clear from its further development: an oratory was transformed into apartments and a church was built just north of the former shrine and between the two, a tomb was placed. Further guesthouses were added and in the final stage, the complex contained several structures interpreted by Makowiecka as guesthouses, an oratory for visitors, several kitchens and refectories as well as two churches.

A similar development is found at the White Monastery. Here, textual sources suggest that a whole range of sacred sites developed, which could be visited individually or attended as a part of a longer sequenced series of visits to different stations on a processional route.[75] The attractions included shrines in the monastery's desert hinterland as well as two churches within the monastery itself. A liturgical text from the fifteenth century, suggests that one church was associated with the tomb of the monastery's patron saint, Shenoute, while the other held relics with healing properties.[76] Shenoute's fifth-century reference to visitors staying in the gatehouse predates these texts by almost a thousand years and there is no evidence – textual or archaeological – that suggests in which part of the monastery visitors could have stayed. However, it seems clear that the restrictions for visitors to remain at the monastery's gatehouse were no longer valid.

---

73   See Makowiecka 1995 for a detailed description of this development accompanied by a series of plans. See also Descaeudres 1995.

74   Makowiecka 1995.

75   Blanke 2017.

76   See, for example, Blanke 2017; Davis 2008, 114; Timbie 1998; 2008.

Comparative examples from modern pilgrimage practice could imply that the accommodation provided by monasteries need not necessarily have comprised architectural units that were incorporated into the built environment. The annual celebrations of Egypt's *moulids* (meaning birthday, but referring to the day of death of the saint) often include temporary accommodation in the form of tent camps, attested, for example, at the annual *moulid* to the White Monastery in celebration of Shenoute.[77] Such temporary installations would often be overlooked in the archaeological record as they could occupy an area that was separate from the main monastic complex and thus not examined by archaeologists.

The physical configuration of monasteries into areas that were either accessible to monastics and visitors (public) or accessible to only monastics (private) provides important insights into the relationship between the monastics and their visitors. The separation served to protect the monastics' ascetic practice, while at the same time reinforcing the otherness of the community and the visitors' experience of being (almost) in the presence of the holy men.

A clear division between public and private spaces is found in the tenth-century restructuring of the monastery of Deir Anba Hadra (Fig. 10.5). The monastery was built on an escarpment with a 5.5m drop between the upper and the lower parts of the complex. The monastery's public area (the lower part) is accessed through a narrow gateway with a bent axis in the complex's east wall. The public area was centred on a small courtyard from which five individual rooms could be reached. Each room was equipped with three beds and a window and the courtyard also contained shared kitchen facilities as well as a platform that was interpreted by Monneret de Villard as a sleeping space for the less well-off visitors to the monastery.[78] From here, visitors could access the monastery's main church, a small adjoining baptistery and a shrine within a cave, which presumably was associated with the monastery's patron saint: *The Life of Anba Hadra* recounts how he lived for a time within a cave in the desert.[79] The *vita* further recounts how the saint carried out miracles of healing while residing in the desert.[80]

The architectural configuration suggests that the church, baptistery and shrines were used by both visitors and monastics, but further access to the monastic complex was limited to a single point of access. A narrow staircase restricted the movement between the public part of the monastery and the

77   Pers. comm. Elizabeth Bolman 2005, also Father Shenoute (White Monastery) 2006.
78   Monneret de Villard 1927, 14–24.
79   Timm 1984–2007, 665.
80   Timm 1984–2007, 665.

FIGURE 10.5   Plan of the Monastery of Anba Hadra near Aswan. Note the division
between the public eastern part (right) and the private western part (left)
(after Monneret de Villlard 1927, fig. 176).

monastic cells, kitchens and production areas. The number of sleeping spaces suggests that up to 25 visitors could have stayed in relative comfort in the monastery. This number seems realistic considering that the permanent population may have included around 75 monastics. This number derives from calculations made from the available seating spaces within the refectory, assuming that the refectory was built to hold all monastics at one sitting.[81]

5   Pricing Salvation: an Economy of Visitation

The case studies outlined above show how visitation became gradually more incorporated into the monasteries' built environments. This increase in visitation to the monasteries corresponds with a decline in the range of income-generating activities available to the monasteries and it seems that some monasteries actively sought to increase their number of visitors.[82] At Kellia, the gradual merging of two dwellings into a complex of churches, shrines, kitchens and accommodation suggests a response to popular demand as well as an encouragement of its further development. At the White Monastery, the number of ritual activities made accessible to visitors also seems to have increased through time, while the entire monastery of Anba Hadra was constructed with visitation in mind. The economic benefits from visitation were perhaps particularly important for the monastics at Anba Hadra, as the archaeological remains suggest that the capacity of the production area was minimal and probably designed for consumption by the residents only.

Although the presence of visitors is articulated in the monasteries' archaeological remains, it is much more difficult to identify the ritual practices that drew the visitors to the sites. Fortunately, the rich corpus of both literary and documentary sources supplies some insights into the spiritual exchange that took place at the shrines. Interaction between monastery (patron saint) and visitor was centred on the monasteries' provision of services at the critical stages of life and in the mediation between God and the earthly world. At the White Monastery healing and the redemption of sins were important attractions for visitors, while provision of prayer and in time also baptism and funerary rites were services provided by the monasteries in return for a payment of some kind.[83]

---

81   Blanke 2019.
82   The production of hagiographies in this period support this claim, see Papaconstantinou 2012.
83   Blanke 2017.

It is not possible to quantify the value of these spiritual services, but the message conveyed in the rich corpus of hagiographies and documentary sources is clear: 'even though saints are said to [for example] heal for free they actually only offer their services against payment.'[84] Documentary sources from the eighth and ninth centuries give details of bequests of land, buildings and animals, while money, goods and even labour were donated in return for services or to be further distributed among the poor.[85] The category of labour represents an interesting type of donation that is found in both hagiographies and documentary sources. A group of more than twenty eighth-century papyri from the monastery of Phoibammon at Thebes is perhaps the best-known example of the donation of labour.[86] These papyri tell us how male children were donated by their parents to the monastery as living testimonies to the miraculous healing (of the children) granted by the monastery's patron saint. The children were donated, not to join the ranks of monks, but to serve the monastery as labourers for the rest of their lives.[87] Although of much earlier date, the presence of children in the White Monastery is documented in Shenoute's *Canons*, but their role within the monastery and how they came to live there in the first place is unclear.[88]

The donation of land to monasteries through wills has been studied by Arietta Papaconstantinou.[89] She describes a series of important examples in which land and material goods were donated to monasteries. The reasons stated in the documents for the donations are listed as, for example, 'offering for mercy at God's tribunal' and 'for the salvation of his soul.'[90]

6   Conclusion

In this chapter, I have examined the development of monastic economies in response to socio-political conditions in late antique and early Islamic Egypt. I have argued that while late antique monasteries relied on many different types of income, the financial pressure on monasteries in the early Islamic period through taxation necessitated an increased reliance on the income

---

84   Papaconstantinou 2012, 75.
85   See, for example, Papaconstantinou 2012.
86   See, for example, MacCoull 1979; Papaconstantinou 2002; Schenke 2016; Schroeder 2009.
87   Schenke 2016.
88   Layton 2014, 55.
89   Papaconstantinou 2012.
90   Papaconstantinou 2012, 79.

from visitation. Within this framework, funerals, baptism, blessings, healing and prayers should be perceived as commodities, which generated indirect payment through donations from the Christian communities. The monasteries' sacred economy is not easily quantified, as the size of the donations was dependent on the means of the donors. The successful continuation of this system of exchange hinged on the monasteries' local reputation and their perceived importance in the eyes of contemporary Christians. The textual sources and the remains of sites such as Kellia show that visitation was already important prior to the Islamic conquest, but these sources suggest an accelerated growth from the eighth century onwards. In order to explain this development, I have concentrated on the economic function of visitation. It is, however, important to note that the increase in visitation was also reflective of the changing role of monasteries in a society, where Christianity gradually became a minority religion. Other factors such as the recurrent travel bans on Christians under Umayyad and Abbasid rule (641–969) also contributed towards new social dynamics in which monasteries and local Christian communities became increasingly dependent on each other and monasteries developed into important centres of local social identity and cohesion.

Bibliography

Abu Salih the Armenian. 1895. *The Churches & Monasteries of Egypt and Some Neighbouring Countries*, Oxford.

Bagnall, R.S. 2001. "Monks and Property: Rhetoric, Law, and Patronage in the Apophthegmata Patrum and the Papyri", *Greek, Roman, and Byzantine Studies* 42, 7–24.

Blanke, L. 2017. "The Allure of the Saint: Late Antique Pilgrimage to the Monastery of St Shenoute", in *Excavating Pilgrimage: Archaeological Approaches to Sacred Travel and Movement in the Ancient World*, eds. T.M. Kristensen and W. Friese, Abingdon, 203–233.

Blanke, L. 2019. *An Archaeology of Egyptian Monasticism: Settlement, Economy and Daily Life of the White Monastery Federation*, New Haven.

Booth, P. 2013. "The Muslim Conquest of Egypt Reconsidered", in *Constructing the Seventh Century*, ed. C. Zuckerman, Paris, 639–70.

Boud'Hors, A. *et al.* 2009. *Monastic Estates in Late Antique and Early Islamic Egypt. Ostraca, Papyri, and Essays in Memory of Sarah Clackson*, Cincinnati.

Brooks Hedstrom, D.L. 2007. "Divine Architects: Designing the Monastic Dwelling Place", in *Egypt in the Byzantine World 300–700*, ed. R.S. Bagnall, Cambridge, 368–89.

Brooks Hedstrom, D.L. 2017. *The Monastic Landscape of Late Antique Egypt: An Archaeological Reconstruction*, Cambridge.

Brooks Hedstrom, D.L. and Bolman, E.S. 2012. "The White Monastery Federation Project: Survey and mapping at the monastery of Apa Shenoute (Dayr al-Anba Shinuda), Sohag, 2005–2007", *Dumbarton Oaks Papers* 66, 333–64.

Brown, P. 2016. *Treasure in Heaven: The Holy Poor in Early Christianity*, Charlottesville – London.

Clackson, S.J. 2008. *It is our Father who Writes: Orders from the Monastery of Apollo at Bawit*, Cincinnati.

Clarke, W.K.L. ed. 1918. *The Lausiac History of Palladius*, London.

Coquin, R.-G. *et al.* 1991. "Kellia", in *The Coptic Encyclopedia*, ed A.S. Atiya, New York, 1396–410.

Daumas, F., Guillaumont, A., and Garcin, J.-C. 1969. *Kellia I Kom 219: fouilles exécutées en 1964 et 1965*, Cairo.

Davis, S.J. 2008. *Coptic Christology in Practice: Incarnation and Divine Participation in Late Antique and Medieval Egypt*, Oxford.

Davis, S.J. 2010. "Archaeology at the White Monastery, 2005–2010", *Coptica* 9, 25–58.

Descaeudres, G. 1995. "Mönche als pilger und als pilgerziel", in *Akten des XII. Internationaen kongresses für Christliche archäologie*, eds. E. Dassmann and J. Engemann, Münster, 682–8.

Emmel, S. 2004. *Shenoute's Literary Corpus*, Leuven.

Emmel, S. and Layton, B. 2016. "Pshoi and the Early History of the Red Monastery", in *The Red Monastery Church: Beauty and Asceticism in Upper Egypt*, ed. E.S. Bolman, New Haven, 11–5.

Frank, G. 2000. *The Memory of the Eyes: Pilgrims to Living Saints in Christian Late Antiquity*, Berkeley.

Gabra, G. *et al.* 2001. *Be thou there: The Holy Family's Journey in Egypt*, Cairo.

Gabra, G. and Takla, H.N. eds. 2008. *Christianity and Monasticism in Upper Egypt*, Cairo – New York.

Gascou, J. 1991. "Monasteries, economic activities of", in *The Coptic Encyclopedia*, ed. A.S. Atiya, New York, 1639–45.

Gascou, J. 2008. "Le cadastre d'aphrodito (SB 20.14669)", in *Fiscalité et société en Egypte Byzantine*, ed. J. Gascou, Paris, 247–305.

Goehring, J.E. 1986. "New Frontiers in Pachomian Studies", in *The Roots of Egyptian Christianity*, eds. B.A. Pearson and J.E. Goehring, Philadelphia, 236–57.

Goehring, J.E. 1992. "Through a Glass Darkly: Diverse Images of the Apotaktikoi(ai) of Early Egyptian Monasticism", *Semeia* 58, 25–45.

Goehring, J.E. 2007. "Monasticism in Byzantine Egypt: Continuity and Memory", in *Egypt in the Byzantine World 300–700*, ed. R. Bagnall, Cambridge, 390–407.

Goehring, J.E. 2008. "Pachomius and the White Monastery", in *Christianity and Monasticism in Upper Egypt. Vol 1. Akhmim and Sohag*, eds. G. Gabra and H.N. Takla, Cairo – New York.

Gonis, N. 2004. "Arabs, Monks, and Taxes: Notes on Documents from Deir el-Bala'izah", *Zeitschrift für Papyrologie und Epigraphik* 148, 213–24.

Grossmann, P. 1993. "Ruinen des klosters Dayr al-Balaiza in Oberaegypten. Eine Survey-Aufnahme", *Jahrbuch für Antike und Christentum* 36, 171–205.

Grossmann, P. 2002. *Christliche Architektur in Ägypten*, Leiden – Boston – Köln.

Grossmann, P. *et al.* 2004. "The Excavation in the Monastery of Apa Shenute (Dayr Anba Shinuda) at Suhag, with an Appendix on Documentary Photography at the Monasteries of Anba Shinuda and Anba Bishoi", *Dumbarton Oaks Papers* 58, 371–82.

Grossmann, P. *et al.* 2009. "Second Report of the Excavation in the Monastery of Apa Shenute (Dayr Anba Shinuda) at Suhag", *Dumbarton Oaks Papers* 63, 167–219.

Jones, A.H.M. 1973. *The Later Roman Empire, 284–602: A Social, Economic and Administrative Survey*, Oxford.

Kahle, P.E. 1954. *Bala'izah*, London.

Kasser, R. 1983. *Survey archéologique des Kellia (Basse-Egypte): Rapport de la campagne 1981*, Louvain.

Kasser, R. 1984. *Le site Monastique des Kellia (Basse-Egypte): Recherches des années 198–1983*, Louvain.

Kemp, B. 2000. "Soil (including Mud-brick Architecture)", in *Ancient Egyptian Materials and Technology*, ed. P.T. Nicholson and I. Shaw, Cambridge, 78–104.

Kennedy, H. 1998. "Egypt as a Province in the Islamic Caliphate, 641–868", in *The Cambridge History of Egypt*, ed. C.F. Petry, Cambridge, 62–85.

Kuhn, K.H. 1954. "A Fifth Century Egyptian Abbot. I. Besa and his Background", *Journal of Theological Studies*, 36–48.

Layton, B. 2002. "Social Structure and Food Consumption in an Early Christian Monastery: The Evidence of Shenoute's *Canons* and the White Monastery Federation A.D. 385–465", *Le Muséon* 115, 25–55.

Layton, B. 2007. "Rules, Patterns, and the Exercise of Power in Shenoute's monastery: The Problem of World Replacement and Identity Maintenance", *Journal of Early Christian Studies* 15.1, 45–73.

Layton, B. 2014. *The Canons of our Fathers. Monastic Rules of Shenoute*, Oxford.

Leipoldt, J. 1903. *Schenute von Atripe und die Entstehung des national äegyptischen Christentums*, Leipzig.

MacCoull, L.S.B. 1979. "Child Donations and Child Saints in Coptic Egypt", *East European Quarterly* 13.4, 409–15.

MacCoull, L.S.B. 2011. "Monastic and Church Landholding in the Aphrodito Cadaster", *Zeitschrift für Papyrologie und Epigraphik* 178, 243–6.

Makowiecka, E. 1995. "Monastic Pilgrimage Centre at Kellia in Egypt", in *Akten des XII. Internationalen kongresses für Christliche archäologie*, eds. E. Dassmann and J. Engemann, Münster, 1002–15.

Maspero, G. 1906. "Le Couvent de Saint Simeon près d'Assouan", *Revue Archéologique* 4.8, 155–62.

Munier, H. 1930–1931. "Les stèles coptes du monastère de Saint Siméon à Assouan", *Aegyptus* 11, 257–300, 433–84.

Monneret de Villard, U. 1927. *Il monastero di S. Simeone presso Aswan*, Milano.

Papaconstantinou, A. 2002. "Notes sur les actes de donation d'enfants au monastère Thébain de Saint-Phoibammon", *Journal of Juristic Papyrology* 32, 83–105.

Papaconstantinou, A. 2007. "The Cult of the Saints: A Haven of Continuity in a Changing World?", in *Egypt in the Byzantine World 300–700*, ed. R. Bagnall, Cambridge, 350–67.

Papaconstantinou, A. 2012. "Donation and Negotiation: Formal Gifts to Religious Institutions in Late Antiquity", in *Donations et donateurs dans la société et l'art byzantins*, eds. J.-M. Spieser and É. Yota, Paris, 75–95.

Patrich, J. 2004. "Monastic Landscapes", in *Recent Research on the Late Antique Countryside*, eds. W. Bowden, L. Lavan, and C. Machado, Leiden, 413–45.

Petrie, W.M.F. 1907. *Gizeh and Rifeh*, London.

Petrie, W.M.F. 1908. *Athribis*, London.

Richter, T.S. 2009. "The Cultivation of Monastic Estates in Late Antique and Early Islamic Egypt. Some Evidence from Coptic Land Leases and Related Documents", in *Monastic Estates in Late Antique and Early Islamic Egypt. Ostraca, Papyri, and Essays in Memory of Sarah Clackson*, ed. A. Boud'hors *et al.*, Cincinnati, 205–15.

Rousseau, P. 1985. *Pachomius. The Making of a Community in Fourth-century Egypt*, Berkeley.

Schachner, L.A. 2005. *Economic Production in the Monasteries of Egypt and Oriens, AD 320–800*, unpublished PhD dissertation, University of Oxford.

Schenke, G. 2016. "*The Healing Shrines of St. Phoibammon*: Evidence of Cult Activity in Coptic Legal Documents", *Zeitschrift für Antikes Christentum* 20.3, 496–523.

Schroeder, C.T. 2009. "Children in Early Egyptian Monasticism", in *Children in Late Ancient Christianity*, eds. C.B. Horn and R.R. Phenix, Tübingen, 317–38.

Sijpesteijn, P.M. 2006. "The Arab Conquest of Egypt and the Beginning of Muslim Rule", in *Egypt in the Byzantine World, 300–700*, ed. R.S. Bagnall, Cambridge, 437–59.

Sijpesteijn, P.M. 2009. "Landholding Patterns in Early Islamic Egypt", *Journal of Agrarian Change* 9.1, 120–33.

Seybold, C.F. 1912. *Alexandrinische Partriarchengeschicte von S. Marcus bis Michael I., 61–767: nach der ältesten 1266 geschreibenen Hamburger Handschrift*, Hamburg.

Somers Clarke, G. 1912. *Christian Antiquities in the Nile Valley*, Oxford.

Swanson, M.N. 2010. *The Coptic Papacy in Islamic Egypt (641–1517)*, Cairo – New York.

Szkilnik, M. ed. 1993. *Rufinus of Aquileia, L'histoire des moines d'Égypte; suivie de, La vie de saint Paul le Simple*, Genève.

Timbie, J. 1998. "A Liturgical Procession in the Desert of Apa Shenoute", in *Pilgrimage and Holy Space in Late Antique Egypt*, ed. D. Frankfurter, Leiden, 415–44.

Timbie, J. 2008. "Once More into the Desert of Apa Shenoute: Further Thoughts on BN 68", in *Christianity and Monasticism in Upper Egypt*, ed. G. Gabra and H.N. Takla, Cairo – New York, 169–78.

Timm, S. 1984–2007. *Das christlich-koptische Ägypten in arabischer Zeit: eine Sammlung christlicher Stätten in Ägypten in arabischer Zeit, unter Ausschluss von Alexandria, Kairo, des Apa-Mena-Klosters (Dēr Abū Mina), der Skētis (Wādi n-Naṭrūn) und der Sinai-Regio*, Wiesbaden.

Ward, B. 1975. *The Sayings of the Desert Fathers*, Kalamazoo.

Wipszycka, E. 1972. *Les ressources et les activités économiques des églises en Égypte du IVe au VIIIe siècle*, Bruxelles.

Wipszycka, E. 1999. "L'organisation économique de la congrégation Pachomienne: critique du témoignage de Jérome", in *Ägypten und Nubien in Spätantiker und Christlicher zeit*, ed. S. Emmel *et al.*, Wiesbaden, 411–21.

Wipszycka, E. 2009. *Moines et communautés monastiques en Égypte*, Warsaw.

Wipszycka, E. 2011. "Resources and Economic Activities of the Egyptian Monastic Communities (4th–8th Century)", *Journal of Juristic Papyrology* 41, 159–263.

Wipszycka, E. 2013. "A Look at the Origins of Monasticism in Egypt from a Geographical Point of View", *Przeglad Humanistyczny* 2, 109–26.

Wüstenfeld, F. 1847. *Macrizi's geschichte der Copten*, Göttingen.

Zereteli, G. and Jernstedt, P. 1925–1935. *Papyri russischer und georgischer Sammlungen*, 5 vols., Tiflis.

CHAPTER 11

Do ut des: The Function of *Eulogiai* in the Byzantine Pilgrimage Economy

Max Ritter

It is the will of the general synod that whisperings, divinations, magic knots, amulets and incantations shall not be used among all Christians. But if there is one who is sick and who is tempted by Satan, let him be brought to the churches and monasteries where there is the treasure of the bones of the saints. Oil and *Ḥnānā* shall be given them and they shall offer a prayer over them.[1]

∴

It is clear from this example, the sixty-fourth canon of the East Syrian collection on the First Council of Nicaea, dating from the fifth century, that *eulogiai* such as the aforementioned oil and *hnānā* (sacred dust) were regarded as a legitimate substitute for amulets and other items. Initially, *eulogiai* (εὐλογίαι; Latin *benedictiones*; Syriac *burkāṭā*) were small perishable gifts first blessed by clerics or monks and then distributed to either catechumens or clerics of other Churches on special occasions, such as reciprocal visits.[2] Most often, these were alimentary offerings such as bread or fruits.[3] This habitual early Christian practice became a widespread phenomenon of everyday life across the Byzantine Empire and it became a more regularised and institutional gift-giving process when pilgrimage activities became a widespread development at the turn of the fourth/fifth centuries CE. At the same time, the use of relics proliferated,

---

1 Marutae episcopi Maipherkatae Canon 64 (Vööbus I 106–107; *eodem* II 88–89). Most parts of this East Syrian collection also circulated in the Melkite Churches of Syria and Egypt and the Maronites at least in the eighth century – most probably by a lost West Syrian intermediary – but this explicit canon was then left out.

2 Gregorii Vita Basilii iunioris I 25 (Sullivan/Talbot/McGrath 114); Schauta 2008, 81–2; Vikan 2010, 13; Drews 1898, *passim*; Stuiber 1966, 920–8.

3 Itinerarium Egeriae III 6 (Franceschini/Weber 40); Anastasii Sinaïtae Viae dux I 2, 120 (Uthemann 16).

© KONINKLIJKE BRILL NV, LEIDEN, 2020 | DOI:10.1163/9789004428690_012 and many visitors of sacred sites longed to acquire relics. Based on both developments, a new type of *eulogiai* evolved: *pilgrim's eulogiai*. These *eulogiai* were by contrast not foodstuffs, instead, they were contact relics – in most cases less perishable liquids, soil or wax whose value was believed to be derived from the healing or apotropaic power contained within them, and were thus able to be bottled and transported.[4] Because of their very different character, it is convenient to specify these items by calling them 'pilgrims' *eulogiai*', although the sources do not differentiate between the former and the latter.

Their use had significant implications for the economic relationship between sanctuaries and believers. This chapter is concerned with charting diachronic processes of change in Byzantine pilgrimage with the help of economic theory, and to analyse the phenomenon of *eulogiai* as an important part of this. In order to do so I want to start with some introductory remarks about the sources, methodology and state of research before going into the topic.

My approach in this chapter is to attempt to reconstruct economic patterns in the past that are not mentioned in the sources, because Byzantine sources do not explicitly concern themselves with the mechanisms of their sacred economy. I will use deductive methods to build an economic interpretation from fairly well-known material phenomena: the pilgrim's *eulogiai*. There is much literature on this group of objects both in art history and archaeology,[5] but the few attempts that have been made to explore their economic role have almost always been done without the use of economics. Most often the approach to the economic function of these items is simplistic, biased and descriptive. My approach therefore begins with an exploration of what the sources offer for an economic interpretation before examining different aspects of available economic theory to find the most suitable approach for explaining the pattern found in both the textual sources and the archaeological material, in order to interpret the economic mechanisms that drove the phenomena we witness.

The written sources at our disposal for this venture include saints' lives, miracle collections, pilgrimage reports and itineraries, and some historiography (both secular and ecclesiastical). In the case of the material remains – the ceramic containers of the *eulogiai* – we have a tiny proportion of the vessels that were produced (estimated at less than 0.1%) and of these, an arbitrary selection which can be analysed archaeologically and art historically. A complete economic interpretation of this phenomenon has to rely on both written and archaeological sources in tandem. Due to the constraints of the written sources, I bring together diachronic testimonies from both Late Antiquity through

---

4   Caner 2006, 331–3.
5   Ousterhout 1990; Frank 2006; Vikan 1995, 380 and 1998; Foskolou 2012; Bangert 2007.

to the Middle Byzantine period in order to reveal both common patterns and telling differences over this period of time.

1 *Eulogiai*: Functions and Types

The main religious function of *eulogiai* is to transport the miraculous power of relics and holy places somewhere else, in order to access and use the sacred power at a place other than that where the holiness is located. Most cases mentioned in the sources imply that *eulogiai* were primarily used by pilgrims during their return journey in order to protect themselves against the dangers of travel.[6] We find examples of such use of *eulogiai* in the fifth-century *life* of Simeon Stylites the Elder,[7] where the dust was applied to the hull of a ship. In all the following cases the *eulogia* was supposedly thrown into the turbulent, stormy sea, which then miraculously became calm: In the *life* of Simeon Stylites the Younger at the turn of the sixth to the seventh century,[8] in a depiction of a stylite's *ampulla* found in Sardis,[9] in the *life* of Niketas Patrikios who, after a pilgrimage to Cherson was trapped in a storm on the Black Sea,[10] and in Xiphilinos' miracles of Eugenios of Trebizond.[11]

The acquisition of a *eulogia* acted to intensify the experience of visitors at the pilgrimage shrine itself through its haptic and olfactory features,[12] and they were also taken home to be used for healing, either for relatives, or for the pilgrim himself.[13] In such cases the oils or dust were applied to the sick body

---

6   Ioannis Chrysostomi Homilia in martyres (PG 50, col. 664); Vikan 1995, 384.

7   Vita syriaca Symeonis Stylitae, chap. 71 (Assemani 334; Doran 151): 'He rubbed handfuls of that ḥnānā on all sides of the ship while everyone as they lay down cried out 'Mar Simeon, ask your Lord, help us by your prayer'.'

8   Arcadii episcopi Constantiensis Vita Symeonis Stylitae iunioris, chap. 235, 13–17 (van den Ven 212).

9   Rautman 2005, 720.

10   Vita Nicetae patricii, chap. 30 (Papachryssanthou 347): Πρὸς δὲ τὴν πόλιν Χερσῶνος ἐπειγόμενοι, ἐξῆλθον τοῦ σκάφους αὐτῶν καὶ τὸν τάφον τοῦ ἁγίου προσεκύνησαν. ἀπιέναι δὲ μέλλοντες ἐν ἀγγείῳ ἔσπευσαν ἁγίῳ ἐλαίῳ λήψασθαι, καὶ οὕτως τῶν ἐκεῖσε ἀπεκίνησαν. καὶ δὴ πρὸς μέσον τοῦ πελάγους γενόμενοι σφοδραῖς ἀνέμων βίαις ὑπεβλήθησαν· ὅθεν τῇ συστροφῇ τῶν ἀνέμων τρικυμίαις πολλαῖς χειμαζόμενοι εἰς παντελῆ τοῦ ζῆν ἀνελπιστίαν συνήλασαν. εἷς οὖν ἐξ αὐτῶν περὶ τῆς τοῦ ἐλαίου εὐλογίας τὸν ναύκληρον ἀναμνήσας, ἐπιπέμψαι τοῦτο παρ' αὐτοῦ τῇ θαλάσσῃ προσετάττετο. ὁ δὲ τὴν τοῦ ὁσίου ἁγίαν πρεσβείαν ἐπικαλεσάμενος τῇ ἀγριαινούσῃ καὶ κυμαινομένῃ θαλάσσῃ τὸ εὐλογημένον καὶ ἅγιον κατέχεεν ἔλαιον.

11   Ioannis Xiphilini Miracula Eugenii, mir. 9 (Rosenqvist 196).

12   Hunter-Crawley 2012.

13   Examples for this: Thessalonica to Thebes: Gregorii presbyteri Vita Theodorae Thessalonicensi, chap. 56 (Paschalides 178; Talbot 212). Hosios Lukas and its surrounding:

or used by pregnant women. They were accepted as proof that the pilgrimage had been undertaken,[14] and as an apotropaic item over the rest of one's life, especially those in containers specifically produced for this purpose. They were worn on the body, most often around the neck[15] as we know from archaeological evidence[16] as well as from visual representations.[17] One lively testimony comes from the mid-seventh century *life* of the Bishop Spyridon:

> The saint held his crosier in his hands and wore a headscarf wreathen with palm twigs on his head – which is called by some *tiara*, by others helmet – and he also wore a clay vessel, in which there was oil of the holy and life-giving Cross.[18]

They were also stored in the house as an apotropaic item against demons. Theodoret of Cyrrhus hung a small oil flask (ληκύθιον) filled with martyr's oil near his bed,[19] and other uses in domestic contexts are testified to in the archaeological record.[20]

The theological foundation of this religious function was based on the belief in relics and the holiness of places in early Christianity: as such, *eulogiai* were transmitters of holy power (δύναμις).[21] Pilgrim's *eulogiai* as a constitutive feature of pilgrimage only developed in the fifth century, when immediate access to the relics at many shrines became restricted. At Abu Mena,[22] St. Peter's in

---

Vita Lucae iunioris Steiriotis, chaps. 80, 21–24 (Connor 130–132) and 84, 24–32 (Connor 138–40). Nikon Metanoeite: Vita Niconis Metanoeite, chap. 50 (Sullivan 166). See for this subject in general: Talbot 2002, 160–1.

14 Maraval 2004, 233.

15 Engemann 2002, 169.

16 Kötzsche-Breitenburg 1984, 239: in this instance, remnants of a red-dyed leather strap were recorded. Jasaeva 2012, 477, obj. 102: here in a grave context, an ampulla of the tenth/eleventh c. had been fastened on a silver necklace.

17 Engemann 1973, 13.

18 Theodori episcopi Paphensis Vita Spyridonis episcopi Trimithuntis, chap. 8 (van den Ven 43): Ὁ γὰρ ἅγιος εἶχεν ἐν χερσὶν τὴν ποιμαντικὴν αὐτοῦ βακτηρίαν καὶ ἐπὶ τῆς κεφαλῆς αὐτοῦ κειμένην κίδαριν ἐκ βαΐων φοινίκων πεπλεγμένην, ἥτις τιάρα παρά τισιν ὀνομάζεται, παρὰ δὲ ἄλλοις περικεφαλαία ἤτοι κάσσις, ἐπιφερόμενος κἀκεῖνο τὸ ὀστράκινον σκεῦος ἐν ᾧ ἦν τὸ ζωτικὸν ἔλαιον τοῦ τιμίου καὶ ζωοποιοῦ σταυροῦ (trans. by author).

19 Theodoreti episcopi Cyrrhensis Historia religiosa XXI 16 (Canivet II 96).

20 Anderson 2004, 87.

21 Vikan 1998, 234; Vikan 1995, 382.

22 Redigolo 2012, 35.

Rome[23] and other major sanctuaries,[24] pilgrimage shrines started to physically channel the pilgrimage crowds through the construction of architectural features such as parallel staircases, and to screen the relics. Since contact with the sacred was now impossible, pilgrims required compensation, furthermore, it seems that pilgrims now wanted to take something back home as a testimony to their piety – perhaps to mark their social status as wealthy enough to travel, perhaps to confer the blessing of the shrine onto their home community more generally. Both developments contributed to the invention of *eulogia*. Even as early as the fifth century, it was considered unusual and rude when visitors of an important sacred site were dismissed without even receiving a *eulogia*.[25]

The basic substance of the *eulogiai* themselves was always cheap and easily replenished,[26] collected by clerics or monks at the site.[27] Solid substances used included dust[28] (Syriac ḥnānā; Greek μάννα – 'powder') or wax; liquids included olive oil, tree resin,[29] 'blood',[30] and water.[31] These basic substances were often mixed. For example, *kerote/kerion* was a solid mixture of oil and wax imprinted with a seal, which could be melted at body temperature in order to be applied to the sick body;[32] In the sources they are called seals.[33] Another example are ḥnānā tokens, which were made of terracotta and ḥnānā dust.

---

23   Brenk 1995, 73–9.

24   *E.g.* the 40-Martyrs-Church in Saranda, north of Bouthroton/Butrint, cf. Mitchell 2004, 176–7.

25   Theodoreti episcopi Cyrrhensis Historia religiosa XXI 33 (Canivet II 118–120).

26   Patlagean 1984, 45–6.

27   Maraval 2004, 239.

28   Outside of Syria, dust or earth *eulogiai* are testified in Ephesus and Amastris, for the latter *cf.* Nicetae Paphlagonis Laudatio in Hyacynthum Amastrenum, chaps. 21–22 (PG 105, cols. 437–440).

29   Itinerarium Antonini Placentini, chap. 39 (Geyer 149; Wilkinson 87): 'lump of gum'.

30   In the St. Euphemia church of Chalcedon: Theophylacti Simocattae Historiae VIII 14 (Boor/Wirth 311–2; Whitby 233–234); Naumann *et al.* 1979, 26. In the tenth century, further testimonies are: Vita Athanasii Athonitae secunda, chaps. 67–77 (Noret 202–9; Greenfield/Talbot 335–57) and Vita Mariae iunioris Bizyensi, chap. 12, 16, 18 (AASS Nov. IV 697–9; Laiou 269–72).

31   An early, fifth-century example for this is: Callinici Vita Hypatii Rufinianae, chap. 38 § 4–5 (Bartelink 228). Later, tenth-century, examples are Gregorii presbyteri Translatio Theodorae Thessalonicensi, chap. 3 (Paschalides 194–5; Talbot 221); Vita Eliae Spelaeotes monachi in Calabria, chap. 96, 20–9 (AASS Sep. III 886); and Vita Theophanus imperatricis, chap. 26 (Kurtz 18, 27–19,2).

32   Miracula Cosmae et Damiani, mir. 30, 54–60 (Deubner 175); Miracula Artemii, mir. 3 and 33 (Papadopoulos-Kerameus 3–4 and 50; Crisafulli 83 and 177). Definition by Festugière 1971, 100 fn. 5; further references to this: Caseau 2007, 645; Maraval 2004, 239.

33   Miracula Artemii, mir. 16 (Papadopoulos-Kerameus 17; Crisafulli 109).

Kerote was typical for healing sanctuaries (Menouthis, Kosmidion, sanctuary of St. Therapon in Perama) whereas ḥnānā was common in Syria.

Olive oil was widely used in various mixtures (*e.g.* with wine or dust[34]). Most often the oil was perfumed and taken either from the 'inextinguishable' lamps burning in front of the respective saint's tomb[35] or channelled past the saint's bones within the sarcophagus.[36] The latter was referred to as *myron* from the seventh century onwards,[37] and could be used as an ointment, salve or as a beverage. From the ninth century, it became the most prominent *eulogia* within the empire.[38] In addition, sacred water from springs or streams such as the Jordan River[39] or from different *hagiasmata*[40] (holy springs) were thickened with mud to be applied to the body or consumed.

It is very important to differentiate analytically between the *eulogiai* themselves and the containers of *eulogiai* (in Latin sources called *ampulla*, but with no equivalent Greek term other than the ordinary σκεύη – 'vessel'). In most cases – most prominently for the *ampullae* of Abu Mena, Jerusalem and the

---

34   *E.g.* at Phantinos the Younger: Vita Phantini iunioris, chap. 58 (Follieri 464).

35   See Talbot 2015, 224–5 with examples from the tenth century onwards. The earliest testimony is from the sixth century: Cyrilli Scythopolitani Vita Euthymii, chap. 54 (Schwartz 76; Price 74).

36   Gregorii presbyteri Vita Theodorae Thessalonicensi, chaps. 49–51 (Paschalides 165–70; Talbot 206–9).

37   Caseau 2005, 149. The earliest examples, all in the seventh and eighth c., are to be found in Amathous: Leontii episcopi Neapolitanis Vita Ioannis Eleemosinarii, chap. 60 (Festugière 409); in Myra: references in Anrich 1913/17, 516–17 and Caseau 2013, 72; in Constantinople: Miracula Therapontis, chaps. 21 and 26 (Deubner 130 and 133); and in Patras: Gregorii episcopi Turonensis Liber in gloria martyrum, chap. 30 (Krusch 55–6), see Caseau 2013, 175–7.

38   C. the turn of the eighth/ninth century: Vita Philothei Opsiciani (AASS Nov. prop. 47–48) and Eustathii episcopi Thessalonicensis Laudatio in Philotheum Opsicianum, chap. 20 (Tafel 151). Ninth century: Sabae Miracula Petri Atroënsis, chap. 98 (Laurent 149); Constantini episcopi Tiensis Translatio corporis Euphemiae, chap. 5 (Halkin 89); Sabae monachi Vita Macarii abbatis Pelecetae, chaps. 21–22 (Gheyn 163). Tenth century: Vita Mariae iunioris Bizyensi, chap. 12 (AASS Nov. IV 697; Talbot 268–9); Vita Lucae iunioris Steiriotis, chaps. 69, 73 and 84 (Connor 114, 122 and 140); Vita Demetriani episcopi Chytraei, lineae 631–635 (Grégoire 236); Vita Pauli iunioris Latrensi, chap. 47 (Delehaye 133–4); Nicetae Paphlagonis Vita Ignatii patriarchae Constantinopolitanis, chap. 83 (Smithies/Duffy 112); Basilii episcopi Vita Euthymii iunioris Thessalonicensi, chap. 26 (Petit 191; Greenfield/Talbot 79–81); and Vita Theophanus imperatricis, chap. 31 (Kurtz 22, 30–23, 3).

39   Itinerarium Antonini Placentini, chap. 11 (Geyer 135; Wilkinson 82): '[...] and draw out holy water. This water they use for sprinkling their ships when they are about to set sail.'

40   An early example for water as healing eulogia is (mid-fifth c.): Callinici Vita Hypatii Rufinianae, chap. 38 § 4–5 (Bartelink 228); Maraval 2004, 239.

so-called 'Asia Minor *ampullae*' – the term εὐλογία was given to the *container* due to the fact that this word is written on them; however, this word most certainly did not designate the container, but rather its content.[41] Tellingly, the depictions on the items – at least in those from Jerusalem – refer to the pilgrimage shrine itself and the corresponding liturgy taking place there.[42]

However, of course liquids had to be bottled for transport. For this reason, specific *eulogia* containers were produced and fulfilled a particular economic role. The first *eulogia* containers we know of are from the very end of the fifth century,[43] much later than the attestation of the first pilgrim's *eulogiai*. Prior and contemporaneously to this, *eulogia* liquids were carried in non-specific containers and vessels. The distinctive containers of the sixth and seventh centuries are mostly made of terracotta, sometimes of metal alloys like pewter for more prestigious pilgrims, and while *eulogiai* were a common feature of all pilgrimage shrines at all times from the fourth century onwards, these specific containers were only produced at a few large pilgrimage centres, and only during certain periods (Fig. 11.1). Their formulation and iconography often resemble amulets from the same period.[44]

Eulogiai and their containers were products controlled by the administrative staff of the local Church. Pilgrimage sites were led by either *oikonomoi* as in the case of Abu Mena in Egypt, or *prosmonarioi/paramonarioi* as at Euchaita and Chonai in Asia Minor. Those sites were administrated by them on behalf of the local bishop, who was the nominal owner of the pilgrimage site. The clerical staff relied on offerings (προσφοραί) made by pilgrims because their regular stipends were insufficient to support them,[45] and the surplus was given to the diocese. In some cases, the administrators of a pilgrimage site could come into conflict with the local Church over the profits or treasures (as we see in Seleukeia/Meriamlik versus Tarsus[46]) and some bishops moved their see to a pilgrimage church in time of crisis (as was the case in Chonai, Myra, Germia and Ephesos).

---

41   *Pace* Witt 2000, 13 and 66.

42   Krueger 2015, 118.

43   Kiss 1989 *passim*.

44   Engemann 1995a, 224; Engemann 2002, 168; Spier 1993. For a survey on amulets of the Greek period see Kotansky 1991.

45   Herman 1942, 430.

46   Miracula Theclae, mir. 32 (Dagron 374–6; Talbot/Johnson 129–31).

FIGURE 11.1   Map of pilgrimage sanctuaries distributing pilgrim's *eulogia* and specific
eulogia containers at different times.
BY AUTHOR

2   *Eulogiai* and Their Containers: Holy Sepulchre, Abu Mena, and Qal'at Sem'an

In Jerusalem the earliest mention of the distribution of *eulogiai* to pilgrims is not, as often stated, the itinerary of Egeria,[47] but the report of the Piacenza pilgrim. In his time (*c.* 570) contact oil from the True Cross was placed in special containers and given out at the rock of Golgotha.[48] Oil from the lamps

---

47   Itinerarium Egeriae XXXVII 2 (Franceschini/Weber 81). The cases gathered by Maraval
from the fourth/fifth c. point to distribution of relics of the True cross but not *eulogiai*:
Maraval 2004, 234.

48   Itinerarium Antonini Placentini, chap. 20 (Geyer 139; Wilkinson, Jerusalem Pilgrims 83):
'[...] and they offer oil to be blessed in little flasks. When the mouth of one of the little
flasks touches the Wood of the Cross, the oil instantly bubbles over, and unless it is closed
very quickly it all spills out.' For this: Engemann 1973, 11. Another testimony for the True
Cross' oil provides Pope Gregory I who had received it as a gift from the Exconsul Leontius

in the *Anastasis* rotunda was given to pilgrims at around the same time. Both the Piacenza pilgrim[49] and Augustine[50] mention that sand was collected in the rotunda and given to pilgrims as *eulogiai* as early as the fifth century. This practice is well-attested by a ninth-century *authentica* stored in the Lateran church [Terra de sepulchro domini].[51] Furthermore, from the eleventh century onwards, wax was given to pilgrims in connection with the famous Easter light miracle.[52]

These containers were produced in Jerusalem in the sixth and seventh centuries (Fig. 11.2).[53] The most well-known examples are found in the church treasuries of Monza and Bobbio in northern Italy,[54] which alone provide us with thirty-six specimens.[55] They came into the possession of these objects in the early seventh century as offerings made by the Lombard Queen Theodolinda (589–627) who in turn perhaps received them from Pope Gregory I.[56] But they were also found in excavations, for instance in Istanbul (Yenikapı[57]) and in Coptic tombs.[58] There are about one dozen more in museum collections worldwide but their provenance is in most cases uncertain.[59]

After the Arab conquest of Jerusalem, the production of *eulogia* containers halted for reasons as yet unknown, although pilgrimage and oil distribution continued.[60] It was not until the second half of the twelfth century that

---

in 598 on the occasion of the latter's assumption of office in Sicily: Gregorii I papae ep. VIII 33 (Norberg 557–9; Martyn 528–9).

49   Itinerarium Antonini Placentini, chap. 18 (Geyer 138; Wilkinson, Jerusalem Pilgrims 83): 'Earth is brought to the tomb and put inside, and those who go in take some as a blessing.' For this: Klausen-Nottmeyer 1995, 923; Schauta 2008, 83.

50   Augustini episcopi Hipponiensis De civitate Dei XXII 8 (Green VII 244–50).

51   Luchterhandt 2017, 45–6.

52   Jaspert 2015. The Easter miracle involved the autonomous lighting of the lamp in the tomb, see Külzer 1994, 203; Pratsch 2011, 62–6; earlier major study: Canard 1965.

53   Anderson 2004, 80; Engemann 1995b, 34. Models of very similar ampullae were found in Jerusalem itself, see Piccirillo 1994.

54   Engemann 2002, 161. Weitzmann wanted to see in them rudiments of a Palestinian 'loca sancta iconography', see Weitzmann 1974, 39–40 and 49.

55   Engemann 1973, 26.

56   Lambert – Pedemonte Demeglio 1994, 218; also Elsner 1997. This thesis was recently persuasively questioned by Filipová 2015, who argues that the queen got the ampullae from private persons in her kingdom. The assumed relation with Gregory is based on the relic authenticates for *brandea* of Roman martyr tombs, see Tjäder 1955, vol. II 205–22.

57   Sever Georgousakis 2016, 39–41.

58   Kötzsche-Breitenburg 1984, 233.

59   Filipová 2015, 5 n. 6.

60   Luchterhandt 2017, 46; Frolow 1961, 174–5. *E.g.* Vita Stephani thaumaturgi arabica, chap. 52 (Lamoreaux 81–3).

FIGURE 11.2   Holy Sepulchre *ampulla* (so-called Monza-Bobbio *ampullae*
type), sixth century CE
DUMBARTON OAKS, BYZANTINE COLLECTION/
WASHINGTON DC, BZ 1948.18

they were produced again. Although on a small scale, wide-necked, and made
of lead,[61] they roughly follow the Monza-Bobbio scheme[62] and in this way
resemble their late antique predecessors. Their contents certainly were oil
from the lamps burning at the tomb, depicted on the ampullae.[63] However,
their rarity – to date only five are known[64] – in this period suggests they
were only given to selected aristocratic pilgrims as a gift by the royal court.
Ordinary pilgrims to Jerusalem at this time were also able to receive *eulogia*,
but these containers were produced in Acre, the main landing point for pilgrims to the Crusader kingdom of Jerusalem in the thirteenth century. Acre

61   Kötzsche 1988.
62   Vikan 1998, 260; Kötzsche 1995, 283.
63   Boertjes 2012, 184–5.
64   Boertjes 2012, 175–81 with figs and refs.

had no celebrated shrines of its own, however, and it seems that these containers, which have extraordinary wide necks and a non-specific decoration,[65] were empty when acquired. Their shape indicates that they could have held different *eulogiai* from diverse pilgrimage shrines acquired in or en route to Jerusalem in Samaria or Galilee.[66] Although a later example, this observation is very important for the economic interpretation I wish to make.

Most known *eulogia* containers come from Abu Mena in northern Egypt:[67] Monica Gilli collected 762 specimens.[68] They were always made of terracotta (Fig. 11.3)[69] and filled with oil from the tomb of St. Menas beneath the bema of his martyrium church[70] or, alternatively, from a lamp in front of his tomb as indicated in the miracle collections.[71] All the containers are dated to the period between the end of the fifth to the seventh century,[72] as proven by stratigraphically secure finds in Kom el-Dikka (Alexandria). However, the examples show a wide iconographic range. Furthermore, a minority of preserved examples do not depict St. Menas at all, but unknown local saints,[73] as well as St. Theodore Tiron and St. Isidore of Chios,[74] and sixteen containers showing St. Thekla.[75] Thekla was venerated in a small sanctuary in the Mareotis (in at-Tūm), but not in Abu Mena itself.[76] It was suggested that these containers represent a gendered model for pregnant women,[77] but it is much more likely that that the sanctuary of Thekla was founded by a Cilician auxiliary unit (*numerus*) stationed nearby by the Emperor Zeno[78] and was also visited by the same

65   Foskolou 2012, 73; Syon 1999.

66   Syon 1994/99.

67   Vikan 1998, 240.

68   Gilli 2002, 10. Circa 200 were taken to Frankfurt by Abu Mina's excavator Carl Maria Kaufmann. For some areas, there are special studies on this group, *e.g.* for Merovingian contexts (12 specimens): Delahaye 2005.

69   There are four ampullae made of pewter recorded in Cairo, but I was not able to verify the information given by Witt 2000, 27.

70   Engemann 1995a, 226.

71   Miracula Menae coptica, mir. 5 (Drescher 118–19); Miracula Menae arabica, mir. 25 (Jaritz 240); George 1974, 38; Grossmann 1998, 285.

72   Bangert 2007, 27; Kiss 1989 *passim*.

73   Durand 1992, 156–7.

74   Metzger 1981, 15; Davis 1998, 311–12.

75   Davis 2001, 117–9; Davis 1998; Durand 1992, 156–7.

76   Miracula Menae graeca, mir. 3–4 (Drescher 116–118); Miracula Menae arabica, mir. 9 (Jaritz 168–169); Jaritz 1993, 298; Davis 2001, 127–9; Davis 1998, 314–17; Varinlioğlu 2007, 293; Delahaye 1910, 130.

77   Davis 1998, 313; Davis 2001, 124.

78   Witt 2000, 54–5; Gascou 2008, 69–71. This interpretation is based on: Cyrilli Scythopolitani Vita Sabae, chaps. 1, 9 and 25 (Schwartz 87, 92, 109; Price 95, 101, 118); Sabas' father served in that unit.

FIGURE 11.3   St. Menas *ampullae*, made of terracotta,
               sixth century CE
               WALTERS ARTS MUSEUM/BALTIMORE, 48.2541,
               PURCHASED IN 1987

pilgrims as Abu Mena. Whatever the case may be, two facts become obvious. First, the *ampullae* were produced not only for Abu Mena, but also for other sanctuaries in the area under the control of the bishop of Alexandria;[79] and secondly, there is a huge iconographic variation in the Abu Mena *ampullae* which can be addressed through an economic interpretation.

As a last example, I want to examine the rather puzzling evidence from Qal'at Sem'an (between Antioch and Aleppo). At first, in the mid-fifth century, as the different *lives* of St. Simeon the Elder relate, only pure ḥnānā (dust of

---

79   Regarding ecclesiastical control in Abu Mena, cf. Caseau 2007, 647.

FIGURE 11.4   Token of St. Simeon Stylites the Elder, made of terracotta,
               sixth century CE
               WALTERS ARTS MUSEUM/BALTIMORE, 48.1939,
               PURCHASED IN 1946

the mountain mixed with oil)[80] was given, by the saint himself, to visitors.[81] The ḥnānā could be dissolved with water, rendering it applicable to the body. Schachner was surprised that there are no containers known from that time,[82] but this relatively solid ḥnānā either did not need any container or was carried in leather bags that have long since perished. From the sixth and seventh centuries, however, different *eulogiai* of Simeon appear (Fig. 11.4), many showing the

---

80   Vita syriaca Symeonis Stylitae senioris, chap. 88 (Assemani 357–8; Doran 167).
81   o.c., chaps. 61 (Assemani 318–319; Doran 141) and 33 (Assemani 290–291; Doran 120). The latter one: '[…] he [the saint] answered, 'In the name of Lord Jesus Christ, take some of this dust and go out and apply it to her' (for there was no oil there to give, nor was it yet the custom to give hnana for he [Simeon] had been there only fourteen months). The moment that dust touched her in the name of Christ, she leapt up and stood healed.'
82   Schachner 2010, 365.

adoration of the magi, which makes a sixth-century date or later most likely.[83] Found both in the archaeological record of Qal'at Sem'an itself, in nearby cities and out of context in European collections, they amount to around 250 pieces. The so-called tokens (Greek σφραγίδες/σφραγίδια – 'imprints') are made of terracotta mixed with dust, in rare cases also wax,[84] and in one case coated with metal.[85] In other words, the ḥnānā is still part of the recipe, but clay predominates. It is not surprising that these *eulogiai* are not mentioned in the *lives* of the fifth century, because they did not exist at that time.

The French excavators analysed the clay of these tokens, showing that they were produced adjacent to the mountain.[86] In recent years, excavations at the gate to the so-called *Via sacra* revealed five tokens accompanied by coin weights and bronze cross-pendants in the booths VS01 and 02 in a late sixth-century context, which suggests that they were sold in this location.[87] A wide range of scenes is depicted upon them: although most show Simeon,[88] there are also many other images.[89] Vikan is correct in stating that 'tokens are functionally related to pilgrim *ampullae*'[90] in that they have to be treated like *eulogiai* encompassed by a container. As with the Abu Mena containers and the Acre *ampullae* we can observe a surprising iconographic variation on the containers. Instead of interpreting them art historically or from a liturgical point of view,[91] as has been done in the past, this also has economic implications, as I will show.

As we have seen, while *eulogiai* themselves were distributed at all pilgrimage destinations and times since the fourth century, *eulogia* containers were first produced only from the late fifth to the seventh century and then only at some sanctuaries. It is therefore clear that *eulogiai* were normally put into nondescript containers which were brought by the pilgrim, supported by an extract from the eleventh-century life of Nikon Metanoeite where it is explicitly stated that the pilgrim filled a random container with the *myron* from

---

83   Krueger 2014, 84–6.
84   Sodini 1993, 141.
85   Peña – Castellana – Fernandez 1975, 176.
86   Sodini *et al.* 1998, 9–11.
87   Pieri 2009.
88   Vikan 1998, 236.
89   Bangert 2007, 319–20; Sodini 2010, 310–4; Vikan 2010, 59–61.
90   Vikan 1991.
91   Krueger 2014, 77–8, 84–6 and 94.

the saint's tomb.[92] We also have a similar testimony from the Black Sea area around the same time.[93]

In the twelfth/thirteenth centuries, specific containers were produced again, but only in some places, including Acre, Jerusalem, and Thessalonica. Usually the medallions related to the *Mons Admirabilis* (near Antioch) are mentioned in that context, although they do not resemble *eulogiai* containers.[94] Apart from these, Ephesos[95] and Corinth[96] may have produced some *ampullae* again at around the same time, but evidence is very slight. The containers were made of pewter or lead, or glazed pottery. In other words, there is a 400-year gap in production between the end of the seventh until the twelfth century.[97] This lacuna has been explained as being a result of the Arab expansion and the subsequent breakdown of the pilgrimage economy in the Middle East. However, Ephesos remained within the Byzantine empire but bears witness to the same trend (although the distribution of containerless *eulogia* continued there as well). Exactly when and where *eulogia* container production started again is not yet known. It may have been re-introduced in the Crusader kingdoms due to an increase in pilgrimage traffic, but it is also possible that it spread from within the eleventh-century Byzantine empire to the Levant.

3 The Economy of *Eulogiai*

First, we must stress again how important it is to differentiate between *eulogiai* and their containers. Vicky Foskolou has recently convincingly shown that

---

92 Vita Niconis Metanoeite, chap. 50 (Sullivan 166): Ὁ στρατηγὸς Βασίλειος ὁ Ἀπόκαυκος […], ἐπεχωρίασε τῇ Λακεδαίμονι ἐφ᾽ ᾧ προσκυνῆσαι τὴν τιμίαν σορὸν τοῦ μάκαρος καὶ τὸν πρὸς αὐτὸν ὡς οἷόν τε ἀφοσιώσασθαι πόθον. ἐν δὲ τῷ μέλλειν τῆς Λακεδαίμονος ἀπαίρειν, ἔν τινι σκεύει λαβὼν τοῦ ἁγίου μύρου οἴκαδε ἀπεκόμισεν εἰς ἁγιασμὸν καὶ δεινῶν ἀπαλλαγὴν καὶ νόσων ἀλεξιτήριον. (The strategos Basil Apokaukos […] was visiting Lacedaimon to do reverence to the honoured coffin of the blessed one and to satisfy his love for him as much as possible. Being about to leave Lacedaimon, he took some of the holy ointment in a vessel and he brought it home for sanctification and relief from misfortunes and remedy for diseases.)
93 Ioannis Xiphilini Miracula Eugenii, mir. 9 (Rosenqvist 196).
94 However, a Middle Byzantine mould preserved in the Gaziantep museum was designed to produce ampullae for St. Simeon the Younger. No ampullae are known so far, but the mould testifies to a reactivation of production; see Laflı – Ritter – Boura, "A Pilgrim Flask Casting Mold with the Depiction of St. Simeon the Stylite the Younger from Gaziantep" (forthcoming).
95 Buora – Laflı – Kan Şahin 2015, no. 21.
96 Davidson 1952, 75–76 no. 576.
97 Vikan 1998, 257.

the former were always given free to the pilgrims,[98] however, she conflates the testimonies regarding *eulogiai* with those about the containers, and concluded that the latter had also been given out free of charge. But I argue that the related economic mechanism is much more complex: here, I shall first investigate the economics of *eulogiai*, and then that of the containers.

As Foskolou shows, there is considerable evidence that *eulogiai* were given to pilgrims for free by the clergy and it is for this reason that Daniel Caner coined them "disinterested gifts".[99] But was this in fact so simple? How did pilgrimage centres make a profit from *eulogiai* if they were given for free? The obvious answer is by the receipt of counter-gifts. Gifts and offerings were expected to be given by the pilgrims according to the means of each.[100] This was the common exchange mechanism when pilgrims experienced miracles, as we shall see, and the same pattern on a smaller scale can be construed also for *eulogiai*. Because they were gifts which could not be refused, and whose power was only to be felt at a later time so that they could not be returned, a counter-gift was due immediately.

When money is mentioned in relation to *eulogiai* in the sources, then it is always as a counter-gift, not in relation to fixed prices to be paid. A rather late example supports this: a certain monk near Jericho in the twelfth century received money for giving *eulogiai*, which were self-made wooden crosses: '[...] we will produce [wooden] crosses, which we will give to those who come to pray for the sake of a blessing [τοῖς ἐπευχίταις χάριν εὐλογίας]. According to the inclination of each they will hand over some small change with which we can buy supplies for me and you.'[101]

Put in economic terms, *eulogiai* belonged to the class of goods defined by Karl Polanyi as reciprocal.[102] For those goods the major issue is social embeddedness, which means that their transaction features and their value are defined almost *in toto* according to the prevalent cultural habits of the communities involved. Consequently, when cultural habits change, such goods may lose their value. Furthermore, reciprocity is rather an inefficient mode of transaction due to the manifold uncertainties accompanying its execution: it is

---

98   Foskolou 2012, 60–1 and 80–1; Caner 2006, 358 n. 102; *pace* Campbell 1988, 544–5.

99   Caner 2013 *passim*.

100   Theodoreti episcopi Cyrrhensis Graecarum affectionum curatio VIII 64 (Raeder 217; Müller 315): Καὶ οἱ μὲν ἐκ χρυσοῦ, οἱ δὲ ἐξ ὕλης πεποιημένα. δέχεται γὰρ ὁ τούτων δεσπότης καὶ τὰ σμικρά τε καὶ εὔωνα, τῇ τοῦ προσφέροντος δυνάμει τὸ δῶρον μετρῶν.

101   Ioannis Ducac Descriptio Terrae sanctae, chap. 23 (Troïckij 21). The pilgrim was the Grand Hetairiarch Ioannes Doukas, on a diplomatic mission to Jerusalem in 1177. For the identification: Messis 2011.

102   Polanyi 1944, 71–87.

almost impossible to guarantee an appropriate 'counter gift' without thorough negotiation prior to the gift-giving.

Pilgrimage centres developed mechanisms to minimise factors of inequality in exchange transactions in three ways. First, they wanted precious metals and immovable property like land; in other words, commutable goods, and in general, of high value (1). Second, they wanted to have the gift at once and not promises of gift-giving at a later date, which could be easily forgotten (2). Third, they needed to protect themselves against broken promises, for example, gifts being smaller when given than what was promised (3). Examples of all these can be found in the sources, usually in punishment miracles (which were especially popular in the eighth and ninth centuries but can be also found in other periods).[103]

The subject of high-value gifts (1) is common. The pilgrim was expected to donate according to his wealth and the miracle he had experienced. This is usually expressed by the terms 'μετὰ τῆς ὀφειλούσης τιμῆς, ὅσον πρὸς τὸ δυνατὸν αὐτῷ'[104] and '[...] τὰ εἰκότα εὐχαριστήσας τῇ Θεομήτορι.'[105] When the tenth-century monk Ioannes Peperis from Chaldia offered all his liquid assets (i.e. 3 *solidi*) to the Theotokos in exchange for his cure, She accepted the offer and he readily fulfilled his promise thereafter,[106] a successful incidence of bartering. Time as an economic factor (2) is apparent in the miracles for St. Eugenios, in which we hear of the saint torturing a woman suffering from dysmenorrhoea for as long as she hesitated in fulfilling her promise to donate a golden oil lamp.[107] However, it is the problem of a reduction in the promised gifts (3) that is the most common subject in the sources. A pilgrim to Abu Mena wanted to offer St. Menas a silver dish with the saint's name engraved on it, but changed his mind and was punished by the saint.[108] In the eighth-century Arabic collection for the same saint a camel driver vowed the first foal born of his infertile camel, but as he did not give any foal to the saint, even after three were born, the saint took the camel and all three foals by force.[109] In Rupprecht's miracle

---

103   Papaconstantinou 2012, 84.

104   Miracula Artemii, mir. 17 and 26 (Papadopoulos-Kerameus 17 and 37; Crisafulli 109 and 149); 'with appropriate value, as much as he is able [to give]'; Déroche 2006, 154 n. 12.

105   Miracula Deiparae ad fontem, chap. 38 (AASS Nov. III 887; Talbot/Johnson 285): '[...] giving the appropriate thanks [i.e. *charisteria*] to the Mother of God.'

106   'καὶ ταῦτα δεκτά μοι καὶ οὐκ ἀπόβλητα.'

107   Ioannis Lazaropuli Miracula Eugenii, chap. 4, 351–416 (Rosenqvist 264–8).

108   Part of the second miracle of the saint in the Greek collection, dated to the seventh century: Miracula Mena graeca, mir. 2 (Duffy 70–2). This narrative is to be found with minor changes also in: Miracula Menae coptica, mir. 3 (Drescher 114–6) and Miracula Menae arabica, mir. 7 (Jaritz 167–8).

109   Miracula Menae arabica, mir. 17 (Jaritz 175–6).

collection for Sts. Cosmas and Damian a pilgrim with a cataract met a blind beggar in front of the Kosmidion in Constantinople. The saints punished him because, instead of donating to them for healing, as promised, he gave alms to the beggar in front of the church,[110] hoping to receive a cure instead by this act of mercy. After the realisation of his mistake he donated to the saints and was healed. In a later period, a pilgrim to St. Eugenios in Trebizond decided to give fifteen gold coins for his cure when he was back home. According to the fourteenth-century miracle collection compiled by Ioannes Lazaropoulos he sent his son to the sanctuary to deliver it, but the son was overtaken by greed [φιλαργυρία] and kept five of the coins for himself when he entered the sanctuary. The saint appeared at night in his dreams and turned them into nightmares. Thereafter the son gave not just the fifteen promised coins, but five of his own in addition.[111]

There are no sources for counter-gifts after the receipt of *eulogiai*, but such mechanisms for countering reciprocal unevenness that we find in regard to miracles can be used as evidence to reason that the same mechanism was at work on a smaller scale with *eulogiai*. We have to keep in mind that in some cases, such as at the Kosmidion in Constantinople and Menouthis near Alexandria it was the *kerote* which was applied as a *pharmakon* and only through its use miracles were to be expected. In other words, *eulogiai* were a basic necessity to experience miracles in healing sanctuaries. But there are also other factors which promoted reciprocity. Because pilgrims were used to the Christian moral of *do ut des* (give and it will be given to you; Lk 6.38), they were supposed to give, and they did give. This is how the Christian sacral economy functioned in public space: as a generalised reciprocity[112] which provided the sanctuary with donations from all pilgrims, poor and wealthy alike, which in turn created the overall profit for the shrine.

Gift-giving was a common feature of pilgrimage sites even before they started distributing *eulogiai*. I would argue that the rationale for *eulogia* distribution on a larger scale was to include all visitors to the pilgrimage site in this gift-giving process, regardless of whether they experienced miracles or not. In the case of a miracle happening during one's stay at the pilgrimage centre, the pilgrim was inclined to give again, only this time certainly much more.

In sum: the introduction of *eulogiai* in pilgrimage sanctuaries had a prominent economic aspect. By receiving *eulogiai*, visitors felt much more compelled to make a reciprocal counter-gift during their stay. In this way the main income

---

110   Miracula Cosmae et Damiani, mir. 18 (Rupprecht); Wittmann 1967, 27.
111   Ioannis Lazaropuli Miracula Eugenii, chap. 29 (Rosenqvist 350).
112   Elwert 2004, 137.

of the sanctuaries – which were pilgrim's offerings – was increased, making it likely that this was the main reason for the distribution of *eulogiai* at almost all pilgrimage sites in the Byzantine world.[113] As it had become common practice to distribute *eulogiai* in many places, it became mandatory for sites developing later to follow that practice too, if they wanted to promote their sanctuary or spread its fame.

4   The Economy of *Eulogia* Containers

However, I believe that the *containers* follow economic rules different to those of *eulogiai* themselves. Contrary to Foskolou's interpretation, I argue that while the distribution of *eulogiai* worked economically through channels of expectation and reciprocity, the distribution of their containers did not. Traditionally, however, *eulogiai* and their containers are not differentiated, as if they only existed in combination. This confusion is found in the written sources themselves, where the containers are rarely mentioned and the combined item is called simply '*eulogia*', after its precious content. But, as I have shown above, specific containers are a rather rare phenomenon restricted to only some periods and very few pilgrimage sites.

The most obvious feature of late antique containers is their variation in material, size and iconographic depictions. The material differences can be explained by their value. The more valuable containers were produced for wealthier pilgrims, as we can see from the Monza-Bobbio collections assembled at the Lombard royal court. However, some pilgrimage sites produced containers of only one material, where we must assume that the material had no strong economic implication. But if different materials were used, we must surely understand that *eulogia* containers were intended for purchase. However, this is not the conclusion that most scholars have come to – partly because the written sources give us no hints in that direction.

The distribution patterns of the containers with regards to their place of origin have led to various economic interpretations,[114] and are significantly different from region to region: 71 % of the *ampullae* found in Syria are from Abū Mīnā, 21 % from Jerusalem and 7 % from Asia Minor, whereas 82 % of those found in Asia Minor are from Asia Minor itself. At the same time, the

---

113   See also Blanke, this volume, exploring the economic implications of increased visitor numbers at monastic institutions in Egypt at this time.

114   Esp. Lambert – Pedemonte Demeglio 1994; it is their data which given here. Some remarks on the subject found in: Maraval 2004, 212; Anderson 2007, 225 and 238–9.

Abu Mena *ampullae* are found all over the Mediterranean[115] while those from Anatolia have been to date recorded outside Asia Minor only in the Balkans and the Black Sea region. It seems that the tokens of Qal'at Sem'an actually never left Syria.[116]

What is clear is that the distribution of the containers is unlike other products; like pottery, for instance.[117] Consequently, it seemed plausible to many scholars that they were sold and to some even that they were traded.[118] But their sale is not recorded in any text, quite the opposite. Gregory of Tours underlined that filled *ampullae* received their power through prayer at the place of their origin and not by bottling.[119] Thus, trade conflicted with two principles: the illicit purchase of sanctified goods and theological considerations. For these reasons, the different distribution patterns should not be interpreted as evolving from trading networks, but rather as evidence for diverging catchment areas of the respective pilgrimage shrines.

Here we cannot rely on the written sources, because they tend to stay silent on financial matters within the sacred economy, a well-known phenomenon: even the most obvious and common financial transactions are not to be spoken about when being carried out within the sacred confines of a ritual economy, as sociologist Pierre Bourdieu observed, coining for this sector the term 'good-faith-economy'.[120] For this reason we have to be cautious about the containers, especially because the sources never talk about the mode of transaction applied to them. Because the written sources are silent on the question of the economic role of the containers, we will now look at the archaeological material itself in more detail.

As we have seen in all the instances presented here, there is a huge variation in the iconographic depictions on the containers from the same sites and which contained the same *eulogia*. This observation can be made for all containers, from all periods. How can we explain this variation, if we imagine a situation where all pilgrims were given a container for free? I argue that variations only make sense if pilgrims were able to select for themselves a container from the broad range available. In other words, this variation had to have an addressee. The only feasible explanation is that the recipient of the container

---

115   Overview by Sodini 2011, 86–92 and Witt 2000, 71–2. Even as far north as the ancient settlement of Meols on the Wirral near Liverpool (UK) an *ampulla* of St. Menas has been found.

116   Sodini 2011, 92–101.

117   Anderson 2004, 89.

118   Campbell 1988, 544–5. Objection by Sodini 2011, 139–40.

119   Gregorii episcopi Turonensis Liber in Gloria confessorum, chaps. 9–10 (Krusch 304).

120   Bourdieu 1983, 184–5.

chose the container he wanted to have. This selection process would be superfluous and involve too much friction if the containers were given for free.[121] However, choice makes perfect sense in a preference system, in other words, in a transaction involving purchase. Without explicit testimony from the written sources, the production of specific containers in order to sell them cannot be proven but considering the archaeological remains – both the containers themselves, but also moulds and production sites[122] – there is a strong indication that this was the case.

If we accept that containers were bought, how high was the price and how much did the containers contribute to the sanctuary's income? I suspect that they did not generate a great deal of profit, because the production of *eulogia* containers is too restricted in time and to a few places only. Nevertheless, they served other purposes. Their distinctive appearance authenticated and identified their content. It made the *eulogia* within them even more valuable because the containers, specifically produced for them, guaranteed authenticity. The containers also promoted the sanctuary in distant regions, serving as a brand. I think this is the main reason why they were produced in those sanctuaries where we find them: they enabled pilgrimage centres to enlarge their catchment areas by promoting their power across a much larger area than minor pilgrimage sites were able to do. Every common pilgrimage site distributed *eulogiai*, but those did not have the ability to attract pilgrims from other regions or advertise their holy power to pilgrims from far away.

As a case in point I can again refer to Qal'at Sem'an. Here the ḥnānā dust was distributed at the end of the fifth century, being a *eulogia* which did not need a container at all. But at the moment when the sanctuary wanted to produce containers in order to attract pilgrims from far off, as Abu Mena or Jerusalem were able to do, it required an innovation. Instead of producing a container the sanctuary mixed the dust-oil tokens with terracotta, manufacturing the only item in the empire which combined the features of *eulogia* and containers. I argue that the production of specific containers started at the very end of the fifth century (first attested in Abu Mena), but only in those pilgrimage sites which intentionally wanted to attract pilgrims outside of their original catchment area. Contrary to the *eulogiai* which were always given for free, the containers were purchased for a small fee on the site before being filled up with the respective *eulogia*.

---

121 For the preference system which demands selection *cf.* Berghoff – Vogel 2004, 20–1; Jones 2014, 57.

122 *E.g.* in eighth or ninth-century Bet She'an/Skythopolis: Reynolds 2015, 374–5; Tsafrir 2006; Rahmani 1993; and in twelfth-century Acre: Syon 1994/99.

Acknowledgements

This research on the Byzantine pilgrimage economy had been part of a dissertation project and would have been impossible without the financial support of the Romano-Germanic Central Museum in Mainz and its joint project.[123] "For the Sake of Salvation and Happiness: Byzantine Pilgrimage and its Origins". I want to thank Troels Myrup Kristensen (Aarhus), Claudia Sode (Cologne), Sabine Schrenk (Bonn), Ina Eichner and Ewald Kislinger (both Vienna) for their support of my work on the chapter's topic over the last few years.

Primary Sources

Hagiography (Sorted by Saint)

Miracula Artemii (BHG 173). A. Papadopoulos-Kerameus, ed. 1909. *Διήγησις τῶν θαυμάτων τοῦ ἁγίου καὶ ἐνδόξου μεγαλομάρτυρος καὶ θαυματουργοῦ Ἀρτεμίου*, St. Petersburg, 1–75. V.S. Crisafulli, trans. 1997. *The Miracles of St. Artemios*, Leiden, 76–225.

Vita Athanasii Athonitae secunda (BHG 188). J. Noret, ed. 1982. *Vitae duae antiquae sancti Athanasii Athonitae* (CCSG 9), Turnhout, 127–213. R.P.H. Greenfield and A.-M.M. Talbot, trans. 2016. *Holy Men of Mount Athos*, Cambridge, MA, 129–367.

Gregorii Vita Basilii iunioris (BHG 263–264f). D.F. Sullivan, A.-M.M. Talbo, and S. McGrath, eds. and trans. 2014. *The Life of Saint Basil the Younger: Critical Edition and Annotated Translation of the Moscow Version*, Washington, DC, 64–753.

Miracula Cosmae et Damiani (BHG 372–392). L. Deubner, ed. 1907. *Kosmas und Damian: Texte und Einleitung*, Leipzig, 87–225. Egyptian collection: E. Rupprecht, ed. 1935. *Cosmae et Damiani sanctorum medicorum vitam et miracula e codice Londinensi*, Berlin.

Miracula Deiparae ad fontem (BHG 1072). AASS Nov. III, cols. 878–889. A.-M.M. Talbot and S.F. Johnson, trans. 2012. *Miracle Tales from Byzantium*, Cambridge, MA, 205–97.

Vita Demetriani episcopi Chytraei (BHG 495). H. Grégoire, ed. 1907. "Saint Démétrianos, évêque de Chytri (île de Chypre)", *Byzantinische Zeitschrift* 16, 217–37.

Vita Eliae Spelaeotes monachi in Calabria (BHG 581). AASS Sep. III, cols. 848–887.

Ioannis Xiphilini Miracula Eugenii (BHG 610). J.O. Rosenqvist, ed. and trans. 1996. *The Hagiographic Dossier of St Eugenios of Trebizond in Codex Athous Dionysiou 154*, Uppsala, 170–203.

---

123 This has since been published: Ritter 2019.

Ioannis Lazaropuli Miracula Eugenii (BHG 613). J.O. Rosenqvist, ed. and trans. 1996. *The Hagiographic Dossier of St Eugenios of Trebizond in Codex Athous Dionysiou 154*, Uppsala, 246–359.

Constantini episcopi Tiensis Translatio corporis Euphemiae (BHG 621). F. Halkin, ed. 1965. *Euphémie de Chalkédoine: légendes byzantines* (SubsHag 41), Brussels, 84–106.

Cyrilli Scythopolitani Vita Euthymii (BHG 647). E. Schwartz, ed. 1939. *Kyrillos von Skythopolis*, Leipzig, 5–85. R.M. Price and J. Binns, trans. 1991. *Cyril of Scythopolis: The Lives of the Monks of Palestine*, Kalamazoo, MI, 1–83.

Basilii episcopi Vita Euthymii iunioris Thessalonicensi (BHG 655). L. Petit, ed. 1903. "Vie et office de Saint Euthyme le Jeune", *Revue de l'Orient Chrétien* 8, 168–205. R.P.H. Greenfield and A.-M.M. Talbot, trans. 2016. *Holy Men of Mount Athos*, Cambridge, MA, 3–125.

Nicetae Paphlagonis Laudatio in Hyacynthum Amastrenum (BHG 757). PG 105, cols. 417–440.

Callinici Vita Hypatii Rufinianae (BHG 760). G.J.M. Bartelink, ed. and trans. 1971. *Callinicos, Vie d'Hypatios* (SC 177), Paris.

Nicetae Paphlagonis Vita Ignatii patriarchae Constantinopolitanis (BHG 817). A. Smithies and J.M. Duffy, eds. and trans. 2013. *The Life of Patriarch Ignatius* (CFHB 51), Washington, DC.

Leontii episcopi Neapolitanis Vita Ioannis Eleemosinarii (BHG 886). A.-J. Festugière and L. Rydén, eds. and trans. 1974. *Léontios de Néapolis, Vie de Syméon le Fou et Vie de Jean de Chypre*, Paris, 343–409.

Vita Lucae iunioris Steiriotis (BHG 994). C.L. Connor and W.R. Connor, eds. and trans. 1994. *The Life and Miracles of St. Luke of Steiris*, Brookline, MA, 2–142.

Sabae monachi Vita Macarii abbatis Pelecetae (BHG 1003–1003c). I. van de Gheyn, ed. 1897. "S. Macarii monasterii Pelecetes hegumeni acta graeca", *Analecta Bollandiana* 16, 142–63.

Vita Mariae iunioris Bizyensi (BHG 1164). AASS Nov. IV, cols. 692–705. A.-M.M. Talbot, trans. 1996. *Holy Women of Byzantium: Ten Saints' Lives in English Translation*, Washington, DC, 253–89.

Miracula Menae arabica. F. Jaritz, ed. and trans. 1993. *Die arabischen Quellen zum Heiligen Menas*, Heidelberg.

Miracula Menae coptica. J. Drescher, ed. and trans. 1946. *Apa Mena: A Selection of Coptic Texts Relating to St. Menas*, Cairo.

Miracula Menae graeca (BHG 1256–69). J. Duffy and E. Bourbouhakis, eds. and trans. 2003. "Five Miracles of St. Menas", in *Byzantine Authors: Literary Activities and Preoccupations*, ed. J.W. Nesbitt, Leiden, 68–81.

Vita Nicetae patricii (BHG 1342b). D. Papachryssanthou, ed. 1968. "Un confesseur du second iconoclasme: la Vie de du patrice Nicétas (†836)", *Travaux et Mémoires* 3, 325–51.

Vita Niconis Metanoeite (BHG 1366–67). D.F. Sullivan, ed. and trans. 1987. *The Life of Saint Nikon*, Brookline, MA, 26–270.

Vita Pauli iunioris Latrensis (BHG 1474). H. Delehaye, ed. 1913. "Monumenta Latrensia hagiographica", in *Der Latmos. Milet: Ergebnisse der Ausgrabungen und Untersuchungen* 3,1, ed. T. Wiegand, Berlin, 105–135.

Vita Philothei Opsiciani. AASS Nov. prop., cols. 47–48.

Eustathii episcopi Thessalonicensis Laudatio in Philotheum Opsicianum (BHG 1535). G.L.F. Tafel, ed. 1832. *Eustathii metropolitae Thessalonicensis opuscula accedunt Trapezuntinae historiae scriptores Panaretus et Eugenicus*, Frankfurt a.M., 145–51.

Sabae Miracula Petri Atroënsis (BHG 2365). V. Laurent, ed. 1958. *La vita retractata et les miracles posthumes de Saint Pierre d'Atroa* (SubsHag 31), Brussels, 133–71.

Vita Phantini iunioris (BHG 2366z). E. Follieri, ed. and trans. 1993. *La vita di san Fantino il Giovane: introduction, testo greco, traduction, commentario e indici* (SubsHag 77), Brussels, 400–71.

Cyrilli Scythopolitani Vita Sabae (BHG 1608). E. Schwartz, ed. 1939. *Kyrillos von Skythopolis*, Leipzig, 85–200. R.M. Price and J. Binns, trans. 1991. *Cyril of Scythopolis: The Lives of the Monks of Palestine*, Kalamazoo, MI, 93–209.

Theodori episcopi Paphensis Vita Spyridonis episcopi Trimithuntis (BHG 1647). P. van den Ven, ed. 1953. *La légende de S. Spyridon, évêque de Trimithonte*, Louvain, 1–103.

Vita Stephani thaumaturgi arabica. J.C. Lamoreaux, ed. and trans. 1999. *The Life of Stephen of Mar Sabas* (CSCO Scriptores arabici 50/51), 2 vols., Louvain.

Arcadii episcopi Constantiensis Vita Symeonis Stylitae iunioris (BHG 1689). P. van den Ven, ed. 1962. *La Vie ancienne de S. Syméon Stylite le Jeune (521–592)*, vol. 1. (SubsHag 32), Brussels.

Vita syriaca Symeonis Stylitae senioris. S.E. Assemani, ed. 1748. *Acta sanctorum martyrum orientalium et occidentalium: in duas partes distributa, adcedunt acta S. Simeonis Stylitae omnia nunc primum nub auspiciis Johannis V. Lusitanorum regis e Bibliotheca Apostolica Vaticana prodeunt*, Rome. R. Doran, trans. 1992. *The Lives of Simeon Stylites*, Kalamazoo, MI, 103–98.

Miracula Theclae (BHG 1717). G. Dagron, ed. 1978. *Vie et Miracles de Sainte Thècle: texte grec, traduction, et commentaire* (SubsHag 62), Brussels. A.-M.M. Talbot and S.F. Johnson, trans. 2012. *Miracle Tales from Byzantium*, Cambridge, MA, 3–183.

Gregorii presbyteri Vita Theodorae Thessalonicensi (BHG 1737). S.A. Paschalides, ed. 1991. Ὁ βίος τῆς ὁσιομυροβλυτίδος Θεοδώρας τῆς ἐν Θεσσαλονίκῃ: Διήγησῃ περὶ τῆς μεταθέσεως τοῦ τιμίου λειψάνου τῆς ὁσίας Θεοδώρας, Thessalonica, 66–189. A.-M.M. Talbot, trans. 1996. *Holy Women of Byzantium: Ten Saints' Lives in English Translation*, Washington, DC, 163–217.

Vita Theophanus imperatricis (BHG 1794). E. Kurtz, ed. 1898. "Zwei griechische Texte über die Hl. Theophano, die Gemahlin Kaisers Leo VI.", *Memoires de l'Academie Imperiale des Sciences de St. Petersbourg* 8ᵉ s. 3/2, 1–24.

Miracula Therapontis (BHG 1798). L. Deubner, ed. 1900. *De incubatione capita quattuor*, Leipzig, 120–34.

Other Sources (Sorted by Author)

Itinerarium Antonini Placentini. P. Geyer, ed. 1965. *Itineraria et alia geographica* (CCSL 175), Turnhout, 129–153.

Itinerarium Egeriae. A. Franceschini and R. Weber, eds. 1965. *Itineraria et alia geographica* (CCSL 175), Turnhout, 37–90. J. Wilkinson, trans. 1999. *Egeria's Travels: Translated with Supporting Documents and Notes*, third edition, Oxford.

Anastasii Sinaïtae Viae dux. K.-H. Uthemann, ed. 1981. *Anastasii Sinaitae Viae dux* (CCSG 8), Turnhout – Leuven.

Augustini episcopi Hipponiensis De civitate Dei. W.M. Green, ed. and trans. 1972. *Saint Augustine, The City of God against the Pagans*, 7 vols., Cambridge, MA.

Gregorii episcopi Turonensis Liber in gloria martyrum. B. Krusch and W. Arndt, eds. 1969. *Gregorii episcopi Turonensis miracula et opera minora* (MGH SS rerum Merovingicarum), third edition, Hannover, 34–111.

Gregorii I papae epistolae. D.L. Norberg, ed. 1982. *S. Gregorii Magni registrum epistularum* (CCSL 140), 2 vols., Turnhout. J.R.C. Martyn, trans. 2004. *The Letters of Gregory the Great*, 3 vols., Toronto.

Ioannis Chrysostomi Homiliae. PG 47–65.

Ioannis Ducae Descriptio Terrae sanctae. I. Troickij, ed. and trans. 1889. Ioanna Phoki Skazanie vkratc' o gorodach' I stranach' ot' Antiochii do Ierusalima, takže Sirii, Finikii I o svjatych' mestach' v' Palestin, koncha XII veka. *Pravoslavnyj Palestinskij Sbornik* 8/2, St. Petersburg, 1–28.

Marutae episcopi Maipherkatae Canones. A. Vööbus, ed. and trans. 1982. *The Canons Ascribed to Mārūtā of Mapherqat and Related Sources* (CSCO 439/40), 2 vols., Louvain.

Theodoreti episcopi Cyrrhensis Graecarum affectionum curatio. J. Raeder, ed. 1904. *Theodoreti Graecarum affectionum curatio*, Leipzig.

Theodoreti episcopi Cyrrhensis Historia religiosa. P. Canivet and A. Leroy-Molinghen, eds. and trans. 1977/79. *Théodoret de Cyr, Histoire des moines de Syrie* (SC 234/57), 2 vols., Paris.

Theophylacti Simocattae Historiae. C. de Boor and P. Wirth, eds. 1972. *Theophylacti Simocattae historiae*, second edition, Leipzig. M. Whitby and M. Whitby, trans. 1986. *The History of Theophylact Simocatta*, Oxford.

Bibliography

Anderson, W. 2004. "An Archaeology of Late Antique Pilgrim Flasks", *Anatolian Studies* 54, 79–93.

Anderson, W. 2007. "Menas Flasks in the West: Pilgrimage and Trade at the End of Antiquity", *Ancient West and East* 6, 221–43.

Anrich, G. 1913/17. *Hagios Nikolaos: der Heilige Nikolaos in der griechischen Kirche*, 2 vols., Leipzig.

Bangert, S. 2007. "Menas Ampullae: A Case Study of Long-Distance Contacts", in *Incipient Globalization? Long-Distance Contacts in the Sixth Century*, ed. A. Harris, Oxford, 27–33.

Berghoff, H. and Vogel, J. 2005. "Wirtschaftsgeschichte als Kulturgeschichte: Ansätze zur Bergung transdisziplinärer Synergiepotentiale", in *Wirtschaftsgeschichte als Kulturgeschichte: Dimensionen eines Perspektivenwechsels*, eds. H. Berghoff and J. Vogel, Frankfurt, 9–41.

Boertjes, K. 2014. "The Reconquered Jerusalem Represented: Tradition and Renewal on Pilgrimage Ampullae from the Crusader Period", in *The Imagined and Real Jerusalem in Art and Architecture*, eds. J. Goudeau, M. Verhoeven, and W. Weijers, Leiden, 169–89.

Bourdieu, P. 1983. "Ökonomisches Kapital, kulturelles Kapital, soziales Kapital", in *Soziale Ungleichheiten. Soziale Welt*, Sonderband 2, ed. R. Kreckel, Göttingen, 183–98.

Brenk, B. 1995. "Der Kultort, seine Zugänglichkeit und seine Besucher", in *Akten des 12. internationalen Kongresses für christliche Archäologie, Bonn 1991*, eds. E. Dassmann and J. Engemann, Münster, 69–122.

Buora, M., Laflı, E., and Kan Şahin, G. 2015. "Some Ampullae from Western Asia Minor", in *Arheologia mileniului I p. Chr. 4: Nomazi şi autohtoni în mileniul I p. Chr.*, ed. B. Ciupercă, Bucharest, 273–92.

Campbell, S.D. 1988. "Armchair Pilgrims: Ampullae from Aphrodisias in Caria", *Mediaeval Studies [Toronto]* 50, 539–45.

Canard, M. 1965. "La destruction de l'église de la résurrection par le Calife Hakim et l'histoire de la descente du feu sacré", *Byzantion* 35, 16–26.

Caner, D.F. 2006. "Towards a Miraculous Economy: Christian Gifts and Material 'Blessings' in Late Antiquity", *Journal of Early Christian Studies* 14, 329–77.

Caner, D.F. 2013. "Alms, Blessings, Offerings: The Repertoire of Christian Gifts in Early Byzantium", in *The Gift in Antiquity*, ed. M. Satlow, Malden, MA, 25–44.

Caseau, B. 2005. "Parfum et guérison dans le christianisme ancien et byzantin: des huiles parfumées des médecins au myron des saints byzantins", in *Les pères de l'église face à la science médicale de leur temps*, eds. V. Boudon-Millot and B. Pouderon, Paris, 141–91.

Caseau, B. 2007. "Ordinary Objects in Christian Healing Sanctuaries", in *Objects in Context – Objects in Use: Material Spatiality in Late Antiquity*, eds. L. Lavan, E. Swift, and T. Putzeys, Leiden, 625–54.

Caseau, B. 2013. "Experiencing the Sacred", in *Experiencing Byzantium: Papers from the 44th Spring Symposium of Byzantine Studies*, eds. C. Nesbitt and M.P.C. Jackson, Aldershot, 59–77.

Davidson, G.R. 1952. *Corinth 12. The Minor Objects*, Cambridge, MA.

Davis, S.J. 1998. "Pilgrimage and the Cult of Saint Thecla in Late Antique Egypt", in *Pilgrimage and Holy Space in Late Antique Egypt*, ed. D. Frankfurter, Leiden, 303–39.

Davis, S.J. 2001. *The Cult of Saint Thecla: A Tradition of Women's Piety in Late Antiquity*, Oxford.

Delahaye, G.-R. 2005. "Le culte de saint Ménas: témoignage des relations entre l'Égypte copte et la Gaule mérovingienne", in *La Méditerranée et le monde mérovingien: témoins archéologiques*, eds. X. Delestre, P. Périn, and M. Kazanski, Aix-en-Provence, 257–70.

Delehaye, H. 1910. "L'invention des reliques de Saint Ménas à Constantinople", *Analecta Bollandiana* 29, 117–50.

Déroche, V. 2006. "Vraiment anargyres? Don et contredon dans les recueils de miracles protobyzantins", in *Pèlerinages et Lieux Saints dans l'Antiquité et le Moyen Âge. Mélanges offerts à Pierre Maraval*, eds. B. Caseau, J.-C. Cheynet, and V. Déroche, Paris, 153–8.

Drews, P.D. 1898. "Zur Geschichte der 'Eulogien' in der alten Kirche", *Zeitschrift für praktische Theologie* 20, 18–39.

Durand, J. 1992. *Byzance: l'art byzantin dans les collections publiques françaises*, Paris.

Elsner, J. 1997. "Replicating Palestine and Reversing the Reformation: Pilgrimage and Collecting at Bobbio, Monza and Walsingham", *Journal of the History of Collections* 9, 117–30.

Elwert, G. 2005. "Sanktionen, Ehre und Gabenökonomie: Kulturelle Mechanismen der Einbettung von Märkten", in *Wirtschaftsgeschichte als Kulturgeschichte: Dimensionen eines Perspektivenwechsels*, eds. H. Berghoff and J. Vogel, Frankfurt, 117–42.

Engemann, J. 1973. "Palästinensische Pilgerampullen im F.J. Dölger-Institut in Bonn", *Jahrbuch für Antike und Christentum* 16, 5–27.

Engemann, J. 1995a. "Eulogien und Votive", in *Akten des 12. intern. Kongresses für christliche Archäologie*, eds. E. Dassmann and J. Engemann, Münster, 223–33.

Engemann, J. 1995b. "Das Jerusalem der Pilger. Kreuzauffindung und Wallfahrt im Frühmittelalter", in *Akten des 12. internationalen Kongresses für christliche Archäologie*, eds. E. Dassmann and J. Engemann, Münster, 24–35.

Engemann, J. 2002. "Palästinensische frühchristliche Pilgerampullen: Erstveröffentlichungen und Berichtigungen", *Jahrbuch für Antike und Christenum* 45, 153–169.

Festugière, A.-J. 1971. *Sainte Thècle, Saints Côme et Damien, Saints Cyr et Jean* (*extraits*), *Saint Georges*, Paris.

Filipová, A. 2015. "On the Origins of the Monza Collection of Holy Land Ampullae: The Legend of Gregory the Great's Gift of Relics to Theodelinda Reconsidered", *Arte Lombarda* 173/74, 5–16.

Foskolou, V. 2012. "Blessing for Sale? On the Production and Distribution of Pilgrim Mementoes in Byzantium", *Byzantinische Zeitschrift* 105, 53–84.

Frank, G. 2006. "Loca Sancta Souvenirs and the Art of Memory", in *Pèlerinages et Lieux Saints dans l'Antiquité et le Moyen Âge. Mélanges offerts à Pierre Maraval*, eds. B. Caseau, J.-C. Cheynet, and V. Déroche, Paris, 193–201.

Frolow, A. 1961. *La relique de la Vraie Croix: recherches sur le développement d'un culte*, Paris.

Gascou, J. 2008. "Religion et identité communautaire à Alexandrie à la fin de l'époque byzantine, d'après les 'Miracles des saints Cyr et Jean'", in *Alexandrie médiévale* 3, eds. J.-Y. Empereur and C. Décobert, Cairo, 69–88.

George, B. 1974. "Menaslegenden und Pilgerindustrie", *Medelhavsmuseet Bulletin* 9, 30–9.

Gerard, M., Metzger, C., Person, A., and Sodini, J.-P. 1998. "Argiles et eulogies en forme de jetons: Qal'at Sem'an en est-il une source possible?", in *Materials Analysis of Byzantine Pottery*, ed. H. Maguire, Washington, DC, 9–24.

Gilli, M. 2002. *Le ampolle di San Mena: religiosità, cultura materiale e sistema produttivo*, Rome.

Grossmann, P. 1998. "The Pilgrimage Center of Abû Mînâ", in *Pilgrimage and Holy Space in Late Antique Egypt*, ed. D. Frankfurter, Leiden, 281–302.

Herman, E. 1942. "Die kirchlichen Einkünfte des byzantinischen Niederklerus", *Orientalia Christiana* 8, 378–442.

Hunter-Crawley, H. 2012. "Pilgrimage Made Portable: A Sensory Archaeology of the Monza-Bobbio Ampullae", *HEROM* 1, 135–56.

Jaritz, F. 1993. *Die arabischen Quellen zum Heiligen Menas*, Heidelberg.

Jasaeva, T.J.J. 2012. *The Legacy of Byzantine Cherson: 185 Years of Excavation at Tauric Chersonesos*, Sevastopol – Austin.

Jaspert, N. 2015. "Eleventh-Century Pilgrimage from Catalonia to Jerusalem: New Sources on the Foundation of the First Crusade", *Crusades* 14, 1–47.

Jones, D.W. 2014. *Economic Theory and the Ancient Mediterranean*, Chichester.

Kiss, Z. 1989. *Alexandrie 5. Les ampoules de Saint Ménas découvertes à Kôm el-Dikka* (*1961–1981*), Warsaw.

Klausen-Nottmeyer, S. 1995. "Eulogien: Transport und Weitergabe von Segenskraft Ergebnisse einer Zusammenstellung von Pilgerandenken", in *Akten des 12. Internationalen Kongresses für christliche Archäologie, Bonn 1991*, eds. E. Dassmann and J. Engemann, Münster, 922–7.

Kotansky, R. 1991. "Incantations and Prayers for Salvation on Inscribed Greek Amulets", in *Magika Hiera: Ancient Greek Magic and Religion*, eds. C.A. Faraone and D. Obbink, Oxford, 107–37.

Kötzsche, L. 1988. "Zwei Jerusalemer Pilgerampullen aus der Kreuzfahrerzeit", *Zeitschrift für Kunstgeschichte* 51, 13–32.

Kötzsche, L. 1995. "Das Heilige Grab in Jerusalem und seine Nachfolge", in *Akten des 12. Internationalen Kongresses für christliche Archäologie, Bonn 1991*, eds. E. Dassmann and J. Engemann, Münster, 272–90.

Kötzsche-Breitenburg, L. 1984. "Pilgerandenken aus dem Heiligen Land: drei Neuerwerbungen des Württembergischen Landesmuseums in Stuttgart", in *Vivarium: Festschrift Theodor Klauser zum 90. Geburtstag*, ed. E. Dassmann, Münster, 229–46.

Krueger, D. 2014. *Liturgical Subjects: Christian Ritual, Biblical Narrative, and the Formation of the Self in Byzantium*, Philadelphia.

Krueger, D. 2015. "Liturgical Time and Holy Land Reliquaries in Early Byzantium", in *Saints and Sacred Matter: The Cult of Relics in Byzantium and Beyond*, eds. C.J. Hahn and H.A. Klein, Washington, DC, 111–31.

Külzer, A. 1994. *Peregrinatio graeca in terram sanctam: Studien zu Pilgerführern und Reisebeschreibungen über Syrien, Palästina und den Sinai aus byzantinischer und metabyzantinischer Zeit*, Frankfurt.

Lambert, C. and Pedemonte Demeglio, P. 1994. "Ampolle devozionali ed itinerari di pellegrinaggio tra IV e VII secolo", *Antiquité Tardive* 2, 205–31.

Luchterhandt, M. 2017. "The Popes and the Loca Sancta of Jerusalem: Relic Practice and Relic Diplomacy in the Eastern Mediterranean after the Muslim Conquest", in *Natural Materials of the Holy Land and the Visual Translation of Place 500–1500*, eds. R. Bartal, N. Bodner, and B. Kuehnel, London, 36–63.

Maraval, P. 2004. *Lieux saints et pèlerinages d'Orient: histoire et géographie des origines à la conquête arabe*, second edition, Paris.

McCulloh, J.M. 1976. "The Cult of Relics in the Letters and Dialogues of Pope Gregory the Great", *Traditio* 32, 145–84.

Messis, C. 2011. "Littérature, voyage et politique au XIIe siècle: l'ekphrasis des lieux saints de Jean 'Phokas'", in *Ekphrasis: la représentation des monuments dans les littératures byzantine et byzantino-slaves réalités et imaginaires*, eds. V. Vavřínek, P. Odorico, and V. Drbal, Prague, 146–66.

Metzger, C. 1981. *Les ampoules à eulogie du musée du Louvre*, Paris.

Mitchell, J. 2004. "The Archaeology of Pilgrimage in Late Antique Albania: The Basilica of the Forty Martyrs", in *Recent Research on the Late Antique Countryside*, eds. W. Bowden, L. Lavan, and C. Machado, Leiden, 145–86.

Ousterhout, R.G. 1990. "Loca Sancta and the Architectural Response to Pilgrimage", in *The Blessings of Pilgrimage* (Illinois Byzantine Studies 1), ed. R.G. Ousterhout, Urbana, IL, 108–24.

Papaconstantinou, A. 2012. "Donation and Negotiation: Formal Gifts to Religious Institutions in Late Antiquity", in *Donations et donateurs dans la société et l'art byzantins*, eds. J.-M. Spieser and É. Yota, Paris, 75–95.

Patlagean, E. 1984. "Theodora de Thessalonique: Une sainte moniale et un culte citadin (IXe–XXe siècle)", in *Culto dei santi, istituzioni e classi sociali in età preindustriale*, eds. S. Boesch Gajano and L. Sebastiani, Rome, 39–67.

Peña, I., Castellana, P., and Fernandez, R. 1975. *Les stylites syriens*, Milan.

Piccirillo, M. 1994. "Uno stampo per eulogia trovato a Gerusalemme", *Liber Annuus* 44, 585–90.

Pieri, D. 2009. "Saint-Syméon-le-Stylite (Syrie du Nord): les bâtiments d'accueil et les boutiques à l'entrée du sanctuaire", *Comptes-rendus des séances de l'Académie des Inscriptions et Belles-Lettres* 153, 1393–420.

Polanyi, K. 1944. *The Great Transformation*, New York.

Pratsch, T. 2011. "Der Platz der Grabeskirche in der christlichen Verehrung im Osten", in *Konflikt und Bewältigung. Die Zerstörung der Grabeskirche zu Jerusalem im Jahre 1009*, ed. T. Pratsch, Berlin, 57–66.

Rahmani, L.Y. 1993. "Eulogia Tokens from Byzantine Bet She'an", *'Atiqot* 22, 109–19.

Rautman, M.L. 2005. "A Stylite Ampulla at Sardis", *Travaux et Mémoires* 15, 713–21.

Redigolo, A. 2012. *San Mena: iconografia, origini e diffusione del culto*, unpublished Ph.D. dissertation, Venice.

Reynolds, D. 2015. "Monasticism in Early Islamic Palestine: Contours of Debate", in *The Late Antique World of Early Islam: Muslims among Christians and Jews in the East Mediterranean*, ed. R.G. Hoyland, London, 339–91.

Riiter; M. 2019. *Zwischen Glaube und Geld: Zur Ökonomie des byzantinischen Pilgerwesens (4.-12. Jh.)*, Mainz.

Schachner, L.A. 2010. "The Archaeology of the Stylite", in *Religious Diversity in Late Antiquity*, eds. D.M. Gwynn and S. Bangert, Leiden, 329–97.

Schauta, M. 2008. *Die ersten Jahrhunderte christlicher Pilgerreisen im Spiegel spätantiker und frühmittelalterlicher Quellen*, Frankfurt.

Sever Georgousakis, D. 2016. "A Pilgrim's Self-Identification: Sixth-and Seventh-Century Lead Pilgrim Flasks from the Holy Land", *Diogenes* 4, 35–48.

Sodini, J.-P. 1993. "Qal'at Sem'an: ein Wallfahrtszentrum", in *Syrien von den Aposteln zu den Kalifen*, ed. E.M. Rupprechtsberger, Linz, 128–43.

Sodini, J.-P. 2010. "Saint Syméon: l'influence de saint Syméon dans le culte et l'economie de L'Antiochène", in *Les sanctuaires et leur rayonnement dans le monde méditerranéen de l'antiquité à l'époque moderne*, eds. J. Leclant, J. de la Genière, and A. Vauchez, Paris, 295–322.

Sodini, J. P. 2011. "La terre de semelles: Images pieuses ramenées par les pèlerins des Lieux saints (Terre sainte, martyria d'Orient)", *Journal des savants* 1, 77–140.

Spier, J. 1993. "Medieval Byzantine Magical Amulets and their Tradition", *Journal of the Warburg and Courtauld Institutes* 56, 25–62.

Stuiber, A. 1966. "Eulogia", in *Reallexikon für Antike und Christentum* 6, Stuttgart, cols. 900–28.

Syon, D. 1994/99. "A Crusader Token Mould from Akko", *Israel Numismatic Journal* 13, 13–6.

Syon, D. 1999. "Souvenirs from the Holy Land: A Crusader Workshop of Lead Ampullae from Acre", in *Knights of the Holy Land: The Crusader Kingdom of Jerusalem*, ed. S. Rozenberg, Jerusalem, 111–5.

Talbot, A.-M. M. 2002. "Pilgrimage to Healing Shrines: The Evidence of Miracle Accounts", *Dumbarton Oaks Papers* 56, 153–73.

Talbot, A. 2015. "The Relics of New Saints: Deposition, Translation, and Veneration in Middle and Late Byzantium", in *Saints and Sacred Matter: The Cult of Relics in Byzantium and Beyond*, eds. C.J. Hahn and H.A. Klein, Washington, DC, 215–30.

Tjäder, J.-O. 1955. *Die nichtliterarischen lateinischen Papyri Italiens aus der Zeit 445–700*, 3 vols., Lund.

Tsafrir, Y. 2006. "Four Eulogia Tokens Found in Bet Shean, Scythopolis (Israel)", in *Akten des 14. Internationalen Kongresses für christliche Archäologie* 2, eds. R. Harreither, P. Pergola, R. Pillinger, and A. Pülz, Città del Vaticano, 731–4.

Varinlioğlu, G. 2007. "Living in a Marginal Environment: Rural Habitat and Landscape in Southeastern Isauria", *Dumbarton Oaks Papers* 61, 287–317.

Vikan, G. 1991. "Pilgrim Tokens", in *The Oxford Dictionary of Byzantium*, third edition, Oxford, 1678.

Vikan, G. 1995. "Early Byzantine Pilgrimage Devotionalia as Evidence of the Appearance of Pilgrimage Shrines", in *Akten des 12. Internationalen Kongresses für christliche Archäologie, Bonn 1991*, eds. E. Dassmann and J. Engemann, Münster, 377–88.

Vikan, G. 1998. "Byzantine Pilgrims' Art", in *Heaven on Earth. Art and the Church in Byzantium*, ed. L. Safran, University Park, PA, 229–66.

Vikan, G. 2010. *Early Byzantine Pilgrimage Art*, second edition, Washington, DC.

Weitzmann, K. 1974. "'Loca Sancta' and the Representational Arts of Palestine", *Dumbarton Oaks Papers* 28, 31–55.

Witt, J. 2000. *Staatliche Museen zu Berlin. Skulpturensammlung und Museum für Byzantinische Kunst. Werke der Alltagskultur 1, Menasampullen*, Wiesbaden.

Wittmann, A. 1967. *Kosmas und Damian: Kultausbreitung und Volksdevotion*, Berlin.

CHAPTER 12

Festivals, Fairs and Foreigners: Towards an Economics of Religion in the Mediterranean *Longue Durée*

Barbara Kowalzig

Ματ' είδαν τα ματάκια μου, εψές στο πανηγύρι,
Άρπαξ' ο λύκος το παιδί 'πο την 'γκαλλιάν της μάννας,
χίλιοι πεζοί ετρέξανε και πεντακόσ' καβάλα
κανείς δεν τον εζύγωσε εκείνη τον ζυγώνει.
η μάννα πούχε τον καϋμόν, πούχε τη σκορπιμάρα
εκείνη τον εζύγωσε εκείνη τον ζυγώνει
άφσε λύκε το παιδί και πάρε με εμένα
να φας κριάσ' και κόκκαλα, να φας και ν'απομείνη,
δεν θέλω παλυοκρίασα, να φάγω και να μείνουν,
και το παιδί της έκρινε 'πο του λύκου το στόμα,
μάννα κακή, μάννα τρελλή πώχεις γυναικογνώσι
θυμάσαι όντας επούλαγες, τ' αλεύρι με τη στάχτη,
και το κρασί με το νερό, το λάδι με μολόχα,
το βούτυρο με χοιράλλειμα, το στάρι με το χώμα,
σύρε μάννα στο σπίτι σου, σύρε στην ερημιά σου
κτύπα και το κεφάλι σου με δυό μαύρα λιθάρια,
ειπέ και του πατέρα μου να μάθη να ζυγιάζη,
κι όντας να στίψ' η θάλασσα να γένη περιβόλι
κι όντας ν' ασπρίσ' ο κόρακας να γένη περιστέρι
τότε κ' εγώ θελαβγώ 'πο του λύκου το στόμα

What did my eyes see, yesterday at the panegyri,
The wolf seized the child from its mother's embrace,
A thousand people ran after him and five hundred horsemen
But no one could approach him, but she comes close.
The mother held by grief and confusion,
She approached the wolf, she comes close to the wolf,
Let go, wolf, of my child and take me instead,
So that you eat flesh and bones, that you eat and he may live,
I don't want your damn flesh to eat that they may live

And her child answered from the belly of the wolf,
Bad mother, mad mother with women's knowledge,
Do you remember how you sold flour mixed with ash,
Wine mixed with water, oil with mallow,
Butter with lard, wheat with soil,
Take yourself, mother, to your house, to your loneliness
And beat your head with two black rocks,
Tell my father that he should learn to weigh
And when the sea dries up and turns into an orchard
And the crow turns white to become a dove
Then I will happily come out of the wolf's belly.

Folk song, attested in 19th-century Epeiros

∴

1 Introduction

According to tradition, in the Epeiros of bygone days near an old monastery, a *panegyris* used to be held, a festival with a market fair lasting a whole month, or twelve days in other accounts, and attracting a great mass of people (πλῆθος ἀνθρώπων). The location bore many names: 'Niziani', a Slavic word, meaning 'bundle of coins' (ἀμρμάθους νομισμάτων), or 'contested place' (τόπος φιλονικούμενος), or Zambrechon, after its founder Zambros, who had established the fair to boost commerce in the region. A certain Krisaras, a wealthy man who dressed his only son in golden clothes, traded there with his wife. He sold adulterated wares, mixing flour with ash, wine with water, oil with corn, butter with pork fat. God, the story goes, did not approve and sent a wolf to snatch the child from his mother's arms. The fair was at once dissolved and never revived, leaving only its name, 'στο χαμένου', the place of the person 'who has lost his wits'. In the late 19th century, local old women still told this tale 'with great skill', cursing the couple, and the folk song above echoing the child's lament from the world beyond continued to be transmitted as proof of the story and the festival.[1]

---

1 Mystakides 1899; some time later, the *panegyris* was apparently revived elsewhere. I am grateful to Angelos Chaniotis, Kyriaki Chryssomalli-Henrich, Aneurin Ellis-Evans, Erika Milburn, Teresa Morgan, Ian Rutherford, Antigone Samellas and the two editors for reading partial or whole drafts of this chapter; all errors remain my own.

The story and its song suggest that festivals with market fairs were special transactional spaces, outside or with limited institutional control, with their own rules, their own ways of fostering trust, and their own enforcement mechanisms: an intertwining of shared notions of value, popular morality and divine justice guaranteed the validity of transactions. At fairs, the religious and the economic meshed in many ways. There is the idea of investment in the festival in order to stimulate trade in a rural area; at the same time, the fair presents a temptation to generate wealth at the expense of others. There is honesty as part of a social contract; and if any participant disregards it, the whole community will suffer — hence the cursing of the couple by the old women of the region. The monastery's gravitational pull is crucial to the market's success, and the religious framework key to the functioning of the story and the fair alike, implying that there is much more to market fairs than their economic importance.

In antiquity, market fairs attached to religious festivals form an important, but neglected element within the broader context of what may be termed 'pilgrimage economy'.[2] Graeco-Roman fairs have mostly been studied from an economic point of view, for their role in local, regional or international circuits, and in the context of economic transformation. Although the phenomenon itself existed and must have been widespread, detailed evidence is comparatively meagre (see also Kristensen, this volume). Superficially there are only a few and apparently not very useful literary references to what is known as *panegyris* for the archaic and classical periods.[3] There is a somewhat larger but still not huge corpus of inscriptions related to festivals with market fairs in Hellenistic and Roman Greece – at Ilion, Aktion, Andania, Eretria, Kyzikos and others.[4] In a substantial article, Chandezon discusses most of the known

---

2   'Pilgrimage' is a handy, yet somewhat misleading term given the very different nature and organisation of Greek *theoria*: Rutherford 2013; Rutherford does not engage with the economic dimension of ancient 'pilgrimage'.

3   While *panegyris* is a frequent term for 'festival with market fair', it is neither the only term, nor does *panegyris* always imply a market, though in later periods the meaning 'festival with market' prevails. On the terminology for fairs, including a discussion of *heorte, agora, panegyris*, see most recently Chandezon 2000, 82–4. *Cf.* also Vryonis 1981, 198–200; Calame 1991.

4   De Ligt 1993, App. 1–2, 243–59 conveniently lists sources for fairs from archaic Greece to Late Antiquity. Some relevant Greek inscriptions are: Tegea: *LSCG* 67, 26–7 (fourth century); Eretria: *LSCG* 92, 32–5 (=*RO* 73, *c.* 340 BCE); Aktion: *LSS* 45.31–4 (*c.* 216 BCE); Samos: Lupu 2005, 18 (*c.* 245/4 BCE); Magnesia at the Maeander: *LSAM* 33A, 33–5 (second century); Andania: *Syll.*[3] 736 = *LSCG* 65 = Gawlinski 2012 (first century); Ilion: *I. Ilion* 10, 11 (fourth century); Kyzikos: *SEG* 4.707, 10–11; 13–14 =*IGR* iv, 144=*IMT Kyz Kapu Dağ* 1431 (first century CE). Literary texts: *e.g.* Plb. 5.8.4–7 Thermon (third century BCE); Paus. 10.32, 13–17, at Tithorea in Phokis. See also Horster, this volume.

examples, largely in terms of their administration and financing. The apparent focus on wholesale transactions in grain, livestock, wool and cloth, precious metals; on craftsmanship and luxury items, and the specialisation in the sale of slaves led him to conclude that fairs served as an 'economic irrigation of rural Greece', periodically making goods accessible to geographical areas not located at a node of connectivity.[5]

Fairs in the Roman period were long victim of the modernist-primitivist debate in the wake of Rostovzeff: as Jean Andreau points out, in his desire to assimilate the Roman economy to that of the 17th/18th century, Michael Rostovtzeff chose to ignore the evidence for fairs. De Ligt's very useful book *Fairs and Markets in the Roman Empire* is an important counterweight, but is principally interested in the role of fairs and periodic markets within the larger system of the Roman economy.[6] The Byzantine *panegyris* has fared a little better, with an important study by Speros Vryonis on both the economic and festive aspect of these events that stresses continuity from Greek antiquity as well as their international dimension.[7] In the Middle Ages, the Fairs of Champagne, rising from a regional to an international market for long-distance trade and growing into a locus of finance and banking between the 12th and 13th centuries, are the best known and most discussed among numerous other examples. In contrast to antiquity, market fairs were not always held during religious festivals and studies are chiefly concerned with fairs in the context of rising and declining local, regional and international economies, often in the face of political crisis.[8]

---

5   Chandezon 2000, esp. 92–6. Apart from this contribution, the literature on Greek fairs remains scarce with only one somewhat more comprehensive treatment by De Ligt – De Neeve 1988 (with *SEG* 38.1953); brief summary discussions elsewhere: Nilsson 1955–1961, 871; Robert 1966, 24–5; 1963, 67–9; Gauthier 1989, 108–9; Horden – Purcell 2000, s.v. 'fair', esp. 432–4; Dillon 1998, 216–20; Dignas 2002, 157–9; Davies 2007, 63–5; Parker 2011, 173 n. 7; Thonemann 2011, 117–24; McInerney 2013, 191–5; Bresson 2015, 237–8, 257; Harris – Lewis 2016, 11.

6   Andreau 2001; De Ligt 1993; a highly inspiring piece on Roman fairs is MacMullen 1970; see also Nollé 1982; Frayn 1993, esp. 133–44; and now Holleran 2012, 159–93.

7   Vryonis 1981; 1971, esp. 15–16, 39–41, 160–1; also Laiou 1980/1 and 2000; an older account is Koukoules 1949, iii. 270–83. Some major fairs of the 11–12th centuries are St. Phokas at Sinope, St. Eugenios at Trebizond, St. John at Ephesos; St. Theodore at Euchaita; St. George at various places in Paphlagonia, and St. Michael at Chonai; but also a number in the Peloponnese: Koukoules 1949, 274–6.

8   Helpful overviews are still Verlinden 1963; Lombard-Jourdan 1984; Epstein 1994 applies a New Institutional Economics perspective to medieval fairs, arguing for their role in economic growth. The economic dimension of pilgrimage in medieval western Europe is a major topic within a complex contemporary discourse on e.g. usury and sacred finance, materiality of belief, social and economic mobility. There is a vast bibliography, *e.g.* Zika 1988; Bynum 2007. The classic treatment on religious profiteering is Little 1978.

Interesting as it might be to track individual economic circuits and relate them to cycles of growth and decline, I am drawn to a different set of questions that have largely remained neglected. For the evidence from antiquity to the late Byzantine period, scattered and limited as it is, insinuates that festivals with fairs constituted exceptional spaces of exchange. At *panegyreis*, religious and economic behaviour came to intersect in interesting ways, and seem to have been mutually stimulating, intimating that the fair's significance went beyond the mere opportunism of those with something to sell making use of a crowd of people assembled for a different purpose. Indeed, I will proceed to argue that such interaction between the religious and the economic produces an *ad hoc* community that at least conceptually provides an imperative for 'fair' behaviour. If transactions at festivals with fairs, be they religious or economic, are on the whole less regulated and instead subject to supervision by the divine, this in turn entails that the borders of right and wrong are subject to speculation — which might explain why cheating is frequent. And if individuals' dishonesty, while severely punished, causes proportionately more severe economic consequences for the entire community, this indicates that the functioning of the fair relies on mechanisms that help build trust between participants.

In what follows, I will disentangle different strategies deployed by *panegyreis* to create a religious community that is at the same time an economic community. I will argue that the constant overlapping of religious and economic stimuli produces an atmosphere, a disposition among participants in which religious and economic experience become one and the same (section 1). When holding myth or legend against ritual practice, we can observe how a community of giving and receiving religious goods converges with a community of selling and buying merchandise. Festivals with market fairs thus break down separate spheres of exchange in the attempt to create a community of moral interdependence (section 2). It is not least for this reason that fairs can develop into thriving economic hubs, and I will look next at how investing in the collective memory of a fair provides a powerful incentive for trade at times of economic crisis (section 3). And lastly, the physical and symbolic delineation of specific transactional spaces in the service of a ritualisation of economic relations at work during festivals with markets helps to build the framework of trust that makes the *panegyris* a popular, and apparently secure, site of cross-cultural trade (section 4). Festivals with fairs offer a privileged context for the meeting of religious and economic behaviour, so that gaining a more differentiated understanding of them might take us some way towards pinpointing the interactions between religion and the economy more broadly, in antiquity and perhaps beyond.

A number of caveats must be made immediately. First, the subject is too vast and too fundamental to command a single line of argument, and I merely hope to open up avenues for more detailed investigations. Second, if I seem to move relatively freely through time and space from archaic Greece to Late Antiquity to Byzantine Greece to the early Middle Ages throughout the Mediterranean and the Black Sea, this results from the patchy nature of the evidence for any given period. A *longue-durée* perspective reveals patterns in the practices and mentality of Mediterranean peoples that would otherwise remain invisible, even if precise historical analogies or comparisons cannot be made and ultimately the detail of such patterns remains distinctive of certain times and places.

And third, for Greek antiquity I do not attempt to draw a sharp distinction between festivals with market fairs and festivals of *theoria*, 'pilgrimage', in the carefully circumscribed administrative and institutional sense recently set out by Ian Rutherford (2013). This is to reduce the complexity of the problem and to avoid further diminishing the already scarce ancient evidence, but also because most non-urban sanctuaries in ancient Greece (with or without an attested fair) had a 'theoric' dimension, acting as cult centres with a regional catchment area even where there is no evidence for rigorous organisation.[9]

2   Crowding into a Common Experience

Looking at the literary evidence for fairs cross-culturally and over time, there are striking similarities between what these reports choose to say, as if over many centuries and across different types of texts and contexts, a common semantics for talking about festivals with market fairs had developed.[10] Two constants stand out immediately and universally in textual attempts to convey the atmosphere of market fairs. There is, firstly, a marked emphasis on the 'crowds' attending (Greek *plethos*), on the overwhelming throngs of people visiting the sanctuaries and markets. Texts speak of thousands, myriads, countless and infinite numbers; these are often matched by the abundance and diversity of products on offer. So Menander, comparing life on earth itself to a *panegyris*, mentions a crowd (*ochlos*), a market, entertainments – and thefts. Demosthenes cites plentiful merchandise as a sign of a successful

---

9   As argued throughout Kowalzig 2007.
10   De Ligt 1993's collection of texts provides a useful starting point for such an analysis (243–59); Koukoules 1949 assembles much literary evidence from the Byzantine periods not often used elsewhere.

panegyris, again using the word *plethos* (τὸ τῶν ὠνίων πλῆθος ὁρῶντες καὶ τὴν εὐετηρίαν τὴν κατὰ τὴν ἀγοράν), while the temple of Ceres on Pliny's estate 'may be rather old and small, but on the appointed day it is extremely crowded ... a great gathering of people assembles from the area, much business is done, many prayers are made, and many answered'.[11] Dio Chrysostom considers the coming and going of vessels and the 'excess' (*hyperbole*) of people, goods and ships a 'suitable topic for the praise of a fair, a harbour, a market'. Elsewhere, he lists the varied range of profiteers at the Isthmian games: sophists, writers, poets, conjurers, fortune tellers and countless lawyers and 'not a few' petty traders, all cheating one another. The idea of a 'mass' is underlined by the repetition of 'many' (*polloi*): 'at the temple of Poseidon, you could hear *many* of x, *many* of y, *many* of z'. He also stresses the 'infinite crowd' at the *panegyris* at Roman Apamea.[12] Church fathers claim that at Immae, some forty kilometres from Antioch, 'a *panegyris* was held attracting a number beyond counting'; a *myrion plethos* attends the miracles of Saint Thekla at Seleukeia in Cilicia in the late fifth century CE, a festival so enormous that 'the earth becomes too small, and the sea too narrow to hold all the people flooding in, entire populations, houses, clans'.[13] The masses (*plethos*), 'assembling from all nations', coming together at the 11th-century festival of St. Theodore at Euchaita, ca. 50 km west of Amaseia, transform the untrodden desert (*eremia*) into a populous city and countryside just like currents of a river flowing into the sea – as if the *panegyris* were a gateway to the sea itself.[14]

In his vivid depiction of the festival and fair of St. Demetrius at Thessaloniki, the *Timarion*, a 12th-century essay by a mystery satirist in the style of Lucian, speaks of the 'rush of the masses', and later an *asemon plethos*: 'as for the indistinguishable crowd that was following it, both from the countryside and the city, I won't do more than mention its size'.[15] As late as 1897, W.J. Woodhouse, visiting the fair at Tatarna that takes place on the banks of the Acheloos river in

---

11 Men. *PCG* 871 (= 416b Körte); Dem. 10.49–50 (*Phil.* iv); Plin, *Ep.* 9.39 (tr. Horden – Purcell 2000, 432).

12 Dio Chrys. *Or.* 32.37: ἀναγωγαὶ δὲ καὶ κατάρσεις καὶ πλήθους ὑπερβολὴ καὶ ὠνίων καὶ νεῶν πανηγύρεως καὶ λιμένος καὶ ἀγορᾶς ἐστιν ἐγκώμιον; *Or.* 8.9 πολλῶν μὲν σοφιστῶν ... πολλῶν δὲ συγγραφέων ... πολλῶν δὲ ποιητῶν ... πολλῶν δὲ θαυματοποιῶν ... πολλῶν δὲ τερατοσκόπων ... μυρίων δὲ ῥητόρων ... οὐκ ὀλίγων δὲ καπήλων; 35.15, πλῆθος ἀνθρώπων ἄπειρον.

13 Theod. *Hist. rel.* 7.2 = *PG* 82.1365: πλῆθος ἀριθμοῦ κρεῖττον; Thecla *Mir.* 33; 29, 17–24 Dagron.

14 John Mauropous, pp. 130–2; 207–8 Lagarde; 130–4, 207–8 on the *panegyris* of Theodore, a fourth-century martyr.

15 *Timarion* 1.5; 1.7 tr. Baldwin, modified; the description of the entire festival, which is compared to the Panathenaia and the Panionia and deemed 'the most important' in Macedonia: 1.5–1.9. The *panegyris* may have been held as early as the sixth century CE, but is definitely still attested in the 14th century: Koukoules 1949, 275.

the remote countryside of Aitolia, comments that 'thousands ... attend the Fair [which 'seems more largely attended than ... any other in Northern Greece'] ... so great is the throng at the time of the Panégyris that the river barely suffices to supply the needs of men and animals'.[16] We could cite many more such passages; it is clear that the image of the masses attending was intrinsic to the idea of the *panegyris* itself.

These crowds are international, and the two concepts obviously go together: Timarion observes the 'native and indigenous throng' (*autochthon ochlos kai ithagenes*) pouring in but also pilgrims (*hiketai* and *theoroi*) of every conceivable region and ethnicity: 'Greeks from wherever they happen to live, the entire motley crew of Mysians ...[from] as far as the Danube and Skythia, Campanians, Italians generally, Iberians, Lusitanians, and Transalpine Celts'.[17] The fair of Michael at Chonai in southwestern Anatolia (12th century) features the peoples of Lydia, Ionia, Caria, Paphlagonia, Iconium (Konya).[18] For the festival of St. Cyprian/Leukothea in inland Lucania, Cassiodorus in the sixth century CE counts the whole of southern Italy: Campania, Bruttium, Calabria, Apulia. Sozomen, writing in the fifth century CE, reports on a 'brilliant feast' at the oak of Mamre/Abraham in Palestine prior to Constantine's intervention, to which Phoenicians and Arabians and other buyers and sellers resort, a fair attended 'diligently by all the nations', Jews, Pagans and Christians, praying, libating, burning incense, sacrificing and dedicating a product of their labour 'according to promise as a provision for the feast for themselves and their dependents'.[19] Goods brought from India and China were sold at Batme on the Euphrates. The first-century CE fair in honour of Athena Polias at Kyzikos features 'merchants and foreigners from the whole oi[koumen]e' and 'craftsmen from Asia';[20] Dio Chrysostom lists visitors from Ionia, Sicily, Italy, North Africa, Marseilles, and Borysthenes at Isthmia. This *panegyris* for Poseidon provides the setting for the Romans' declaration of freedom in 196 BCE and, in expectation of what was to come, the most outstanding men from 'nearly the whole world (*oikoumene*)' attend.[21] Pliny praises the

---

16   Woodhouse 1897, 36, quoted by Horden – Purcell 2000, 433.

17   *Timarion* 1.5 tr. Baldwin.

18   See note 36.

19   St. Cyprian/Leukothea: Cassiod. *Var.* 8.33; Mamre: Sozom. *Hist. eccl.* 2.4. According to *Chron. Pasch.* the fair was founded by Hadrian; *PG* 92, 614b.

20   Batme: Amm. Marc. 14.3.3. Kyzikos: *SEG* 4.707, 10–11; 13–14 = *IGR* iv, 144 = *IMT Kyz Kapu Dağ* 1431.

21   Dio Chrys. *Or.* 9.5; Plb. 18.46; cf. Liv. 33.32. Though note Aristid. *Or.* 46.23, likening the city of Corinth to a year-round *panegyris*, in contrast to the Isthmian games which are periodic; see also Str. 8.6.20.

bronzes of Delos at a time when the 'entire world thronged the markets of Delos', a centre of continuous pilgrimage. And finally, to end in the archaic period, the *Homeric Hymn to Apollo* jubilates about 'all men' and the 'glorious tribes of men' on Delos and at Delphi.[22]

These crowds from all over the world form the background against which the spectacle of the *panegyris* itself unfolds. For the second immensely popular recurrent motif is the splendour and brilliance of the fair, routinely termed *theama* or *spectaculum*. In particular, it is the shininess, the glamour, the visual appeal of the fair and its almost blinding effect on the eye that is singled out. Cassiodorus, once again on the festival of St. Cyprian/Leukothea in Lucania, speaks of the charming sights, the attractive people attending. A recurring term is *lampros* or *lamprotes*, 'shining', 'brilliance' and their derivatives, often describing something that emanates from the lamps and torches, the reflections of the gold and silver decorations, the beauty of the glittering clothes worn by participants. Dionysius of Halikarnassos calls the market at the cult of Feronia in Italy *agorai lamprotatai*.[23] Pilgrims visiting St. Thekla in Cilicia admire *to lampron kai phaidron* of her festival. Timarion is asked to speak of 'the size and the brilliance of the fair, the masses and the wealth and the goods for sale'.[24] The 11th-century *panegyris* of St. Theodore at Euchaita in the northern Anatolian hinterland takes place in a shining, brilliant precinct, while Gregory of Nazianzus makes a point of rejecting all 'glamour' at Christian festivals, part of the anti-materiality discourse of the church fathers; the vocabulary used betrays the splendour of the pagan *panegyris*.[25]

The *Timarion* is a good illustration of how the language of splendour used for market fairs blends into that of the religious events. Having described the *theatron* of the carefully arranged, teeming market, a thing 'worth seeing' (*axiotheon*), he continues with the contemporary procession and imminent ceremony driven by desire for further spectacle (ἔρωτι θεαμάτων ἑτέρων): 'As the populace stood agog in front of the entrance, eagerly awaiting the imminent presence [of the archbishop] ... It was a spectacle that gave me no ordinary delight.... As for the ... crowd (*plethos*) ... I won't do more than mention its

---

22   Plin. *HN* 34.4; *Hom. Hymn. Ap.* 57; 537.

23   Cassiod. *Var.* 8.33; Dion. Hal. *Ant. Rom.* 3.32.1.

24   Thecla *Mir.* 33.14–15 Dagron; *Timarion* 1.4 tr. Baldwin μεγέθους τε αὐτῆς καὶ λαμπρότητος, πλήθους τε καὶ πλούτου καὶ ὠνίων πάντων.

25   Euchaita: John Mauropous 208 Lagarde; *cf.* Vryonis 1971, 40 n. 204. Greg. Naz. *Or.* 5, *PG* 35, 708c–12 (paraphrase): no embellishment of our body; no changing of our clothes ... no feasting and drinking, no decoration of the streets with crowns and flowers, nor the tables with perfume, nor the vestibules, so that the houses not be illuminated. For the *lamprotes* of early Christian festivals see Hart 1981, 124–6.

size. The chosen leaders ... made the procession a marvellous sight, being men all in their prime, all glowing with health, all in fact the pupils and initiates of Enyalian Ares the war god, resplendent in their silk and studded garments, their hair thick and gold ... their Arabian horses pranced along ... rearing up as though to leave the ground and fly .... They appeared to blend in with the resounding splendour with all the gold and silver gleaming on their reins; as they kept arching their necks as if to display their glittering harnesses, it seemed as if they were enjoying the gorgeousness of their trappings.'[26] These are followed by the appearance of the governor, a sight likewise causing 'joy in the soul' (χαρμονὴν τῇ ψυχῆι) and 'depth of exaltation' (ἀγαλλιάσεως πλήσμιον, 1.7); the governor himself is a marvellous sight, sparkling eyes and teeth, tall and nimble in stature, and as he began to speak he alternatingly projected 'the grace of Aphrodite ... the vigour of Ares ... the great majesty of Zeus', Hermes' 'sharp and quick-changing glances'; his hair iridescent between several colours, woman and man alike, and mixed with manliness producing *eros*, a 'godlike man' (σεῖος ἀνήρ) himself invoking the martyr to begin the ensuing rites of prayers and antiphonal chanting, itself ubiquitous and all-embracing (1.9–10).

The *Timarion* communicates the sensory, emotional charge and visual effect in a language that resembles ancient descriptions of epiphany, where size, splendour and luminosity, and fragrance are equally synaesthetic experiences of the divine — the most often-repeated instance is the epiphany of Demeter in her *Homeric Hymn*.[27] This charge has a highly impassioned dimension — the *Timarion* is keen to communicate the growing desire of worshippers to be part of the event, whose splendour elicits strong emotions, *eros* among visitors, eager to see (*philotheoroi*), producing joy (γῆθος, χαρμονή, ἀγαλλίασις).[28]

The *Timarion*'s tightly woven, exaggerated and quasi-redundant use of pagan ritual vocabulary to evoke the divine is of course the deliberate literary strategy of a religious satire.[29] But regardless of the treatise's mockery of 12th-century society and aristocracy, and its attempted subversion of Christian faith (in the words of a 14th-century critic), it directs our attention to a similarly suggestive sensory conflation of the religious and economic experiences of worshippers at fairs elsewhere. For example, Cassiodorus' portrayal of the fair

---

26   *Timarion* 1.7, tr. Baldwin. The tightness of the market's arrangement of merchant booths is likened to the body of a centipede: 1.5–6.

27   *Hom. Hymn. Dem.* (2); *Hom. Hymn. Dion.* (7). For the strategies of textual invocation of epiphany, see Platt 2011, ch. 1, esp. 61–72.

28   *Timarion* 1.6–7, tr. Baldwin.

29   It is outside the scope of this article to discuss the role of the *Timarion* in its intellectual milieu, or to try to disentangle the ancient and Byzantine references to competing forms of religiosity. On this intriguing text see *e.g.* Alexiou 1982; Baldwin 1984.

of St. Cyprian/Leukothea uses comparable language in building up to the ceremony, while John Mauropous (11th century) describes the 'brilliance' of the fair of St. Theodore at Euchaita in tones that similarly stress the great throng 'from all nations' passionately gathering to chant, burn incense, pray and bring gifts to the saint.[30]

Libanius offers an additional take on the emotional dimension of the pagan *panegyris* when commenting on the prosperity that festivals with fairs bring to communities: the participating cities benefit from mutual reciprocity and resource complementarity when exchanging goods at festivals with cheer, delight and gain.[31] In other (albeit spurious) passages he offers a glimpse of the emotional anticipation of and readiness for the upcoming festival: 'when the *panegyris* is about to take place, desire (*pothos*) comes to men; there is pleasure (*hedone*) at their occurrence, and remembrance (*mneme*) at their end ... and memory has some utility'.[32] There follows the eager anticipation of an exchange that blurs the spiritual and the material: worshippers are 'in high spirits' (*met'euthumias*) while washing their clothes, preparing their contributions of flocks and wine for the common sacrifice: the masses what they will feast on 'splendidly' (*lamprws*), the prosperous adding gifts to the gods.[33] Elsewhere we hear more detail on the economic aspects of the festival, a time when one 'may see the markets flourishing':

> At first, then, when [the festival] is approaching, it is a much-desired thing (ποθεινόν τι χρῆμα), and time seems to slow down for people, and they are eager to take part in the festival, just as sailors long for land. Then, when it arrives, every man rushes to spend, both the one who has a lot of money and the one who, living frugally, has amassed some silver.

---

30 John Mauropous 134, 207 Lagarde. New or restored Hellenistic festivals employ very similar motifs in order to convey the theatricality and emotionality of processions leading up to the sacrifice: see Chaniotis 1995, 154–60.

31 Lib. *Or.* 11.230: '... sharing their goods with one another by means of the festivals to which they invite the others and are invited, each one in turn summoning the others to it. They enjoy and take pleasure in the same things, and profit by sharing with others their surplus and gaining in return what they need (εὐθυμούμεναί τε καὶ χαριζόμεναι καὶ κερδαίνουσαι), selling some things and buying others ... they earn their wealth with laughter and bustle ...' (tr. Downey); this is then interestingly compared negatively to relying on seaborne trade.

32 Lib. *Progymnasmata* 12.29 (tr. Vryonis): Πανηγύρεων δὲ μελλουσῶν μὲν πόθος ἀνθρώποις, παρουσῶν δὲ ἡδονή, πεπαυμένων δὲ μνήμη. καὶ γὰρ αὖ τὸ μεμνῆσθαι καθίστησι τοὺς ἀνθρώπους ἐγγὺς τῶν ἔργων αὐτῶν ('for indeed, remembering, in turn, brings people close to the events themselves'). ἔχει δέ τινα καὶ ὠφέλειαν ἡ μνήμη.

33 Lib. *Progymnasmata* 12.29.

One man washes his clothes, while another borrows some. (4) And for those who practice farming, everything that the country produces is brought in – among other things, a million types of birds, some domestic, some wild. But for those who make their livelihood with their hands, what comes from the retailers is sufficient; for at that time especially you would see the marketplace flourishing. (5) So, on the day before the festival, gifts are carried through the city, as many as would make a table splendid (τράπεζαν ... λαμπράν), some from the powerful honoring each other, others from the lower ranks to them and from them to the lower ranks, the latter attending to the former's power, the former sharing their luxury with their attendants.

LIBANIUS, *Progymnasmata* 12.3–5 (tr. Gibson)

I will return in the next section to the curious cycle of reciprocity between rich, poor and the divine that Libanius describes. For now, we can say that even a small selection of texts suggests that the conventions for describing the *panegyreis* are part of their interpretation. The passages cited indicate that religious and commercial experience are aesthetically and emotionally very close, even inseparable. The elaborate emphasis on size and splendour, exuding a colourfulness matched by the *poikilia* ('diversity') of the participants, seems to be a strategy for triggering emotional involvement and reflects the mass enthusiasm and anticipation of the festival with fair. Mixing sight, sound, smell and social relations likewise contributes to the psychological charge of the occasion, blending its religious and economic aspects. Dio Chrysostom notes that wherever there are masses at festivals, wealth and prosperity are to be found, implying that the religious dimension of fairs provided stimuli for a different and perhaps peculiar economic intensity.[34]

3   Conflating Spheres of Exchange: Giving and Receiving, Selling and Buying

The emotional charge produced by the overlapping religious and economic sensations at fairs produces the foil for a conflation between religious and economic transactions. It underlies the creation of what I shall term a 'community of giving and receiving' that merges with a 'community of buying and selling', in turn constituting a temporal moral community. To the ancient historian a 'community of giving and receiving' may sound a little too Christian for

---

34   Dio Chrys. *Or.* 35.15–17; *cf.* Dem. 10.49.

comfort, but for once it may be helpful to think in these terms. Fairs offer an opportunity for the convergence of otherwise discrete, or at the very least differently configured, spheres of exchange. In anthropology, the term 'spheres of exchange' refers to an arrangement whereby objects of exchange are assigned to different spheres for transactional purposes, and can only be exchanged within that sphere. Subsistence items, for instance, belong to one sphere, luxury products to another, and while items can be readily exchanged within the same sphere, calculating comparative values between different spheres is difficult and often impossible. In traditional societies, this helps, for example, to prevent powerful individuals or families from capitalising on the needs of poorer ones, thus ensuring equal access to subsistence goods. In what follows, I will suggest that festivals with fairs fuse several discrete spheres of exchange, in the first place, what we might distinguish as religious and economic spheres; and furthermore, different types of markets also seem to merge. The result are several interlinked cycles of exchange that come to forge a moral community whose self-regulation is sponsored by the divine.[35]

3.1 The Byzantine Panegyris

What is at stake is a little easier to demonstrate for the Late Antique and Byzantine periods, but there are analogies in antiquity. The miracles construed around saints with a *panegyris* are at the heart of the process, and it is in itself intriguing that relevant stories cluster around those saints that also boast a festival with a market. The *Timarion*'s description of St. Demetrius' festival already intimated that the spiritual effect of a fair is closely bound up with what the liturgy chooses to remember, represent and celebrate as the saint's doings. Michael Choniates explicitly says that the miracles at Kolossai in Phrygia gave rise to the *panegyris* and drew the masses from all over 'for the sake of selling and buying'.[36] The case of St. Phokas at Sinope is particularly effective in illustrating the connection between miracle story ('myth') and form of worship ('ritual') that resonates in the saint's fair and causes the conflation of different spheres of exchange.

---

35 For the history and use of the expression 'spheres of exchange' in anthropology, see Sillitoe 2006.

36 Michael Choniates (*c.* 1140–1220) i.56, 12–18 Lampros: 'It is the wonders which have occurred at the church of Kolossai which have given rise to so populous a *panegyris*. For these wonders draw people not only from all the neighbouring cities, but also those from beyond the mountains, Lydians, Ionians, Carians, Pamphylians, and Lycians, and what is more even the barbarians of Iconium, for the sake of selling and buying' (ἀποδοῦναι καὶ πρίασθαι).

Sinope, on Anatolia's Black Sea coast, was an important harbour throughout antiquity, and continued to be a major grain port and naval base in the 11th century. It had an important ancient shrine of St. Phokas and a conspicuous later commercial *panegyris*.[37] St. Phokas was the patron saint of merchants and sailors, and performed miraculous rescues at sea. He took care of the sails, prevented ships from running into rocks or captains from falling asleep.[38] The earliest traditions make Phokas a local gardener who grew fruit and vegetables on the site of his future church, 'outside the polis by the Isthmos of Sinope'; he was well known for the hospitality he offered to pilgrims together with the produce of his orchard, the remainders of which were given to the poor.[39] Later aetiologies explaining his maritime cult, set in different towns along Anatolia's Black Sea coast, make him the son of a ship-builder, who neglected his studies to watch the sea all day long. When one day a ship from Alexandria, presumably carrying grain, was stuck at the harbour, and 1500 men were unable to move the vessel, its merchant-owner (*naukleros*) dreamt of a local child with supernatural powers. So Phokas fought and defeated the ship's maritime *daimon* — who introduced himself as 'Herakles' — subsequently saved another boat from shipwreck elsewhere, and rescued a third that hailed from Macedonia.[40]

These events take place variously at Sinope, Herakleia, Amaseia, and Amisos, suggesting an interconnected set of local myths and stressing the saint's broader reach. The texts themselves make much of the fact that Phokas' fame travelled widely, and present entire catalogues of his cult's spread. Early-fifth century Asterios speaks of mariners' hymns being sung not just in the Pontus but also in the Aegean and Adriatic, the Atlantic Ocean and the

---

37   Van de Vorst 1911; the fair was interrupted in the late 11th century during Turkish invasions. Van de Vorst 1911 is a fundamental study of this fourth-century saint and collects a number of relevant texts; see also Oikonomides 1952. The *panegyris* at Sinope is mentioned in the 14th century panegyric by Andreas Libadenos (p. 289) in the context of the restoration of the church at Kardyle near Trebizond after the Turkish invasions (p. 264). The oldest text pertaining to Phokas is the panegyric of Asterios of Amaseia (early fifth century CE), to whom I will refer to as in AS Sept vi, pp. 294–9 (= *PG* 40, 300c–313) for ease of reference (note the edition by Datema 1970; transl. in Leemans 2003). Other texts will be cited as printed in Van de Vorst 1911. For a summary of sources on Phokas in chronological order see the online database *The Cults of Saints in Late Antiquity*.

38   Asterios, AS Sept vi, 298 (fifth century CE); Van de Vorst 1911, 286; 289 (14th century).

39   Asterios, AS Sept vi, 295; 297; see *ODS*, s.v.

40   Van de Vorst 1911, esp. 272–9; 280–1; 292–3. It is notable that Phokas is found battling with Herakles; the Greek hero wrestled with a series of sea-demons, the Old Man of the Sea, Nereus, Proteus.

Eastern Mediterranean.[41] Phokas' cult was already broadly diffused in Late Antiquity, especially in the coastal locations on the Black Sea where his aetiological legends took place, but also near Trebizond and at Constantinople.[42] A charity house was dedicated to him at late antique Cherson/Chersonesos, known from two bread-stamps bearing his image.[43] On the island of Syros, in the bay of Grammata, a well-known haunt for sailors in the Aegean since antiquity, votive inscriptions to Phokas date from the fourth-fifth century CE.[44] Rome seems to have had a significant cult, an early church was built in his honour in Syracuse on Sicily, and he is equally known epigraphically in the fifth century CE Levant.[45]

So Phokas' cult was widespread and popular among seafarers from early on. The ritual customs attested in his honour intriguingly pick up on all his different legends and tie his activities as rescuer of ships and his generosity towards pilgrims and the local poor into the larger economic circuits of maritime trade, not least involving grain. For Asterios, using the language of the Graeco-Roman *theoxenia* — offered among others to the seafaring Dioskouroi — knows that the seamen adopted a custom by which they had Phokas as a guest (συνεστιάτορα) at their common table. To deal with the problem that someone 'bodiless' could not participate in a common meal, every day the sailors divided up their food into equal shares and put aside a portion for Phokas — *meris*, the

41   Asterios AS Sept vi, 298; Andreas Libadenos (286) knows of Phokas' fame throughout the Black Sea, the Bosporos and Anatolia; the Caucasus, Egypt, Ionian and Adriatic Sea (Van de Vorst 1911, 284–9, esp. 286).

42   Black Sea: Sinope, probably Amaseia (Van de Vorst 1911, 252 n. 2; *cf.* the stories set there 276–8; 283) and Amisos (282); *Syn. Eccl. CP* p. 69 speaks of Phokas' activities in all three cities. Trebizond: Andreas Libadenos, Van de Vorst 1911, 264–5. Constantinople, to where Phokas' relics were transferred in the fifth century CE, had several shrines: *ibid.* 255–7. Oikonomides 1952, 215–19 discusses the different localities of Phokas' cults in the Pontos in greater detail; Van de Vorst 1911, 255–9 lists many attested cults elsewhere.

43   Tauric Chersonese: Latichev 1899, 344–9. On these pilgrim tokens (*eulogiae*), dating to the fifth-sixth century CE, Phokas is standing on a boat, carrying a rudder; they bear the inscription: 'Eulogy of Saint Phokas of the poorhouse (πτωχίου) of Cherson': Yashaeva 2011, cat. nos. 371–2.

44   Syros: *IG* xii.5, 712.56; 58 with Klon 1875; see also Rossi, *Bull. Arch. Christ* 1876, 112–16. For Phokas' distribution today in the Black Sea, the Aegean island world, the Levant and southern Italy, the popular article by Michalakopoulou 2018 gives an idea of how interesting a systematic study of this saint might be.

45   Rome: Asterios AS Sept vi, 298 mentions a 'cult and honour among all people' and a conspicuous temple beautifully adorned (δορυφορία πάνδημος καὶ τιμὴ καὶ οἶκος περιφανής, ἠσκημένος εἰς κάλλος) and that Phokas was not worshipped less than Peter and Paul. A shrine has been conjectured at the foot of the Aventine by the Tiber on the basis of 11th century literary sources: Van de Vorst 1911, 255–6; *Bull. Arch. Christ.* 1878, 60–1. Syracuse (fifth century CE): Orsi 1899, 636–41. Levant: Van de Vorst 1911, 257–8.

word also denoting 'sacrificial portion' in antiquity. Every day, a different sailor bought the portion, and when they arrived in the harbour and safely on land, the money collected from the sale was distributed among the hungry. And so 'Phokas' portion' (ἡ μερὶς τοῦ Φωκᾶ) became a benefaction to the poor.[46] In a slightly different version, the sailors always put out a portion of grain (μερίδα σιτίων) for him, collected them all at the end of the journey, and in this way 'paid afterwards what [the saint] had granted them'.[47]

The money and/or grain thus dedicated by the sailors was given to those in need and fulfilled the divine command of giving alms; in some versions, the *naukleros* of a rescued ship would give Phokas one hundred gold coins to distribute to the poor.[48] Indeed, merchants routinely dedicated a share of wheat or other goods to certain saints' shrines in return for safety at sea, which in turn allowed them to profit from the sale of their wares. One merchant pledged to give as much as half of the value of his cargo to St. Lazarus every year.[49]

Legends of St. Nicholas of Myra, the seafaring saint par excellence, give us an idea of how much the saints were implicated in the economic interdependency of their broader worshipping clientele.[50] Despite his later popularity he did not leave traces of a major fair in his city of origin, but several of his miracles establish the same sort of cycle of reciprocity within a festive community (*heorte*). During a food shortage at Myra, St. Nicholas appeared to grain merchants plying the sea between Cyprus and Constantinople, and bought the cargo for 150 gold coins in return for their diverting their boats. When the

---

46   AS Sept. vi, p. 298: ὅθεν καὶ νόμος ἐγένετο ναύταις, Φωκᾶν ἔχειν συνεστιάτορα. καὶ ἐπειδὴ τὸν
        νῦν ἀσώματον, σύσσιτον εἶναι καὶ κοινωνὸν τραπέζης ἀμήχανον· μάθετε πῶς ἄρα φιλευσεβὴς
        λογισμὸς ἐσοφίσατο τὸ ἀδύνατον. καθ᾽ ἑκάστην γὰρ τὴν ἡμέραν τὴν τῶν ὄψων μερίδα πρὸς ἰσο-
        μοιρίαν τῶν ἐσθιόντων ἀποκληροῦσι τῷ μάρτυρι. ταύτην δέ τις τῶν δαιτυμόνων ἐξωνούμενος, τὸ
        ἀργύριον κατατίθεται, καὶ τῇ ὑστεραίᾳ ἄλλος, καὶ ἄλλοτε ἕτερος· καὶ οὗτος ὁ κλῆρος τῆς ἀγο-
        ρασίας περιϊὼν ἅπαντας, δίδωσι καθημέραν τῆς μερίδος τὸν ὠνητήν· ἐπειδὰν δὲ ὅρμος αὐτοὺς
        ὑποδέξηται, καὶ εἰς γῆν ἀφίκωνται, μερίζεται τὸ ἀργύριον τοῖς πεινῶσι· τοῦτο ἡ μερὶς τοῦ Φωκᾶ,
        πενήτων εὐεργεσία.

47   Van de Vorst 1911, 289, ll. 12–13. The link to the cult of the Dioskouroi (but apparently not to
        the *theoxenia*, though see Oikonomides 1952, 189–92) was discussed in some early studies,
        and would perhaps merit a re-assessment: Lübeck 1904; Radermacher 1904; Jaisle 1907,
        52–7. Asterios himself mentions the Dioskouroi as rescuers of seamen: Leemans 2003, 173.

48   Van de Vorst 1911, 282, where the *naukleros*, here at Amisos, gives Phokas praise, one hun-
        dred gold coins, and a horse on which he rides to meet the poor masses (πλῆθος πτωχῶν)
        at the gates of the city of Amaseia; cf. the Armenian life, p. 294.

49   St. Lazarus: AS nov. iii, 532–3.

50   St. Nicholas of Myra, dating back to the time of Constantine: Anrich 1913–17, i.130–2 gen-
        erally on the saint's protection of sailors; i.169–170; i.282–3 rescues at sea; i.415 a Saracen
        merchant who then converted to Christianity. The stories of Nicholas' intervening at sea
        in the different vitae are helpfully collected and briefly analysed in Ševčenko 1981, 99–103.

saint had disappeared, the salesmen, thinking that this was an illusion, continued on their voyage but immediately a storm arose; when they called upon St. Nicholas for help, they found themselves saved in the harbour of Myra. On visiting St. Nicholas' tomb, they were surrounded by the scent of myrrh and recognised the saint; the merchants gave (δέδωκαν) the 150 gold coins to the poor and sold their grain to the people, and held a splendid festival (*lampren heorten*). And so, the text says, the grain (*sitos*) for the people was multiplied (ἐπληθύνθη), as was the gain (*kerdos*) for the merchants.[51]

One might say that in these cases, a cycle of exchange is constructed around the miracles where giving and receiving merges with buying and selling, while at the same time tying local and regional economic circuits into one another. For selling their wares to the saint, the merchants obtain rescue at sea; in return they dedicate the price of the grain to the saint who gives it to the poor; in turn the wealthy merchants are able to sell the remainder of their cargo; the local community is freed from starvation, and a splendid festival is offered to the saint. But the cycle does not finish here — it was not only the merchants who offered goods. The sources are careful to distinguish between contributions from the poor and the rich, between honest and dishonest gifts; and between giving to, and receiving from, the saint on a scale proportionate to one's means.[52] And once again the stories revolve around the saints for whom a *panegyris* is known. So St. Theodore at Euchaita, in whose cult gift-giving was listed as part of worshippers' zeal at his *panegyris*, is honoured by a soldier with a sword, by a farmer with his ox, by a poor woman with a chicken – the relative worth of all three of which is protected by the saint against other devotees' acquisitiveness.[53] There is also the story of a youth from Paphlagonia who, with the help of St. George, managed to get his village's first-fruits (*karpophoria*), amounting to as much as one litra of gold, past a family of robbers all the way to St. Michael at Chonai, host of a thriving fair in the middle Byzantine period. Another tradition tells of a poor boy who dedicated a cake, his trophy from a children's game, to St. George who had many local fairs throughout Paphlagonia; four merchants arrived at the shrine, greedily ate the cake as if the saint had just laid it out there for free, and promptly found themselves shut

51 Anrich 1913–17, i.284–6; see also 160–1; 224. At 251–2, 403 only one merchant receives three gold coins, and 'thus provided gain to himself and release from the famine for the people' (λιμοῦ ἀπαλλαγὴν τῶι λαῶι, 403). See ii.395–8 on the dating and the relationship between the different versions of the grain-ship miracles.

52 *Cf.* Lib. *Progymnasmata* 12.29, as p. 297 above.

53 Sigalas 1924, 328–9; 333–4; 317–18. In all three cases, the gift is taken by someone of higher social status, who is duly punished and on restoration of the gift eventually recognises the power of the saint.

into the church until they had left a substantial sum of money.[54] Saints knew what they were worth, demanded their worth from their worshippers; but they also protected their relative worth from the greed of devotees.

Overall then, if bringing gifts (*dora*) was part of the experience of the *panegyris*, so were returns: on the last day of her festival, St. Thekla sat in her temple, on an elevated, beautifully decorated throne, distributing to those gathered the many and magnificent gifts (δῶρα λαμπρά τε καὶ πολλά) prepared specifically for the *panegyris*, 'worthy of the saint who offered them' (αὐτῆς τῆς παρεχούσης ἄξια). A little further, at the village of Dalisandros, every year at the time of her *panegyris* St. Thekla arrived in a chariot from the mountain's summit at her church in order to distribute her gifts among the assembled people, thereby showing her delight at the festival and her acceptance of the honours offered to her, and giving very nice things in return. Worshippers, regardless of their status, would thus attend a fair with the expectation of giving and in eager anticipation of receiving. This is part of the emotional charge that Libanius attributes to the *panegyris*, and is suggested by many other passages.[55]

One might say then that the *panegyris* concentrated many different cycles of reciprocity into a single occasion and thus brought into focus a community of economic interdependence. The fair and associated stories were bound up with a 'moral economy' tying the needs of poor peasants into the profits of rich merchants, and the saints' festivals functioned as nodes of a special kind of redistribution that nonetheless left the existing distribution of wealth untouched. Shared worship of a saint brought the community of the faithful together in mutually entangled cycles of giving and receiving that fuzzily overlapped with those of buying and selling, blurring the boundaries between otherwise discrete spheres of exchange. Furthermore, by linking international merchants to a local festival, regional and foreign economic connectivity became bound up with local demands for provision while presenting lucrative business opportunities for a non-local clientele. Saints and their festivals thus seem to regulate a moral economy that connects international and local

---

54   The youth and his village's first-offerings for Michael of Chonai: Aufhauser 1913, 107–13, no. 11 (*cf.* Vryonis 1971, 41 n. 211). The boy, the merchants and St. George: Aufhauser 1913, 103–7, no. 10.

55   Thecla *Mir.* 33.38–43 Dagron; *Mir.* 26.30–7; the latter part technically belongs to Paul: 44–6 Dagron. Dagron 1978, 101 and 79 for other examples of gifts at *panegyreis*. St. Theodore at Euchaita (John Mauropous 134 Lagarde (δῶρα προσάγοντες)); Lib. *Progymnasmata* 12.5; see also Vryonis 1971, 40–1. On gifts and anticipation see also the papers by Eidinow and Ritter in this volume.

worshipper, merchant and peasant, rich and poor in a cycle of exchange across different spheres, bringing them together in a temporary moral community.[56]

It is therefore no coincidence that the saints' hold over this moral economy was often construed around something as fundamental to communities as the grain supply. Few places in the Mediterranean produced enough grain for themselves, and it is fair to assume that a majority depended on supplies from abroad, usually from across the sea; furthermore, irregular harvests or political circumstances led to frequent shortages. Grain and grain merchants are hence effective elements in the construction of a moral economy revolving around fairs. It is striking to note that saints who rescue merchants at sea and interfere in the local grain supply typically also enjoy a larger and well-known *panegyris*, and have close connections to the sea and maritime trade. St. Demetrius at Thessaloniki, the saint about whose fair we are so amusingly informed by the *Timarion*, performed such miracles: when the city's grain supply from the interior was compromised after invading Slavic tribes blocked the overland routes (early seventh century), Demetrius felt prompted to open up sea routes by intercepting grain ships from Chios and other northern Aegean ports destined for Constantinople, redirecting them to Thessaloniki.[57] St. Thekla, the saint who commanded a major festival in late antique Cilicia, rescued a Cypriot boat, presumably owned by a grain trader, from a massive storm in the harbour while the family travelling on it were keenly attending the *panegyris*, driven by *pothos* ('desire') for the event.[58] St. Nicholas, in another miracle, once again sought to counter local food shortage at Myra and asked the grain merchants carrying public grain for Constantinople from Egypt to leave behind 100 measures of their load to offset the famine under the promise that they would not have a loss of their cargo. And indeed, on arrival at Constantinople, the grain was weighed, and nothing was missing. Meanwhile, the amount of grain was sufficient for two years' seed and supply.[59] Somewhat different yet similar

---

56   On the concept of 'moral economy' see Thompson 1971.

57   Demetrius *Mir.* 8, 9, pp. 100–8 Lemerle 1979. Interestingly, the cycle of St. Nicholas in the church of St. Nicholas Orphanos at Thessaloniki depicts the story of Demetrius and the grain ships, and is apparently its only known representation: Ševčenko 1983, 102–3.

58   Thecla *Mir.* 15 Dagron; for Cyprus as the origin of much grain see Anrich 1913–17, ii.395–6. Note that there is no explicit mention of a market in the texts, though the length of Thekla's *panegyris* (one week) and the flood of visitors and traders from all over Cilicia and from Cyprus (Thecla *Mir.* 15, 26, 33 Dagron), many arriving by sea, would suggest it. Vryonis 1981, 200–2; Thonemann 2011, 123–4.

59   Anrich 1913–17, i.132–3; cf. 228; 300 There is also the intriguing tradition of the 13th-century St. Nicholas of Tolentino, usually depicted with a breadbasket. Bread blessed in honour of this saint was thrown into the sea to appease the demons of the sea and prevent shipwreck: Hennig 1943.

legends also exist for Michael at Chonai and his enormous, well-documented
fair in central Anatolia, flourishing in the 12th century. In true Heraklean manner, the saint supposedly prevented the spring around which the shrine was
built from being flooded by the two branches of the river surrounding it, presumably helping it remain a node of communications. Though this legend is
not directly related to the grain supply, it still betrays an emphasis on preserv-
ing the location's economic connectivity.[60] In any case, it appears that grain is
so prominent in several of these legends because its provision represents universal access to sustenance and therefore lends itself particularly well to illustrating divine sanction of intertwining cycles of reciprocity and redistribution.

3.2   Eleusis

Returning to antiquity, it is somewhat trickier to demonstrate this intercon-
nectedness of giving and receiving, selling and buying based on the few surviving attestations of festivals with fairs; but there are some striking analogies, if
not in the emotional charge of the cycle, then certainly in its economic significance. A cycle of reciprocity of sorts across different spheres of exchange
is explicitly mentioned in the *Homeric Hymn to Apollo* for the sanctuaries of
Delos and Delphi, when Apollo is seen to receive and distribute offerings from
abroad to locals.[61] On the level of individual behaviour, dedications to gods for
the successful completion of a journey by sea are frequent;[62] several mention
first-fruits or a *dekate*, perhaps indicating that merchants offered a share of
their cargo in exchange for the profits expected from the sale of their merchandise. Whether these dedications were made in the context of a religious
festival, let alone with a fair, is impossible to say.[63]

---

60   Michael Choniatis i.56–9 Lampros on the *panegyris*; numerous icons of the episode sur-
      vive; the church and its mosaics are famous; for the fair see Vryonis 1971, 20.
61   *Hom. Hymn. Ap.* 56–60, on Delos: 'But if you have the temple of far-shooting Apollo, all
      men will bring you hecatombs and gather here, and incessant savour of rich sacrifice will
      always arise, and you will feed those who dwell in you from the hand of strangers; for truly
      your own soil is not rich.' At Delphi: *Hom. Hymn. Ap.* 535–9: 'Though each one of you with
      knife in hand should slaughter sheep continually, yet would you always have abundant
      store, even all that the glorious tribes of men bring here for me. But guard you my temple
      and receive the tribes of men that gather to this place' (tr. Evelyn-White).
62   Wachsmuth 1967; Romero Recio 2000.
63   *E.g. SEG* 28.838 (fourth/third century, Halikarnassos, to Aphrodite); *TAM* II, no. 1184
      (fourth century, Phaselis, to Athena), possibly *CIG* 2660 = *SGDI* III 5731 ('fairly old', Pedasa
      in Caria, to Athena, three individuals from central Greece) with Jim 2014, 143–4; 153–4;
      163–4. *SEG* 61.625 (3) might be a votive graffito by grain dealers who were saved from
      shipwreck by Aphrodite. Note that it is the Samians and not Kolaios himself who put up
      a dedication to Hera as a *dekate* from the profitable trip to Tartessos: Hdt. 4.152. *Cf.* Ael.
      Arist. *Or.* 8.54–5. See also Naiden, this volume.

On the level of interaction between communities rather than individuals there are, however, indications that sanctuaries and their festivals can be involved in, and protective of, the grain supply of their worshipping communities and exploit their shrine's gravitational pull to that effect, just like the shrines of St. Nicholas and St. Demetrius. The sanctuary of Demeter and Kore at Eleusis, administered by Athens for most of its existence, had always been connected to grain, though its exact role in the production and (re)distribution remains unclear. The 'first-fruits decree' dating to the late-fifth century Athenian empire recalls some of the issues just discussed. Without wishing to delve into the contextual intricacies of Athenian imperialism here, it is fair to say that this decree was formulated in such a way as to drive the Greek world into a perpetual process of interrelated real and symbolic obligations: in keeping with a traditional custom, sanctioned by the Delphic oracle, the Attic demes and allies are requested and other cities encouraged to send first-fruits (*aparchai*) of wheat and barley to Demeter and Kore; according to Athenian ideology, this showed their gratitude for having received the art — or should we say the 'miracle'? — of growing grain from the local hero Triptolemos.[64] From the sale, a giant cake (*pelanos*) is to be produced, and sacrifices offered to an array of Eleusinian divinities together with dedications listing those who brought the *aparchai*. In return, 'to those who do this may much good come, and good and plentiful harvests, as long as they do no wrong to the Athenians or to the city of the Athenians or to the two Goddesses'.[65] Unfortunately we do not know whether all the incoming grain was sold at once and to whom; but we do know of major grain storage facilities at Eleusis. The *aparchai* might also have served as a public grain reserve to compensate for a shortage in a given year, as seems to have been the case in 329/8 BCE when this grain was sold below market price to counter a crisis in supply.[66]

Not unlike the legends of the saints, local demands for grain are intriguingly linked to international economic connectivity, possibly converging at a festival with a fair. While the local Proerosia, a pre-ploughing festival in the autumn, are often thought most suitable, we ignore whether the context for civic delegations' transport of the *aparchai* was that of a large theoric festival to Eleusis that might have set off processes similar to those we have observed for the

---

64   *IG* i³ 78a, with Parker 1996, 143–4; Cavanaugh 1996; and recently Jim 2014, 207–19, with previous bibliography.

65   *IG* i³ 78a, 44–6 (tr. Lambert-Osborne).

66   *IG* ii² 1672, esp. 269 96, on which recently Jim ..., ..., building on Jameson 1983, 10 11; see now Bresson 2015, 405–9. A portion of the harvest from the rented land belonging to a temple at Herakleia in southern Italy is to be stored in the public granary: *IG* xiv 645, I, l. 102, with Ampolo 1992.

Byzantine period.[67] We should remember though that Eleusis offered 'mysteries' as one of its 'spiritual' goods, in which the production of grain certainly had a role.[68] Fourth-century bronze coins from Eleusis depict Triptolemos holding grain ears on the one side, and on the other a piglet, the sacrificial offering for Demeter, on top of a mystic staff, connecting mystic initiation, a particularly emotionally engaging religious experience, to grain provision via a means of payment.[69] During the mysteries, says Philostratos, Athens became 'the most populous city of Greece', using the same idioms that we have identified as topical for fair descriptions throughout Antiquity and the Byzantine period. Though the evidence is patchy, we know of a large *panegyris* at Eleusis that in around 100 BCE took place annually, at which Italian wines were sold and a public slave supervised the correct use of weights and measures.[70] Later, Hadrian, who had an interest in Eleusis, picked up on the Athenian urge to figure as the node of Panhellenic grain provision and fused the religious and the economic by depicting himself on silver coins as Ploutos holding stalks of grain, while his wife was worshipped as the 'New Demeter' in Megara and addressed as Euergetis Karpo[phoros] by the 'Panhellenes'.[71] A peculiar tax-exemption for the sale of fish at the festival by none other than Hadrian himself and ratified by as important an institution as the Athenian Areopagus confirms that Eleusis' finely orchestrated use of tradition and religious symbolism fostered a lasting economic gravitation in the interests of the shrine and presumably the administering city of Athens, and an influx of people for religious and economic business alike.[72] We might posit that the late antique *pothos* of Libanius and the miracles of Thekla, the desire to be part of transactional processes across

---

67   See Parker 2005, 143–4; Jim 2014, 100–1 on a possible association with the Proerosia; contra Smarczyk 1992, 184–216 who links the decree with the mysteries. We have no proof that any places outside Attica actually ever delivered the first-offerings; those arriving in 329/8 BCE are from Attic tribes, cleruchies and nearby territories: *IG* ii² 1672, 263–88; *cf. SEG* 30.61 B fr. a 13 (367–48 BCE); ii²140 (353/2 BCE).

68   The possible centrality of the art of grain cultivation in the mysteries cannot be discussed here; see *e.g.* Parker 2005, 354 for some evidence pointing in this direction, with bibliography; the mysteries and Eleusis' more strictly agricultural festivals (*ibid.* 328–33) shared similar associations.

69   Psoma 2007, 229, with the relevant bibliography, a bronze coinage that might have been used by worshippers to pay for practicalities. Apparently international attendance was encouraged in the fourth century.

70   *IG* ii² 1013, 45–9 (public slave, *c.* 100 BCE); Italian wine: Alciphron. *Epist.* 4.13.9; *cf.*, tentatively, Men. *Sicyonians* 57–8; Philostr. *VA* 4.17.

71   Clinton 1989. Hadrian's wife: *IG* ii² 1088, 49; *IG* vii 73–4, with Jim 2014, 215–16.

72   *IG* ii² 1103; Pleket 1964, no. 16; with De Ligt 1993, 233.

different spheres of exchange, worshipper and god, buyer and merchant, was already well established in Antiquity.

4 Towards an Economy of Memory: the *Panegyris* of Athena Ilias

The cycle of giving and receiving, buying and selling at Eleusis as suggested by the *aparche*-decree is tied to a religious past in terms of both myth and ritual, as if commemorating Triptolemos' gift to the world in a traditional ritual custom recalled by the Delphic oracle were an incentive to attend the festival in the first place. More broadly, dwelling on the memory of a *panegyris*, its aetiological myths and its rites, often formed part of an overall investment in a sanctuary, in turn providing a stimulus for trade. Ancient sources are well aware that the memory and affective charge attached to a festival had economic potential. I recall Libanius' claim that the memory (*mneme*) of the emotional involvement experienced at the *panegyris* has some use. When the fair of St. Eugenios at Trebizond, a hub for grain and luxury items such as textiles and spices, was renewed after a period of disruption, a later metropolitan of the city claimed that its memory had been forgotten, as if oblivion were to blame for the economic crisis. We could even think of the renewal of the festival at Delos at the height of the Peloponnesian War on the model of an earlier *panegyris* as motivated by economic as much as political factors. Strabo would later describe the festival as 'an entirely commercial affair'.[73]

The cult and *panegyris* of Athena at Ilion, organised by the *koinon* of cities in the Troad and Propontis, gives an idea of how promoting ancestral traditions, evoking and creating emotional memories associated with a sanctuary and its festivals, could well have been part of an investment aimed at turning the *panegyris* into a site of thriving economic activity. Ilion's Trojan War associations created an obvious opportunity to exploit the past in order to bolster the shrine's appeal to worshippers.[74] In the archaic and classical periods Ilion had few and largely regional connections; being cut off from the interior of Anatolia routinely led to economic depression in the Troad. A

---

[73] Lib. *Progymnasmata* 12.29 (see n. 32 above). St. Eugenios: Papadopoulos-Kerameus 1896/1965, i.59. The festival was established during the reign of Basil I, ninth century, often interrupted and reinstated due to Turkish invasions in the 11th century: Vryonis 1971, esp. 15–16, 39–40, 160, 477. Regional products were sold, but Trebizond was in particular a node for spices, textiles and grain. Delos: Thuc. 3.104; Str. 10.5.4. On ritual and emotional memories see Chaniotis 2006.

[74] See *e.g.* Rose 2015 on how the city of Ilion built on its Trojan war heritage for its urban setting.

fourth-century upswing visible in the archaeological record has been attributed to access to Aegean trade networks at the moment when military activity
and the Achaemenid landed aristocracy supported local production and commerce, where the Troad mediated between Anatolia and the Aegean.[75] It is in
this broader economic context that we should understand the eventual formal
establishment of Ilion as a major regional cult centre, the foundation of the
koinon of Athena Ilias and of the long-lasting *panegyris* at the Panathenaia with
theoric delegations arriving from participating cities. Ilion's increased prosperity and wider range of contacts in the Aegean in the fourth century seem to
have been bound up with building on the cultural capital of a traditional cult
site, over time forging a memory where religious experience and economic interactions came to be intertwined and ensured the festival's continuity.

The federation of at times as many as twelve, mostly coastal, cities was
likely established during Antigonos I's reign in the last decade of the fourth
century BCE.[76] Of some twenty inscriptions revolving around the festival, dating from the late fourth to the late first century CE, many deal with its organisation and the financial arrangements among the cities involved; they attest
the *panegyris'* resilience through a series of economic and political crises, and
the *koinon*'s commitment to keeping it alive.[77] Not unlike the *aparche*-decree
at Eleusis, the *koinon* had developed a number of ways to make sure that individual cities remained obliged to Athena Ilias: notably the cattle and first-fruits
tributes that each city was required to supply, together with a financial contribution and interest on debt owed to the sanctuary. Religious tributes that
marked cities' participation in the cult were here intertwined with financial
commitments so as to keep attracting participants and keep them indebted.[78]

While there is no evidence for an earlier *panegyris*, it is clear that Athena's
shrine looked back to an attractive past and had been recognised by a series
of prominent visitors. The Trojan War traditions were used to connect, rather than to separate, the Aegean and Anatolia, not least because the link had

---

75   This is Lawall's argument (2002) on the basis of a wider range of amphora types in local
      production; Berlin 2002 and Wallrodt 2002 discuss the religious aspects of a fourth-
      century deposit. Note also the Achaemenid-style pottery in the deposit: Berlin 2002,
      33–40. Troy in the fifth and fourth centuries: Rose 2014, 143–57.

76   Ellis-Evans (2018, esp. 24–5) has now argued for satrapal interest in Athena Ilias already in
      the earlier fourth century, possibly setting off the process of placing her at the centre of a
      regional identity.

77   *I. Ilion* 1–18; 82–3; Curty 2015, no. 32 (= *SEG* 53.1373), with Ma 2007. See Robert 1966; *I.Ilion*,
      xi–xv; Knoepfler 2010; Pillot 2016; Lefèvre – Pillot 2015 on the remarkable continuity of the
      koinon's institutions and financial strategies; Ellis-Evans 2016; and most recently 2019, 46–55.

78   See 5, 6 (late third century BCE), 10, 11 (first century BCE), on cattle tribute, and financial
      contributions; also 7–9; 18. *I. Ilion* 10.38–9 for the *aparchai*.

proven economically necessary. During the Trojan War, Athena Ilias was the tutelary goddess of Troy but nonetheless on the side of the Achaians (*Il.* 6.297– 311). Xerxes dedicated 1000 cattle to her as his army came to the Skamander river, hinting at the later centrality of the cattle sacrifice at the Panathenaia. Alexander sacrificed to Athena on arrival, and, promising to invest in the cult, swapped his armour for that of Trojan War heroes deposited in the precinct, an act that has been interpreted as a gesture not of Hellenic superiority but rather of reconciliation.[79]

The first appearance of the *panegyris* seems to put us right at the heart of an 'experience economy' when a certain Malousios of Gargara in *c.* 306 BCE gave an interest-free loan to the *koinon* of more than 5250 gold staters (= 17.5 talents of silver) towards the needs of the *panegyris*, and above all the building of a theatre and associated expenses — could we assume that plays staging the Trojan War were performed, to trigger the memory of the audience for emotional effect?[80] After all, the Bronze Age fortification walls were still clearly visible at this time. A century later, a Kydimos from Abydos was honoured for his services to the *panegyris*, including taking on the expensive office of choregia, the financing of the dramatic chorus. This is followed by the curious remark that it would be beneficial for the *synedroi* to take good care of those who devoted themselves to the enlargement and fame of the festival (ἐπαύξησιν καὶ δόξαν), so that others may be encouraged to do so, too. The growth and reputation of the *panegyris* clearly mattered — for merchants and their customers, for example, they ensured the reliability of the festival as a market opportunity.[81]

How intensely this *panegyris* eventually came to play with the memory of its own past comes across in the long decree of 77 BCE concerning its renewal or refinancing after the Mithridatic Wars, which had caused economic difficulties in all the cities of the Troad.[82] Throughout the Hellenistic period, many

---

79   Pillot 2017. Xerxes: Hdt. 7.43; Alexander: Plut. *Alex.* 15.7–9; Diod. Sic. 17.17.6–18.1; Arr. *An.* 1.11.7–12; Str. 13.1.26, promising investment in the shrine. Other conspicuous visitors include Mindaros: Xen. *Hell.* 1.1.4; Antiochos iii: Liv. 35.43.3; and later a number of Romans.

80   *I. Ilion* 1 (late fourth century), a dossier of six inscriptions; see Csapo – Wilson 2015, 366–7. The city may have been seated by tribes named after Homeric heroes: SEG 44.982 with Rose 2014, 241; 162–70 on the building activity in the early period of the *koinon*, including the theatre.

81   *I. Ilion* 2.19–26 συμφέρει δὲ καὶ τοῖς συνέδροις ἐπιμέλειαμ ποιεῖσθαι / τῶγ καλῶγ καὶ ἀγαθῶν ἀνδρῶν καὶ φιλοτί-/μων εἰς τὰ διατείνοντα πρὸς τὴν τῆς πανη-/γύρεως ἐπαύξησιν καὶ δόξαν, ἵνα τούτου γινο-/μένου προτρέπωνται καὶ οἱ ἄλλοι τὸ καθ᾽ ἑαυ / τοὺς, συναύξειν τὴμ πανήγυριγ καὶ περὶ πλείσ-/του ποιεῖσθαι τὴν εἰς τὰ κοινὰ φιλοτιμίαν·

82   *I. Ilion* 10 (77 BCE). For the sack of Ilion by Fimbria in 85 BCE see Livy *Per.* 83; Julius Obsequens, *Liber de prodigiis* 56b; Str. 13.1.27; App. *Mithr.* 53; Dio 30–35.104.7. The coinage

festivals were abandoned due to war or economic problems, and renewals were frequent. Such renewal inscriptions appear to justify their changes by reference to tradition, even when a given measure is effectively an innovation.[83] What stands out in our inscription is the excessive use of 'καθότι καὶ πρότερον' ('just as before') and related formulae. If all the restorations are correct, there are as many as six instances, possibly topped by the idiom 24–5: κατὰ τὸν πάτρι-] ον [νόμ]ον ('according to the ancestral custom') in relation to the central cattle sacrifice.[84] This emphasis on ostensibly traditional custom might point to an exceptionally critical financial situation of the *koinon* festival, or demonstrate an especially intense awareness of the power of the past of this *panegyris*, or most likely both. We might imagine that in times of crisis, memories had become particularly emotionally charged, and that the past was dwelled upon strategically to retain the festival's role as an economic driver for the entire region.

The sizeable cattle sacrifice, vowed to be twelve by the Trojan priestess Theano (*Il.* 6.308) and enlarged to 1000 by Xerxes, seems to have played a special role in forging evocative ritual memories of a particularly affective nature. We know from earlier inscriptions that each participating city was to contribute its own animal (*I. Ilion* 5.16, 21; 6.7). As opposed to Hellenistic festival renewal inscriptions in general, which elaborate on the procession, the banquet and the agon,[85] our regulation of 77 BCE returns to the older practice of dwelling on the sacrifice, to be conducted 'according to ancient custom' (*I. Ilion* 10.24–5). A conspicuous cattle sacrifice, of which there are depictions on coins first in the late second/early first century and then more frequently in the Roman period, may have held special significance for Ilion's foundation legend.[86] In the first century BCE a certain Agathes is honoured for his services to the *koinon*'s Panathenaia, and for having twice organised 'taurobolia' with more than forty oxen. Whilst it is unclear what exactly this entailed, Athena Ilias' cattle

---

of Athena Ilias apparently continued (see below).

83 See Habicht 2006 for a list of interrupted festivals, often due to war; renewal strategies: Stavrianopoulou 2011.

84 *I. Ilion* 10.22: καθότι καὶ π[ρότερον; 23 [κα]θότι καὶ πρότερον, 26 [ὁμ]οίως κ[α]θότι νενομο-θέτ<η>ται; 34 καθό<τ>ι εἴ<θ>ισται ἐξαιρεῖσθ[αι] καὶ νῦν, 37 [καθότι] καὶ πρότερον; 39 καθό[τι καὶ πρότερον; 24–5 κατὰ τὸν πάτρι-] ον [νόμ]ον.

85 Chaniotis 1995, 154.

86 First occurring on the issue of Melanippides (late second/early first century; Ellis-Evans 2018, 115), coins show a cow hanging from a tree, or a man standing on the back of a cow, possibly to be connected with Ilion's foundation legend: Apollod. 3.12.3; Σ Tz. *Lyc.* 29. von Fritze 1902, 514–16; most recently Riedel 2016, 74–5. For the possible ritual see Nilsson 1906, 92–3; 232–8; von Fritze 1903; Stengel 1903. *Cf. I. Ilion* 32.28–9 = *OGIS* 219.28–9; Dikaiarchos of Messene wrote a treatise 'On the sacrifice at Ilion', perhaps revolving around Alexander's sacrifice. Attalos' gift of cattle to the city: *I. Ilion* 42.

sacrifice must have been an extraordinary spectacle and attending it a memorable experience.[87]

That this 'ritual memory' became intrinsically intertwined with economic and financial transactions may also be deduced from what has been termed 'festival coinage' for Athena Ilias. Tetradrachms and for a time drachms bearing the name and title of the goddess as a legend were issued between the 180/70s BCE and c. 60/50 BCE, i.e. through the Mithridatic Wars, possibly for the specific needs of the *panegyris*, with smaller denominations perhaps indicating a reduction of expenditure. While the question of '*panegyris* coinage' as opposed to 'sanctuary coinage' is disputed, it is beyond doubt that shrines strove to associate religious imagery and the attendant mythical memories with economic transactions, for example by producing their own weights, briefly discussed below.[88]

And finally, grain re-enters the stage, too, playing its own part in furthering the festival's persistence. A third-century decree honours an *agoranomos* ('market-official') for the provision of grain and its sale at the cheapest price ([ὅπως ὡς εὐτελέσ]τατα ὠνῶνται οἱ ἐν[δημοῦντες *I. Ilion* 3.13), and for also having taken care of the other merchandise. *Agoranomoi* can have a role in supplying necessities for attendants of the *panegyris*, but the naming of a particular product is rare.[89] I wonder whether this specification may not have been made with an eye to the bulk sale of grain so typical of market fairs, thus encouraging buyers to attend while guaranteeing a large clientele for sellers. Ilion was situated at the exit from the Hellespont, and ships carrying grain from the Black Sea sailed past from at least the times of Xerxes (Hdt. 7.147). If our festival was modelled on the Athenian Panathenaia, it would have taken place in early August, just at the time when the merchant ships would have been travelling through.[90] For the coastal cities of the *koinon*, the sale of grain could even be seen as a symbol of their interdependence, where surplus and shortage most visibly participate in the same economic process. In any case, the presence

---

87 *I. Ilion* 12, 14–18 (first century BCE): the *taurobolia* may be a bull-hunt, or slaughtering, perhaps by ephebes: *I.Ilion*, p. 49; Robert 1971, 315–16. Knoepfler 2010, 59 n. 120. Cf. installations for mass sacrifice at Magnesia and Dion: Bingöl 2007, 82–3; Pandermalis 2000.

88 Psoma 2008; Robert 1966, 18–46. See now Nollé 2014, doubting the minting of such coins specifically for the *panegyris*; Thonemann 2015, 82–4. Ellis-Evans 2016 provides the fullest discussion of these issues, arguing that they served both for expenditure and as a status symbol; 149–51 for denominations below a tetradrachm appearing in the first century BCE indicating substantial reduction of festival expenditure; also 2019, 48–9.

89 Though in *LSS* 45 (Aktion, third century BCE), ll. 33–5 the *agoranomoi* may be concerned with the sale of slaves in particular; *cf. IGLS* vii.4028, 33–9 (Baitokaike, third century CE): *agoretai* listed before the sale of livestock and slaves.

90 Ellis Evans 2019, 50 briefly raises this possibility.

of the grain ensured the continued existence of a market, for merchants and clients alike.

Certainly, Ilion's connectivity, notably to the Black Sea, was carefully cultivated; it underlay a decree issued at the time of the *koinon*'s foundation by the city of Ilion for four brothers from Tenedos. This was famously an island of *porthmeutai*, ferrymen, according to a recent study quite possibly sailing the Hellespont into the Black Sea on behalf of *naukleroi* from the Aegean who would often have had to wait months until favourable winds enabled them to enter the Dardanelles. Apart from the strictly economic benefits, such as *ateleia* in buying from and selling to anyone at Ilion, this ferry-family also obtained front seats at the Panathenaia. Though issued by the city and not the *koinon*, the decree shows that Ilion's broader economic connectivity was intertwined with the cult's *mise-en-scène*.[91]

Cherishing, reiterating, reinventing 'memory' and 'tradition', including the aetiological stories and miracles that gave rise to the festival in the first place, can thus be seen as part and parcel of any *panegyris* and notably of the theoric economy. In a recent book attempting to deconstruct the opposition of sacred and profane in the contemporary pilgrimage industry, Ian Reader insists that pilgrimage operates within, and draws its success from, a competitive marketplace in which pilgrim sites are promoted, reshaped and invented through strategies of consumerism, and where the acquisition of material goods, many of them evoking the pilgrim experience, is crucial to the success of these sites. In other words, pilgrimage operates *through* the market place.[92] We have not (yet) identified much amounting to souvenirs from festival sites in antiquity.[93] Ancient *theoria*, with its public delegations attending festivals on behalf of their community, employed different strategies to be remembered and to continue attracting its clientele; the phenomenon and immense popularity of 'festival announcements' (*epangelia*), to which Ian Rutherford has dedicated a whole chapter in his book on *theoria* is certainly one of these. As I hope to have suggested in this section, cultivating a memory in which religious and economic experiences overlapped and often merged was a strategy to keep a festival alive, competitive and lucrative.[94]

---

91   *I. Ilion* 24 (*c.* 300 BCE); on Tenedos' ferrymen see the suggestive essay Barnes 2006.

92   Reader 2014; Bynum 2007, 74.

93   Though Ellis-Evans 2019, 32, n. 62 notices a surge in the mass production of terracotta figurines at Ilion in the third/second century BCE.

94   Rutherford 2013, ch. 5. For another intriguing case of furthering a festival alongside economic renewal, see Müller 2014.

5 The Ritual of Buying and Selling

Finally, thinking back to the story and folk song from Epeiros of the beginning, I would like to discuss a final way in which fairs conflated the religious and the economic in order to create special transactional spaces with their own rules and enforcement mechanisms: the physical and symbolic delineation of the transactional space itself.

In the ancient Greek city, defining and controlling the economic domain was key to the security of sale and purchase. From Plato's *Laws* we can glean the importance attributed to determining the exact spaces for economic activity, within which the validity of the sale could be guaranteed by the officiating authorities, such as the civic agora and the emporium. Elsewhere, Plato says, transactions must be made on the basis of personal trust alone.[95]

Ancient and Byzantine sources agree that *panegyreis* form an economic domain of their own. Being less regulated, they offer exceptional opportunities, and do so for everyone. Fifth-century Priscus thinks of fairs as *isonomoi* and as not being dangerous. At late antique Gaza, the abundance of wares fills the bags of rich and poor alike. Fairs are places of spending for those who wish, but it is no secret that price equivalency is not always achieved, so that risk and opportunity go hand in hand: 'who knows how to negotiate gains a lot, and who does not will endure punishment.'[96] As we saw above, as early as Menander, the fair is a metaphor for life with its crowds, markets, thefts, dice-playing, entertainments, an idea that takes on a theological interpretation among church fathers: 'Take this life as a *panegyris*; if you negotiate, you'll win. For greater things will be exchanged for smaller, and transient for eternal things. Once the *panegyris* is over, you will not have another moment'.[97]

Returning to antiquity, we know that Classical and Hellenistic festivals with market fairs did indeed have looser regulations, which together with

---

95   Pl. *Leg.* 11.915d–e. See Bresson 2015, 225–59 for the institutions and regulations of the civic agora; 305–38 of the emporion.

96   Priscus (fifth century) fr. 1.39–40 Bornmann; *cf.* Clem. Alex. *QDS* 32.2 = 181.1 Stählin. Serving rich and poor: Chorikios (sixth century) *Laud. Marc.* 1.83–9; 2.58–65 Förster-Richtsteig; no price equivalency: Basileios (fifth century) *PG* 31, 281c; 32, 1153; benefits depending on ability to negotiate: Joseph Bryennios (14th–15th century), 2.220–1, 416; 3.92, 94 Boulgares, as cited by Koukoules 1949, 271 n. 5.

97   Life as a *panegyris*: Men. *PCG* 871 (= fr. 416b Körte); theological significance: Theologos Gregorios *PG* 37, 930; M. Basileios *PG* 31, 281. See Koukoules 1949, 270–83 for many more passages of related character. But festivals and fairs were also places of excessive spending: e.g. Asterios *Or.* 4.5.1; 4.7.1 Datema; Julian, *Antiochicus* 35.362d.

the popular tax-exemptions were most likely intended to encourage trade.[98] Inscriptions do detail fair regulations, so that at first sight one might think that they pay close attention to the mechanisms of transactions. But their contents suggest that fairs were perceived as a different economic environment, with different types of interference, and one where the religious orchestration was pivotal to generating trust. Fairs had their own ways of circumscribing, physically and symbolically, such environments, as part of their strategies aimed at construing a community of buyers and sellers as a community of worshippers and vice versa.

To begin with, it is clear that different types of markets came together at these fairs and there was a preoccupation with who could trade what. For example, slaves were allowed to sell at the mysteries of Andania, while at the Samian Heraion only licensed shopkeepers were admitted; at the Amarysia at Eretria, anyone could buy and sell whatever they wished, and could do so tax-free.[99] We find details on where exactly in the sanctuary stalls could be set up.[100] A number of *agoranomoi* are attested, but their purview seems rather different from their duties in the civic *agora*. At Andania, which incidentally has a history similar to the *panegyris* of Athena Ilias — likely establishment in the fourth, renewal in the first century BCE — it is the city's weights that were used, and the *agoranomos* had to ensure that the products were sold unadulterated and pure (*adola kai kathara*); he was not, however, allowed to set a price or time for the transaction, limiting his power.[101]

In fact, stories of cheating at fairs abound not just in the popular tradition of 19th-century rural Greece — Dio's verdict on fairs as the arena for the perversion of truths suggests that the temptation was no different in antiquity. Price determination and fairness, alongside the authenticity of the goods, are frequent concerns in the *panegyris*-inscriptions. Perhaps as a response, fairs employed concrete means to mark out an integrated religious and economic space. Economic transactions were cloaked in religious symbolism and imagery and

---

98   See Chandezon 2000, 85–92 on the many examples of tax exemption; De Ligt 1993, app. 1.C; De Ligt-de Neeve 411–13. See also the chapter by Horster, this volume.

99   Slaves at Andania *LSCG* 65.102 = Gawlinski 2012, 86, line 102; Heraion of Samos: Lupu 2005, no. 18; Eretria: *LSCG* 92.32–5 (=*RO* 73). See Chandezon 2000, 85–92 on the many examples of tax exemption; De Ligt 1993, app. 1.C. See also Horster, this volume.

100 Spaces and places set apart for markets/stands: Andania *LSCG* 65.99–101, with Gawlinksi 2012 ad loc.; Tegea *LSCG* 67.26–27; selling in the sanctuary: Eretria *LSCG* 92.32 (=*RO* 73); Panionion: Sokolowski 1970, ll. 2–4; *kapeloi* renting out a specific number of structures at the Samian Heraion: Lupu 2005, 18.5–8; p. 291 for examples from non-*panegyris* contexts.

101 Gawlinski 2012, 86 lines 99–103; 216–18, with Chandezon 2000, 82–3; 79–85 for the differing powers of the *agoranomoi*, for which see also Robert 1963, 67–9. The agoranomos at Andania is also responsible for water management and bathing: ll. 103–10.

even seemingly included in the ritual arrangements. As mentioned above, the existence and use of *panegyris* or festival coinage is debated, but it seems likely that at least some festivals, and certainly major religious centres, had their own currency, not dissimilar perhaps to the Coquille St.-Jacques of the pilgrimage to Santiago de Compostela, which became itself an object of exchange. Special weights and measures also participated in the symbolic delineation of discrete transactional spaces: weights have been found belonging to a shrine's divinity, whose name was inscribed in the genitive, the best example being the nearly 500 specimens from the sanctuary of Zeus at Olympia, but (in much smaller numbers) also at Delphi. Apollo's sanctuary at Thermon, which boasted a famous *panegyris*; possibly that of Artemis Amarysia, about whose fair we also know a reasonable amount; the Heraion at Samos and the Amphiaraion at Oropos provide further examples of the practice. Here it was the gods who supervised the correct weight and value of the merchandise.[102]

The resulting creation of a special sphere of exchange was promptly matched by the establishment of mechanisms enabling access to it. Inscriptions show a recurrent concern with the conversion of currency, weights and measures. So the Delphic Amphictyony set a standard exchange rate; Athenians decreed weights and measures valid during the festival at Eleusis.[103] Money changers and lenders were typical sights at *panegyreis*, a significant and feared presence at festival markets whose exact financial activity across time might deserve a separate treatment.[104]

---

102 Hitzl 1996, esp. 77; 96–104; 121–32. At Olympia, 1 silver and 483 bronze weights have been found; two of these ended up in the sanctuary of Artemis at Lousoi and at Aigeira. These weights are inscribed with the names of their deities, perhaps vouching for their value: Διός (Olympia); Ἀμφιαράου (Oropos, Petrakos 1997 no. 748–9); Ἥρης (Samos, inscribed on all four sides, see Hitzl 1996, 77 no. 504; 126–7, pl. 42a, b); Delphi, inscribed *hiera* ibid. 122 (Perdrizet 1908, nos. 708–9 (other weights: nos. 708–24)). Thermos: *IG* ix² 1, 83; *SEG* 40.461: Ἀπόλλωνος | Μ(νᾶ) | Θερμίου (*c.* 200 BCE). Amarynthos: a lead weight inscribed with Amarysia allegedly from the area of the sanctuary of Artemis Amarysia (*AE* 1890, 21); *cf.* Fachard, *AR* 2016–17 on the recently identified shrine. A classical bronze weight inscribed Ἀπόλλωνος Δηλίο has recently been found at Zara, near Karystos *SEG* 51.1128; 56.1042 (A. Chatzidimitriou, *AD* 52 B2 (1997) [2003], 407–9). Cf. *SEG* 63.250 (between Troizen and Hermione, possibly of Apollo Platanistiou).

103 Delphic Amphictyony: *Syll.*³ 729=*CID* iv.127 (late second century); Eleusis: *IG* ii² 1013, 49ff (late second century); *cf.* the use of bronze coins only at Pergamon under Hadrian: *OGIS* 484. Note also the dedication by an *agoranomos* of the *panegyris* of a Hermes *zygostates* at Ilion: *I Ilion* 1 (imperial).

104 Presence of money changers: Thonemann 2011, 117–18; Dagron 2012; Horden – Purcell 2000, 432, noting 109 moneychangers with some twenty-five associates and assistants in their train at the fair of St. Gilles in the Provence in 1148 CE.

Finally, we could also read into some of the surviving documents that an intimate connection was felt to exist between ritual and economic procedures. In a fourth-century inscription detailing the *panegyris* at the Panionion, another festival renewal, the regulation on sacrificial procedure immediately follows that governing the sellers. A more pointed integration of religious and economic business may be seen in the second-century festival for Artemis Leukophryene at Magnesia on the Maeander. Recalling the glamorous processions of the Byzantine fairs discussed above, the setting up of the statue, procession, sacrifice and the 'management of the sales' constitute the proceedings of the first day, in the presence of an 'agora filled up' (πληθυούσης ἀγορᾶς l. 38) with a host of dignitaries 'in conspicuous robes' (ἐπισήμοις l. 39).[105]

More broadly then, we might conclude that festivals with fairs and their sanctuaries expended a lot of effort upon the creation of an *ad hoc* community of exchange, which in turn provided a level of trust and an enforcement mechanism in a temporary economic environment. Such a sense of community may be particularly relevant when seen in the wider context of the mentalities underlying buying and selling in the ancient world. Nicholas Purcell has recently reminded us that buying and selling, the transfer of property, were highly loaded, psychologically complex processes in a society where market exchange was rare, novel, or both. The article has a telling title taken from Varro's *De re rustica* '*Quod enim alterius fuit, id ut fiat meum, necesse est aliquid intercedere*' – 'For something which has belonged to someone else to become mine, something needs to happen in between', loosely interpreted as 'transactions ... cannot help but modify ... who both parties are, and the differences between them ..., as well ... as the nature of what is transferred ... '.[106] In other words, the economic transaction resembles a ritual *process*, which also entails a change of interpersonal identity. Varro cites the Republican jurist Manius Manilius, who notes that for some nine, marginally different kinds of sale, state regulation laid out a particular practice, involving highly formulaic, lengthy declarations on the quality of the object to be sold, differing for different forms of livestock: sheep, goats, horses, and, in particular, herdsmen and, in the Aedilian edict, complex consumer protection rules for the selling of slaves. Without getting into the thorny issue of Roman contract law, it is helpful to keep in mind that property transfers were conceptualised as protracted, highly ritualised processes even when backed by state institutions.[107]

---

105   Panionion (350–23 BCE): Sokolowski 1970, ll. 1–4; Magnesia (first half of second century BCE): *LSAM* 33A, 34–5, with Gauthier 1990.

106   Varro, *Rust.* 2.1.15; Purcell 2012, 81–2.

107   Varro *Rust.* 2 *passim*; 2.10 on slaves.

Against this background fairs might be seen to have their own forms of ritualisation of exchange. The 'making of community' through the constant overlap of religious and economic stimuli and symbols, behavioural imperatives, and interactions across social boundaries at fair festivals becomes so important as it builds up to what Marcel Mauss has termed a continued state of 'effervescence' characteristic of ancient attitudes towards buying and selling, producing the anticipation and excitement conveyed in the reports of *panegyreis* through the ages.[108] Purcell's notion that the religious dimension of festivals delineates social relations among worshippers that parallel their economic interaction could be taken a step further: fairs aim to blend the religious and economic dimensions; and if 'the encounter between buyer and seller deserved ... a part in the religious framework', it is the blurring of the difference between giving and receiving, selling and buying within that religious framework that facilitates the transaction.[109]

Seen in this light, it is no coincidence that many ancient and Byzantine fairs especially traded in those goods for which transactions were of greater complexity, and thus required a greater degree of ritualisation — that is to say, cattle and slaves in particular.[110] A late-third century inscription relating, once again, to the renewal and reorganisation of an old festival, of Apollo at Aktion in Western Greece, is particularly concerned with the slave market.[111] Once again, the fair is in a state of financial disarray. It is to be bailed out by the Akarnanian *koinon* which in return seizes 50% of the revenue from slave sales: the most complex transaction in the ancient conception of sale is here facilitated by enlarging the catchment area, publicising the fair as a league festival to a significantly broader audience and potential community of buying worshippers, or worshipping buyers. Once again, religious appeal and a cultic framework are used to increase revenues, in turn supporting and furthering

---

108   Mauss 1923/4, 96–7.

109   Purcell 2012, 96.

110   Cattle and slaves dominate, but precious metals, textiles and other livestock are also mentioned: *e.g.* St. Cyprian/Leukothea: Cassiod. *Var.* 8.33, *c.* 527 CE, slaves, livestock, textiles; Ps. Ioh. Chrys. *Hom. Suppl.* 3.3 (*PG* 64.436b) garments and cattle; Pylaia: *Paroemiogr.* 1, no. 36, 135: slaves; Aktion: *LSS* 45, 31–4 slaves; Tithorea: Paus. 10.32.15: slaves, livestock, clothes, precious metals. Baitokaike: *IGLS* vii, 4028.D 37–9 with Dignas 2002, 157: slaves, cattle and other animals; Epict. *Diatr.* 2.14.23–9: livestock, oxen. Working animals and slaves grouped in a law from Abdera: Chandezon 2003, no. 23. For war-booty sold at *panegyreis*, see Chaniotis 2005, 133; Plb. 4.77.5. The same set of products stand out in Byzantine fairs: Koukoules 1949, 278–80; Vryonis 1971, 15–16; De Ligt, De Neeve 1988, 400–3 on comparative evidence; Chandezon 2000, 93–4.

111   *IG* ix.1² 2, 583=Pouilloux 1960, no. 29=*LSS* 45 (216 BCE); Str. 7.7.6; Habicht 1957; Blawatsky 1974; Czech-Schneider 2002.

the religious attraction. We might suppose that the high degree of ritualisation required for the selling of slaves was more easily achieved in a religious environment.

And to bring in a final point, the same joint religious and economic dynamic of community creation might well be what made fairs an important node of international trade and attractive to foreign merchants. Instead of the regulations and bureaucracy of the Athenian agora or the urban market of Byzantine Thessaloniki, the enhancement of cohesive processes of 'even imperfectly understood shared religion lubricates economic reciprocity and helps to guarantee trust'.[112] The ancient sources know well that shared ritual often counters the uncertainty accompanying cross-cultural trade. The most famous instance of ritualised exchange is that of the 'silent trade' between the Phoenicians and the gold-trafficking people of the desert described by Herodotus, which took place somewhere at the edges of the earth beyond the pillars of Herakles (with parallels in many other societies).[113] Ultimately, at fairs everyone was a *xenos* and fairs can be seen as particularly powerful mechanisms for turning *xenoi* (foreigners) into *xenoi* (guest-friends). An inscription from Kyzikos regarding a tax-free fair attended by 'merchants and foreigners from the whole *oikoumene*' and praised for its philanthropy, explicitly prescribes that foreigners must be given a portion of the sacrificial meat, as if to overcome cultural boundaries through communal feasting. In the Byzantine record, there are numerous examples of Muslim merchants attending Greek *panegyreis*, sometimes resulting in conversion.[114]

If fairs always existed in a milieu of uncertainty, security sometimes lay in their liminality — often geographical, in rural places; always temporal, given their limited duration. Incidentally, an archaic institution in Attica were the *ephoriai agorai*, as if to push trade with non-locals as far as possible to the edges of the state. One of the archaic lead tablets attesting cross-cultural trade found in southern France states that the transaction is to take place in

---

112   Purcell 2012, 96.

113   Hdt. 4.196; on silent trade worldwide, see e.g. Bovill 1929; de Moraes Farias 1974.

114   Kyzikos: *SEG* 4.707=*IGR* iv 144=*IMT Kyz* Kapu Dağ, 1431 (41–54 CE). This *panegyris* is known particularly for its itinerant traders, who must also have included travelling artisans for whom such institutions were vital in marketing their skills. Perhaps the many mythical mobile craftsmen in Greece, such as the Telchines, who might have gone from festival to festival, give us a hint of the importance and frequency of *panegyreis*. Conversions of seafaring merchants after rescue: the Saracen merchant turning Christian; an Egyptian fisherman: Anrich 1913–17 i. 408–9; 415. For a list of conversion stories in the saints' lives see Vryonis 1971, 39. *Cf.* Thonemann 2011, 126–7 on riots breaking out between Christians and Turks at Chonai; 127 n. 80 on the religious and ethnic mixture at *panegyreis* in various periods.

the no-man's land, on a boat in the middle of the Rhône.[115] Ancient authors were acutely aware that geographical liminality could become commercial and cross-cultural centrality: Livy describes the festival of Poseidon at Isthmia, opportunely located between the two opposite seas (... *propter opportunitatem loci, per duo diversa maria* ...), as 'furnishing mankind with abundance of all wares', and where 'the market was a meeting-place for Asia and Greece'.[116] The seeming paradox that Isthmia's location at the edges of two seas actually made it a nexus nicely illustrates how liminality and hybridity — geographical, temporal, cultural — might turn into economic opportunity.

6   Conclusions

I hope to have offered some ideas on how the religious and the economic were intrinsically interlinked at festivals with market fairs, from the archaic to the Byzantine period. A long-term perspective helps to make sense of a number of lasting features common to both ancient and Byzantine *panegyreis*, and may be justified as heuristic despite the differences in cultural, belief and economic systems. Fairs appear to have been construed as discrete transactional spaces with enforcement mechanisms different from those deployed by civic or other authorities. Central to the functioning of these fairs was a religious community that was at the same time also an economic community, where social relations in a religious context not only came to mirror, but were eventually inextricably intertwined, with those in an economic context.

Throughout this essay, I have tried to disentangle some of the strategies festivals deployed to construe such a community of worshippers as a community of buyers and vice versa. Broadly, these strategies can be grouped into four different areas. Firstly, the fair was an overwhelmingly sensory experience, communicated in the literary accounts through dwelling on the crowds and the splendour attending the events, and characterised by a synaesthesia of religious and economic stimuli, where ritual arena and market turn into one and the same venue. Secondly, the resulting emotional charge, a continuous state of 'effervescence', underlies the breaking down of the boundaries between otherwise discrete spheres of exchange. Myth/legend and ritual tie into one another to create a joint religious-economic community where giving and receiving, selling and buying blend into a single set of transactions, entangled in several cycles of reciprocity and creating a community of moral

---

115   Ampolo 1999; Pech-Maho tablet: SEG 38.1036.
116   Liv. 33.32.2 (tr. after Sage); Str. 8.6.20.

interdependence. On the one hand, the religious sphere of exchange with the divine becomes enmeshed with the economic sphere among humans; on the other, different types of markets also come together: as is particularly evident in the fairs of Byzantine Anatolia, *panegyreis* integrated international economic mobility and local demand.

Thirdly, investing in an often traditional *panegyris* can boost trade in times of economic crisis. In antiquity, festivals with market fairs, though ubiquitous, are on the whole poorly represented in the record. The case of the comparatively well-documented *panegyris* of Athena Ilias has shown how capitalising on the memories associated with the *panegyris* with all their affective charge could ensure the continued attractiveness and gravitational pull of the festival through periods of economic downturn. The success of a fair festival lay in the quality of the promotion of the shrine and its worshipping community in an ever-widening catchment area. Forging and dwelling on a memory can be seen to form part of an aggressive advertising strategy to which the collective consumption of beliefs and rituals is as central as material transactions within a temporary community of exchange.

And finally, in environments of uncertainty and anonymity it is important to draw attention to the high degree of ritualisation in many exchange practices in antiquity as a prerequisite for building trust. In the international, often cross-cultural and trans-religious milieu of the *panegyris*, festival- or sanctuary-specific weights and coinages contributed to the symbolic delineation of this separate sphere of exchange, and facilitated trade between *xenoi* by furthering the inseparability of religious and economic transactions. In theory, then, the transaction's validity lay within the purview of the god in question; in practice, we might wonder whether the particular version of Maussian effervescence typical of fairs — synaesthetic stimulation, overpowering emotion, being dazzled by all the spiritual and material goods to be exchanged — may not actually have intensified the peculiar feature of exchange often thought especially characteristic of life of the Mediterranean Sea from antiquity through the early modern period: that is, the persistent cohabitation of glut and starvation, of risk and opportunity.

Bibliography

Alexiou, M. 1982. "Literary Subversion and the Aristocracy in Twelfth-Century Byzantium: A Stylistic Analysis of the *Timarion* (ch. 6–10)", *Byzantine and Modern Greek Studies* 8, 29–45.

Ampolo, C. 1992. "The Economics of Sanctuaries in Southern Italy and Sicily", in *Economics of Cult in the Ancient Greek World: Proceedings of the Uppsala Symposium 1990*, eds. T. Linders and B. Alroth, Uppsala, 25–8.

Ampolo, C. 1999. "La frontiera dei Greci come luogo del rapporto e dello scambio: i mercati di frontiera fino al V secolo a.C.", in *Confini e frontiera nella grecità d'Occidente: atti del trentasettesimo Convegno di studi sulla Magna Grecia, Taranto, 3–6 ottobre 1999*, ed. A. Stazio, Taranto, 451–64.

Andreau, J.M. 2001. "Markets, Fairs, and Monetary Loans: Cultural History and Economic History in Roman Italy and Hellenistic Greece", in *Money, Labour and Land: Approaches to the Economies of Ancient Greece,* eds. P. Cartledge, E.E. Cohen, and L. Foxhall, London, 113–29.

Anrich, G. 1913–1917. *Hagios Nikolaos: der heilige Nikolaos in der griechischen Kirche. Texte und Untersuchungen*, Leipzig.

Aufhauser, J.B. 1913. *Miracula S. Georgii*, Leipzig.

Baldwin, B. trans. 1984. *Timarion: Translated with Introduction and Commentary*. Detroit.

Barnes, C.L.H. 2006. "The Ferries of Tenedos", *Historia* 55, 167–77.

Berlin, A. 2002. "Ilion before Alexander: A Fourth Century B.C. Ritual Deposit", *Studia Troica* 12, 131–65.

Bingöl, O. 2007. *Magnesia am Mäander*. Istanbul.

Blawatsky, T. 1974. "Über den Sklavenmarkt am Aktion", *Klio* 56.2, 497–500.

Bresson, A. 2015. *The Making of the Ancient Greek Economy. Institutions, Markets and Growth in the City-States*, Princeton.

Boulgares, E. and Mandakases, T. eds. 1768–84. *Ioseph monachou tou Bryenniou ta heurethenta*, 3 vols. Leipzig.

Bynum, C.W. 2007. *Wonderful Blood: Theology and Practice in Late Medieval Northern Germany and Beyond*, Philadelphia.

Calame, C. 1991. "'Mythe' et 'rite' en Grèce: des catégories indigènes?", *Kernos* 4, 179–204.

Cavanaugh, M.B. 1996. *Eleusis and Athens: Documents in Finance, Religion, and Politics in the Fifth Century B.C.*, Atlanta.

Chandezon, C. 2000. "Foires et panégyries dans le monde grec classique et hellénistique", *Revue des Études Grecques* 113, 70–100.

Chandezon, C. 2003. *L'Élevage en Grèce (fin Ve–fin Ier s. a.C.) : l'apport des sources épigraphiques*, Bordeaux.

Chaniotis, A. 1995. "Sich selbst feiern? Städtische Feste des Hellenismus im Spannungsfeld von Religion und Politik", in *Stadtbild und Bürgerbild im Hellenismus: Kolloquium, München, 24. bis 26. Juni 1993*, eds. M. Wörrle and P. Zanker, München, 147–72.

Chaniotis, A. 2006. "Rituals between Norms and Emotions: Rituals as Shared Experience and Memory", in *Ritual and Communication in the Graeco-Roman World*, ed. E. Stavrianopoulou, Liège, 211–38.

Chaniotis, A. 2005. *War in the Hellenistic World. A Social and Cultural History*, Malden, MA.

Clinton, K. 1989. "Hadrian's Contribution to the Renaissance of Eleusis", in *The Greek Renaissance in the Roman Empire: Papers from the Tenth British Museum Classical Colloquium*, eds. S. Walker and A. Cameron, London, 56–68.

Csapo, E. and Wilson, P. 2015. "Drama Outside Athens in the Fifth and Fourth Centuries BC", *Trends in Classics* 7.2, 316–95.

Curty, O. 2015. *Gymnasiarchika. Recueil et analyse des inscriptions de l'époque hellénistique en l'honneur des gymnasiarques*, Paris.

Czech-Schneider, R. 2002. "Das Apollonheiligtum von Aktion in hellenistischer Zeit: Überlegungen zum wirtschaftlichen Verhältnis zwischen Heiligtum und profanem Inhaber", *Klio* 84, 76–100.

Dagron, G. trans. 1978. *Vie et miracles de Sainte Thècle: texte grec, traduction et commentaire*, Brussels.

Dagron, G. 2012. *Idées byzantines*, vol. 2, Paris.

Datema, C. 1970. *Asterius of Amasea, Homilies I–XIV: Text, Introduction and Notes*. Leiden.

Davies, J.K. 2007. "The Origins of the Festivals, especially Delphi and the Pythia", in *Pindar's Poetry, Patrons, and Festivals: from Archaic Greece to the Roman Empire*, eds. S. Hornblower and C. Morgan, Oxford, 47–69.

De Ligt, L. 1993. *Fairs and Markets in the Roman Empire: Economic and Social Aspects of Periodic Trade in a Pre-industrial Society*, Amsterdam.

De Ligt, L. and De Neeve, P.W. 1988. "Ancient Periodic Markets: Festivals and Fairs", *Athenaeum* 66, 391–416.

Dignas, B. 2002. *Economy of the Sacred in Hellenistic and Roman Asia Minor*, Oxford.

Dillon, M. 1998. *Pilgrims and Pilgrimage in Ancient Greece*, London.

Ellis-Evans, A. 2016. "The Koinon of Athena Ilias and its Coinage", *American Journal of Numismatics* 28, 105–58.

Ellis-Evans, A. 2018. "Memnon and Mentor of Rhodes in the Troad", *Numismatic Chronicle* 178, 33–69.

Ellis-Evans, A. 2019. *The Kingdom of Priam. Lesbos and the Troad between Anatolia and the Aegean*, Oxford.

Epstein, S.R. 1994. "Regional Fairs, Institutional Innovation, and Economic Growth in Late Medieval Europe", *Economic History Review* 47, 459–82.

Frayn, J.M. 1993. *Markets and Fairs in Roman Italy. Their Social and Economic Importance from the Second Century BC to the Third Century AD*, Oxford.

von Fritze, H. 1902. "Die Münzen von Ilion", in *Troja und Ilion: Ergebnisse der Ausgrabungen in den vorhistorischen und historischen Schichten von Ilion, 1870–1894*. Vol. 2, ed. W. Dörpfeld, Athens, 477–534.

von Fritze, H. 1903. "Zum griechischen Opferritual. Αἴρεσθαι und Καταστρέφειν", *Jahrbuch des Deutschen Archäologischen Instituts* 18, 58–67.

Gauthier, P. 1989. *Nouvelles inscriptions de Sardes II*, Geneva.

Gauthier, P. 1990. "Epigraphica", *Revue de Philologie* 64, 61–70.

Gawlinski, L. 2012. *The Sacred Law of Andania. A New Text with Commentary*, Berlin.

Habicht, C. 1957. "Eine Urkunde des Akarnanischen Bundes", *Hermes* 85, 86–122.

Habicht, C. 2006. "Versäumter Gottesdienst", *Historia* 55, 153–66.

Hart, M. 1981. "La dénonciation des festivités profanes dans le discours épiscopal et monastique, en Orient chrétien, à la fin du IVᵉ siècle", in *La Fête, pratique et discours: d'Alexandrie hellénistique à la mission de Besançon*, ed. F. Dunand, Paris, 123–47.

Harris, E. and Lewis, D. eds. 2016. *The Ancient Greek Economy: Markets, Households and City States*, Cambridge.

Hennig, J. 1943. "St. Nicholas' Bread", *Béaloideas* 13, 264–9.

Hitzl, K. 1996. *Die Gewichte griechischer Zeit aus Olympia*, Berlin.

Holleran, C. 2012. *Shopping in Ancient Rome. The Retail Trade in the Late Republic and the Principate*, Oxford.

Horden, P. and Purcell, N. 2000. *The Corrupting Sea: A Study of Mediterranean History*, Oxford.

Jaisle, K. 1907. *Die Dioskuren als Retter zur See bei Griechen und Römern und ihr Fortleben in christlichen Legenden*, Tübingen.

Jameson, M. 1983. "Famine in the Greek World", in *Trade and Famine in Classical Antiquity*, eds. P. Garnsey and C.R. Whittaker, Cambridge, 6–16.

Jim, T. 2014. *Sharing with the Gods. Aparchai and Dekatai in Ancient Greece*, Oxford.

Klon, S. 1875. *Epigraphai tes nesou Surou*, Athens.

Knoepfler, D. 2010. "Les agonothètes de la Confédération d'Athéna Ilias: une interprétation nouvelle des données épigraphiques et ses conséquences pour la chronologie des émissions monétaires du Koinon", *Studi Ellenistici* 14, 33–62.

Koukoules, P. I. 1949. *Βυζαντινῶν βίος καὶ πολιτισμός*, Athens.

Kowalzig, B. 2007. *Singing for the Gods. Performances of Myth and Ritual in Archaic and Classical Greece*, Oxford.

Lagarde, P. de ed. 1979. *Iohannis Euchaitorum Metropolitae quae in codice Vaticano Graeco 676 supersunt*, Amsterdam (reprint of the Göttingen 1882 edition).

Laiou, A.E. 1980/81. "The Byzantine Economy in the Mediterranean Trade System: Thirteenth–Fifteenth Centuries", *Dumbarton Oaks Papers* 34/35, 177–222.

Laiou, A.E. 2000. "Exchange and Trade: Seventh–Twelfth Centuries", in *The Economic History of Byzantium* 2, ed. A.E. Laiou, Washington DC, 696–770.

Lampros, S.P. ed. 1879. *Michaēl Akominatou tou Chōniatou Ta sōzomena*, 2 vols., Athens.

Lawall, M.L. 2002. "Ilion before Alexander: Amphoras and Economic Archaeology", *Studia Troica* 12, 197–243.

Leemans, J. ed. 2003. *'Let Us Die That We May Live': Greek Homilies on Christian Martyrs from Asia Minor, Palestine and Syria (c. AD 350–AD 450)*, London.

Lefèvre, F. and Pillot, W. 2015. "La confédération d'Athéna Ilias: administration et pratiques financières", *Revue des Études Grecques* 128.1, 1–27.

Lemerle, P.E. 1979. *Les plus anciens recueils des miracles de Saint Démétrius et la pénétration des Slaves dans les Balkans*, Paris.

Little, L. 1978. *Religious Poverty and the Profit Economy in Medieval Europe*, Ithaca, NY.

Lombard-Jourdan, A. 1984. "Fairs", in *Dictionary of the Middle Ages*, vol. 4, ed. J.R. Strayer, New York, 582–90.

Lübeck, K. 1909. "Der hl. Phokas von Sinope", *Historisches Jahrbuch* 30, 743–61.

Lupu, E. 2005. *Greek Sacred Law. A Collection of New Documents (NGSL)*, Leiden.

Ma, J. 2007. "Dating the New Decree of the Confederation of Athena Ilias", *Epigraphica Anatolica* 40, 55–7.

MacMullen, R. 1970. "Market-Days in the Roman Empire", *Phoenix* 24, 333–41.

Mauss, M. 1923/24. "Essai sur le don: forme et raison de l'échange dans les sociétés archaïques", *L'Année sociologique n. s.* 1, 30–186.

Müller, C. 2014. "A *koinon* after 146? Reflections on the Political and Institutional Situation of Boeotia in the Late Hellenistic Period", in *The Epigraphy and History of Boeotia: New Finds, New Perspectives*, ed. N. Papazarkadas, Leiden, 119–46.

Mystakides, N. 1899. "Ἀρχαιολογικαὶ μελεταὶ Μαυροπούλου καὶ Ἱεριαχίου", *Δωδώνη* 2, 73–82.

Nilsson, M.P. 1906. *Griechische Feste von religiöser Bedeutung, mit Ausnahme der attischen*. Leipzig.

Nilsson, M.P. 1955–1961. *Geschichte der griechischen Religion*, second edition, Munich.

Nollé, J. 1982. *Nundinas habere et instituere. Epigraphische Zeugnisse zur Einrichtung und Gestaltung von ländlichen Märkten in Afrika und der Provinz Asia*, Hildesheim – Zurich – New York.

Nollé, J. 2014. "Panegyris Coinage – eine moderne Geisterprägung", *Chiron* 44, 285–323.

Oikonomides, N. 1952. "Hagios Phokas o Sinopeus. Latreia kai diadosis autes", *Archeion Pontou* 17, 184–219.

Orsi, P. 1899. "Nuove chiese byzantine nel territorio di Siracusa", *Biblische Zeitschrift* 8, 613–42.

Pandermalis, D. 2000. "Δίον 1998: Ἑκατόμβες καὶ Σωτήρια", *Τὸ Ἀρχαιολογικὸ Ἔργο στη Μακεδονία και στη Θράκη* 12, 291–8.

Papadopoulos-Kerameus, A. 1896. *Sbornik istochnikov po istorii Trapezundskoĭ imperii I*, (repr. Amsterdam, 1965) St. Petersburg.

Parker, R. 1996. *Athenian Religion. A History*. Oxford.

Parker, R. 2004. "New 'Panhellenic' Festivals in Hellenistic Greece", in *Mobility and Travel in the Mediterranean from Antiquity to the Middle Ages*, eds. R. Schlesier and U. Zellmann, Münster, 9–22.

Parker, R. 2011. *On Greek Religion*, Ithaca, NY.

Perdrizet, M.P. 1908. *Fouilles de Delphes V.1. Monuments figurés: Petits bronzes, terres-cuites, antiquités diverses*, Paris.

Petrakos, V. 1997. *Hoi epigraphes tou Oropou*, Athens.

Pillot, W. 2016. "Ilion, Athéna Ilias et les Détroits, d'Alexandre le Grand à Antiochos III. Identité régionale d'une communauté politique et de son sanctuaire, au carrefour d'influences européennes et asiatiques", in, *Identité régionale, identités civiques autour des Détroits des Dardanelles et du Bosphore (Ve siècle av. J.-C. – IIe siècle apr. J.-C.)*, eds. M. Dana and F. Prêteux, Paris, 133–70.

Platt, V. 2011. *Facing the Gods: Epiphany and Representation in Graeco-Roman Art, Literature, and Religion*, Cambridge.

Pleket, H.W. 1964. *Epigraphica: Texts on the Economic History of the Greek World I*, Leiden.

Pouilloux, J. 1960. *Choix d'inscriptions grecques: textes, traductions et notes*, Paris.

Psoma, S. 2007. "Profitable Networks: Coinages, Panegyris and Dionysiac Artists", *Mediterranean Historical Review* 22.2, 237–55.

Psoma, S. 2008. "Panegyris Coinage", *AJN* 20, 227–55.

Purcell, N. 2012. "'Quod enim alterius fuit, id ud fiat meum necesse est aliquid intercedere' (Varro). The Anthropology of Buying and Selling in Ancient Greece and Rome: An Introductory Sketch", in *Anthropologie de l'Antiquité*, eds. P. Payen and E. Scheid-Tissinier, Turnhout, 81–98.

Radermacher, M.L. 1904. "St. Phocas", *Archiv für Religionswissenschaft* 7, 445–52.

Reader, I. 2014. *Pilgrimage in the Marketplace*, London.

Riedel, S. 2016. *Darstellungen der Göttin Athena auf den Münzen von Pergamon und Ilion*, Bonn.

Robert, L. 1966. *Monnaies antiques en Troade*, Paris.

Robert, L. 1963. "*Samothrace. Vol. 2 part 1: The inscriptions on stone* by Karl Lehmann, P.M. Fraser", *Gnomon* 35, 50–79.

Robert, L. 1971. *Les Gladiateurs de l'orient grec*. Amsterdam.

Rose, C.B. 2014. *The Archaeology of Greek and Roman Troy*, New York.

Rose, C.B. 2015. "The Homeric Memory Culture of Roman Ilion", in *Cultural Memories in the Roman Empire*, eds. K. Galinski and K. Lapatin, Los Angeles, 134–52.

Rutherford, I. 2013. *State Pilgrims and Sacred Observers: A Study of Theoria and Theoroi*, Cambridge.

Schmitt-Pantel, P. 1981. "Le festin dans la fête de la cité grecque hellénistique", in *La Fête, pratique et discours: d'Alexandrie hellénistique à la mission de Besançon*, ed. F. Dunand, Paris, 85–99.

Ševcenko, N.P. 1983. *The Life of Saint Nicholas in Byzantine Art*, Turin.

Sigalas, A. 1924. "Ή διασκευή των υπό του Χρυσίππου παραδεδομένων θαυμάτων του αγίου Θεοδώρου," *ΕΕΒΣ* 1, 295–339.

Sillitoe, P. 2006. "Why Spheres of Exchange?", *Ethnology* 45, 1–23.

Smarczyk, B. 1990. *Untersuchungen zur Religionspolitik und politischen Propaganda Athens im Delisch-Attischen Seebund*, München.

Sokolowski, F. 1970. "Règlement relatif à la célébration des Panionia", *Bulletin de Correspondance Hellénique* 94, 109–12.

Stengel P. 1903. "Zum griechischen Opferritual. Αἴρεσθαι und Καταστρέφειν", *Jahrbuch des deutschen archäologischen Instituts* 18, 113–23.

Stavrianopulou, E. 2006. "Normative Interventions in Greek Rituals: Strategies for Justification and Legitimation", in *Ritual and Communication in the Graeco-Roman World*, ed. E. Stavrianopulou, Liège, 131–49.

Thonemann, P. 2011. *The Maeander Valley. A Historical Geography from Antiquity to Byzantium*, Cambridge.

Thonemann, P. 2015. *The Hellenistic World: Using Coins as Sources*, Cambridge.

Thompson, E.P. 1971. "The Moral Economy of the English Crowd in the Eighteenth Century", *Past and Present* 50, 76–136.

Van de Vorst, C. 1911. "Saint Phocas", *Analecta Bollandiana* 30, 252–95.

Verlinden, C. 1963. "Markets and Fairs", in *The Cambridge Economic History of Europe from the Decline of the Roman Empire 3: Economic Organisation and Policies in the Middle Ages*, eds. M.M. Postan, E.E. Rich, and E. Miller, Cambridge, 119–53.

Vryonis, S. 1971. *The Decline of Medieval Hellenism in Asia Minor and the Process of Islamization from the Eleventh through the Fifteenth Century*, Berkeley, CA.

Vryonis, S. 1981. "The Panegyris of the Byzantine Saint", in *The Byzantine Saint: University of Birmingham 14th Spring Symposium of Byzantine Studies*, ed. S. Hackel, London, 196–227.

Wachsmuth, D. 1967. *Πόμπιμος ὁ δαίμων. Untersuchungen zu den antiken Sakralhandlungen bei Seereisen*, Berlin.

Wallrodt, S. 2002. "Ritual Activity in Late Classical Ilion: The Evidence from a Fourth Century B.C. Deposit of Loomweights and Spindlewhorls", *Studia Troica* 12, 179–96.

Woodhouse, W.J. 1897. *Aetolia: Its Geography, Topography, and Antiquities*, Oxford.

Yashaeva, T. 2011. *The Legacy of Byzantine Cherson*, Sevastopol – Austin.

Zika, C. 1988. "Hosts, Processions and Pilgrimages: Controlling the Sacred in Fifteenth-Century Germany", *Past and Present* 118, 25–64.

CHAPTER 13

Gods of Trust: Ancient Delos and the Modern Economics of Religion

Dan-el Padilla Peralta

1 Introduction: the Power of a Statue

In the second century of the Common Era, the Greek periegetic writer Pausanias commented in his *Description of Greece* that the island of Delos in the Aegean had previously been believed to be safe for traders on account of the god Apollo, singling out a wooden statue of the god that had long stood in Delos before making its way to another place sacred to Apollo on the Peloponnesian coastline.[1] Through this mention of the statue, the reader is invited to reflect on the connection between its previous abode in Delos and Delos' run of success as a major port. The illusion of mercantile security perpetuated by the statue was rudely shattered in 87 BCE, when the forces of King Mithridates VI of Pontos under the command of his lieutenant Menophanes sacked Delos in the course of their campaign against Rome and its allies in the Greek East. During the ensuing chaos and destruction, one of his soldiers hurled the statue into the sea. Yet according to Pausanias the aftermath of the sack confirmed the vindictive power of the offended god and his mistreated statue: Menophanes died in a confrontation with outraged merchants on his way out of Delos, and his king (much) later would commit suicide.[2] The statue itself fared fine in the end, bobbing on the waves of the Aegean until it arrived at its new destination on the Peloponnesian coast. The port and island of Delos, however, did not, sliding into a slump that worsened after a second exogenous

---

1   Paus. 3.23.3: 'For the (wooden) statue of Apollo which is now there [at Epidelion on the Peloponnesian coastline] used to stand at Delos. When Delos was a trading hub for the Greeks and was held to be secure for merchants on account of the god ...' (τὸ γὰρ τοῦ Ἀπόλλωνος ξόανον, ὃ νῦν ἐστιν ἐνταῦθα, ἐν Δήλῳ ποτὲ ἵδρυτο. τῆς γὰρ Δήλου τότε ἐμπορίου τοῖς Ἕλλησιν οὔσης καὶ ἄδειαν τοῖς ἐργαζομένοις διὰ τὸν θεὸν δοκούσης παρέχειν ...). I cannot explore here Pausanias' literary aims or the ambitions and generic standing of periegetic literature in the Second Sophistic. Usefully on his work and life, see Habicht 1985 for a fresh take on his work's 'shuttling' between local and translocal identity-formation, Whitmarsh 2010, 14–16.

2   Paus. 3.23.3–5, with Habicht 1985, 153–4 on the author's relish for stories of divine vengeance; cf. Strabo 10.5.4; Plut. *Sull.* 11; App. *Mith.* 28; Florus 1.40.8.

shock courtesy of an assault by pirates in 69. Three-quarters of a century later, the Augustan-era geographer Strabo remarked that in his time the island still had not recovered from the destruction unleashed by Mithridates' troops. Archaeological signs – chiefly in the form of a dramatic fall-off in monumental and commercial activity – and an apparent decline in population seem to bear him out.[3]

This essay will take Pausanias' characterisation of this statue and of the presence of the god on the island as a prompt for re-evaluating the entanglement of the sacred and the economic on Delos. One reading of this passage has construed the phrase 'on account of the god' (*dia ton theon*) as emphasising a 'system of commercial oaths and curses': both Greek and Roman merchants swore on statues and on altars near statues to finalise agreements.[4] But I will argue that Pausanias' words open the door to a more far-ranging reconstruction of the linkages between economic activity and religious observance. Specifically, I will contend that sacred artefacts such as statues *influenced* human behaviour, and in particular the behaviour of travellers and traders wary of being hustled or cheated, at sites that did double duty as centres for pilgrimage and hubs of commercial activity. This influence was by no means unidimensional or one-directional; it will be one of the secondary objectives of this contribution to explain why the interaction between the sacred and the mercantile on Delos is not simply another testament to the 'embeddedness' of religion in ancient life but evidence for the indispensable role of religious praxis in lowering barriers to economic transactions. Although pointing the arrow of influence in this direction is no indemnification against the charge of distorting ancient material to fit modern conceptual rubrics,[5] this chapter will have served its main purpose if it clarifies how modeling the causal and mediating role of religion in economic activity can contribute to a 21st-century understanding of the experience economy of Graeco-Roman religious observance.

What makes ancient Delos a fertile – if challenging – site for elucidating and testing a model with this aim in mind? Already in the eighth and seventh centuries, Delos, famed as the birthplace of the gods Apollo and Artemis, was a prominent node for Aegean cultic activity. By the late archaic and early classical period, the island's annual festival in honour of the god Apollo had become central to the religious self-identification, communal socialisation, and networking not only of resident Delians but of inhabitants of the neighbouring

---

3 Fundamental on Delos' archaeology: Bruneau 1970.
4 For this reading see Rauh 1993, 288; on the efficacy of oaths, n. 50 below.
5 Cautionary notes on this problem: Clark 2011, 247–8; but *cf.* Acton 2014, 16–22 for a spirited response to this line of argument and to the 'embeddedness paradigm' more broadly.

islands and of the European and Asia Minor coastlines.[6] Pausanias' remark about the location's appeal to traders alludes to the next phase of its development: an island of initially rather unprepossessing economic indicators, Delos eventually outclassed insular neighbours such as Gyaros and became the Aegean's most prosperous and dynamic *entrepôt*, in no small part because Apollo's festival and cult incentivised pilgrimage to the island – with an assist from the imperial Roman Republic, to be detailed further below.[7] Already in 1919, the French scholar Jean Hatzfeld hit the nail on the head: *because* Delos was a sanctuary and pilgrimage site, it became an international centre; *because* it was an international centre, it became a focus for commerce.[8] However, Hatzfeld's confidence in this causality has been somewhat elided in more recent work on the economic prowess of the island. Teasing out the relationship between religious activity and economic performance on Delos has, with the notable exception of Nicholas Rauh's publications, not assumed pride of place in the scholarly literature.

In the passage from Pausanias with which I began, the author attributes part of the commercial allure of Delos to the presence of Apollo, as embodied in the god's statue. I propose to demonstrate below how the built-up landscape of religious praxis on the island – the statues and shrines and votive dedications that attested devotion not only to Apollo but to other gods as well – augmented Delos' commercial appeal to travellers whose reasons for visiting toggled between pilgrimage and trade, in that blur characteristic of Mediterranean sojourners in other times and periods.[9] The key to grasping the full force of the island's charisma is to read this monumentalised landscape as generative of social capital among potential economic agents; the storage of this social capital in artefactual and monumental forms in turn encouraged cooperation and good dealing among future waves of visitors to the island.

Motivating this chapter's line of argument are two considerations. First, the importance of religious practices to generating social capital among economic actors in the ancient Mediterranean remains underappreciated. In light of the emerging consensus that for much of the first millennium BCE the ancient

---

6 Constantakopoulou 2007, ch. 2 offers a full account of this centuries-long development, with equal attention to the literary testimonies and to the archaeological evidence. Brief but incisive on Delian connectivity: Parker 2017, 15–16.

7 For the piddling tribute that Gyaros could barely muster in the Augustan age, see Strabo 10.5.3 with Reger 1994, 1.

8 'Parce que Délos était un sanctuaire, elle est devenue une ville internationale: parce qu'elle était une ville internationale, elle est devenue une place de commerce': Hatzfeld 1919, 36–7.

9 'Hem ziyaret hem tifaret': Horden – Purcell 2000, 445.

Mediterranean benefited from periods of sustained economic growth, it is all the more necessary to determine the role played in this development by religious and cultic practices. These practices, it will be shown, are far from being epiphenomenal and do not merely 'veil' commercial transactionality, as Filippo Coarelli would have it.[10] They may not be *drivers* of macro-economic growth to the same extent that demographic changes or large-scale alterations in production and consumption patterns are, but they did propel and maintain behaviours conducive to growth. Second, scholars studying the interface of religion and economics in the historical record, especially those working on cases and religions where doctrinal statements are lacking and access to the inner minds of devotees is unobtainable, can benefit from an approach that pairs material culture with the probabilistic modelling of those psychological states that facilitated the decision to engage in risky behaviour.

Ultimately, what is at stake in this contribution is not only how to theorise the relationship of economics and religion at sites of pilgrimage, but whether and to what extent ancient economic growth piggybacked on forms of religious observance. After furnishing some narrative context for the general economic efflorescence within which Delos reached its peak, this chapter will zero in on the private association as one of the main features of this efflorescence at Delos before proceeding to a re-interpretation of the materiality of religious observance on Delos through the bifocal lens of social-capital theory and ecological signalling theory.

2   Delos at the Crossroads of 'Wealthy Hellas' and Hegemonic Rome

The economic efflorescence of the Archaic, Classical, and early Hellenistic eastern Mediterranean worlds of the eighth through third centuries BCE has been the subject of multiple recent studies.[11] While the exact quantitative parameters of this efflorescence remain open to dispute, archaeological indices and demographic modelling point to several centuries of increasing *per capita* consumption and production, first in the eastern and then in

---

10   Coarelli 1984, 467.

11   Morris 2004, Ober 2010, and Ober 2015 make the case and provide the evidence for economic growth. On the new 'consensus' see also the essays on Greece in Scheidel *et al.* 2007 and the application of New Institutional Economics to Greek economic history in Bresson 2016; Manning 2018 for a history of Mediterranean economies. For the absence of religion from studies of the ancient economy see the Introduction to this volume. Demographic parameters: Hansen 2006.

the western Mediterranean.[12] Especially across the eastern Mediterranean, quality of life, real wages, and overall rates of economic growth reached premodern heights rivalled only by the economic efflorescence of the Dutch Republic in the late 16th and early 17th centuries. Numerous indications in the material and environmental record signal that this economic boom continued over the course of the last three centuries BCE and first century CE, the period of Rome's imperial ascendancy: a spike in the number of recovered shipwrecks, suggestive of increasing seaborne commerce; the intensification and commercialisation of agricultural production, as reflected *inter alia* in the large-scale traffic in slaves, for which Delos came to be an important hub; the acceleration of monetisation, driven by Roman minting on a scale surpassed only by Han China among premodern imperial formations; and, to sustain this monetisation, the unprecedented and centuries-long exploitation of mines, the environmental consequences of which are corroborated by Greenland ice-core samples that unequivocally show substantially higher concentrations of lead pollution in the atmosphere for this period.[13] There is no agreement on the direction of the causal arrows, on appropriate or even viable measures for quantifying GDP, or on the precise timing of the Roman economy's wax and wane. I will sidestep the vigorous debates surrounding each of these points and simply note that the economy of the Roman world, much like that of the Greek world which it took over, benefited from a favorable economic dispensation whose extension into the first and second centuries of the Common Era seems to bear out Gibbon's famous encomium to the Empire's felicity in the time of the Antonines.

Graeco-Roman economic growth was high *by premodern standards*: the presence of devastating diseases for which there was no cure, such as malaria,

---

12   A single-author account of the economics of the Hellenistic world to update Rostovtzeff 1941 remains to be written. For a descriptive overview, see Davies 1984; Hellenistic material is incorporated in Migeotte 2014 and Bresson 2016; among edited volumes Archibald *et al.* 2011 is the most comprehensive. Regional studies whose foci and lines of interpretation bear directly or indirectly on this section: Reger 1994 and 2007.

13   The literature on the economic boom is vast and continues to grow; for an analytic summary of the major bodies of evidence and an orientation to the main interpretive debates see Scheidel 2009. For late Hellenistic Delos' centrality to the traffic in slaves see Str. 14.5.2. A lively debate persists as to whether the Agora of the Italians functioned as a slave market: see Coarelli 2005 and the bibliography cited in Zarmakoupi 2018, 32–3 with 40 ns. 28–9. I cannot agree with Silver 2016 that the absence of firm archaeological evidence for the warehousing and auctioning of slaves on the island means that the majority of those being trafficked were 'self-sellers.' For the feedback loop between the traffic in slaves, eastern Mediterranean landholding patterns, and agricultural production see Eberle – Le Quéré 2017.

the absence of truly transformative and broadly disseminated technological innovations, and a variety of other social and institutional pressures acted to prevent first Greek and then Roman societies from breaking through the Malthusian ceiling and reaching higher levels of social and economic development.[14] It is a matter of ongoing controversy as to which of these factors – technological limitations, disease regimes, institutional and ideological configurations – was most responsible for the inability of the Graeco-Roman world to escape the Malthusian trap.[15] Ultimately, the efflorescence came to a brutal end: the motor of economic progress, possibly already grinding to a halt by the end of the first century CE, was halted by the second-century plagues that according to some calculations may have carried off a third of the Empire's population. Then came the military and political disasters of the third century, from which the western Empire was never able to fully recover; North Africa and the Greek East experienced a second economic uptick as the western Mediterranean began to unravel, only to experience their own plague-fueled economic implosion in the decades leading up to the Arab Conquest.[16]

With this *longue durée* trajectory outlined, we are now in position to come to grips with the specific case of late Hellenistic Delos. Already a bustling port during the Classical and early Hellenistic periods, Delos took off as the preeminent node for eastern Mediterranean commerce in the years after 167/6 BCE, when the Roman Senate granted *ateleia* to the island and entrusted its management and supervision to Athens.[17] Over the next several decades, the island underwent a hitherto unprecedented surge in urbanisation and in commercial activity. The main evidence for these processes has survived to us in archaeological form: the expansion and renovation of harbour and storage facilities, the expansion and renovation of the island's residential quar-

---

14   On the disease environment see Sallares 2007; on demographic constraints and the Malthusian ceiling, Scheidel 2007; on institutions, Frier – Kehoe 2007.

15   Scheidel 2009; note also the social development index proposed in Morris 2010 and explained at greater length in Morris 2013.

16   For the drivers of the economic transition from High Empire to Late Antiquity see now Harper 2017.

17   With (intentionally) catastrophic effects for Rhodes, previously the dominant Aegean port. Computation of January and July travel-times and travel expense from three major Italian ports – Ostia, Puteoli, Brundisium – to the Aegean through the ORBIS platform (orbis.stanford.edu) confirms that it was cheaper and quicker to get to Delos than to Rhodes, but only by about a full day during the winter and slightly less than half a day during the summer. Such a difference is not significant enough to account independently for the swing in Italian/central Mediterranean trade away from Rhodes (where an Italian merchant is attested c. 250: *CIL* I².404 = *ILindos* 92) and toward Delos over the course of the 2nd century.

ters, and – crucially for our purposes – the building of shrines, sanctuaries, and clubhouses dedicated to the worship of specific gods by private associations whose names, functions, and officer lists are in multiple cases preserved on inscriptions.[18]

Excavations conducted on Delos by French archaeologists since the late 1800s have brought to life the staggeringly eclectic array of cultic and religious practices on the island and the tremendous energy and resources lavished on these practices by private associations of Delian merchants, both those resident on the island year-round and those coming in on regular trips.[19] The associations, at least twenty-four of which are documented epigraphically,[20] reflect the geographic diversity of the mercantile and pilgrim influx into Delos throughout this period. Not only Greek but Italian and Phoenician merchants came together in corporate units that carried out ritual and cultic observances and paid for the construction of religious structures on the island. While membership in these bodies seems to have been largely dependent on ethnic background, there is substantial evidence for openness and mobility; Italians and Phoenicians in particular seem to have had relatively few scruples about joining in or subsidising the activities of religious associations that offered cult to gods not worshipped in their homelands.[21] Willingness to participate in cult to a god or goddess who was not natively one's own was emblematic of a syncretistic mode of religious cognition that prevailed throughout the Mediterranean in the centuries before the spread of Christianity. Gods and goddesses slipped across regional, ethnic, and political boundaries largely because believers became disposed to accept equivalencies between X god of one community and Y god of another, in the context of the animated intercultural encounters that occurred in highly frequented international sanctuaries and

---

18   Zarmakoupi 2013 summarises the island's fluctuation in population; urbanisation and residential expansion in the decades after 167/6 is detailed in Zarmakoupi 2018. For an assessment of the commercial networks radiating out of second-century Delos see Eberle – Le Quéré 2017.

19   The standard synthesis of this religious activity is Bruneau 1970, supplemented now with the focused work of Claire Hasenohr on the Agora of the Competaliastai and the activity of the Competaliastai (2000, 2001, 2003); *cf.* Flower 2017, 175–91. Note also Trümper 2006 and 2011 on the association clubhouses.

20   The overview of the evidence for these Delian associations in Roussel 1987 remains fundamental. For succinct comment on their Hellenistic context see Reger 2007, 477.

21   For more on these two groups see Hasenohr 2007a; on the cultural lability of the Italians, Hasenohr 2007b; for a prosopographic catalogue of the Italians on the island, Ferrary *et al.* 2002; generally on the second- and first-century diaspora of Italian *negotiatores*, Eberle 2017. As best we can tell, membership in any one ethnically or religiously oriented association did not preclude membership in others.

sacred precincts.[22] Among the most renowned of these syncretisms harmonised the Phoenician Melqart to the Greek-Roman Herakles/Hercules.[23]

Syncretism continuously interacted with the propagation of a shared transregional language of cult and divinity to underwrite the formation and growth of religious associations. A local instantiation of a Mediterranean-wide process that intensified rapidly during the Hellenistic period, the emergence of Delian religious associations has elicited much discussion since Erich Ziebarth and Franz Poland published pioneering works on the topic at the turn of the twentieth century. The rise of these associations, comprised for the most part of itinerant merchants, is important not only to the cultural arc of ancient Delos but to the historical entwinement of economy, religion, and tourism in the eastern Mediterranean of the last few centuries BCE. With growing vigour, modern studies of pilgrimage and tourism have underlined the need to reckon with the 'co-existence of a multiplicity of truths' in tracing the motivations that guided humans towards sacred destinations.[24] Ancient Delos, which functioned both as a sanctuary site and as a high-traffic port, is a deserving candidate for the application of this principle: it became home to a network of associations in which the economic and the religious productively cross-fertilised. Examining the how and why of this feedback system is our next task.

3   The Religious Association and Its Artefactual Outcomes

In the decades leading up to the publication of Erich Ziebarth's *Das griechische Vereinswesen* in 1896, considerable ink was spilled on speculation as to why the ancient Greeks, for all their advances in specialised and increasingly sophisticated craft and artistic production, never developed anything quite along the lines of a guild. Ziebarth and thirteen years after him Poland were among the first to discern that the commercial and professional associations which emerge in the Hellenistic period do exhibit some of the properties of a guild, and that their distinctive configuration in the form of cult groups and under theophoric names (*e.g., Hermaistai* or 'worshippers of Hermes,' *Apolloniastai* or 'worshippers of Apollo,' etc.) needed to be taken into account when assessing the broad

---

22   One such conversation between a Greek and a Phoenician: Paus. 7.23.7–8, with Habicht 1985, 157–59 for scholarship on the passage.

23   In addition to discussions of *interpretatio* in standard works on Greek and Roman religion (see *e.g.* Burkert 1985, Bremmer 1994; Beard *et al.* 1998), note Assmann 2004 for the Greek side of things and Ando 2008 for the Roman. For the special case of Melqart and Herakles-Hercules see Daniels 2017.

24   Quotation and discussion: Collins-Kreiner 2009.

spectrum of their social and economic utilities. These associations, often but not always of traders and merchant-ship owners (*emporoi* and *naukleroi*) and in quite a few cases of non-Greeks transacting at Greek ports, are attested from the late fourth century, and not only at Delos: from Athens, we know of associations of Egyptians, Tyrians, and Sidonians, among others; at Rhodes, for a century and a half the dominant Mediterranean port until the Roman intervention in Delos, approximately two hundred associations – Greek and non-Greek – are documented. The blossoming of this so-called *fenomeno associativo* has been variously construed: (1) as a real-time referendum on the diminishing powers of the Greek *polis*;[25] (2) as an institutionalised expression of the need for small, frequently face-to-face groups to undertake the vetting, enforcement, and regulatory operations without which the viability of medium – and long-distance commercial activity would be seriously imperilled.[26]

Responses to these interpretations have taken issue with the premise that the *polis* was in a state of terminal decline during the Hellenistic period. In an effort to play up the continuing importance of the *polis* in economic matters, scholars have mobilised the considerable evidence for city-provided regulators and administrators at the major ports of Athens, Delos, and Rhodes.[27] To be sure, any trader or merchant who felt himself cheated and sought support from city-appointed adjudicators would shoulder financial, opportunity, and possibly reputational costs in the pursuit of justice. The question, presently unanswerable given the state of our evidence, is when and to what extent those costs were accounted for and offset in the design of the institutional apparatus for arbitrating disputes. There is some evidence to suggest, for example, that Athens sought to lower the costs of appealing to a city-appointed adjudicator in instances where the validity of a coin as good currency was being disputed.[28] From the perspective of those seeking to do business with a minimum of

25   On the *polis* as 'doomed to extinction' see Runciman 1990; for a vigorous re-affirmation of the vitality of the Hellenistic *polis* see Habicht 1997.

26   The *fenomeno*'s expression in Delian clubhouse construction: Trümper 2011. Merchant self-policing: *cf.* Terpstra 2013 on commercial associations in the Roman Empire, fusing theory and scrutiny of the available evidence to reconstruct this enforcement but commenting only sparingly on religious practice. Hawkins 2013, 186–93 investigates private-order enforcement in the operations of Roman *collegia*. On the membership fees and admission requirements of Ptolemaic religious associations as commitment-enhancing devices see Monson 2006.

27   For a helpful overview of this evidence see Bresson 2008, ch. 4.

28   See e.g. van Alfen 2005 and Ober 2008, ch. 6 on the famous Athenian coinage decree of 375/4. Generally on the emergence and efficacy of *polis*-based institutional controls and oversight see van Alfen 2011. On the magistrates at Delos see Hasenohr 2012, 100–2. For other efforts to lower transaction costs note the improvements to port facilities and

friction, another option was the social lubricant of currying favour, not infrequently through the commissioning and erection of honorific statues; the presence of such private monuments in public spaces at Delos should not be decoupled from the economic imperatives that spurred and rewarded a long-term investment in the grammar of commemorative honours.[29]

Strategies for forging and sustaining social relations amidst the high-octane commercial activity of Delos and other economic centres also made regular use of cultic praxis, as the evidence for offerings and dedications to the gods on the part of individuals and private associations makes abundantly clear. Yet in most studies of these associations, the dynamic and multifaceted role of religion is usually acknowledged only then to be sidelined. The extent of this oversight is most apparent in studies of the *fenomeno*'s Roman manifestations from the late Republic onward, normally taken to be one consequence of an urban explosion that incentivised the rise of small groups for the articulation and strengthening of support networks; it is rare for the religious content of Roman associations to be folded into the detailed exposition of the factors behind the growth of these networks.[30] This oversight becomes all the more problematic when one considers how much in the way of time and resources private associations funneled towards religious activity. In the decades after the Greek Mediterranean came under Rome's thumb, why did resident and itinerant merchants join together in cultic associations, and why were they so willing to lavish resources on the material appurtenances of religious devotion? The volume of sacred dedications, architecture, and inscriptions generated by the activity of Delian residents and travellers in the period 167/6 to 88 is impressive, especially in comparison to preceding and later periods. And the *location* of this build-up is significant: much of it, notably the significant percentage traceable to the activity of Italian merchants and their private associations, takes place in the immediate vicinity of or at a short distance from the port. Why in this location, and to what effect(s)? An easy answer to the

---

infrastructure, presumably with an eye to luring and keeping traders: Burke 1985, 259 on the former; Duchêne – Fraisse 2001 on the latter.

29   The evidence from the Agora of Theophrastos: Ma 2013, 192 with n. 222 for epigraphic references.

30   Review and critique of the scholarship on Roman associations: Bendlin 1999, 9–15; Rüpke 1999, 41–2. Terpstra 2013 is skimpy on the religious dimension of mercantile associations. For a meticulous reconstruction of the "religious aesthetic" of *collegia* in imperial Ostia see Egelhaaf-Gaiser 1999; on the cultic propensities of associations of Roman citizens abroad, Ramgopal 2016, 63–72. Networks and religion in the Roman Empire: Collar 2013, 40–78.

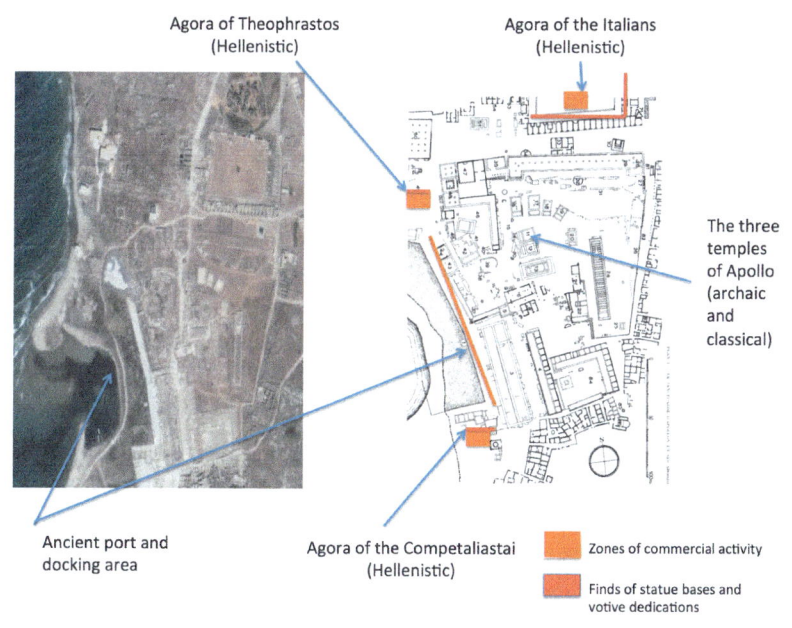

FIGURE 13.1   Location and layout of the ancient port and adjacent area
IMAGE SOURCES: THE MAP ON THE LEFT WAS GENERATED THROUGH
GOOGLE EARTH; THE ARCHAEOLOGICAL PLAN ON THE RIGHT
IS PLAN 1 IN BRUNEAU AND DUCAT 1983 WITH MY OVERLAYS. BY
"ZONES OF COMMERCIAL ACTIVITY," I INDICATE ZONES OF *LIKELY*
COMMERCIAL ACTIVITY: WHILE THE PRECISE *LIEUX D'ÉCHANGE* AT
DELOS REMAIN A SOURCE OF DEBATE, I GROUND MY DESIGNATIONS
IN HASENOHR'S (2012) CAUTIOUS OVERVIEW OF THE EVIDENCE FOR
THE SITES MARKED IN ORANGE.

question of *why* is 'conspicuous display,' but such an interpretation only begins
to scratch the surface.

Stressing the 'positive network externalities' at work in the structuring of
Delian associations, Robert Wright has located their appeal to prospective
members in the fact that each association was 'both a database and a network
of useful contacts' through which merchants could glean 'useful information
from other merchants and shippers.' It is not immediately apparent, however,
why *religious* and *religiously* themed associations emerged as the means for
redressing the information asymmetries that medium – and long-distance
merchants frequently encountered. Another provisional explanation can be
derived from recent work on trust and social capital.[31] In his attempt to con-
textualise the rise and proliferation of private religious associations, Vincent

---

31   Wright 2009, 290. Broadly on religion as social capital see Witham 2010, 172–4.

Gabrielsen has characterised them as 'brotherhoods of faith' in which the performance of repeated acts of religiosity and piety created 'faith in other people' – a foundation for the long-distance trust required for geographically wide-ranging commercial activity.[32] These 'brotherhoods of faith' enshrined and promoted a very specific kind of social capital, in the form of a sense of kinship with the fellow association members who participated in the praxis of cult. Such an enhanced connection will have lowered transaction costs, clearing the way for economic exchange either immediately after the cult act or further down the line.[33]

One example may serve as demonstration. When Publius Sextilius Philo and eleven other men came together as representatives of several distinct *collegia* to make a bilingual dedication to Hercules in 113 BCE,[34] they engaged in a form of collective action that unlocked opportunities for learning not only about the individual tendencies of the other members of the dedicating group, but about the prospects of working together as a group in a multilingual and multiethnic environment. Presumably enacted on a festival day to Hercules, this offering advertised those responsible for its dedication as capable of bridging any differences in background and status to act in concert. The Italian onomastics of the dedicators mask the peninsular diversity of their origins, while the bilingualism of the inscription attests to knowledge of and possibly even native familiarity with Greek for those six dedicators of freedman status. The possibility that the dedication was timed to coincide with a festival is also charged with significance. As was true for other major religious centres in the Graeco-Roman Mediterranean, Delian festival culture was a conduit for the distribution of information about human economic actors.[35] The efficacy of festivals as sites for the collection and dissemination of information relied heavily on the public visibility of acts such as dedications. Indicative of a prosocial orientation towards cult, dedications were instructive not only for those parties who undertook them, but for those other travellers and traders on the island who either saw the dedication in real time or who came across the inscription that commemorated it.

In light of the difficulties with establishing and maintaining reputation that sellers and merchants alike faced at commercial *emporia* throughout the Mediterranean, the social capital that was accrued in the praxis of making an

---

32   Gabrielsen 2008, especially 196 on associations as 'repositories of religiosity and piety.' On long-distance trust as a requirement for the mobility of capital see *e.g.* North 1990, 125–6.

33   Manning 2018, 253–4, following Gabrielsen.

34   Dürrbach no. 116 = *ID* 1753 = *ILLRP* 759; the *collegia* represented are the *Hermaistai*, the *Apolloniastai*, and the *Poseidoniastai*.

35   Festival sites and the circulation of information: Rutherford 2017, 203–9.

offering went a long way towards creating the conditions for the trust that enabled parties to an economic transaction to hurdle over the barriers of risk and uncertainty. At the same time that it promoted trust, the ritual act also interacted with the multitude of ritual acts already marking the landscape of Delos, both to re-affirm the safety of Delos in the eyes of future travellers and merchants and to re-enact a generally shared commitment to maintaining that safety. For a merchant newly arrived on the island who was eager to do business, what may have registered as the most compellingly tangible sign that his likely partners would act in good faith? If we follow Pausanias' lead, it was the wooden image of Apollo – conjoined with and articulated to the ritualisation of sacralised collective action, as denoted by the dedications, altars, and shrines surrounding the island's various *agorai*. In the aggregate, these ritual acts transformed late Hellenistic Delos into a palimpsest, its urban spaces riddled with memorials to the cultic activity of individuals and groups; the impression left by this "virtual presence" of past dedicators on those arriving on the island, whether to admire its sanctuary spaces or to engage in trade, will have been profound.[36] It was in the midst of this visual profusion of monumentality that social capital was minted and deposited.

Although social capital approaches to the study of Hellenistic associations have lately gained some traction, the methodological apparatus behind these approaches is not without its shortcomings.[37] One repeatedly voiced concern is that the procedures for the creation and transmission of this social capital are left underelaborated or unstated. In the case of Delos, it would be important to establish where, how, and with what consequences social capital came to be produced and circulated through the collective action of private associations. How do we know that this social capital was being generated? How do we know that its transmission was taking place? One answer can suffice for both questions: the material record of ritual and sacred activity that these associations left behind. Our understanding of the palpable impacts of social capital on networking, trust-formation, and norm compliance is greatly enhanced if we view the almost hypertrophic output of dedications and offerings to the gods at Delos not as some static marker of piety but as a dynamic agent in the landscape of individual choices. People *responded* to the statue of Apollo, and to the many other statues dotting the landscape as well.

---

36   My application of the terms 'palimpsest' and 'virtual presence' follows the lead of Petsalis-Diomidis 2017.

37   Critique of the major schools of social-capital theory: Seubert 2009. For (measured) application of social-capital models see Kierstead 2013 on Athenian associations.

4   Signalling and Priming Environments at Delos

The number of religious offerings, shrine dedications, and physical monuments to cult practice that sprouted all over Delos, and especially in heavily frequented areas of the island during the late Hellenistic period, is best understood by reference to what Joseph Bulbulia, Marcus Frean, and Paul Reddish have described under the rubrics of 'cooperative ecology' and 'ecological signalling.'[38] In order to demonstrate how these related concepts can be applied to the study of late Hellenistic Delos, a brief sketch of the intellectual background against which and in dialogue with which they were formulated is in order. Psychological studies over the past two decades have confirmed the sensitivity of individual and group norm compliance or defiance to external environmental cues. In a much-cited 1990 article, Robert Cialdini and his colleagues presented and analysed an experiment in which observed participants were much more likely to litter in dirty environments than in clean ones. Their conclusion was that the presence of a dirty environment subconsciously primed individuals into an act of norm defiance (littering) they would have far less likely to commit otherwise.[39] Successive studies modelled along similar lines have corroborated the same principle in a variety of contexts and domains, although it should be borne in mind that some of these studies are now embroiled in the replication crisis that has consumed behavioural psychology and economics over the past several years.[40]

The overall picture emerging from this research, fraught and contested though it is, is that priming and activation effects operate at subconscious levels to guide individual behaviour. Bulbulia and his colleagues have been quick to grasp how the lessons of these studies can be applied to the study of religion.[41] According to their simplifying evolutionary scheme for the

---

38   Bulbulia *et al.* 2013, a substantially beefed-up version of the 'coordination by sacred cues' model set out by Bulbulia and Frean 2009.

39   Cialdini *et al.* 1990 on what has since come to be known as the 'Cialdini effect' (incorrectly spelled in Bulbulia *et al.* 2013 as "Caildini").

40   See *e.g.* Vohs 2006; Berger *et al.* 2008; Keizer *et al.* 2008. Stapel – Lindenberg 2011 was tantalising in its report of a link between disorderly environments and a specific form of anti-social behaviour (racism), but the article was retracted following the lead author's admission to fraudulent data generation. In response to Kahneman 2011, ch. 4's accessible and general synopsis of the important studies, Schimmack *et al.* 2017 subjected these to a scalping, contending that "priming research is a train wreck"; but defenders of this line of research have contended that replication may not be the best standard for adjudicating the merits of studies on priming.

41   Bulbulia – Frean 2009 and Bulbulia *et al.* 2013 present a simplified cooperation-defection game (a "stag hunt") to clarify how cue-based signalling works.

connection between religious belief and enhanced prosocial behaviour, 'religions evolve to generate representations – explicit and implicit – that spread optimism and restore order.' In their account, 'the exogenous mechanisms that evolve to facilitate such a spreading of order' are *ecological signals*, which take two forms. In addition to what they term '*declarative* components of religious cognition' – the shared memories and beliefs often formalised through speech and transmitted through texts – Bulbulia and his colleagues have also scrutinised 'non-declarative cognitive states.'[42] Among the different strategies for initiating and sustaining these states, bodily movement is regularly singled out for particular consideration. One of the most promising lines of research in behavioural psychology has focused on the ways in which forms of mimicry and synchronised movement induce cooperative engagement.[43] I propose extending their signalling model beyond the ritualisation and choreographing of the physical body to encompass the material structures created and continuously modified by religious activity. In other words, we should interpret the inscribed dedications, altars, offerings, sacrifices, and shrines of the Delian landscape as ecological signals capable of priming individuals into prosocial behaviour: they were testimonies to ritual movements that, frozen and recorded in time and space, acted to structure and route the movements and habits of travellers and traders who experienced the force of their palimpsestic impact.

Pausanias' observation about the sense of commercial security promoted by Apollo's statue acknowledges the operation of one such ecological signal, the image of the patron god of the island. While we have no direct evidence for subconscious effects – the ancients were not, to the best of our knowledge, conducting psychological experiments on each other from which they could glean and report such effects – the inhabitants of the ancient Mediterranean were very aware of the emotional and communicative potency of statues, especially divine ones. The second-century BCE Roman satirist Lucilius, who besides being a contemporary of the Delian economic boom may have travelled to the island, had some choice remarks about individuals who reacted too gullibly to statues of the gods:

> The bogeymen and witches that your woodland prophets and your ancient kings instituted, he trembles at them, he stakes everything on them. Just as children before they can speak believe all bronze statues to be

---

42   Bulbulia *et al.* 2013, 103.

43   In addition to the research summarised in Bulbulia *et al.* 2013, 105–6, note also the "ideomotor link" demonstrated to striking effect in Mussweiler 2006.

living and to be human, so too those adults think all those moulded objects are real – they think there is sentience in the bronze statues.[44]

Although Lucilius' mockery of this species of piety conforms to the expectations of (a nascent) genre, we should not for its literary stylings alone dismiss its value as an evocation of the social and affective realities of tremulous worship.[45] There is a voluminous literature on responses to cult statues in the Graeco-Roman world whose conclusions I will not reprise here.[46] For our purposes we need only consider three dimensions of the Greek and Roman engagement with divine statuary. First, the praxis of worship was conceptualised as taking place in front of or in the immediate vicinity of a cult statue. Second, the physical environment of cities, and especially their port and commercial infrastructures, was saturated with images of and testimonia to cult. And third, far from being compartmentalised within the walls of the shrine or temple, participation in cult enjoyed a reasonably high degree of public visibility, since Graeco-Roman cult was primarily an outdoor activity.

The person trembling on his approach to the divinity did so within a public space, and in the sight of other worshippers and passers-by. Often installed in the interior of temples or shrines, cult statues of divinities were usually apprehended from the outside by those participating in festivals or making dedications; sacrifices were almost always conducted on altars erected in front of the temple, within the *temenos* or sacred precinct but outside the physical structure of the edifice that housed the statue.[47] How many of those watching the quavering worshipper were inclined to think along the same lines as Lucilius' satiric persona, and either found themselves casting a sceptical glance at the proceedings or simply dismissing them as bogus? Perhaps some chuckled, their snickering proceeding in much the same vein as Theophrastos' stereotyping of the superstitious man (*Characters* 16); but others nearby might have

---

44   Lucilius frs. 484–8 Marx = 490–4 Krenkel (tr. Feeney 1998: 93, modified): *terriculas, Lamias, Fauni quas Pompiliique / instituere Numae, tremit has, hic omnia ponit. / ut pueri infantes credunt signa omnia aena / uiuere et esse homines, sic isti somnia ficta / uera putant, credunt signis cor inesse in aenis.* For the poet's awareness of Delos see fr. 123 Marx = 124 Krenkel with Cichorius 1908, 49–50.

45   See the comments of Padilla Peralta 2018, xxxvii with n. 33.

46   Overview of this debate and its multiple moving parts in Feeney 1998, 92–7. See also Collins 2008, 19, on Graeco-Roman cultures 'liv[ing] the reality' of statues as animate beings; Collins felicitously invokes the model of "real physical interactions" with divinity proposed by Alfred Gell in his influential 1998 work. For an attempt to build up a 'cognitive archaeology' of statuary and its many uses see Schnapp 1994; for epiphanic encounters with cultic statuary see Platt 2011.

47   For an accessible account of this feature of Graeco-Roman religions see McLean 1996.

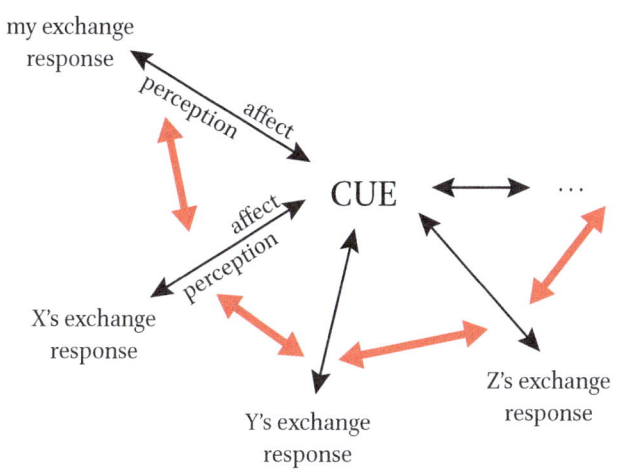

FIGURE 13.2   Bulbulia *et al.*'s cooperative ecology model, modified
                (after Bulbulia *et al.* 2013, Fig. 6.1. I have added the
                red lines).

been moved to exhibit a more visible piety of their own. Venturing into the
nitty-gritty of ecological signalling with the help of a simple model can give us
a better sense as to why.

Fig. 13.2 modifies Bulbulia *et al.*'s visualisation of a cooperative ecology to
bring into clearer focus the *interdependence* of individual responses to specific
environmental cues. While research into the dynamic features of ecological
response is still very much in its infancy, it is not a stretch to assume that any
one individual's response to a specific cue was not unmediated. Routinely and
in many cases unconsciously, the responses of others around the individual
worshipper will have imprinted themselves on him prior to and during the formulation of his own. In the example of Lucilius' gullible trembler, the statue
that inspires such fear in him is the primary cue, while he and his embodied
response are important *secondary* cues.

A person in the immediate neighbourhood will have taken the measure of
the statue and of the gullible trembler in formulating his consciously explicit
response to the scene. Subconsciously, however, he would also be processing
other aspects of the environment in which the interaction between human
and statue was unfolding – a *tertium quid* that had the capacity to steer his
actions in a very targeted way. Two recent studies, one on the effects of priming 'God' concepts and the other on the priming effects of the 'gaze,'[48] offer
some insight into the nature and outcomes of this processing. In the first study,

_____

48   Shariff – Norenzayan 2007; Bateson *et al.* 2006.

subjects for whom notions of God had been implicitly activated were significantly more generous in an anonymous dictator game; in the second, contributions to an office honesty box in a university coffee room rose considerably
when an image of a pair of eyes was placed above the coffee and tea. Despite
being conducted on modern subjects, these studies are useful for elucidating
how a person at Delos might have been primed by the sacralised monumental landscape. For an individual navigating a landscape that was studded with
reminders of divinity, some of which took the form of statues – of gods and
persons – with eyes,[49] several psychological mechanisms conducive to prosocial and cooperative behaviour will have clicked into place.

What if this individual happened to have travelled to Delos with the intention of pursuing commercial activity? On the assumption that this person had
been socialised into thinking that statues embodied a living god, or even into
thinking that most of his peers believed that statues embodied a living god, he
will have been subconsciously primed not only into being more generous but
into acting on an implicit belief that the people around him were, if not fundamentally pious, then at least inclined to be pious whenever in close physical
proximity to statuary, votive offerings, and shrines or temples. Any oath invoking the gods that he took or was nudged into taking would have impressed
itself even more deeply on his consciousness as a result.[50] Pausanias may not
have been far off the mark after all.

The next question to ask is whether the scope and intensity of this priming
effect can be gauged in more precise terms than the merely impressionistic.
Ancient Delians are not around today for us to run controlled experiments on
them, so any attempt at quantification will be indirect and loosely approxima-
tive at best. As a tentative first step and illustration of concept, I offer a simple
probabilistic (Bayesian) model that seeks to identify *where* in the decision-
making process of any one traveller or merchant the effects of priming might
have been most acutely – or most consequentially – felt.[51] Suppose that I, a
Delos-based trader, am considering a transaction with a new arrival to the
island about whom I know nothing. The transaction he is proposing is very

---

49   The evidence of our hardwired, unconscious reaction to human faces is strong and grow-
      ing; on the "neuroethology" of the social gaze see Emery 2000.

50   *Pace* Ramgopal 2016, 63 n. 130 (following Terpstra 2013, 25–6), I see no reason to discredit
      fear of the gods as a prod to good behaviour. On the legal efficaciousness of oaths in
      Roman courts see (purely *e.g.*) Crook 1967, 76.

51   Bayes' Theorem: $xy / [xy + z(1\text{-}x)]$, where x = prior probability, y = probability conditional
      on hypothesis being false, and z = probability conditional on hypothesis being true. For an
      introduction to Bayesian approaches see Silver 2012, ch. 8 (popular); Buck *et al.* 1996 and
      Wonnacott – Wonnacott 2008 (technical).

Baseline	Priming intervention I	Priming intervention II
	*Priming raises x	*Priming raises y (and lowers z)
Prior probability (x) = 0.25	x = 0.35	x = 0.25
Conditional, (y) = 0.5	y = 0.5	y = 0.6
Conditional, (z) = 0.5	z = 0.5	z = 0.4
Posterior probability = 0.25	Posterior = 0.35	Posterior = 0.48
	Priming intervention I, t2	Priming intervention II, t2
	new x = 0.45	new x = 0.48
	y = 0.5	y = 0.6
	z = 0.5	z = 0.4
	Posterior = 0.45	Posterior = 0.58

FIGURE 13.3   Bayesian trust on oath. Bayes's Theorem: $xy / [xy + z(1-x)]$, where x = prior probability, y = probability conditional on hypothesis being false, and z = probability conditional on hypothesis being true.

profitable, but I am extremely risk-averse and have no independent reason to trust him. Let us assume a decently low prior probability of 25% that I will trust him enough to accept the proposed transaction and do business.[52] To encourage me to accept the proposal, the merchant next offers to swear by the gods; he even proposes to go the extra mile and set up some kind of offering to the gods on our behalf, or to join me and my colleagues in the activities of our private association. This new offer gives me information I can use to assess his trustworthiness. While I am taken with his apparent godfearingness, I remain a hardened sceptic, and therefore refrain from swinging too quickly in the direction of trust: *conditional on the new offer* I reckon it a 50–50 prospect that he is trustworthy (Fig. 13.3). Using Bayes' Theorem, we arrive at the entirely unsurprising posterior possibility of 25% for the likelihood that I will trust him enough to accept the offer. Nothing has changed.

Let us now tweak one of the model's parameters by assuming that, throughout the period of my initial reflection on the proposal, I had been primed by

---

52   We will also assume purely for the sake of this exercise that the only factor in my decision to cooperate is my degree of trust in the merchant (*i.e.*, no other explicit determinative considerations).

the surrounding environment of statues and sacred artefacts into being more prosocial and inclined towards cooperation. This priming will have raised the prior probability of my being trusting enough to agree to the transaction from 25% to 35%. When the merchant makes his offer to swear by the gods and to join my private association, again I am split evenly on the question of whether his willingness to do so augurs trustworthiness or its opposite. The posterior possibility that I will agree to his offer is, then, simply 35%. It is now time for another tweak: let us assume that the priming effect operates not by raising the prior probability of my trusting him enough to cooperate, but by upgrading his trustworthiness in my eyes once he makes his supplemental offer – to the extent that, conditional on that offer, there is now a 60% chance that I will discard my previous inhibitions and find him trustworthy enough. Perhaps the priming intervenes at this juncture because I am seeing or have seen other travellers and merchants engaging in ritualised activity, or because I am in an environment dotted with evidence of that activity. In any case, the posterior probability that I will agree to the transaction now swings up to 48%. The ten-percent primed uptick in my assessment of his good faith returns a higher posterior probability than if I had simply entered the transaction slightly more primed to cooperate. If we run this game through a second iteration, representative of my next interaction with another new arrival unknown to me until our encounter in one of the Delian *agorai*, the gap remains: with a priming effect that acts to raise my generic inclination to trust to 45% (but holding conditional probabilities constant at 50–50), the likelihood of my agreeing to the transaction will keep pace at 45%; however, with a new confidence level of 48%, and with a priming effect that alters the conditional probabilities to make me 10% more likely to trust, the likelihood of my agreeing to the transaction will rise to 58%.

If priming to induce greater cooperation was in fact taking place in the sacralised trading environments of Delos, the payoff would have been larger if that priming influenced the assessment of potential economic partners once a transactional dialogue was already under way. On this reading, Pausanias' statue (and the full-spectrum sacralised urban fabric of which it was emblematic) will have had its maximum effect not by preconditioning individuals into blind trust, but by edging individuals towards trust if their transactional counterparts advertised themselves as willing to undertake ritual acts in order to build that trust, and with it social capital. It is this simple but powerful mechanism that may have fueled a virtuous feedback loop of ritual action on late Hellenistic Delos. For those travelling to the island, for those resident on the island, and for those private associations that emerged as a consequence of repeated interactions between individuals from these two groups, priming ensured not only a lowering of the transaction costs that might otherwise stand in the way of commercial activity, but the continuous reproduction of the sacred landscape that was foundational to that priming in the first place.

5 Conclusion

This chapter has sought to advance the dialogue between ancient economics and ancient religion by moving in three directions: first, to Hellenistic Delos with its wealth of religious practices; second, across media, from text to material artefacts; and third, from material culture to psychological and probabilistic models. The interpretations I have proposed make no claims to being comprehensive, all-encompassing, or even verifiable in a directly testable sense. What they do afford is a strategy for relating the substantial material output of sacred artefacts in late Hellenistic Delos to the sense of security travellers and traders felt in encountering each other on the island. Further work is required to put the priming effects of statues and sacred artefacts on a firmer conceptual, empirical, and comparative footing. For now, I offer three takeaways:

1. The *priming* effects of sacred environments on commercial activity, as sparked by the *material form* of those sacred environments, should be placed on a level with other forms of socio-religious capital currently receiving attention in the scholarly literature.
2. Understanding these priming effects is important to reconstructing the cycles of virtuous behaviour and norm compliance that contributed simultaneously to enhancing economic performance and high-visibility ritual acts.
3. At sanctuary and pilgrimage sites such as Delos, travel, religion and economics were deeply co-implicated, seamlessly collaborating across a range of languages, media, and cognitive dispositions in the constitution of the island's experience economy.

One final issue remains to be confronted. In examining the matrix of choices and incentives that structured the decision of voluntary travellers to Delos, I have not taken into account the transformative force of conspicuous religious observance for the many who came to the island unwillingly: the hundreds of thousands if not millions of slaves for whom the shining marble of dedications and petrified ritual acts heralded their commodification into chattel. How the experiences of coerced travel to Delos interacted with the sights of the island – one whose monumentalisation was largely underwritten by the profits of the slave trade – to leave a lasting impression on the subjectivities of these involuntary migrants is sorely in need of investigation.[53] As for those who trafficked in human bodies, it may well have been the reassurance of the island's sacred monumentalisation that emboldened them to travel to the island and transact their *mercatura sordida*. Ultimately, the story of sacred travel and commerce at Delos cannot be written without recognition of those persons for whom the vibrant religious life of private associations with their public cult acts meant nothing more, and nothing less, than social death.

Acknowledgements

A rough-hewn version of this essay was first presented at the 2013 Annual Meeting of the Association for the Study of Religion, Economics, and Culture; my thanks to co-panelists John Larrivee and Robert Mochrie and audience members Reza Varjavand and Laurens de Rooij for genially tolerating an interloper. For additional feedback, bibliography, and encouragement, I thank Barbara Kowalzig. My greatest debt is to Anna Collar and Troels Myrup Kristensen, for steering this contribution into the fold of this volume and for bearing my dilatory devils with humour and grace.

Bibliography

Acton, P. 2014. Poiesis: *Manufacturing in Classical Athens*, Oxford.

Ando, C. 2008. *The Matter of the Gods: Religion and the Roman Empire*, Berkeley, CA.

Archibald, Z., Davies, J.K., and Gabrielsen, V. eds. 2011. *The Economies of Hellenistic Societies, Third to First Centuries BC*, Oxford.

Arnaoutoglou, I. 1998. *Ancient Greek Laws: A Sourcebook*, London.

Assmann, J. 2004. "Monotheism and Polytheism", in *Ancient Religions*, ed. S.I. Johnston, Cambridge, MA – London, 17–31.

Bateson, M., Nettle, D., and Roberts, G. 2006. "Cues of being watched enhance cooperation in a real-world setting", *Biology Letters* 2, 412–4.

Beard, M., North, J., and Price, S. 1998. *Religions of Rome. Volume 1: A History*, Cambridge.

Bendlin, A. 1999. "Gemeinschaft, Öffentlichkeit und Identität: Forschungsgeschichtliche Anmerkungen zu den Mustern sozialer Ordnung in Rom", in *Religiöse Vereine in der*

---

53   Concentrating mainly on Roman Italy, Padilla Peralta 2017 probes some aspects of this problem.

römischen Antike. Untersuchungen zu Organisation, Ritual und Raumordnung, eds. U. Egelhaaf-Gaiser and A. Schäfer, Tübingen, 9–40.

Berger, J., Meredith, M., and Wheeler, S.C. 2008. "Contextual Priming: Where people vote affects how they vote", *PNAS* 105, 8846–49.

Bremmer, J. 1994. *Greek Religion*, Oxford.

Bresson, A. 2008. *L'économie de la Grèce des cités (fin VIe–Ier siècle a.C.). II: Les espaces de l'échange*, Paris.

Bresson, A. 2016. *The Making of the Ancient Greek Economy: Institutions, Markets, and Growth in the City-states*, trans. S. Rendall, Princeton, NJ.

Bruneau, P. 1970. *Recherches sur les cultes de Délos a l'époque hellénistique et à l'époque impériale*, Paris.

Bruneau, P. and Ducat, J. eds. 1983. *Guide de Délos*, third edition, Paris.

Buck, C.E., Cavanagh, W.G., and Litton, C.D. 1996. *Bayesian Approach to Interpreting Archaeological Data*, Chichester.

Bulbulia, J. and Frean, M. 2009. "Coordination by Sacred Cues", available at: http://tinyurl.com/bqawx62 (last accessed 16 August 2018).

Bulbulia, J., Frean, M., and Reddish, P. 2013. "Ecological Signalling", in *A New Science of Religion*, eds. G.W. Dawes and J. Maclaurin, New York, 100–10.

Burke, E.M. 1985. "Lycurgan Finances", *Greek, Roman and Byzantine Studies* 26, 251–64.

Burkert, W. 1985. *Greek Religion*, trans. J. Raffan, Cambridge, MA.

Cialdini, R., Kallgren, C., and Reno, R. 1990. "A Focus Theory of Normative Conduct: A Theoretical Refinement and Reevaluation of the Role of Norms in Human Behaviour", *Advances in Experimental Social Psychology* 24, 201–34.

Cichorius, C. 1908. *Untersuchungen zu Lucilius*, Berlin.

Clark, A. 2011. "*Magistri* and *ministri* in Roman Italy: Associations with Gods", in *Priests and State in the Roman World*, eds. J.H. Richardson and F. Santangelo, Stuttgart, 347–72.

Coarelli, F. 1984. "Iside Capitolina, Clodio e i mercanti di schiavi", in *Alessandria e il mondo ellenistico-romano: studi in onore di Achille Adriana*, eds. N. Bonacasa and A. Di Vita, Rome, 3.461–75.

Coarelli, F. 2005. "L'Agora des Italiens': lo *statarion* di Delo?", *Journal of Roman Archaeology* 18, 196–212.

Collar, A. 2013. *Religious Networks in the Roman Empire: The Spread of New Ideas*, Cambridge.

Collins, D. 2008. *Magic in the Ancient Greek world*, Malden, MA – Oxford.

Collins-Kreiner, N. 2009. "Researching Pilgrimage: Continuity and Transformations", *Annals of Tourism Research* 37.2, 440–56.

Constantakopoulou, C. 2007. *The Dance of the Islands: Insularity, Networks, the Athenian Empire, and the Aegean world*, Oxford.

Crook, J.A. 1967. *Law and Life of Rome*, Ithaca.

Daniels, M. 2017. "Annexing a Shared Past: Roman Appropriations of Hercules-Melqart in the Conquest of Hispania", in *Rome, Empire of Plunder: The Dynamics of Cultural Appropriation*, eds. M.P. Loar, C.S. MacDonald, and D. Padilla Peralta, Cambridge, 237–60.

Eberle, L.P. 2017. "Making Roman Subjects: Citizenship and Empire Before and After Augustus", *Transactions of the American Philological Association* 147.2, 321–70.

Eberle, L.P. and Le Quéré, E. 2017. "Landed Traders, Trading Agriculturalists? Land in the Economy of the Italian Diaspora in the Greek East", *Journal of Roman Studies* 107, 27–59.

Egelhaaf-Gaiser, U. 1999. "Religionsästhetik und Raumordnung am Beispiel der Vereinsgebäude von Ostia", in *Religiöse Vereine in der römischen Antike. Untersuchungen zu Organisation, Ritual und Raumordnung*, eds. U. Egelhaaf-Gaiser and A. Schäfer, Tübingen, 123–72.

Emery, N.J. 2000. "The Eyes Have It: The Neuroethology, Function and Evolution of Social Gaze", *Neuroscience and Biobehavioral Reviews* 24.6, 581–604.

Feeney, D. 1998. *Literature and Religion at Rome: Cultures, Contexts, and Beliefs*, Cambridge.

Ferrary, J.-L., Hasenohr, C., and Le Dinahet, M.T. 2002. "Liste des Italiens de Délos", in *Les Italiens dans le monde grec, IIe siècle av. J.-C. – Ier siècle ap. J.-C. Circulation, activités, intégration*, eds. C. Müller and C. Hasenohr, Paris, 183–239.

Davies, J.K. 1984. "Cultural, Social and Economic Features of the Hellenistic world", in *Cambridge Ancient History*, second edition, 7.1, 257–320.

Duchêne, H. and Fraisse, P. 2001. *Le paysage portuaire de la Délos antique. Recherches sur les installations maritimes, commerciales et urbaines du littoral délien*, Paris – Athens.

Flower, H.I. 2017. *The Dancing Lares and the Serpent in the Garden: Religion at the Roman Street Corner*, Princeton, NJ.

Frier, B.W. and Kehoe, D.P. 2007. "Law and Economic Institutions", in *The Cambridge Economic History of the Greco-Roman World*, eds. W. Scheidel, I. Morris, and R. Saller, Cambridge, 113–43.

Gabrielsen, V. 2001. "The Rhodian Associations and Economic Activity", in *Hellenistic Economies*, eds. Z.H. Archibald, J.K. Davies, and V. Gabrielsen, New York – London, 215–44.

Gabrielsen, V. 2007. "Brotherhoods of Faith and Provident Planning: The Non-public Associations of the Greek World", *Mediterranean Historical Review* 22.2, 183–210.

Gell, A. 1998. *Art and Agency: An Anthropological Theory*, Oxford.

Habicht, C. 1985. *Pausanias' Guide to Ancient Greece*, Berkeley, CA.

Habicht, C. 1997. *Athens from Alexander to Antony*, Cambridge, MA – London.

Hansen, M.H. 2006. *The Shotgun Method: The Demography of the Ancient Greek City-state culture*, Columbia, MS.

Harper, K. 2017. *The Fate of Rome: Climate, Disease, and the End of an Empire*, Princeton, NJ.

Hasenohr, C. 2000. "Les sanctuaires italiens sur l'Agora des Compétaliastes à Délos", *Revue archéologique* 1, 198–202.

Hasenohr, C. 2001. "Les monuments des collèges italiens sur l'Agora des Compétaliastes à Delos", in *Constructions publiques et programmes édilitaires du IIe s. av. J.-C. au Ier s. ap. J.-C. Actes du colloque organisé par l'École française d'Athènes*, eds. J.-Y. Marc, J.-C. Moretti, and D. Viviers, Athens – Paris, 329–48.

Hasenohr, C. 2003. "Les Compitalia à Délos", *Bulletin de correspondance hellénique* 127.1, 167–249.

Hasenohr, C. 2007a. "Les Italiens de Délos: entre romanité et hellénisme", in *Identités ethniques dans le monde grec antique. Actes du colloque international de Toulouse organisé par le CRATA, 9–11 mars 2006*, ed. J.-M. Luce, Toulouse, 221–32.

Hasenohr, C. 2007b. "Italiens et Phéniciens à Délos: organisation et relations de deux groupes d'étrangers résidents", in *Étrangers dans la cité romaine. Actes du colloque de Valenciennes (14–15 octobre 2005)*, eds. R. Compatangelo-Soussignan and C.-G. Schwentzel, Rennes, 77–90.

Hasenohr, C. 2012. "Athènes et le commerce délien: lieux d'échange et magistrats des marchés à Délos pendant la seconde domination athénienne (167–88 a.C.)", in *Stephanèphoros. De l'économie antique à l'Asie Mineure. Hommages à Raymond Descat*, ed. K. Konuk, Bordeaux, 95–110.

Hatzfeld, J. 1919. *Les trafiquants italiens dans l'Orient hellénique*, Paris.

Hawkins, C. 2013. "Manufacturing", in *The Cambridge Companion to the Roman Economy*, ed. W. Scheidel, Cambridge, 175–94.

Horden, P. and Purcell, N. 2000. *The Corrupting Sea. A Study of Mediterranean History*, Malden, MA.

Iannaccone, L. and Boser, F. 2011. "Funding the Faiths: Toward a Theory of Religious Finance", in *The Oxford Handbook of the Economics of Religion*, ed. R. McCleary, Oxford, 323–42.

Kahneman, D. 2011. *Thinking, Fast and Slow*, New York.

Keizer, K., Lindenberg, S., and Steg, L. 2008. "The Spreading of Disorder", *Science* 322, 1681–85.

Kierstead, J. 2013. *An Association of Associations: Social Capital and Group Dynamics in Democratic Athens*, unpublished PhD dissertation, Stanford University.

Kloppenborg, J.S. and Wilson, S.G. eds. 1996. *Voluntary Associations in the Graeco-Roman World*, London – New York.

Ma, J. 2013. *Statues and Cities: Honorific Portraits and Civic Identity in the Hellenistic World*, Oxford.

Manning, J.G. 2018. *The Open Sea: The Economic Life of the Ancient Mediterranean World from the Iron Age to the Rise of Rome*, Princeton, NJ.

McLean, B.H. 1996. "The Place of Cult in Voluntary Associations and Christian Churches on Delos", in *Voluntary Associations in the Graeco-Roman World*, eds. J.S. Kloppenborg and S.G. Wilson, London – New York, 186–225.

Migeotte, L. 2014. *Les finances des cités grecques aux périodes classique et hellénistique*, Paris.

Morris, I. 2004. "Economic Growth in Ancient Greece", *Journal of Institutional and Theoretical Economics* 160, 709–42.

Morris, I. 2010. *Why the West Rules – For Now: The Patterns of History, and What They Reveal about the Future*, New York.

Morris, I. 2013. *The Measure of Civilization: How Social Development decides the Fate of Nations*, Princeton, NJ.

Monson, A. 2006. "The Ethics and Economics of Ptolemaic Religious Associations", *Ancient Society* 36, 221–38.

Mussweiler, T. 2006. "Doing is for thinking! Stereotype Activation by Stereotypic Movements", *Psychological Science* 17, 17–21.

Ober, J. 2008. *Democracy and Knowledge: Innovation and Learning in Classical Athens*, Princeton, NJ.

Ober, J. 2010. "Wealthy Hellas", *Transactions of the American Philological Association* 140.2, 241-86.

Ober, J. 2015. *The Rise and Fall of Classical Greece*, Princeton, NJ.

Padilla Peralta, D. 2017. "Slave Religiosity in the Roman Middle Republic", *Classical Antiquity* 36.2, 317–69.

Padilla Peralta, D. 2018. "An Aristocratic Dilemma: Do it right, or do it better?", *Histos* 12, xxiv–xlvi.

Parker, G. 2017. "Environmental Perspectives on Ancient Communication", in *Mercury's Wings: Exploring Modes of Communication in the Ancient World*, eds. F.S. Naiden and R.J.A. Talbert, Oxford, 3–22.

Petsalis-Diomidis, A. 2017. "Palimpsest and Virtual Presence: A Reading of Space and Dedications at the Amphiareion at Oropos in the Hellenistic Period", in *Excavating Pilgrimage: Archaeological Approaches to Sacred Travel and Movement in the Ancient World*, eds. T.M. Kristensen and W. Friese, Abingdon, 106–29.

Platt, V.J. 2011. *Facing the Gods: Epiphany and Representation in Graeco-Roman Art, Literature and Religion*, Cambridge.

Poland, F. 1909. *Geschichte des griechischen Vereinswesens*, Leipzig.

Ramgopal, S. 2016. *Romans Abroad: Associations of Roman Citizens from the Second Century BCE to the Third Century CE*, unpublished PhD dissertation, University of Chicago.

Rauh, N.K. 1993. *The Sacred Bonds of Commerce: Religion, Economy, and Trade Society at Hellenistic Roman Delos, 166–87 BC*, Amsterdam.

Reger, G. 1994. *Regionalism and Change in the Economy of Independent Delos*, Berkeley.

Reger, G. 2007. "Hellenistic Greece and Western Asia Minor", in *The Cambridge Economic History of the Greco-Roman World*, eds. W. Scheidel, I. Morris, and R. Saller, Cambridge, 460–83.

Rostovtzeff, M. 1941. *The Social and Economic History of the Hellenistic World*, 3 vols., Oxford.

Roussel, P. 1987. *Délos, colonie athénienne*, eds. P. Bruneau, M.-T. Couilloud-Le Dinahet, and R. Etienne, Paris.

Rüpke, J. 1999. "*Collegia sacerdotum*: Religiöse Vereine in der Oberschicht", in *Religiöse Vereine in der römischen Antike. Untersuchungen zu Organisation, Ritual und Raumordnung*, eds. U. Egelhaaf-Gaiser and A. Schäfer, Tübingen, 41–67.

Runciman, W.G. 1990. "Doomed to Extinction: The *polis* as an evolutionary dead-end", in *The Greek City: From Homer to Alexander*, eds. O. Murray and S. Price, Oxford, 348–67.

Rutherford, I. 2017. "Pilgrimage and Communication", in *Mercury's Wings: Exploring Modes of Communication in the Ancient World*, eds. F.S. Naiden and R.J.A. Talbert, Oxford, 195–210.

Sallares, R. 2007. "Ecology", in *The Cambridge Economic History of the Greco-Roman World*, eds. W. Scheidel, I. Morris, and R. Saller, Cambridge, 15–37.

Scheidel, W. 2007. "Demography", in *The Cambridge Economic History of the Greco-Roman World*, eds. W. Scheidel, I. Morris, and R. Saller, Cambridge, 38–86.

Scheidel, W. 2009. "In Search of Roman Economic Growth", *Journal of Roman Archaeology* 22, 46–70.

Scheidel, W., Morris, I., and Saller, R. eds. 2007. *The Cambridge Economic History of the Greco-Roman World*, Cambridge.

Schimmack, U., Heene, M., and Kesavan, K. 2017. "Reconstruction of a train wreck: how priming research went off the rails." https://replicationindex.wordpress.com /2017/02/02/reconstruction-of-a-train-wreck-how-priming-research-went-of-the-rails/ (last accessed 12 August 2018).

Schnapp, A. 1994. "Are Images Animated? The Psychology of Statues in Ancient Greece", in *The Ancient Mind: Elements of Cognitive Archaeology*, eds. C. Renfrew and E.B.W. Zubrow, Cambridge, 40–4.

Seubert, S. 2009. *Das Konzept des Sozialkapitals. Eine demokratietheoretische Analyse*, Frankfurt.

Shariff, A.F. and Norenzayan, A. 2007. "God is watching you: priming God concepts increases prosocial behaviour in an anonymous economic game", *Psychological Science* 18, 803–809.

Silver, N. 2012. *The Signal and the Noise: Why so many predictions fail – but some don't*, New York.

Stapel, D.A. and Lindenberg, S. 2011. "Coping with Chaos: How disordered contexts promote stereotyping and discrimination", *Science* 332, 251–53.

Terpstra, T.T. 2013. *Trading Communities in the Roman world: A Micro-economic and Institutional Perspective*, Leiden.

Trümper, M. 2006. "Negotiating Religious and Ethnic Identity: The Case of Clubhouses in Late Hellenistic Delos", *Hephaistos* 24, 113–40.

Trümper, M. 2008. *Die 'Agora des Italiens' in Delos: Baugeschichte, Architektur, Ausstattung und Funktion einer späthellenistichen Porticus-Anlage*, 2 vols, Rahden.

Trümper, M. 2011. "Where the non-Delians met in Delos. The Meeting-places of Foreign Associations and Ethnic Communities in Late Hellenistic Delos", in *Political Culture in the Greek City after the Classical Age*, eds. O.M. Van Nijf and R. Alston, Leuven, 49–100.

van Alfen, P.G. 2005. "Problems in Ancient Imitative and Counterfeit Coinage", in *Making, Moving, and Managing: The New World of Ancient Economies, 323–31 BC*, eds. Z.H. Archibald, J.K. Davies, and V. Gabrielsen, London, 322–54.

van Alfen, P.G. 2011. "Social Controls, Institutions, and the Regulation of Commodities in Classical Aegean Markets", in *Marburger Beiträge zur antiken Handels-, Wirtschafts- und Sozialgeschichte*, Band 28., eds. H.-J. Drexhage, T. Mattern, R. Rollinger, K. Ruffing, and C. Schäfer, Leidorf, 197–229.

Vohs, K. 2006. "The Psychological Consequences of Money", *Science* 314, 1154–56.

Whitmarsh, T. 2010. "Thinking Local", in *Local Knowledge and Microidentities in the Imperial Greek World*, ed. T. Whitmarsh, Cambridge, 1–16.

Witham, L. 2010. *The Marketplace of the Gods: How Economics explains Religion*, Oxford.

Wonnacott, T.H. and Wonnacott, R.J. 1990. *Introductory Statistics*, fifth edition, New York.

Wright, R. 2009. *The Evolution of God*, New York.

Zarmakoupi, M. 2013. "The Quartier du Stade on late Hellenistic Delos: A Case Study of Rapid Urbanization (Fieldwork Seasons 2009–2010)", *ISAW Papers* 6: http://dlib .nyu.edu/awdl/isaw/isaw-papers/6/ (last accessed 16 August 2018).

Zarmakoupi, M. 2018. "The Urban Development of Late Hellenistic Delos", in *Ancient Urban Planning: New Research Directions*, eds. S. Martin-McAuliffe and D.M. Millette, London, 28–49.

Ziebarth, E. 1896. *Das griechische Vereinswesen*, Leipzig.

Index

Printed in the United States
By Bookmasters